THE WORLDS OF ROBERT E. SHERWOOD

Mirror to His Times
1896-1939

BOOKS BY JOHN MASON BROWN

The Worlds of Robert E. Sherwood—Mirror to His Times
Dramatis Personae
Through These Men
As They Appear
Daniel Boone—The Opening of the Wilderness
Still Seeing Things
Morning Faces
Seeing More Things
Seeing Things
Many a Watchful Night
To All Hands—An Amphibious Adventure
Insides Out
Accustomed as I Am
Broadway in Review
Two on the Aisle
The Art of Playgoing
Letters from Greenroom Ghosts
The Modern Theatre in Revolt
Upstage

EDITED BY JOHN MASON BROWN

The Ladies' Home Journal Treasury
The Portable Charles Lamb
The American Theatre—1752-1934—as Seen by Its Critics
(WITH MONTROSE J. MOSES)

THE WORLDS OF
ROBERT E. SHERWOOD

Mirror to His Times
1896-1939

John Mason Brown

HARPER & ROW, PUBLISHERS
New York

To
All of the Many People
Who Made This Book Possible
with Thanks
Beyond Adequate Expression

ACKNOWLEDGMENTS

My grateful acknowledgment to *Horizon*, in which "Three Speeches, Three Worlds, Three Men" appeared in May, 1962, as "The Worlds of Robert Sherwood," and portions of "Mr. Benchley," "Mrs. Parker," "Mr. Sherwood," "The Algonquin Group," and "Round Tablers All" in July, 1962, as "High Spirits in the Twenties"; to *Horizon* and also to Al Hirschfeld for permission to use Hirschfeld's drawing of the Algonquin Round Tablers; to *Vogue*, in which the section on M.E.W.S. in "From These Roots" appeared in February, 1962, as "Self-Appointed Arbiter of Everything"; to Norman Cousins and the *Saturday Review* for permission to reprint portions of "Inaugural Parade"; to Charles Scribner and Charles Scribner's Sons for their graciousness in giving me access to their Sherwood files and allowing me to quote from Sherwood's book reviews written for *Scribner's Magazine* and from the prefaces to his plays which were published by Scribner's; to Franklin D. Roosevelt, Jr., for allowing me to print Mrs. Roosevelt's letter to Sherwood; to Mrs. Robert Benchley for her kindness in giving me access to her husband's diaries.

CONTENTS

ILLUSTRATIONS

BY WAY OF INTRODUCTION

You cease living your own life when you start writing someone else's. You want to. You have to. But neither your having to nor wanting to is the true cause for the change that occurs. Without your being aware of it, you are no longer alone within yourself. Your mind and heart have a new tenant. Once he has moved in, you find that he requires more and more space, space which you are delighted to let him have. His every concern becomes yours as does everything that concerns him. Day and night he is in the background of your thoughts even when he is not, as he most often is, in the foreground of your thinking. I have lived happily with this knowledge for the past nine years during which, in spite of unavoidable interruptions, I have been living with the life of Robert Emmet Sherwood.

I confess I did not realize how far the subway was to carry me beyond the stop at which I got off when, one September morning in 1956, I went down to Wall Street to take my first glance at Sherwood's letters and papers stored at the United States Trust Company of New York. I made the trip at the suggestion of Harper's Cass Canfield and with the permission of Sherwood's widow, Madeline, and of John Wharton, the lawyer for his estate.

Cass Canfield had in mind a collection of Sherwood's correspondence and wondered if I would be interested in editing it and writing a commentary. To help me, he had asked Marguerite Hoyle, an able editor of his (who, incidentally, had worked on Sherwood's *Roosevelt and Hopkins*), to go through the files and extract a sampling from the thirty thousand items with which they bulged.

I had planned to spend a few days going over this material before deciding. Almost at once, however, as I dipped into Sherwood's letters to and from Woollcott, the Lunts, Edna Ferber, the Garson Kanins, Geoffrey Kerr, Samuel Goldwyn, S. N. Behrman, and Maxwell Anderson, or William Allen White, Elmer Davis, Felix Frankfurter, Franklin D. Roosevelt, Winston Churchill, Averell Harriman, Adlai Stevenson, Truman, and Eisenhower (to mention only a few), I knew I was the captive of what was before me. Within hours I was taxiing uptown to Harper's to admit this to Cass Canfield.

Soon thereafter Sherwood's files began to arrive, one by one, at my apartment and to rise like a cluster of green office buildings in my already hopelessly overcrowded study. The new tenant had moved in, although I could not then guess, welcome as he was, the length of his stay or the extent to which he would take over.

As the weeks and months slipped by and I dug deeper into the files, the more certain I became of one thing. I did not want to stop with editing the letters. There was too much else that tempted me. Those files soon ceased for me to be repositories of crumbling clippings, fading photographs, thousands of old letters, the drafts of speeches long since delivered, and manuscripts abandoned or completed. Increasingly I came to realize that very much alive in them was an exceptional man who had touched his times in many ways.

The whole man was not in the files. Unquestionably, the whole man is not in this book. But the search for as much of the whole Sherwood as I could track down, understand, and assemble from these fragments of his thinking and living became for me an absorption that quickly swelled into an obsession. The more I knew about Sherwood the more I wanted to know. The files had pushed me into the unanticipated role of biographer. Shaw once described a dramatic critic as a man who leaves no turn unstoned. A biographer is different. He cannot live with himself if he leaves one pebble unexamined or unweighed, and he is haunted by the fear that another pebble will come to light after he has combed the beach.

Few of our contemporaries have lived so many lives with such abundance as Sherwood. Few have so reflected the changing decades with their changing issues, interests, and climates as this skyscraper of a man, mournful of face, gay at heart, slow in talk, fluent with pen, and serious of purpose, who could seem solitary even in company.

His files, copious as they were, covered mainly the sixteen years before Sherwood's death at fifty-nine in 1955. They were rich in their random revelations about his activities and experiences. Yet, much as the files revealed and indispensable as they have proved, they did not disclose all or even enough. They were as tantalizing in their omissions as in their inclusions. Sherwood's family backgrounds and relationships, his youth, his growing up personally and professionally, his service in World War I, his pioneering work as a movie critic, his private appraisals of himself and his contemporaries, and the impression he made upon others—all of these naturally were missing, stated piecemeal, or only hinted at.

For help in acquiring this and other information I am indebted to a host of people who touched Sherwood's life in all of its periods and phases. These include the many I have interviewed, the many who have written me in illuminating detail, the many who have turned over their Sherwood files and records to me, and the many with whom over the past years I have talked casually. Their names are given on page 391, though such an impersonal reference to them is a woefully inadequate expression of my gratitude. Of course, too, I have consulted every book I have been able to get hold of containing any reference to Sherwood or dealing with any aspects of his career. With the invaluable assistance of Elisabeth Sill, who again has functioned as a collaborator, I have pored over the magazines and newspapers for which Sherwood wrote and, as far as possible, those in which his plays, books, movies, and television scripts were reviewed or in which he was mentioned at any length. My profound thanks also to Harper's for assigning Miss Hoyle to me as editor. She, like Miss Sill, has steered and sustained me by giving first-rate aid at many needed moments.

My debt is boundless to Sherwood's family, his brother and sister-in-law, Philip and Elsie Sherwood; his daughter, the late Mary Elms;

his nieces, Lydia McClean and Elizabeth Townsend; his aunt, Mrs. Wilfrid de Glehn; his nephew, Arthur M. Sherwood, III; and, above all, his sister, Rosamond Sherwood, who by family agreement is "Official Guardian of the Archives." Their kindnesses have been unfailing in supplying me with letters, diaries, recollections, photographs, clippings, and memorabilia. Without Rosamond Sherwood's attic, memory, and warmhearted encouragement, this book would not have been possible. Needless to say, it would also have been impossible without the wholehearted and unflinching cooperation of Madeline Sherwood. It was she who with great courage trusted me with the intimate diaries her husband kept sporadically from 1936 to 1955, and with the long, frank, loving letters, meant to be read by her and her alone, which he sent to her daily whenever they were separated.

Let me make certain things very clear at once. This book is not a commissioned "family" biography. I would never have considered doing such a book, strait-jacketed in its opinions and purchased in its praise. Nor (and of this I am confident) would Robert Sherwood ever have wanted such a book written about him. I have been on my own, free to reach my own conclusions, state my own thoughts, and make my own mistakes, as Sherwood was when he wrote of Harry Hopkins.

Like Sherwood, I have an aversion to the interruption of footnotes. In his introduction to *Roosevelt and Hopkins* he wrote that as "an inveterate reader of history and biography" he had long been "plagued, angered, and aged prematurely" by pages "which were pockmarked with asterisks, daggers, and other nasty little symbols" which pulled his eye down to small type at the bottom of a page. Accordingly, I have avoided footnotes by seeking to make the text self-contained.

Bob Sherwood had close friends and an army of distant close friends. He was a man easy to admire and hard to know. Many who loved and admired him and knew him long and intimately have told me this. Their experience, I admit, was mine. I did not know him as a friend until the war years in London, when he was Overseas Director of the OWI and I a transient in the Navy. I had known about him, of course, since his *Barnum Was Right* was produced by the Hasty Pudding in 1920 when I was a freshman at Harvard, and had followed his work since, in the twenties, I read his movie reviews in *Life*. From 1927 and *The Road to Rome* on, I had reviewed all his plays that were done professionally in New York, damning some, praising others.

We had corresponded about a few of these, and had our emphatic disagreements in print. We had met two or three times stiffly and self-consciously, because a dramatist and a critic are apt to have a Montague and Capulet relationship. It took a war to bring about an armistice between us. Even when I saw him in London and much more intimately thereafter in New York, and had come to love him, I cannot say that I knew him. I mean really knew him on the easy terms that we know most friends.

Naturally, I know him much better now, this long-time tenant of my interest. Biography is by obligation an invasion of privacy. This is its privilege and its point. Bob Sherwood's papers have given me insights into him that I could never have hoped to gain when he was alive, and a chance to know him at closer range than I do friends whom I think and feel I know best. They have also given me insights into people and events which I had observed from the outside. He was only four years older than I, hence his times were mine. The difference was that, though we shared many interests, he had lived through the altering decades importantly as a participant, often near or at the center of many worlds which I had followed from the sidelines.

When Sherwood died he was not only a playwright who had written about Lincoln but a person who in the public mind had wrapped around his shoulders a portion of Abe Lincoln's shawl. He was an individual who had become a myth, a personage in addition to a dramatist, a literary figure who had emerged as a delegate-at-large for the American conscience. Like the rest of us, he was not one man but many men. He, however, was a bigger man than most, therefore his contradictions seem the larger and are the more interesting. "History," Garson Kanin once wrote him lovingly, "will surely remember you as a soldier, author, monstrosity, playwright, lover, songwriter, wit." This was before he had turned biographer with *Roosevelt and Hopkins.*

Sherwood's life was divided into two periods by the events that led up to the Second World War. This volume, *Mirror to His Times,* deals with his emerging years and the changing worlds in which he moved between the two World Wars. His association with Roosevelt and his activities during the war and in the years that followed will be the subject of a second volume, *On a Larger Stage.* That he was a mirror to his times is one of the reasons for his abiding interest as a man and a writer.

JOHN MASON BROWN

New York, N.Y.
1965

THE WORLDS OF ROBERT E. SHERWOOD

Mirror to His Times
1896-1939

Prologue

THREE SPEECHES, THREE WORLDS, THREE MEN

JUNE 13, 1914

In the crowded schoolroom that Saturday morning at Milton Academy, ten miles from the heart of Boston, Robert Sherwood at eighteen was already sitting on those tenterhooks which years later he was to describe as "the upholstery of the anxious seat." Outside, the June sun brightened the green of the school's wide lawns and the red bricks and white columns of its Georgian buildings, and created the illusion of the calm which is supposed to be academic.

This was an illusion to which young Sherwood did not at the moment surrender. He was a gawky, squab-chested giant, more bone than flesh, whose body within the past two years had stretched another unneeded two inches until it rested, towering uneasily at six feet seven. As one of the seventeen members of the graduating class, he was unnaturally clean for the occasion and wore the uniform of the day—white flannels, a dark-blue coat and vest, a school tie of orange and blue stripes, and the kind of choking high stiff collar in which Herbert Hoover would have found comfort. He was one of two classmates whose hair was jauntily parted in the middle, a fashion which was to be the hallmark of a generation of American males. His lantern face, young and assured as it was, however, knew no jauntiness, and his stomach no June warmth.

1

He was a little pale, a little nervous, and with reason. Not because scarlet fever, then a common menace, had bedded several of his classmates in the shining new infirmary. Nor because he and his parents had been informed that, as a result of his sustained gift for gathering appallingly bad marks, he would not receive a diploma for work done well but a certificate for having been physically present. This was bad news, though stale. He and his family had lived with it for two unhappy weeks.

The reason for young Sherwood's disquiet was the copy of the "Programme for Commencement" which he held in his hands. It was a disturbing reminder (as if he needed one) of what lay inexorably ahead. The first three of the items it listed were a hymn, a prayer, and the award of prizes; the last three, the award of diplomas by the President of the Board of Trustees, an address by Harvard's Professor Bliss Perry, and the school song. Sandwiched in the middle of these traditional features was the announcement which read, "Valedictory: Robert Emmet Sherwood," an honor, by the way, which had been conferred on him by the vote of his classmates. The announcement was tucked in the middle of the program even as tucked in the inner pocket of Sherwood's dark-blue coat was his script. Tucked as surely within his heart was the lack of ease of the speaker who has not yet been called on.

When his turn came, he extricated himself from his chair, unfurled his body, walked to the lectern, spread his manuscript, waited for the applause to end, and then began to read, having to stoop to the podium like a feeding crane to bring his pages into focus.

What did he say to this audience of three hundred, composed of parents and families, who had driven out in carriages or Stanley Steamers and Model-T Fords, and of boys, new and old, the squeaky and squirming small fry as well as his frog-throated and attentive classmates? What did he say at this school in which the recurrent names were Saltonstall, Forbes, Wolcott, Hallowell, Pierce, Robbins, Wigglesworth, and Sherwood? What do all valedictorians say, at least in part even now, in schools public and private, up and down the country, almost by obligation, when the hour of liberation is at last at hand and the voice of the boy orator is heard in the land?

To his credit Sherwood did not exhume, "And this above all, to thine own self be true," as if he had heard the first Polonius speaking it for the first time. Yet in his own way, rediscovering the old truths as the young will and making them theirs by the sincerity of their wonder, he pulled out the unvarying stops of nostalgia, responsibility, and trust. He spoke, as doubtless thousands of his contemporaries were speaking from thousands of platforms that early June, when the skies above them appeared to be almost cloudless, when their futures were theirs to make as they chose, when oceans were still oceans, when foreign affairs were foreign indeed, and America the beautiful still seemed smiling and secure.

He spoke from within the walls of his years, his school, his experiences there, his emotions at parting, his expectations, and the universal confidence. He thanked his teachers. He thanked his school because Milton, in spite of his grades and his mountain of black marks, had meant much to him and was always to hold a special place in his heart. He spoke of the better realization that he and his classmates had gained there of "the ideals of sincerity, simplicity, and uprightness which make for better men." To buttress his optimism he turned automatically in those days to Browning. His was the double vision of the valedictorian. He looked forward and backward, backward with affection, forward with assurance, aware that he and his classmates were making the "somewhat dangerous leap across the chasm which separates school and college and youth from manhood."

There were Sherwood touches in the valedictorian's ever-recurrent themes—schoolboy sproutings of his humor and foretastes of his fluent clarity and mixed realism and idealism. He spoke of escape. Escape into what? Of course, into "that unknown which lies beyond and into which we are about to pass," a world vaguely felt to be "a marvelous place" where "the perfect freedom may be found."

He then appraised his own class, apologizing for its lack of distinction in scholarship and athletics. "Are we not, after all," he asked, "a commonplace lot, not to be remembered with any more interest or respect than is held for every class which graduates from this school?" In the future lay atonement. "There will come a time—it seems a long way off," said he, "when we shall be old men returning on Graduates' Day. . . . We are determined that we shall then bring

some offering of attainment to increase the good name of the
school."

He was climbing to his peroration, as planes and speakers will for
altitude. His was the pious valedictory hope that it would be ultimately said of his class "when we pass through the gates for the very
last time" that "we of the class of 1914" had indeed, in terms of the
school motto, dared to be true.

He was through. The ordeal was over. The "Programme" continued to its close, after which luncheon (cold salmon and potato
salad, no doubt) was served at Robbins House. His masters, his
classmates, and their parents said their good-byes and dispersed.
They clucked to their horses or cranked their cars, leaving this
Norman Rockwell scene in its Sargent setting, many of them soon to
sail for what they expected to be a carefree summer in Europe.

Sherwood within a few days headed for the state of Washington to
visit his eldest brother, Arthur. They were all in a vacation mood. A
new world was at hand, but it was not to be the world that he and his
contemporaries took for granted. Two weeks later, in distant Sarajevo, a student assassinated the Austrian Archduke Ferdinand and
his Duchess with results which were to involve America in ways
that could not be foreseen. A prophecy for a class had been turned
into a farewell to an age.

JUNE 14, 1940

Another commencement, again at Milton. Sherwood faced his
audience this time as an aroused individual, passionately committed.
He was a man very much in the news and the news was very much in
him. Two and a half months before, *There Shall Be No Night* had
opened in New York making it clear that the fate of Finland had
forced Sherwood, like his peace-loving scientist Dr. Valkonen in that
play, to reach an agonized decision. It was that in a world imperiled
by Nazi, Fascist, and Soviet forces the time comes when "there is
only one form of work that matters—resistance—blind, dogged, desperate resistance."

The previous month Sherwood had made his position even clearer
by joining William Allen White on the Committee to Defend Amer-

ica by Aiding the Allies. Only four days before he came to speak at Milton the full-page "STOP HITLER NOW" advertisement, which he had written for that committee and for the publication of which he and some friends paid, had created a sensation when it was run in newspapers across the country from New York City to Portland, Oregon. By bluntly asserting that "Anyone who argues that the Nazis will considerately wait until we are ready to go to war is either an imbecile or a traitor," it had infuriated those living on the sedatives of impossible hopes. At a White House press conference, however, it had won the public endorsement of President Roosevelt, whom Sherwood then did not know. Dr. Joseph Goebbels's response from Berlin was acid in its realism. "Stop Hitler? With what?" he had sneeringly asked.

This time nine hundred people, including thirty-three students from war-torn countries overseas, were in the Robert Saltonstall gymnasium, built since Sherwood had spoken as valedictorian. Expectancy was as crisp in the June warmth as the bite of frost in winter. When the audience was gathering, a graduate said to a master, "I'll bet Bob Sherwood will launch out and outdo himself today because of what has been on the air." What had been on the radio, what had turned the day's headlines into mourning bands, what was on the mind of everyone, was the news that Paris had fallen to Hitler. With France conquered by the Nazis, it appeared inevitable that England's turn would come next and that she would be conquered quickly.

Sherwood had seen the papers the night before as he took the midnight train to Boston, and the news of the fall of Paris had seemed to him "to mark this as the blackest day in all history." He could not sleep. He did not want to. He was racingly awake. After such a catastrophe he knew that he neither would nor could deliver the next morning the traditional Commencement address he had prepared. Accordingly, he tore it up and sat up all night in his compartment trying to write down what he really felt about "the obscure and terrible future."

At forty-four Sherwood returned to Milton as an alumnus bringing "an uncommon offering of attainment." He had made his name in journalism as the editor and motion-picture critic of *Life*. He was a fabulously successful and ever-deepening playwright who had twice won the Pulitzer Prize for drama. He had prospered in Hollywood as well as on Broadway. He was a past president of the Dramatists Guild, a cofounder of the Playwrights' Company, and a member of the National Institute of Arts and Letters. Yet it was not only because of his successes and distinction that he aroused interest as he jackknifed his long body into his chair on the platform. The man mattered more than the playwright that morning; the man at last awake in an America for the most part sleeping; the controversial figure praised by those alerted in his fashion but condemned by isolationists and America Firsters as a pacifist who had become a warmonger.

If tired from his ordeal on the train, Sherwood did not show it. His tension routed his fatigue. Beneath his shaggy eyebrows the darkness of a darkening world was in his deep-brown eyes. His head seemed small, coming as a climax to a body so extended. His broad mouth was thinned by resolution. In spite of the gray in his short-cropped mustache, his hair, no longer parted in the middle but at the right, was a smooth black. He had the look of a youngish man with energies well used and a reservoir of energies untapped. In appearance he was more worldling than aesthete. Well tailored though casual, he was totally American. Yet he suggested, until he spoke, a lean, trim, elongated British major in mufti.

Some think they remember that he began haltingly, with pauses which sounded like intermissions. Others recall only the speed with which they were possessed by the intensity of feeling which plainly possessed him. According to one master, his address was "electric in its communicated emotion"; according to another, it was "one of the four or five most moving speeches" he ever heard. Sherwood was conscious of the "ugly responsibility" he faced in having to stand up and talk to a group of boys who were going from a school he cherished into the dreadful world that confronted them. He chose as his theme the threats of that world, and the follies and failures which had brought it into being. He did not pull his punches.

Inevitably, he went back to 1914 to re-create, for the young to whom he spoke, the world of his youth as he had known it eight or nine years before the oldest boy in his audience was born. He confessed that he and his classmates on their Commencement Day had foreseen no complications in the future. They did not watch the skies for bombers, fearing an invasion from the air, because "at that time, it was all an airplane could do to fly as far as from Providence to Boston." They did not listen to alarming news broadcasts because there was no radio, and if there had been the news would not have been alarming. "In our innocence, and our ignorance, we had virtually nothing to worry about."

He mentioned Sarajevo and the shots there which had started a chain of explosions that had blown this other world to bits. "In the twenty-six years that have passed since then," he added grimly, "all efforts to reassemble that world, or to construct a newer, more reasonable world, have failed tragically. Our world now resembles chaos worse confounded." He referred to his three years at Harvard and his experiences overseas in The Canadian Black Watch in World War I when, wounded, he had been a patient in a long series of hospitals in England and France. "I never wanted to see war again," he admitted, "and I firmly believed that I never should."

Then he turned to the twenties, castigating them for their "disastrous folly" and as "the age of disillusionment, which sowed the seeds of despair which were to grow into the present calamity." Proudly he recalled how the United States had gone into the First War "in the finest spirit." With shame he remembered how we came out of it, cynically announcing that we had fought in vain, that our young men had died for nothing, and that we flatly refused to do our share toward keeping the peace we had helped to win.

He minced no words in attacking "the appalling corruption of the Harding administration," "the hysterical revelry in paper profits of the Coolidge 'boom,'" "the hypocrisy and crime of Prohibition," and the literature of futility which had grown up in this country and in England, France, and Germany. In particular, he narrowed his attention to three books which in June, 1929, he had reviewed for *Scribner's Magazine* a few months before the Wall Street crash. The three, all war books and all written by German soldiers, were *All Quiet on the Western Front* by Erich Remarque, *War* by Ludwig Renn, and *The Storm of Steel* by Ernst Junger. He had admired the first two books, different as they were in their statements against war, but recalled shuddering when he read Junger's account written from the point of view of a fire-eating Prussian officer who enjoyed the sight of dying French and English men. Only recently Sherwood had shuddered again on seeing in a newspaper that Junger was one of the extremist leaders of the Nazi party who had constantly urged Hitler on in his career of destruction.

Sherwood told the young they had the right to ask their elders why, instead of a more perfect civilization, there had been such retrogression to savagery and the jungle since 1914. This was the tormenting question that he asked himself, too. He was fully aware of the enormous developments in communications made possible by the automobile, the airplane, radio, and motion pictures; the vast social reforms in the emancipation of women, the strides in collective bargaining, the recognition in all democracies of certain essential human rights; the ambitious experiment in the Soviet Union; the inspiring advance of the medical profession in psychology and the exploration of the infinite mysteries of the human mind; and the heartening, remarkable spread of education in all parts of the earth.

Then came the avowal of the hideous truth he had faced which he felt it his duty to call to the attention of the young. When on this June morning Sherwood quoted the words "Dare To Be True," the George Herbert line on the Milton shield, he did so to remind his hearers of the inscription that used to be over the portals of Heidelberg. Its beautiful assurance was that the university was dedicated "To the Living Truth." This the Nazis had changed to read "To the *German* Truth." "You cannot 'Dare To Be True,'" said Sherwood, "in a world ruled by Hitler. You cannot dare to be free, or even to be human. You can only dare to die."

"I'm afraid," he added, "that, as Commencement addresses go, this one rates among the gloomiest ever delivered." He asked forgiveness by saying on this historic day "we have learned of the fall of Paris" and "my mind is full of that terrible knowledge." One and only one expression of hope he gave to the graduating class. His own essential faith in the goodness that is in man still survived after these tragic twenty-six years, and he was confident that it would continue to do so as long as he lived. "I hope that you will find in your own lives that this faith is justified. I hope you will see a world in which men at last have found a way to live in peace."

In the next weeks Sherwood had letters from two of the mothers who were present that day. They upbraided him for his depressing speech, and in effect asked, "How could you look into those innocent, hopeful faces and say such awful things?" He could only reply to these good ladies that he had been unable to bring himself to tell lies to their sons.

APRIL 28, 1954

It was to honor Milton's graduates who had dared to die for their country that he mounted the platform in the gymnasium this Wednesday night, fourteen years and two wars later. Twenty-three men had given their lives in the First War, two of them his classmates in 1914; forty-four in the Second War, including four of the "innocent" and "hopeful" who had heard him in 1940; and four during the Korean conflict. Seventy-one of the approximately 1,900 enlisted alumni was a small number compared to the more than 557,000 Americans who had died in the three wars, but it was a large number for Milton because Milton was a small school. The tragic aggregate was gallantly represented in the fraction.

Many of the families, friends, and teachers of the dead were crowded in the gymnasium, along with the young, to hear this Alumni War Memorial Foundation lecture. It was the twentieth to be delivered since 1924 on the subject of "The Responsibilities and Opportunities Attached to Leadership in a Democracy." The previous speakers had ranged from former Assistant Secretary of the Navy Franklin D. Roosevelt, and Canada's Vincent Massey, to Boston's Bishop William Lawrence, Germany's ex-Chancellor Bruening, Britain's John Buchan, and America's Newton D. Baker and General George C. Marshall. Sherwood was the second Miltonian to be asked to speak, and, remembering 1914 and 1940, he had written the headmaster, Arthur B. Perry, Bliss Perry's son, "It would seem to be a mistake to invite me, associated as I am with doom." He was associated with much more.

He had earned his place among the eminent. Everyone knew of his involvement with events. Everyone knew that he had worked on Roosevelt's speeches and been his friend, that he had served as Overseas Director of the OWI, and that there were few in high positions in the free world unknown to him. He was a distinguished playwright who had evolved into an acclaimed biographer, a man of the theatre very much at home on the larger stage of affairs. In addition to achieving fame for his talents, he had become famous for his goodness. Because of his prestige, he faced the hazards of being turned into a national institution, the fluent and fearless spokesman of the democratic faith. Every good cause and every committee turned to him as a sponsor and his susceptible conscience permitted him to decline few.

His honors had multiplied. He had won two more Pulitzer Prizes, one for drama with *There Shall Be No Night*, the other for biography with *Roosevelt and Hopkins*, and many other awards. In *The Best Years of Our Lives* he had written a film that had collected nine Oscars. He had been elevated from the National Institute to the Academy, served as Trustee of Milton and an Overseer at Harvard, and received honorary degrees from Dartmouth, Yale, Harvard, and Bishop's University. He had grown and grown—but never stodgy. He could be as gay as ever, was as fond of frivolity, and as grateful for laughter. Yet on his face that night was a sadness which tugged at the hearts of perceptive spectators; a weariness, too.

Most people took his height to be the measure of his strength. Uncommonly strong he was, but only with a strength resolute enough to triumph over frequent illness and the torture of having had to live for years with a recurrent and terrible facial nervous disorder, double *tic douloureux*, which had attacked him again only the week before. The pain which he had become accustomed to rising above was on his face that evening.

He looked twenty-five years older, not fourteen, as he sat on the platform with the lights stressing the gray streaks in his dark hair, the white plumes of his still scraggly eyebrows, the darkness of his mourning eyes, the whiteness of his crisp mustache, and the strong downward pull of the lines under his lower lids and around his nostrils and mouth. The British major that a Royal Academician could have painted in 1940 had been transformed by the years into an El Greco in a dinner jacket.

Sherwood's day had been exhausting. He had spoken that morning at the Naval War College in Newport on the political aspects of strategy, and speaking had become for him an ordeal. He had guessed he would be nervous at Milton, and he was. To take his mind off his speech, he had asked his old friend, tutor, and favorite master, Albert W. Hunt, to dine with him at the Ritz-Carlton in Boston. Though they had talked pleasantly of old times, his nervousness grew. It was even greater when they had driven to Milton. There, to subdue it, he took a giant's slug of gin, uncontaminated by ice, ten minutes before he walked onto the platform with Mr. Perry.

It was not only conquered pain or the fatigue of a tiring day which pinched his face and accentuated the puffs under his eyes as he towered above the podium. It was the accumulated weariness of days and nights and years of living and giving and working as if his superb energies were endless. It was the secret fear that haunts the creator, the fear which tormented Sherwood, the fear that his gift had left him because he had not had a successful new play produced on Broadway in fourteen years.

It was the sorrow and the emptiness of the letdown after the death of Roosevelt and after the dizzying tensions and excitements of the war years spent close to the White House and to great events. It was the heartbreak of seeing the heroic efforts and sacrifices of a Second World War end in disenchantment, with Hitler and the other marchers stopped but with victory not even bringing a true peace. It was the deep alarm with which he recognized the threats of nuclear power and his realization that this time he spoke not only in a different world but in a different age.

Sherwood had tried to tell the unflinching truth as he saw and felt it in 1940 when Paris had fallen. He tried to do the same thing now as, with his long, nervous fingers spilling communication, he opened his manuscript and began to read, having put on his reading glasses. These turned the audience for him into a blur except for the attentive students in the front rows.

He was seeking to pay tribute to and to justify the war dead at a frightening and frightened time. The needs of peace had long brought unprotesting acceptance of the country's first peacetime conscription. Unrest and menace were everywhere. The once veiled language of diplomacy had become an open rivalry in invective. Old empires

were tottering and slumbering continents awakening. Nationalism
was once again a panacea. Dienbienphu was about to fall. An uneasy truce existed in Korea.

The Cold War was always hot. The balance of power had been
replaced by the balance of terror. The United States had been cata-
pulted into a pre-eminence among the free nations that it did not
want, did not like, and was not as yet equipped to occupy. Soviet
might was catching up with Soviet bluster. The death struggle between Communism and Capitalism was a phrase on many tongues
and a fact dreaded, though accepted, by most minds. McCarthyism
was at its ugly height, and within ten days "point of order . . . point
of order" was to be heard on the air, with the insistent buzz of a
pneumatic drill in an idiot's hands, as the junior senator from Wis-
consin intimidated the Army before television cameras as in public
and in private he had intimidated the Administration and millions of
Americans. Due to the atmosphere of fear McCarthy epitomized, J.
Robert Oppenheimer had been badgered and bullied and smeared
before the Gray Board in a proceeding in which few, if any, could
take pride. It was not a comfortable moment at which to speak of the
fruits of victory made possible by the sacrifices of the gallant dead.
Nor did Sherwood minimize the darkness of the hour.

The valedictorian of eighteen was now the elder statesman of fifty-
eight, and spoke as one. Arms and the man was his theme—the new
arms, the new America, the new Russia, and the new age—and his
plea, in the name of survival, was for a war on war. His was a long,
discursive speech, prepared to fill that obligatory hour which is the
common expectation and tolerance of an audience that has come to
hear a "lecture." Though poorly organized and somewhat tired, it
made its telling points, showed in many passages Sherwood's facile
expository skill, and was blessed with fervor. It found Sherwood,
again like his own Dr. Valkonen in a threatened schoolroom, still
speaking as an idealist of the jungle world outside but this time
asserting with more hope than confidence that there shall be no
night.

Once again he turned back to the lost tranquillity of 1914, when
to young Americans "major war was something that was buried in
the cemetery at Gettysburg," and the putting on of uniforms in order

to fight was unthinkable. He referred to 1940, too, pointing out that there was one piece of news which he had not mentioned when Paris fell because he had not known it, and which he could not have mentioned if he had. On the day after his Commencement address, Franklin Roosevelt had at the White House signed an order to Dr. Vannevar Bush authorizing him "to study into the possible relationship to national defense of recent discoveries in the field of atomistics, notably the fission of uranium." That was the beginning of the new age, and, as Sherwood said, by 1954 the A-bomb had already become "antiquated."

As a militant pacifist in the years following Wilson's failure at Versailles, he deplored the folly of high-minded pacifism and disarmament that had only made possible the rise of the dictators in Germany, Italy, Japan, and Russia. He quoted at length from an ignored article in the *New York Times* of three weeks before by William L. Laurence on the cobalt bomb and the life-taking radioactive dust it was capable of spreading for thousands of miles across lands and oceans. He stressed the futility of outlawing the worst of weapons, insisting that we face up to the fact that "war is a dirty business and those who engage in it must be prepared and even eager to fight it in the dirtiest manner possible," never forgetting that world disarmament is the ultimate goal.

Once more he apologized for the "shocking unpleasant subjects" which he had felt compelled to discuss, and with manifest effort tried to rise above doom as he had written Mr. Perry that he would. "Every major challenge," said he, "that has been hurled at our people has been met and greatly met," and those who died meeting these challenges did not die in vain. From Milton's Honor Roll he singled out three names which had for him "a particular emotional meaning." From the First War he cited Charlie Reynolds, the head monitor of his class in 1914; from the Second, his brother's son, Philip Burr Sherwood; and from the Korean, the son of an old and dear friend, George Lee.

His conclusion, though by obligation hortatory, was bound to be inconclusive. It was, "We have the strength, if only we assert it." The strong faith was qualified, the "if only" insistently strong. Sherwood needed to believe, and still believed, but his beliefs were sorely tried.

He spoke as a man made melancholy by the spectacle of human folly and the terrible and needless possibilities of doom brought about by a progress that was in so many ways retrogressive.

He spoke as someone who, as he saw the darkness deepen in the postwar years, had considered it "a privilege to escape from the appalling and inexplicable present" and to relive the confident greatness of the war years by writing *Roosevelt and Hopkins*. He spoke as a man too aware of the threats of the new age not to be sad in a world that had changed almost beyond knowing since the sunnily secure days of his youth and childhood.

In three speeches delivered in the same place over a span of forty years, Sherwood had supplied a rough chart of his times and of the challenges with which he had lived and from which he had written.

1

FATHER TO THE MAN

That "Biggest Baby"—The Growing Up and Up—A Handful Who Could Be a Hellion—Early Plays and Productions—Long-Legged Peer Gynt—Multiple Ambitions

"That was a happy morning for me," his mother wrote him on his forty-fourth birthday, "when I looked out the window and saw snow heaped on the red tassels of the maple tree and heard the doctor say, 'This is the biggest baby I ever saw.'" That "biggest baby," born at eight in the morning on April 4, 1896, in New Rochelle, New York, in a house known prophetically as Tall Hall, was Robert Emmet Sherwood, who was to expand into the tallest playwright of his time.

He was the fourth of the five children of Rosina and Arthur Murray Sherwood, and his mother was forty-one when he was born. He followed Arthur Jr. by eight years, Cynthia by seven, Philip by five, preceded Rosamond by three, and was to become the tallest of them all by uncomfortable inches. Although the Sherwoods were inclined to height, Bobby had by fifteen pulled out to reach his father's six feet three, and by eighteen, his bones scantily covered, was a gaunt, gangling six feet seven, a giraffe in the human zoo. Since he weighed fifteen pounds at birth, he had plenty to grow on. And grow—and grow—and grow—he proceeded to do.

He was a handsome, laughing baby, his ruddy complexion accentuating his dark hair. He held his head high and looked at the world through far-spaced, shining dark eyes. His appetite was the twin of his size and, according to his mother, would have been more readily lulled if his bottles had been mixed in pails.

15

His energy was explosive, a force unpredictable and uncontrollable. He was good-natured but forever tense, with his every muscle and cord apt to be vibrating and "his brow damp with perspiration from just striving and struggling without cessation." He was so quick and darting that he was hard to photograph and harder to paint. One of the things that years later he admired most in the painting which his cousin, Ellen Emmet Rand, did of him as an infant in his mother's arms was that, plainly, he had not "sat" but "squirmed" for it, because in it he was "unmistakably on the move." Even at fifteen months in the outdoor portrait of him by his aunt, Lydia Field Emmet, he seems ready to be off, restrained only for an inquisitive moment by the sizable peonies behind which he is penned.

He did not learn to walk until he was well over a year old, but as soon as he did he ran away. His alarmed mother, finding no Bobby in the house they had at Delhi, New York, was calmed only when a passer-by told her he had seen a little child in a white dress racing through the village. She dispatched a boy on a bicycle to retrieve him, and, when the boy failed to return, she sent out the caretaker by buggy to continue the search, which he did until in the middle of a road far beyond the village he found Bobby desperately resisting the boy's attempts to capture him.

By the time he was two, he was definitely on the run. Other children might be content to walk holding their nurses by the hand. Not he. He neither sought protection nor could hold himself down to a walk. Released from his go-cart, he would break away from tiny Delia Gilligan, the loving and loved Irishwoman who was long a part of the family. To her powerless annoyance, he would tear into other people's stables, chase the biggest dogs, and come home soggy with sweat and "covered with wagon grease & mud & various fertilizers." Clean or dirtied, his clothes presented a problem. He was always in need of new ones because of shooting up so swiftly that he could never wear the old ones out.

His mother noticed early that his face was going to be long and rightly feared that his lengthening nose would keep pace with his growth. Although enormous from the start, he did not at first feel the singularity of his height. His mother thought it amusing that he towered over the little Jay children in the kindergarten he attended with them in Westport on Lake Champlain, and that he could not get his legs under the tables. By five his height did not amuse him. He needed an explanation for it. Being an imaginative child, he came up with one very much his own which he, his mother, and a boy to whom he gave it were to remember many years afterward.

One summer day this boy was playing by the road in the orchard on the Fuller Farm at Westport when he looked up and saw a stranger. It was another small boy. Or, rather, it was a very tall small boy.

"I'm Bobby—Bobby Newcomb," the first boy said.

"I'm Bobby," replied the other, "Bobby Sherwood."

"I'm five years old."

"I'm five years old, too!" echoed the tall boy.

"But you *can't* be!" said Newcomb, looking up and down the length of Sherwood. "Why . . ."

"Oh, that's all right," Sherwood responded reassuringly. "You see, I was one year old when I was born."

That strange statement stuck in Robert M. Newcomb's mind and he thought about it many times. Forty-four years later, not having seen Sherwood since but having followed his career, Newcomb, then a lieutenant commander in the Pacific, wrote to him suggesting three possible explanations for what Sherwood had said as a very tall small boy. Had he said it because at an early age he had already developed great insight and wanted to keep Bobby Newcomb from feeling inferior because of being short? Or was young Sherwood building a defense mechanism of his own as a person who knew even then that he was destined to bear the cross of never being able to fit into a Pullman berth? Or was it, as Newcomb preferred to believe, considering the wisdom shown by Sherwood since, that he was in fact born one year old?

Sherwood remembered their meeting perfectly. He admitted that at the time he was convinced he was at least a year old when born, but rejected all three explanations. "Although I was to develop in later years into a relatively meek individual," he wrote Newcomb, "as a child I evidently had an ego which might have become as dangerous as Hitler's. There is a story in my family—and I hope it is apocryphal—that once when I was being pushed around in a baby carriage, the usual kindly old gentleman came up and made some approving remarks about my appearance and asked me what was my name, to which I replied indignantly, 'Do you mean to tell me you have never heard of Robert Emmet Sherwood?' That fits in with the attitude of superiority which I inflicted on you when first we met. I just had to be something phenomenal—and I must have been a pretty obnoxious specimen of childhood."

Sherwood persisted in remembering the young Bobby Sherwood as "an objectionable little egomaniac who craved attention and stopped at nothing in the way of criminality to get it." This was an image as amiably distorted as was his later picture of himself as one of those tall men who, because all their energies have gone into growing tall, become diffident, unassertive, and easily imposed upon. Most children crave attention and are diabolically ingenious in contriving to get it. Bobby's ingenuity was dazzling. From the start he knew by instinct where the center of the stage was, and took it. The one thing he could not tolerate, the one thing he resented, was being ignored. He even thrived on such proofs of attention as his brother Arthur gave him when, eight lordly years his elder, he sometimes beat the pants off him ("well, not literally, because the pants were removed first"). He may not have enjoyed those many occasions when his father had reason to apply a disciplinary shingle. But the shingle meant a scene and a scene guaranteed an audience of at least one, and was therefore no doubt preferable to the lonely punishment of being sent to bed for a supper of bread and milk.

His isolating tallness was a problem which he sensed at an early age he was condemned to live with, and one which he recognized could never diminish and would only increase. Increase it did year by year as he inched his way up to that altitude, achieved at eighteen, when other children, self-deceived in thinking themselves original, yelled at him, "How's the weather up there?" Although his energy remained detonating, his health was not helped by his too rapid growth, which reduced his resistance and made him subject to colds. At forty, he would write his mother that he felt better than at any time since he started to grow.

His keeping pace with his growth was a debilitating ordeal. A fat man lives with the hope that someday he will discover the magic diet that will make him thin. Bobby soon began to realize that he was to be denied this consolation. He was "constantly, painfully aware that nothing short of surgical amputation" would make him short. By his own confession he was "extremely sensitive and self-conscious" about his height as a child and youth and cultivated the inevitable slouch to lessen it. From the beginning, however, he stood out for other reasons than being tall.

Rosina, Bobby's mother, sensed this early. She was an enchanting woman, zestful and giving, with the long, lean, highbred, race-horse face of Virginia Woolf or Margot Asquith. Although a painter by instinct and profession, she was a great lady as well as a capable artist, unconventional but not Bohemian, and one of the most vital of very human beings. She loved all of her children with the copiousness she brought to living, and every day they sat for her without their knowing it. She loved them protectingly, ardently, proudly, with Irish warmth and Irish gaiety, spoiling but correcting them, and magnifying their virtues from hope without, as a realist, minimizing their faults. Their every worry, their every success, their illnesses, their displays of talent, their goings and comings, their friends and problems, their progress and setbacks, and everything that touched them were her clear-eyed though doting concern.

From the start she seems to have perceived a difference in Bobby, and not merely because of his misdeeds which would have set him apart in any family. He was not always easy to love. She knew that. He was a handful who could be a hellion. She acknowledged this, too, with a smile and almost with pride. He had a will, a way, and a world of his own. Beyond question he was at times the "horrible little boy" he remembered being. His whims were sudden and unexpected. His sense of humor was often beyond prediction or comprehension. His revenges were unorthodox and merciless. And he was given to retreating into a private universe to which no one was invited and which no one could find. With this knowledge Rosina lived unalarmed and inwardly amused.

After all, as a child he did creep into the bedroom of his paralyzed grandmother, sneak up behind her wheelchair, and, from a long horsewhip, dangle a live beetle over her face. When her feeble cries at last brought a horrified rescuer, Bobby's sole explanation, given calmly, was, "I'm tickling up Grandma." As a little boy he used to treat his adoring baby sister, Rosamond, as if she were Nancy Hanks and he Bill Sykes. Once he even nailed her up in a crate.

He painted every white object in his mother's dressing room yellow, including her shoes. On a visit to his grandfather, while his mother was abroad, Bobby sought to humble the old man's pride in the one flush toilet in the house by emptying the contents of his toy Noah's Ark into the bowl. The summoned plumber, who had installed the fixture, after being upbraided by the grandfather because it did not work, investigated and reported, "It is a good closet, Mr. Emmet, but it won't flush elephants." The visit was difficult both for Mr. Emmet and for Bobby, whose comment on returning home was "I'm thoroughly sick of Grandpa."

Plainly, Bobby could be a problem and was sometimes the kind of little child that it would be nice not to have around, or, if around, to have literally underfoot. There were, however, the long intervals between the monster moments when he was "perfectly sweet and good," and Rosina even seems to have been more entertained than angered by the monster moments. She was torn between writing of Bobby as a "little wretch" when he was bad and a "poor lamb" when he was punished. In her maternal vocabulary he progressed from "cunning" and "a delight" to "glorious," and, at eight, to "a bright and radiant being, and the greatest joy in life is to be with him."

It was not merely because Rosina liked his blazing cheeks, his shining eyes, his cherry-lipped smile that showed all his teeth, or his colorful distortions of the language as a baby that she prized Bobby. Or because by four he shared with her the passion for flowers which was always to stay with him, and could burst in on her lugging a pot filled with a hash of dandelions and earth, and cry, "A flower! I made it! A lovely decent flower!" Or because, at the same age, again as was to remain true of him, he took a sharp interest in women's clothes, and could ask her severely when she was going out, "Where is your bonnet with the gold around it?" Or because he relished country fairs as she did, and the fresh, clean air of mountains.

What caught her eye, what caught her heart, was the excess of exuberance in Bobby with which she also was charged. He had her same "quick excitement." With delight she noted his "ability to take fire," that quality which warmed her long life. Bad though Bobby could be, Rosina realized that he was original even in his badness. She liked his independence, appreciated his sweetness, and respected the private world into which he retreated because she had one of her own. She put up with his faults, sensing as an artist that in this lengthening child there might be an artist of some kind who should be disciplined but must not be destroyed.

When he was five her curiosity about his future and the futures of her other children led her, at Lydia's recommendation, to a fortune-teller in Westport. Gifted, bright, and decisive as Lydia was, she was a gloriously gullible woman who was always going to fortunetellers and gypsies. Rosina, though less surrendering, had just enough Irish in her to be unable to resist fortunetellers entirely.

Throughout their session the "resident Djinn" mistook Rosina for Lydia, a confusion which Rosina found a little discouraging in a soothsayer. Yet, in spite of this, she was convinced the woman had some sixth sense, and found her easy to believe because of the agreeable things she said.

About Bobby, Rosina reported to Lydia, she was "simply inspired and prophetic. She described his appearance and said that if there was one thing I could count on utterly in the universe it was that child and his great nature and genius. She fairly laughed over the sureness of Bobby's success. I must never doubt him, never fear for him . . . he is a great old soul in a child's body and I am to be his star & guide." Rosina was, of course, entranced. Wanting to believe, she half-believed, though her honesty forced her to ask herself, "I wonder if it can be true? Or if it is some hope down in my heart and of which I am unconscious but which I communicate to her?"

She not only nourished this secret hope for Bobby but showed it by reporting his doings fully to her sisters and by preserving, from his babyhood on, his crayon scratchings, his doodlings, his songs and jingles, his attempts at fiction, his programs for his embryonic plays, and his letters, almost as if to aid a future biographer. Rosina was a keeper by nature in a family of keepers. She was not one of those enemies of history, the discarders, who are so busy tidying up the present that they throw out the past. Furthermore, she lived in houses which had attics, and attics are the vanishing guarantees that foregrounds have backgrounds.

She had a lot to save, a lot to record. At two, Bobby, who as a

grown man was to confess, "My ballpen loves to write," was already
dipping a pencil, which he called a "biddy," into an inkwell and
beginning to make flourishes on paper. At four, launched even then
as a song writer and singer, he came up with a new number, probably
about the sunken *Maine*, which he called "Oh! De Big Battleship"
and described as a "very poor song," meaning it was a sad one. At
seven, he was editing a penciled newspaper, *The Children's Life*. At
eight, a veteran of the theatre who had long since been creating and
producing plays himself, and acting in them, he sat unmoved, while
little Rosamond wept, at a tent production of *Uncle Tom's Cabin*
which was "quite beneath" his "superior taste." Two years later at
school he rewrote *A Tale of Two Cities* because he disliked the
shabby way in which Dickens had killed off Sydney Carton at the
end.

Plays of all kinds spilled from him, plays which he committed on
the family but not to paper. As dramas spoken rather than written
not even Rosina could preserve them. What, for example, was the
surprise in *Tom Ruggles' Surprise* has eluded recollection. All that is
known is that Bobby played Tom and surprised Rosamond and his
audience by asking her to play all the other parts. A gaily crayoned
playbill does make clear that *How the King Was Saved* was in several scenes: "The Sorrowful Queen," "The Witches Den," "The
Beautiful Fairy," and "The Meating" (*sic*). The curtain rose at 3:15
on Sunday afternoon, December 31, 1905, and the "caracters" included the King, played by Bobby, the Fairy played by Rosamond,
and the Queen played, in ways hard to figure out, by both of them.
By eleven he was steeped in Scott's novels, and so absorbed in theatrical matters that he told his mother he and Rosamond "had decided during the Christmas holidays to appear in *Repertoire*." They
were going to revive some of his old plays and then present a new
one, *The Curse of Bacchus*, in which eight-year-old Rosamond was
to be a barmaid.

In most of these earlier productions Rosamond was Bobby's valiant assistant, and the variety of the parts with which he afflicted her
cannot have been made the easier for her by his working methods.
Even at thirteen, as Gretchen Finletter remembered in *From the Top
of the Stairs*, "he brooded alone and dreamed his dreams which must

have been clear to him, but he never wrote a scene down or explained to his cast what he expected of them. If he saw a drama perfect and whole in his head, it was unbelievable to him that a few muttered words through his nose would not create a snappy and sparkling scene. He would become indignant, then furious . . . and look elsewhere for actors who were not so dumb."

Rosamond seems to have been more intuitive than most. She survived, or rather endured, as a permanent member of his troupe, featured, if not exactly costarred. She was an honored, happy slave who so loved Bobby that, when she was five and he was away at the Fay School, she was "a little widowed thing" who, as Rosina noted, "ate her breakfast with his napkin ring beside her to remind her of him."

Bobby had a gift for making people want to do what he wanted done. He showed this when, the summer before *The Curse of Bacchus*, he staged a "Fair" of his own at Westport as his first public effort for a worthy cause. The idea was his and he pursued it doggedly and unaided, his face set, his mind aflame, as he circled the countryside collecting the weirdest of strange things that could be put up for sale. He set the day, wrote the invitations, and, according to Rosina, gradually infected the whole community with interest by his "fiery energy and enthusiasm." Every odd bit of rubbish somehow found a buyer, and the receipts were $16. This was sufficient in those days, when the dollar's purchasing power had a greater reality, to enable Bobby to send three mothers and their babies to the seashore for a week and to give four other children a day's outing.

Other "Sea Breeze Fairs" followed, growing in scope and growing in profits, taking in $120 the second summer, $260 the third, $100 the fourth, and $107 the fifth, all of which was donated to the *Life* Summer Camp Fund. Rosina would offer to paint a portrait to be raffled, and circus numbers were added, because Bobby saw himself not only as a Booth, a Belasco, a Bulwer-Lytton, and a George M. Cohan, but a Barnum, too. In these circuses, the ever-serviceable, ever-willing Rosamond was once billed as "Rollicking Rosamond The Bareback Specialist." Another time she was driven around in a small cart on which was printed "Grandmother of All the Freaks."

Although his plays at this period may have been composed largely

in his head, Bobby was always writing. That is, when he was not
fishing, playing tennis, singing, opening a store with Rosamond,
being shingled by Arthur and his father, or reading history with a
talent already remarkable for seizing upon and remembering the sali-
ent facts. He was busy, too, worrying about the poor, following
politics and the news, trying his hand at novels, studying French,
picking flowers, or scrambling over the mountains at Westport which
he loved. "It was wonderful," wrote Rosina to her sister Jane after a
climbing expedition in 1907. "Bobby was in one of his most whimsi-
cal idiot boy moods and went skipping from crag to crag with his
long legs, and spouting and declaiming more like Peer Gynt than
ever. He had a crimson jersey and a shawl over his shoulder and an
old pointed felt hat with two huge scarlet maple leaves sticking in its
side."

Next to the theatre, crayon drawings and poetry (or what he
confidently thought was poetry) were his releases. In both media his
sympathies were hotly given and strongly stated. As a little boy he
poured out his rhymed pity for the children of the poor, "The poor,
the poor, the rechid poor, Down in the slums of Broadway," who,
when the children of the rich at Christmas are coasting downhill,
"Will find it quite hard, With a pail full of lard, To be washing the
window sill."

He was ardently pro-"Jappan" in the Russo-Japanese War,
proudly drew the Rising Sun next to the Stars and Stripes, and invented a Japanese language of his own with which to caption his
picture celebrating Togo's victory. When the 1908 election was
looming, he wrote for his financier father a Christmas poem called
"Which?" about such possible Republican candidates as Taft,
Hearst, Cortelyou, Fairbanks, and Theodore Roosevelt, and, in a
jingle that would have amused F.D.R., stated firmly, "By those in
Wall St. resident, One mans been too much felt, The one who is our
President, Old Teddy Roosevelt."

Rosina went about her own full life watching little Bobby's life fill
out with a warm sense of identification. When he was nine he announced his multiple ambitions by saying, "I would like to have the
looks of Philip, and the learning of Mr. Hunt [the tutor of the
Sherwood children] and the voice of Caruso and the taste of

mother." He did have his mother's tastes. Two years later Rosina, in one of her few moments of being downed as a parent, overstated her fleeting despondency to Lydia by saying, "You know I cant account for my childrens tastes or lack of taste. They don't care for any of the things I like and wont read the books or think the thoughts that used to give me pleasure. Of course, I except Bobby who likes everything I ever liked. He is the one who seems to me to live and be young as I understand the joy of youth and life, a joy that unfortunately is very checkered with disappointments. I should not mind being young and being Bobby, though I know what hard times he may have to go through."

There was a lot of the mother in the child, and a lot of his youth abided in her heart. They were not similar; more important, they were sympathetic. Even as a little boy Bobby was a character definite and different, at the same time that he was the chance fusion of traits, aptitudes, and interests of a family in many ways remarkable.

2

FROM THESE ROOTS

*Begat-and-Begottery—The English Sherwoods and the Irish Wilsons—
"Bold Robert Emmet," the Martyr, and His Wiser Brother, Thomas
Addis—The Emmets in America—Contrasted with the Sherwoods—A
Family of Women Painters—The Incredible M.E.W.S.—Self-Appointed
Arbiter of Everything—Abe Lincoln in Illinois Written to Atone for Her*

"Not that it really matters now when any American's family came
over," wrote Sherwood in 1941 to a Boston columnist who had
called him a warmonger and questioned his citizenship. Sherwood
meant this sincerely. Yet it did not displease him to be able to point
out that his family went "back into New England a hundred or
more years before the Revolution."

He was thinking of the English Sherwoods, known in 1640 to be
among the first settlers of Stratford, Connecticut, and long prominent
in society and at the bar in Delhi and New York. Had he been a
bore, addicted to begat-and-begottery, that oldest of barbiturates, he
could have mentioned the Huguenot Hubleys who came to Pennsylvania in 1732 and had a son who was Washington's friend and aide.
Or the English Piersons, one of whom was Yale's first president. Or
the colorful Irish Wilsons who arrived in 1737, settled in New
Hampshire, and produced two congressmen, one of them the mes-
merizingly eloquent General James Wilson, who stood a mere six feet
four, and who in turn produced that exuberant worldling, social
arbiter, and prolific writer, Mary Elizabeth Wilson, who was Sherwood's grandmother.

Had he been a braggart, Sherwood could have boasted that he
came from a people prosperous in the old country before prospering

in the new, a people including some who had surveyed the wilderness, built stockades, fought off Indians, followed Wolfe to the Plains of Abraham, battled with and been imprisoned by the British during the Revolution, attended Harvard College with John Quincy Adams, argued before the Supreme Court in John Marshall's time, gone often to the White House when Dolly Madison was "Queen" at the "Palace," known Jefferson, Clay, Tyler, and Grant, served America in the War of 1812, the Civil War, and the Spanish-American War, been the friends of Robert Fulton, Governor Clinton, Philip Hone, Andrew Carnegie, the Astors, the Roosevelts, the Sedgwicks, John Singer Sargent, the Damrosches, and the Jameses, William and Henry, and made their names and earned their places as generals, admirals, doctors, lawyers, legislators, orators, authors, painters, and engineers.

Being Robert Sherwood, however, he contented himself with saying, with rather haughty irony, "one of my ancestors came to this country as recently as 1804." He had in mind Thomas Addis Emmet, the founding father of multifarious Emmets in America, who that year brought his wife and children to New York. Charged with treason by the English and barred by them from returning to his native Ireland, he had been in France negotiating in vain with Napoleon and Talleyrand for French military aid to gain Irish freedom.

Sherwood's mother, Rosina, it must be remembered, was an Emmet, not that the Sherwoods, including Bobby even when he had grown to be Robert, ever forgot it. Their reasons for remembering were many and understandable. More than being a family, the Emmets were a tribe. But, though tribal in their numbers and their loyalties, they were a tribe of individualists who in generation after generation had distinguished themselves, the men in public services or at the bar, the women as artists.

Not every family, however tribal, has a national hero as its rallying point and icon. The Emmets had theirs in Robert Emmet, "bold Robert Emmet, the pride of old Erin." To be sure, he was only a collateral antecedent, the younger brother of an equally devoted and wiser Irish patriot, Thomas Addis Emmet, that later-comer of 1804, who was Robert Sherwood's great-great-grandfather. But in the public mind, and sometimes in their own minds, the Emmets were children of the children of the childless Robert Emmet. It was not that they failed to remember and revere the sager, more cautious Thomas Addis. It was simply that they could not forget the martyred and more romantic Robert. They wore him like shamrock in their memories even when most of them had ceased to be anything but inconvenienced by St. Patrick's Day parades in which his Napoleonic young profile was emblazoned on banners.

Unlike Thomas Addis, who lived for Irish freedom, Robert died for it, and lives on because of having done so. No uprising could have been more bungled, none more tragically farcical or farcically tragic than the one which this short, slightly pocked, impulsive young idealist headed against Dublin Castle on July 23, 1803, during his older brother's stay in Paris. Accident trailed accident. Directions were given wrongly or not given at all. Fuses for hand grenades were misplaced; firearms, grappling irons, and scaling ladders undelivered. Promised detachments were either told to go home or did not arrive. Throughout it all, in its planning and execution, Robert Emmet was duped, betrayed, and ill-advised.

Sherwood was later to see the Emmet uprising as "a tragedy which could be described by only one word—Irish." To him it had the qualities of a tale told by "a dramatic poet with a comic twist, such as Synge or O'Casey." The heroic, idealistic struggle for independence was "continually darkened by the shadow of the Informer or made tragically ludicrous by the pretensions of the Playboy or the pubward digressions of a Joxer." But from this brave threat which turned into a sorry fizzle, Robert Emmet emerged as one of Catholic Ireland's heroes, the follies of that day forgotten and his Protestantism and English background forgiven.

He was a failure, twenty-three years old, when the British captured him, and an immortal after they had hanged him a month later. During that month he had delivered before the judges who condemned him an impromptu address, extraordinary even in the annals of Irish oratory, which concluded with the echoing words, "When my country takes her place among the nations of the earth, then, and not till then, let my epitaph be written." He was a trusting, ingenuous man, hot of head, light in judgment, and pure martyr at heart, whose courage and eloquence were his only proven gifts of leadership, though both of these were great.

Sherwood, the realist, was aware of Robert Emmet's failings, but Sherwood, the romantic who also championed causes most effectively with words, was stirred by his virtues and proud to be Robert Emmet Sherwood. He valued the name, and knew its value, never taking it too seriously, remembering its remoteness, but treasuring it with affection. He used it modestly though persistently, claiming it yet escaping from it, in ways true to the complexity of his own nature and the war within himself between his love of tradition and the past and his eagerness to break with them. Although he wanted to make, and did make, his own name, he could not quite persuade himself to drop the panache of the name he had inherited.

It was as "R. E. Sherwood" that he appeared on the masthead of *Life* and that he signed most of his articles and reviews there. It was as "Robert E. Sherwood" that he was usually credited for his motion pictures and his later journalism. It was as "Sherwood" that his name was printed on the spines of his published plays and his single novel, and as "Robert E. Sherwood" that it was stamped on their sides. But it was "Robert Emmet Sherwood" that was spread across their title pages, the notable exception among his books being *Roosevelt and Hopkins* where "Robert E. Sherwood" sufficed inside and out. Perhaps it should be added that it was as "Robert (*pause*) EMMET (*pause*) Sherwood," with the "Emmet" struck like a cymbal, that he introduced himself while doing a last-minute radio appeal for Adlai Stevenson in 1952, explaining with a smile, when the broadcast was over, that he never rolled out his full name except in election years when Irish ears were listening.

Closer by blood to Sherwood than Robert Emmet, though as removed from him in time, was his great-great-grandfather, Thomas Addis Emmet. There are thousands of men who loom large in their own days and serve them richly only to vanish as if by a conjurer's trick from history where they seemed certain of a place. With so much to be remembered, it somehow proves easier to forget them. Thomas Addis Emmet is one of the casualties of this convenience. He was a founder and leader of the Society of United Irishmen and was longer and more deeply involved in its development than Robert, his junior by fourteen years.

To his contemporaries Thomas Addis Emmet was an extraordinary man. They were not pouring out mortuary molasses when at his death they called him "pre-eminent," "excellent," a "genius," and even "great." New York City was equally sincere when, on learning he had died, it lowered the flags on its public building to half-mast. So were Governor Clinton, Martin Van Buren, and the army of notables who attended his funeral, and the many who eulogized him in verse and prose. So, too, were his admirers who by national subscription built in his honor the handsome marble obelisk, over thirty feet high, in St. Paul's Churchyard in New York City. But contemporary recognition can be the stuff that bubbles are made of. The lichen of history is different. Robert Emmet had it; Thomas Addis did not.

He was a kindly six-footer who could be as obstinate as only the meek-mannered can be. Precise but fervid of mind, somewhat slovenly of dress, possessed of more character than glamour, he commanded attention in private by his amiability and his often ceremonious manners rather than by good looks. He was a slow-talking, somewhat humdrum conversationalist, except when he took fire at an idea. Then, in his slightly "Corkonian brogue," he could be as eloquent in private as he was in court and no less enlightening. His speaking voice was musical but, when he sang, his singing voice (shades of Sherwood) was a joke to others and himself. Although he could be gay in his abstemious way, the sadness of his face in his later years was a reminder of what he had endured in Ireland. It was a face as long as Sherwood's and not unlike it.

Thomas was the only Irishman among those arrested after the Rebellion of 1798 who was thrown into solitary confinement for six weeks and physically mistreated at Dublin's Kilmainham Gaol. This was due to the intervention of his bitter and all-powerful enemy Lord Castlereagh, of whom Shelley wrote, "I met Murder in the way—He had a mask like Castlereagh." Joined by his wife, Thomas remained there for a year, and was then transferred with her and his children to more comfortable quarters at Fort George in Scotland. When released three years later by a generous jailer, who did not hesitate to ignore the stern orders of his superior, he went into exile with his family, settling in Paris to carry on his fruitless negotiations with Napoleon and Talleyrand. Grief-stricken by Robert's execution, and having come to believe that Napoleon's idea was for Ireland to gain her freedom from England by surrendering it to France, he decided to carry out at last his plan for coming to America.

When Thomas Addis Emmet landed in New York on November 11, 1804, he was a toughened and tested forty. With him he brought his wife, the eldest of his four sons (the other three followed the next year), and his three daughters, one of whom was born at Fort George. He also brought an emerald presented to him by his cousin, Sir John Temple, which as designed as a ring by Robert, with Hibernia cut upon it playing the harp, was intended to be the seal of the Irish Republic. He brought, too, a child's sword given to one of his sons by Bernadotte; letters of introduction from Generals Kosciuszko and Lafayette; and high hopes which soon materialized.

He brought more. He brought those gifts which long before his death twenty-three years later made him outstanding in New York as a lawyer, a citizen, and a member of society. Above all, he brought with him a large and ever-growing family so pronounced in its characteristics that "Emmet" can almost be used as an adjective to describe them. The Emmets may not have thought of themselves as a family apart, but others came to do so. Not without justification, because by the time of Robert Sherwood's growing up, when one maze after another of new Roberts, new Thomas Addises, new Rosinas, Lydias, Janes, and Christopher Temples had appeared, their distinguishing traits had become unmistakable, especially among the women.

They were a clustery, scattering, loyal, impulsive, energetic, and affectionate breed, apt to be talented, certain to be idealistic, often impractical, sometimes flighty, who moved and belonged in the great world without ever being worldly. The good things of life did not surprise them or the costly things impress them. They assumed the best and were as accustomed to comfort as to cultivation. Utterly unsnobbish, they liked informality and excelled at making it gracious. They lived simply, expansively, abundantly, never worrying too much about money, capable of earning it, and assuming that it would always come in, as it always had and always did.

Ever since Thomas Addis bought a place on the Middle Road, way out in the country where 54th Street and Fifth Avenue now are, they had had a house both in town and in the country. But much as they loved the theatre, music, the ballet, the opera, and New York parties, the country was their spiritual home, whether in New Rochelle, East Rockaway, Westport (as in Sherwood's youth), or Stockbridge, Massachusetts. And always, in or out of the city, in the long but often interrupted good years, there were devoted maids (usually Irish), gardeners, coachmen, fräuleins, mademoiselles, and tutors around who were somehow paid, and trips to Europe or the West which were somehow made.

As a family the Emmets were a united movement of determined separatists, strong in their moral sense, quick in their impulses and sympathies, and happily incapable of dogma. They divided people into "livers" and "leaners," and most certainly they were not "leaners." Where the men turned to law, medicine, engineering, the Army, or the Navy, the women gravitated to the arts, which came to them as naturally as the amenities.

There had been an artist among the Emmet women ever since Thomas Addis's daughter Elizabeth studied painting with Robert Fulton. In Sherwood's youth the family swarmed with women who were professional painters—his mother, Rosina; his aunts, Lydia and Jane; his cousins, Ellen Emmet Rand known as "Bay" and Leslie Emmet; and his sister, Rosamond. There were more to come. But even the strong-willed artists bore no resemblance to painters at an artists' colony. They were hard-working professionals who, though they were not conventional, were correct. There was no Bohemia on their seacoast.

Their minds, their hearts, their eyes, their purses, and their doors were always open. Old Thomas Addis once wrote of "the bustle of company" in his house. That bustle was to the Emmets a melody, welcome and familiar. A pen drawing in the Rowlandson manner, done in 1818 by Tom's son, Dr. John Patten Emmet, captures what was to be the pattern of their living. It is a formidable foretaste of "togetherness." In it eleven Emmets are gathered in Tom's country house for a Saturday night family party. One is darning, one reading, two are playing chess, one fiddling, another singing, one attacking the clavichord, others talking, and some perhaps are even listening, while a manservant is passing drinks.

As even the luckiest families have, the Emmets had their bores.

Yet by and large they were a sprightly, unfettered crew, immersed in life and ungiven to complaints, who took courage as much for granted as culture. They loved sports, the outdoors, dogs, flowers, and children as warmly as they loved their family, the arts, their friends, and the mere act of living. Although they unfailingly remembered Robert Emmet and Thomas Addis with the thrill of recollected battle cries, they came to forget Ireland as a cause, to love England for itself (as Sherwood did), and to turn, in the case of Rosina's immediate family, almost uniformly Republican. Even so, they never closed their minds to ideas, their hearts to issues, their eyes to beauty, or their senses to life.

The antitheses between the Emmets and the Sherwoods, always pronounced, had by the time of Robert Sherwood's growing up become Plutarchian. The two families shared such traits as a love of people, an assumption of the best in life and society, an easy articulateness in speech and writing, rich cultivation, an interest in worthy causes, a hunger for fun, and marked talents for mimicry, rhymes, singing, and parlor games. There the similarities ended rather abruptly and the disparities commenced.

Over the decades the Emmets had multiplied and the Sherwoods decreased until so few remained that Sherwood's father used to say he knew anyone was wrong who claimed to be related to them. This difference in their numbers was just the beginning of their differences in Sherwood's youth.

The Emmets were apt to be visionaries and fairly frugal in their tastes; the Sherwoods were inclined to be worldlings, given to extravagance, fond of the stylish, and not averse to the opulent. Both families liked the city and the country, though it was the city that mattered more to the Sherwoods. The real split between them was the ancient one which was to be at the core of much of Sherwood's playwriting—the Sherwoods were at heart Romans or Spartans, the Emmets Athenians. Equals in their virtues, the Emmets were made the more vivid, the Sherwoods the less colorful, by theirs.

Another division was their attitude toward children. The Emmets doted on them, the Sherwoods endured them. Although there was no prudery on either side, the Emmets often did not drink at all, the Sherwoods quite a lot. Both families were pre-eminently respectable but unalike even in their respectability, for where the Sherwoods were resolute conformists the correct Emmets had rebellion in their blood. Furthermore, the Emmet energy persisted through the generations even as the Sherwood strength sometimes lapsed into languor.

Granitic is the adjective reached for by many when struggling to define a basic element of Robert Sherwood's character. Granitic, in the sense of being New England quarried, is the inevitable word for those dimly known early Sherwoods who settled Connecticut's Stratford. Granitic is what Sherwood's great-grandfather, the Honorable Samuel, was. It was he who crossed the Yankee hills, a dauntless fledgling, light of purse but long on the genteel tradition, to settle in Delhi, New York, and to build there, soon after his arrival in 1804, Woodland House which for a century was the Sherwood summer home.

Samuel was a rock-strong, ruler-of-the-roost man, said to be sometimes irascible and occasionally tyrannical, who in time was elected to Congress. Almost at once at Delhi, and later in New York City, he acquired as a lawyer a fortune so sizable that in Robert's youth, when that fortune had diminished, the Sherwood children, instead of rattling off "Where's the peck of pickled peppers Peter Piper picked?" would race through "Where's the sack of shining silver shekels Samuel Sherwood shook?"

Sherwood's grandfather, John, who became his father's partner, also made shining shekels and had granite in him, though the granite was further underground. On his death in 1896 he was praised as "a ripe scholar," "an excellent lawyer," "a most courteous gentleman" who had "traveled much," "made the acquaintance of many public men," had "a retentive memory," was "very social in his habits," and "profited by all he saw and read." No explanation was given, however, for his traveling so much, for his being so social in his habits, or for meeting so many prominent people at home and abroad.

There was a reason and it wore skirts—Mary Elizabeth Wilson, the overwhelming woman that he married, the mother of the charming but ultimately unlucky Arthur Murray Sherwood, and Robert Sherwood's paternal grandmother. The most weathered granite would have been worn down by her. The wonder is that Rosina was not depleted when, by marrying Arthur, she acquired Mrs. John

Sherwood as a mother-in-law. But Rosina liked her, admired her good qualities, put up with her maddening ones, and got along with her well. Literally hundreds of other people liked her, too, though perhaps not as eagerly as she liked them, especially if they were important. Yet like her they plainly did, and having them like her, even if they scarcely knew her, continued to be her pleasure after it had become her profession as the chronicler, panegyrist, and guardian of high society.

Mary Elizabeth Wilson—"Lizzie," as she signed her intimate letters, and "M.E.W.S.," as she was known because of her initials after her marriage to John—was a foolishly bright, brightly foolish woman, disarming in her charm. She was a showy showpiece of society, secure in her place there, who, when she died in 1903, was described by the *World* as "a feminine Ward McAllister." She was much more than that. Cotillions and making up lists of "the Four Hundred" would never have contained her. She had been everywhere, met everyone, and was the self-appointed arbiter of everything —society, literature, interior decoration, morals, etiquette, acting, Europe's treasures, America's Great Houses, the functions of the second footman, and the beauty of God's creations.

In her youth a vibrant, attractive woman with flashing eyes, vivid color, and a curved, life-tasting mouth, she became in old age a stout fortress of fashion, a dowager given to spaniel curls, rich dresses of purple and lilac, trailing trains, ermine capes, and glittering jewelry. Men—and women—were happy to wait upon her, picking up her dropped furs, umbrellas, boxes, and bags, and also her prodigally scattered recollections and pronouncements. Essentially good, working hard and well for the Sanitary Commission during the Civil War, raising money for the Mount Vernon Society, and forever organizing charity benefits or "culture" groups such as the *Causeries*, she was a mountain of complacency and a hurricane of energy.

M.E.W.S. came by her energy naturally, being of the dazzling, hustling Wilson family of New Hampshire and the daughter of General "Long Jim" Wilson, the towering, black-haired orator and congressman from Keene who, by his rolling rhetoric and sudden wit, could hold an outdoor audience of ten thousand spellbound for two hours and make listening travelers glad that he had caused them to miss their trains. To her father she also owed her first exposure to the great world when, after her mother's death, she served in her youth as his hostess in Washington. From the great world she never recovered. With her it became a disease.

She had a strong mind, weakly used. Her gifts were as real as her intentions were good and her values silly. Incredibly well-read, sincerely stirred by beauty, and possessed of a conversational style that was forceful and bright but destroyingly facile, M.E.W.S. was lacking in judgment. Even in her late autumn she never outgrew her worship of the great and near-great and her Daisy Ashford love for small but costly crowns. She was a snob who took her exercise picking up celebrities and dropping their names. Her life (really an interesting one) was a string of diamonds which she managed to turn into costume jewelry.

Sherwood was only seven when she died just before her seventy-seventh birthday, long a victim of rheumatism and for a decade virtually crippled by it. He remembered her vividly, though the view he took of her was dim and smiling. To him she was "a very gaudy old lady until the end," with whom his grandfather could never keep up "either financially or intellectually" and to whose ultimate softening of the brain Sherwood was sure she had made "a substantial contribution."

She was as wildly extravagant with money as with praise, and could never budget either. Her ostentatious habits were a dreadful trial to her family, came near to impoverishing her husband, and, after his death, continued to bleed Sherwood's father, Arthur. They did not crush M.E.W.S. Nothing could have done so. She had a comforting habit of walking out on life when life became uncomfortably real for her. Once on arriving in France she dashed off a typical letter to her husband who had just been forced, because of her, to sell their New York house, the scene of countless brilliant parties. In giddy detail she described the crossing, how well Coquelin had acted at the Ship's Concert, and how loudly she had been applauded for her reading of one of her poems. Then she added, almost as a postscript, "I feel sad, more heartbroken than I can express, at the disruption of our house. Write me of its last hours, and what became of our things."

M.E.W.S. once said that it was a mountain of unpaid bills on her desk which drove her into writing in her late middle years. Whatever she earned, and she earned a lot, was not enough. She turned out hundreds of articles for *Harper's*, the *Times*, and other magazines and newspapers, and gleefully spawned book after book, such as *A Transplanted Rose*, a novel about the slow triumph of a small-town girl in New York and London society, or, more typically, *Amenities of Social Life, The Art of Entertaining, Manners and Social Usages, An Epistle to Posterity*, and *Here & There & Everywhere*. The last, by the way, was the first book in which the name of Robert Emmet Sherwood appeared prominently, he being one of M.E.W.S.'s four grandchildren ("the gems of my last decade") to whom it was dedicated. When he came across a copy years later, it amused him to think that his grandmother could believe that he had been "very attentive" to her account of court life in old Baden-Baden, since he was only two when it was published.

M.E.W.S. did not so much write as pant in print because her enthusiasm for everything was undiscriminating and uncontrollable. If she depended at times on exclamation points, it was because she had to lean on something to support her raptures. In addition to being an unquestioning and unintentional snob, she was a benevolent egotist, one of those misguided authors who think that everything that happens to them must be of interest to everyone else. When she was not laying down the law on decorum, party-giving, how to treat a guest, or floral decorations at home, she was always going to Europe in search of copy as well as pleasure, and returning having found both. Kings and queens were catnip to her, the doings of the tiniest courts matters of the greatest concern, and authors, major or minor, game to be stalked.

She rushed in where Emily Post was never to dare to tread. Queen Victoria gave her a diamond pin, Queen Marguerite of Italy three audiences, the Khedive of Egypt one, and the French government the red ribbon of the Legion of Honor. Webster, Calhoun, Clay, Booth, Emerson, Longfellow, Bryant, Lowell, Lord Houghton, Browning, the Morgans, Ristori, Oscar Wilde, the Vanderbilts, the Roosevelts, Chauncey Depew, and Lord Randolph Churchill were just a few of the people she knew. Her list of friends, or acquaintances, was so telephone-book long that it seems odd that she did not also know the great in times other than her own. Often her books were travelogues which, though well observed, sounded like Ruskin and Baedeker as rewritten by Louisa M. Alcott and Little Rollo. Even in them Society puts Nature in her place, and big names obscure larger views.

She had strong opinions on everything, such as, "It is to be feared that the Declaration of Independence is between us and good service." . . . "The housekeeping of the Quirinal is excellent." . . . "A thousand dollars is not an unusual sum to expend on a lady's lunch in New York for eighteen or twenty-five guests, counting the favours, the flowers, the wines, and the viands, and even then we have not entered the cost of the china, the glass, the porcelain, *cloisonné*, Dresden, Sèvres, and silver, which make the table a picture." . . .

"Certainly if one flunkey is powdered, they should all be powdered." . . . "If it is in winter, the coachmen outside must not be forgotten. Some hot coffee and oysters should be sent to these patient sufferers, for our coachmen are not dressed as are the Russians, in fur from head to foot." . . .

"The hostess should, in furnishing her house, provide a number of bath-tubs. The ones, shaped like a hat, are very convenient, as are also the india-rubber portable baths." . . . "Novels of society are the novels which society loves, and particularly those of Mrs. Humphry Ward. She makes no mistakes in describing the great world. Her heroines are real. They know their trade. . . . Nor has she that socialistic nonsense to promulgate that because a man is dirty and badly dressed therefore he is a hero. Labor is sufficiently honorable in its own place. It should not be transplanted—not at least unless it has washed its hands."

As a society woman, M.E.W.S. also knew her trade, which was society, embodying it, defining it, improving it. She thought of herself as a crusader for better taste, better living, the social graces, and higher standards of culture and beauty, and fought arrogantly and voluminously for the best as she often misunderstood it. Yet she was not merely foolish, in spite of her frequent successes at being so. In her exceptional way, she was representative of a certain manner of life and of certain values, however misplaced, in American society at a particular period in our emergence. From Polk to McKinley she had seen that society change, as money multiplied, châteaux sprouted on Fifth Avenue, and the older simplicities had been expanded into contests in display. Her fight was to codify the correct, to lead common people to fashion, and to equip parvenus to enter precincts which she held sacred.

People read her because she spoke for their hungers when she spoke for herself. She was no gaudier than the society in which she moved and of which she wrote. If she was a snob, her readers were bigger snobs since what she never doubted that she knew was what they were eager to learn. The untraveled turned to her to take trips they had never taken, the less privileged for meetings with the great, the unfashionable for fashion. Propriety, decorum, the chic, the proper, the ultimate in the modish and elegant, and gossip from the highest pinnacles were what she peddled as surely as Hollywood columnists, writing of a very different aristocracy in a later age, were to sell "glamour" to their quiet readers who yearned to feel close to those, the gilded and the publicized, who led lives of noisier desperation.

Sherwood never forgot how M.E.W.S. told him when he was a child about being taken by her father to the White House to see Lincoln. As a very proper lady from Keene, she was mortified because the President of the United States was wearing ragged old carpet slippers. "I have been inspecting troops all day and my feet hurt" was his explanation. "My grandmother," said Sherwood, "confessed that she had been kicking herself ever since because all she noticed about Abraham Lincoln was those slippers. It may be that these old anecdotes led me eventually to try to make atonement for my family by writing *Abe Lincoln in Illinois*."

Sherwood had to smile at M.E.W.S. She was as easy to smile at as to like. Yet in her his life touched briefly the overstuffed, gold-plated, rococo America, before Deals, Square, New, or Fair, were thought of, which was a part of the many changing Americas he was to know. He also owed his mother to M.E.W.S. because M.E.W.S. was zealous in arranging things so that her sons saw much of Rosina Emmet. After all, the Emmets, different as they were in their values and way of life from the Sherwoods, were highly acceptable socially—even to M.E.W.S.

3

FAMILY CIRCLE

*Rosina Emmet and the Sherwood Brothers—Her Marriage to Arthur
—His Love of Acting, Dancing, Singing, Writing, and the Theatre—
A Misfit in Business Succeeds—Rosina an Artist in Life, Fact, and
Motherhood—Arthur's Failure—Sherwood's Tribute to His Parents*

Rosina was thirty-two and a half when at East Rockaway on June
1, 1887, she married Arthur Murray Sherwood. That would be a ripe
age for a woman to be married at today. It was a riper age then.
According to the *New York Times*, the afternoon was sunny, the
Emmet house was filled with wild flowers, Emmets, and Sherwoods,
the bride's dress of white crepe and her long veil of rare old lace were
"unusually becoming," and the wedding was charming in its simplicity, except for one spectacular incident. This was the arrival of
Wendell Goodwin, a strong-willed guest who, having missed the
Long Island's eleven-o'clock train, "suavely demanded a special
engine," paid for it "in good Boston cash," and appeared as the
ceremony began, "pulling his long mustache and as calm and imperturbable as ever."

Had the wedding taken place six or seven years earlier, it seems
safe to say that the groom would not have been Arthur. In 1880,
when Rosina began seeing a great deal of the Sherwood family, there
were three sons from whom she could have chosen—Samuel, who
was one year older than Rosina, Arthur, who was nearly two years
younger, and Philip, her junior by four years. All of them were then
engaging, gifted, slightly du Maurier characters, possessed of the
social graces which M.E.W.S. held necessary. "What a blessing in the
family," she had written, "is the man who can sing comic songs, and

who does not sing them too often." M.E.W.S.'s family was thrice blessed. Her three sons could sing comic songs. They loved the theatre and music. They could dance, ride, write light verse, ice skate, play the piano, recite, and take part in private theatricals.

All of them liked Rosina, and she liked all of them. But Philip, the youngest, was the one to whom Rosina was at first the most drawn even as he was the one most drawn to her. With Philip she played *Tannhäuser* and Beethoven, had lengthy talks, and went frequently to the opera and the theatre. He was the one who was her codefender of Sarah Bernhardt's acting against the supercilious attacks of Arthur and Samuel; the one who visited her again and again in Pelham, wrote her lengthy letters, and sent her long-stemmed roses. It was only after Philip developed lung trouble and died at twenty-five that Rosina turned to Arthur. Even then she waited four years, under the encouraging smiles of M.E.W.S., to marry him.

She had always been entertained by this Brobdingnagian with his laughing Delft-blue eyes, his high cheekbones, his neat mustache, and his outpouring good nature. After Philip's death she came to love him deeply, shieldingly, abidingly. Their growing enjoyment of each other's company is apparent in the diary Rosina kept from 1880 to 1882; in their letters; and in *Out of Town*, the pleasant spoof of suburbia and the commuter's life, which they wrote together in their New Rochelle days and Harper's published two weeks after Robert's birth. The name of Rosina, who did the Charles Dana Gibsonesque illustrations, appeared on the title page; that of Arthur did not. As a businessman he was discreet enough not to be identified in public with frivolity. Both of them in later years claimed to be more ashamed of this featherweight little book than they needed to be. Though quiet and now dated, it was well observed, its writing was tidy, and its smiling reflection of shared attitudes endearing.

Arthur had bounded into Rosina's life as a gay, assured, and debonair young man who, though out of college, could not quite put college behind him. At Harvard, where he was in the class of 1877, he had made a considerable name for himself as an actor and a humorist. He had been a founder and the first president of the *Lampoon* and an active member of the Hasty Pudding. For the latter he had helped adapt a burlesque, *Fair Rosamond*, in which he appeared as King Henry the Two, a character described in the program as "an extremely aff*able* monarch, but not *half-able* to keep himself out of mischief." This was the first Pudding show to be brought to New York, and when it was given at the Union League Club the reviews praised Arthur, commenting on his great height, "his very thin and flexible legs," his assurance behind the footlights, and the way in which his singing and dancing of a ballet were "rapturously encored."

In Rosina he had from the outset an appreciative audience. She was among the many who were amazed and entertained by his musical memory and his playing the piano entirely by ear. In her diary she noted that after dinner, sometimes with Sam, sometimes with Philip, and often alone, Arthur sang "in the most delightful way," keeping the guests in "perfect fits of laughter with the most utter nonsense," and proving on one occasion more amusing than Harrigan and Hart could ever have been. He did "awfully funny" parodies of ballets, too, or recited such of his own limericks as:

> Whereas there was once a galoot
> Who continually played on the flute,
>   Till at last he was slaughtered,
>   Drawn, pickled and quartered,
> May all of his kind follow suit.

The truth is that Arthur, when young, had as a dilettante many of the gifts and interests which his son Robert was to exercise as a professional. In addition to liking to perform, he could write facilely and with humor in prose or verse. He, too, was stage-struck, so stage-struck that, though a member of such very social clubs as the Union, University, Knickerbocker, and Brook, his dream (realized for a few years after the century's turn) was to belong to the gleefully theatrical Lambs. His talents could easily have led him into the theatre, and he might have been happier had he become an actor. There was, however, the handicap of his height. Even more decisive was the example of his conventional friends and clubmates at Harvard. Many of these, once out of college, headed automatically for Wall Street. This was the expected course, the approved way of keeping a collar white. For a short time Arthur tried to escape from it by working as a journalist. Soon, however, he was caught up in the

current of conformity and became a stockbroker, ultimately forming
a partnership with his classmate A. Clifford Tower.

Arthur was a broker until 1917 when he had a heart attack and
shortly thereafter the firm of Tower and Sherwood failed. Thirty-
eight years is a long, long time. To Arthur, no doubt, it seemed a
longer time. These years were happy ones for the Sherwoods as a
family and for Arthur as a family man, but not entirely happy for him
as an individual. He doted on Rosina, who returned his love, and he
delighted her by thinking that no camera could do her justice until
rose-colored lenses were invented. He also enjoyed his children and
the country on the too few occasions when he could get away to it for
a rest. In the city he was so popular that, according to Rosina, they
once had trouble seating a Harvard dinner because "eighty-five men
wanted to sit next to Sherwood."

But fortunate as he was in many ways, Arthur was one of the
luckless whose work and pleasure, in Churchill's phrase, are not one.
By temperament he was a misfit on Wall Street. Even when he had
been out of college a quarter of a century, he could write for his
Class Report:

> Is it a dream? Can it be true
> That we, ungalled by business fetters,
> Four carefree years once loitered through,
> Sojourners in the home of letters?

What is astonishing is not that Arthur finally failed in business but
that he so long succeeded. Rosina once described him as "one of
those agreeable people who has a supreme talent for simply existing
with grace and amenity when he gets a chance." He did not get the
chance as often as she would have wished for him. He comes through
her letters to her sisters as a man often overworked, worried, and
tightly pushed, capable of making but not accumulating. Plainly he
had his downs and ups as panics and depressions came and went. Yet
for nearly four decades he survived, carried along by the times, by an
expanding economy, by his charm, and by knowing the right people.
Never as rich as his rich friends, he was nevertheless prosperous
enough to maintain a large house in New York at 251 Lexington
Avenue, to give Robert and his other children the best of educations,

to build an imposing place on Lake Champlain, to live in great comfort, to pay his bills however effortfully at times, to keep up his membership in many clubs, and even to come to the aid of the ever-spendthrift M.E.W.S.

His life story, had he written it, would have been a slender and urbane volume, gay as a blazer at its beginning. Its middle chapters would have been stodgy but as easing as a clubman's worn brown leather chair by the window, and its concluding pages gray as a December sky when, after his illness and failure, he retired from life almost as completely as from business. "I have engaged in no activities of interest" was the way in which the once zestful Arthur, by then portly, bald, and with a flowing white walrus mustache, described his last ten years for his Harvard Class Report in 1920.

Rosina could not have written such a sentence. Once as a young woman she confessed with shame to her diary, "This day, I have done nothing." That was one day, only one day. Rosina was never inactive, never uninterested, never uninteresting, never defeated. Right up until her death at ninety-three in 1948 she was, as Sherwood wrote Alfred Lunt, "amusing and amused." She was at ease with life, but life had to quicken its pace to keep up with her.

If she was late in marrying, it was not because she could not have married early. With her long, responsive face, her high-ridged nose, beautiful brown eyes, shimmering light-brown hair, tapering neck, trim figure, and her warmth and ready laughter, she attracted many men her age and older before her juniors, Philip and Arthur, unaware of any difference in age, were attracted to her.

Among these men was an abbreviated Scottish-born American named Andrew Carnegie, who in 1880 at forty-five was already a colossus of finance. He paid court to ladies by taking them riding in Central Park. Among his frequent companions was Rosina, at whose disposal he put a beautiful new black horse even when he was out of town. Years afterwards, in 1912, at Skibo Castle in Scotland when Rosina, Rosamond, and Robert were visiting the Carnegies (Mrs. Carnegie had later ridden the same horse), Robert looked down from his lonely height on his small host and took his mother aside to ask, "Why didn't you marry Mr. Carnegie, Mother? Then I wouldn't have to bow my head every time I go through a door."

Rosina put off marriage because she was already in love, and understandably so, with the life she led as a young woman. It offered her much, all of which she cherished unstintingly. She was a loving person with too much humor, sense, and strength to be a sentimentalist. She loved her parents, particularly her father. She loved her six brothers and watched over the growth of her younger sisters, Lydia and Jane, with a mother's solicitude. She loved her many friends, too, and she loved to dance. She loved clothes and the attention and society of men. She loved gaiety, gossip, the theatre, music, sports, reading (especially Dickens and "Miss Austen"), the pursuit of languages, travel, small country fairs, big parties in town, and the changeing palette of the seasons. Yet happy as she was when moving at ease and with grace through a society of which Edith Wharton was to write, she never became the prisoner of that society.

Rosina did not have to wait for Ibsen or Shaw to be something of a New Woman in her own way, though not in a way they would have recognized. She was no banner-waver or do-gooder, no Nora, no Ann Whitefield or Major Barbara. Much too feminine to be a feminist, she was too much of an individualist to find pleasure in the huddling of committees. Politically, she was as unrevolutionary as they come, being by instinct no less than inheritance a Republican who remained stalwart even when her son was working closely with Franklin Roosevelt.

She did not have to depend on eccentricities to be "a character" or wait for age to demonstrate the force of her own character. Though polite in disengaging herself from fools, she did not suffer them gladly. Hers were the manners of the heart rather than M.E.W.S.'s ritualistic orthodoxies. She liked society—up to a point, though she was far too sensible and unworldly to take it with her mother-in-law's breathy seriousness. She had all the vital juices of M.E.W.S. but none of her relish for fancy sauces, and shared the same huge appetite for life and work without sharing her tastes and values. They liked and respected each other, these two very dissimilar women, and each, being in her own way unfettered, appreciated the asserted freedom and intelligence of the other.

The so-called "great world" on which M.E.W.S. doted, and in and around which she fluttered, was small indeed compared to the inner world in which Rosina lived. Rosina was an artist as dedicated to her painting after marriage as before. Moreover, she was not only an artist in the tradition of Emmet women but the first of them to be a professional. In that day this was as innovational as for M.E.W.S. to be paid for writing as an insider about society. For young ladies to paint plates or portraits for pleasure was permissible and encouraged. To paint them for money, even needed money, was quite another matter. Mary Cassatt, who was nine years Rosina's senior, was different. Being Pennsylvania Railroad rich, she could afford to paint, driven on only by the urgency of her desire to do so. But even she caused some eyebrows to be raised in Pittsburgh and Philadelphia when, though with her family, she settled in Paris determined to be a painter, and allied herself with Degas and the then unpopular Impressionists.

Rosina had ceased to be an amateur at thirteen when she illustrated a joke, sent it to *Harper's Weekly*, and persuaded her family to let her keep the $12 check she received. By the time of her marriage twenty years later she was securely established as an illustrator and a painter. She had collected and illustrated, in a Kate Greenaway manner, a volume of Irish folk songs, called *Pretty Peggy and Other Ballads*, which was well received in England and America.

With a painting, very Pre-Raphaelite in style, of a sexless choir (really some of her brothers and cousins "sissified" for piety, as they protested), she had won the $1,000 prize in the first competition for Christmas cards held in this country by Louis Prang, the originator in America of such greetings. She had permitted no amount of party-going or fun to interfere with her hard, hard work for several years as a pupil of the gifted and exacting William Merritt Chase. She had been commissioned to paint many portraits, particularly of children; had her oils, water colors, and pastels exhibited and favorably reviewed in New York; and, after Philip's death, had studied for a winter at the Julien Academy in Paris.

When Congreve's Millamant stipulated the conditions upon which she would marry, she added, if they were met, she might "by degrees dwindle into a wife." Rosina, although a devoted wife and mother, never dwindled as an individual after marriage. With a husband to care for, large houses to run, innumerable relatives to keep up with, and five children to raise (the first born when she was thirty-three, the last when she was forty-four), her painting was at times inevitably interrupted. Even so, she continued to paint with such undiminished zeal that she won the silver medal at the Paris Exposition in 1889, the art medal at the Columbian Exposition in Chicago four years later, two bronze medals for water color and drawings at the Pan-American Exposition in Buffalo in 1901, and in 1904 the silver medal at the St. Louis Exposition.

She painted throughout the long years of Arthur's delusive prosperity because painting remained for her an inner need even when it had ceased to be a needed supplement. She painted from talent rather than genius, conventionally, pleasantly, and with facile surety. She painted with her rapturous love of flowers showing in her colors. She painted with her tender regard for the lyricism of youth enlivening her portraits of. the young, and her quick eye for character and composition informing her likenesses of adults.

She was minor, not major; charming and capable rather than powerful and original. More than a "lady painter," she was a lady who painted well and had demonstrated as a professional that she had the gift for pleasing others while pleasing herself. Among those others was John Singer Sargent, who had the highest esteem for her as a water-colorist. That she had a profession to fall back on was to prove a salvaging mercy when, after Arthur's heart attack and retreat into a twilight of retirement and ill-health and the clattering failure of Tower and Sherwood, she, at sixty-two, was suddenly confronted with the challenge of meeting the debts, supporting herself, carrying Arthur, and of being, with Lydia's ever-generous aid, the family's caryatid.

Another stalwart upholder of the family's fortunes when they sagged was Rosina's younger brother William LeRoy Emmet, a bachelor loved by all the children as Uncle Bill. He was Rosina's strong right arm, a magnanimous and wise man who again and again aided Rosina and the children, including Robert, in their hours of need. A graduate of the Naval Academy, he became a prominent engineer and garnered many honors, including the Edison Medal, for his distinguished contributions to the development of the steam turbine.

Rosina could seem lost as, with her handsome patrician head deep in concentration, she sat before a canvas. Her deafness, which struck her in middle age and increased with the years, added to the impression she at times created of being removed. This was particularly true when, as an aging, then an old lady, caring less and less about fashion but always wearing distinction as a uniform, she had to depend for spoken communication on the pivoting head of a long, snakelike ear trumpet, known to the family as Nag, after the big black cobra in *Rikki-Tikki-Tavi*. Vague Rosina often was, though never as vague as pretty, blue-eyed Lydia, who had a way of looking off suddenly into space and who once threw out a check for $5,000 which her painting had earned. Let a crisis overtake Rosina, and she was far from vague. Then the strengths of this down-to-earth, gallant, salty, selfless, and immensely sensible woman mobilized, and she met immediate need with immediate and direct action.

This is how she met her children's problems when these intruded upon her. And Arthur's failure and illness, when the liabilities of his suspended firm were $1,057,358 and the actual assets $607,358. Though not legally responsible, because the properties were in her name and not her husband's, she as a woman of honor instantly sold their house in New York and their beloved place on Lake Champlain, and lived here and there uncertainly until, after having reached for her brushes once again as a professional, she could afford an apartment for the family. Even in her mid-seventies, as Philip was to say, she was making some $10,000 a year "by the work of her hands," while Lydia was making $50,000, and "Bay" still more with her boardroom portraits which gave permanence to figures of evanescent importance.

The inner world into which Rosina often retreated was as genuine a need to her as Sherwood's was to be to him. Much as she loved painting, she was no maiden lovesick only for art. There was too much love in her for that. She was the family switchboard, the forwarder of letters, the relayer of news, the nerve center, the blood bank, the never scolding but always alert and understanding adviser, the friend and matriarch, who gave out to her young people, even when they grew older, the warmth of a centering chimney in a New England home.

Rosina was no more blinded by her painting to the issues of the world around her than Sherwood was to be by his playwriting. She was a participant with a strong moral sense, a woman of conscience, never a prude but also never guilty of the immorality of indifference. "We can't have all Bacchantes & *no* Shaw memorials," she wrote as a realist to Lydia, who was studying with MacMonnies in Paris. Robert was two at the time. Later that year the Dreyfus case choked her up with indignation. Pouring out her heart to Lydia, she confessed, "Everybody is aghast at Zola's sentence and the apparent moral degradation of the French people. I believe anybody now could rout the French army. I shouldn't mind invading France myself. . . . The Dreyfus case is rankling in my very soul. I can't write about it. I wish I could stop thinking of it." She was equally aroused by the blowing up of the *Maine,* and in sentences which read almost as if they were paraphrases of what Sherwood would write with the coming of the Second War, she confessed, "Arthur now calls me 'Grim-Visaged War' after calling me last week 'the President's Peace Party.' . . . I have hoped and prayed for peace, but I have known all along that there are worse things than war. . . . I can't live many hours without newspapers now."

Rosina's involvement with life was not curtailed by Arthur's failure, which she tried to make her children feel was for all of them a wonderful and exciting testing of character. It did bring to a drastic and unhappy end a long and blissful period in the Sherwoods' living which Robert Sherwood was always to look back on with uninhibited appreciation. He never ceased to be on the friendliest terms with his father, whom he did not blame. His affectionate admiration for his mother was only increased by the way she met the challenge. Late in the wisecracking, jazz-loving and disillusioned twenties, when he was the editor of *Life,* he expressed his feelings for them both in a Christmas letter he dashed off to Rosina in which he regretted that the whole family was not to be together.

"Not that it really makes any vital difference," he added, "because after all the Christmases we've had we can never be divided, by space or anything else. Arthur, Cynthia and all the rest of us are thinking of our love and devotion for you and Father, and our gratitude to you for our conception of what Christmas means. You can't get away from those things—and there are marvellous tributes to you in the thoughts that your children have now and always: tributes to your unselfishness, your tolerance, your understanding and your sympathy. Fundamentally, we all still believe in Santy Claus, because you've taught us, or rather, you've shown us, the spirit that is no mere childish myth. There can never be any disillusionment in this."

There never was for him.

4

TIME IS THE RIDER

The Happy Cynics and Sherwood's Bedrock of Faith—Westport as a Focal Point in His Life—The Young Runaway—Meets His First President, Taft—The Fay School—The Green Years, and More Sprouting

Sherwood's infancy was short, his boyhood long. His precocity curtailed the former, his idealism extended the latter. He was always to be a boy, at least in a large segment of his large heart. The intense and intricate sophistication of the life he came to lead was never to deprive him of what John Crosby described as "the courage of his own naïveté, a sort of innocent but stouthearted conviction in the essential goodness of humanity."

The cynics feel that only they mature, and they measure their growing up by the widening rings of their disillusionment. Their doubts are their convictions. They are proud of having shed their faith and lost their sense of wonder. The worst does not surprise them. The sole realities they choose to recognize are those known as "harsh," and, the world being what it is, they do not have to search far to find them. They are at home with the complex and strangers to the simple. Affirmation embarrasses them, and the pleasure they find in negation is positive. They take it as a sign of wisdom to believe that all clouds have leaden linings and that there is a pot of vinegar at every rainbow's end. Looking at life through belittling eyes, they smile at the hero and the heroic and fear that sentiment must be sentimental.

Theirs is one point of view. It was not Sherwood's. From boyhood on, he was not only an idealist and a romantic but on occasions an unblushing sentimentalist who believed in heroes, needed them, and

51

was lucky enough to find them. Grief, despair, self-doubt, insecurity, pain, disenchantment, and recurrent melancholy—all these he was to live with as well as with gaiety, happiness, exuberant nonsense, love, confidence, success, and fame. Yet, in spite of the tremors of his living, the bedrock of his faith, though shaken, was never long dislodged. He was an optimist at heart, not unthinking and often inundated by gloom but still an optimist.

As a growing boy he accepted faith hungrily. Even as an older man he held onto it tenaciously. The simplicity of his abiding basic beliefs was among the many contradictions of this man, so much in and of the world, upon whose face its sorrows came to be headlined. He was strengthened, not embarrassed, by the verities. The Milton school motto, "Dare To Be True," more than being a phrase was a factor in his living. He believed resolutely in the Judaeo-Christian virtues and the goodness that lurks in mortals. He recognized the need for men, if they are to survive or deserve to, to be better than they are, and he thought they could be. His hopes were to remain at the core of his convictions, his unsmudged qualities the center of his strength.

Places, certain places, were to mean more to him than to most people. None, however, had for him a deeper meaning than Westport or stirred him more abidingly—and with reason. Pelham, Rosina's "charming archipelago," with its woods, islands, and sparkling inlets, had, like adjoining New Rochelle, mattered greatly to the Emmets and to Rosina as a young woman. To Sherwood it naturally mattered little except as a place to visit, since his family had moved from New Rochelle to New York a year after his birth. Woodland House at Delhi, the stronghold of the older Sherwoods, where he spent his second and third summers in the shadows of M.E.W.S. and the Catskills, also had no real meaning for him. Westport was different, very different, and far more than a summer home. It was the capital of one of his personal worlds, the scene of his first dreaming, a place where he had lived which continued to live in him.

He lived there off and on from the time he was three until he was twenty-one, first in the spreading comfort of Beech Hill, a gray stone house with incongruous Tudor gables, and, after 1906, in the comfortable beauty of Skene Wood, the stately forty-room adaptation of a Georgian mansion which Rosina designed with Stanford White's aid. For Skene Wood, with its three hundred acres and its fine view of the lake and the mountains, he had a special affection.

Westport was for him the anchorage of his youth, the base from which he reluctantly took off and to which he joyfully returned. There he outgrew his cotton dresses and patent leather shoes, his Dutch haircut, his sailor and Indian suits, and the chubby anonymity of early childhood. There his ever-lengthening legs shrank the knickers that he came to wear and, when he had graduated to them, kept his long pants short. There, as time tugged at it, his body thinned down to the structural necessities of a building going up, his hands and feet became giant-large, and little by little his face pulled out to its adult length.

When as a boy writer the sun in his vocabulary was still a "peeping Apollo," he wrote an unfinished story about the building of Skene Wood in which, after condemning the commonplaceness of Westport as a town, he lyrically described the ever-changing light on the water of Lake Champlain and the wonders of the Adirondacks to the west and the Green Mountains to the east. In his youthful opinion Westport had been given by "kind old mother nature . . . a wealth of beauty hardly equalled in the world."

As a man, he did not change his mind. When he was fifty-six, thirty-five years after his mother had sold Skene Wood, he wrote his brother Philip, "I was tremendously moved by your description of Westport. I know if I ever went back there I should break down and sob. Almost invariably, when the going has been toughest for me in my life, I have dreamed about getting back to Skene Wood and trying to convince mysterious and hostile strangers that this is really my home, not theirs."

He left Westport for the last time in the First World War when he headed for Montreal to enlist in The Canadian Black Watch and go overseas. He did not see it again until the summer of 1941 when, during the Second War, he flew up to Montreal to take an RAF Command bomber to Britain. "I suddenly realized," he reported to Philip, "that we were going right over Lake Champlain. The plane was flying very low and I could see Ticonderoga and Crown Point and Port Henry very clearly and then I saw Skene Wood and the village and Button Bay and Camel's Hump and I had the feeling that life for me had come full circle. I also had the feeling that I had always thought this was the most beautiful place in the world and now I knew that, by God, I was right!"

When he was a child, he found New York "dark and gloomy." As he shot up—and up—the city was not spacious enough to hold him. Sherwood needed the mountains. Their size was part of his required scale. In them he was small. They did the towering. Their air was his first champagne. He loved to clamber over their foothills, in his Peer Gynt mood. In them he found the freedom and solitude that were essential to him. In them, too, was room for those spaces within himself into which he was always to withdraw precipitately and without warning and from which intruders were barred.

At Westport, as his interests changed with his years, he was free to try his hand at things uncountable and to run country-wild with his imagination in spacious country. One wintry day in his early teens he even, and quite literally, tried his wings there. With his mother standing behind him, waving a large American flag to cheer him on, he attempted in the dawning of the air age to run down an incline and glide off into space in a contraption of his invention, only to plummet at once and ignominiously into the snow.

Bobby liked the view he got of the mountains from Skene Wood and did not want another. He got another when at thirteen he was sent for the summer to Camp Marienfeld in New Hampshire. He was shipped off to the camp with Philip as his bailiff. During the journey there, a circuitous train trip by way of Albany and Boston, Bobby presented Philip with a problem. In Boston Philip took him to a needed dentist's appointment and, when he returned to collect him, discovered that Bobby had disappeared. Although Bobby had no knowledge of Boston, he had found his way to the Public Library where he had read a book for half an hour, then walked to the Public Gardens and taken a ride in a swan boat. A perturbed Philip, who was looking for him, just happened to run into him on the street afterwards and in time to catch their train.

Once deposited at Camp Marienfeld Bobby found that, though the Green Mountains were still visible in the distance, he was on the wrong side of them. Instantly they ceased for him to be invitations and became barriers. Gnawing homesickness set in at once. As soon as he could, he ran away, heading some six miles through the woods for the mountains and finding shelter in a remote farmhouse. Meanwhile consternation raged at Marienfeld and at Skene Wood. The director of the camp, the masters, the counselors, and the older boys were up all night looking for Bobby, and the worst was feared.

When found, he was brought back to camp, rebuked by the director, and expelled. His homecoming was not merry. The Sherwood children were forbidden to speak to him, and he was sent to bed without dinner in his third-floor room where little Rosamond heard him sobbing. Although his mother hated the disciplinarian's role, this time she took it over promptly and with decision. Her real wish was to keep Bobby at home. She longed to do this. She was afraid, however, that if she let him get away with this insurrection his character might be harmed. She wrote at once to the director of the camp and persuaded him to readmit Bobby. One concession about his return was made. Bobby was allowed to take with him a foolish, bandy-legged setter called Rip, known to the children as "Brainstorm." Accordingly, within a few days, leading Rip by a piece of string, he started out for camp again, gawky and subdued, a crestfallen Don Quixote with a canine Sancho Panza.

Apparently, Rosina relented in her disciplining even before she heard that Bobby had been reinstated in camp. In a letter to her sister Jane she interrupts her account of Bobby's running away, and the "pretty bad jolt" it gave her, to describe the excitement she and Rosamond and Bobby had when they went over to Plattsburg for the Tercentenary Champlain celebration "on the most glorious day that was ever seen.

"By a lucky chance we got on the grand stand just behind the President [Taft] and Governors [including New York's Charles Evans Hughes] and Ambassadors and heard the fine speeches and saw the review of troops which was perfectly beautiful. Mr. Bryce, the English Ambassador, said that Parade Ground was the finest setting for a review in the world. The Canadian Highland regiment far surpassed anything we can show for style. The nice President held Rosamond's hand in both of his and beamed at her and the French Ambassador [Jusserand] talked French to her and said, 'Voilà une petite personne instruite!' " This was Sherwood's first meeting with a President of the United States and also his first glimpse of a Canadian regiment.

The pattern of pleasure followed by punishment was not unknown to Bobby. His behavior invited it. Since he was always up to something, he was often in trouble. The dubious youthful delights of feeling misunderstood were, therefore, not denied him. He once boasted to Philip, who as an older brother was worried about him and trying to correct his behavior, "I made up my mind long ago I would never consider the consequences, and that is the rule I am going to live by." Naturally, he was not abidingly faithful to this ungolden rule, though he took his time in relinquishing it. His impulses were strong, and rebellion was in his blood. Even as a child in New York, he solemnly handed his mother a paper headed *Sacred Rules of Park Avenue*, one of which was "Disobey your nurses."

Punishment following pleasure was the reason for his being sent, when only nine, to Fay School at Southborough, Massachusetts. In the spring of 1905 Bobby indulged once too often in his habit of disappearing without warning or permission. To the consternation of Delia and his family's disquiet he vanished one afternoon to spend long hours at a friend's house. Delia, with a nurse's prejudice, thought he had been kidnaped because he was so handsome. Rosina, with a mother's realism, consoled herself momentarily with the realization that "anyone might as well try to kidnap a trolley car." Bobby's father was not amused. He acted swiftly. Without telling Rosina, who was upset when she heard what he had done, he telegraphed Mr. Fay for a place for Bobby and sent him away to school after the Easter vacation.

Bobby spent more than two years at Fay School. They were not pivotal, but they were pleasant. As he wrote his grandmother, "I have been very scarce in letters but I have not been scarce in fun." During these years he played baseball and football. He sent home those Sunday letters about school games which loving parents have to read with summoned concern. He made many friends, pursued his theatrical interests, and showed early the talent which was to stay with him in his school years for winning indifferent or bad grades for his studies and black marks for his conduct.

Prophetic of his future anxiety about plays in rehearsal was the letter he wrote his mother about an unnamed play in which he was to appear at the school: "6 more days. Mercy. Lately our play has gone down like anything. At one time Mr. Staples thought that we couldn't have it, we have done so poorly. But in the last few rehearsals we have pulled up. A full description of my part is 'a perfect fool.' I have asked Mrs. Fay about my costume but she has not yet decided. . . . Please write me when you are coming. Please come early as there are several little things in the play which I need coaching on and you're the person to do it."

His alarming and ever-increasing growth proved costly from the point of view of his health. When, because of constant colds, he was taken out of Fay and kept at Westport for a year, young Sherwood wrote Mr. Fay a disappointed, typically man-to-man letter. "I am terribly sorry that I can't come back and join the team. I want to like anything. You must have had a fine time on your trip through Europe. I should have loved to have done it myself for I'd like to see the places I read about in books. I miss all the boys up here and wish that there was another one who had to stay away from school that I could have him up here. I haven't been very well today having taken some castor oil (the fifth time I have it this summer including laxatives, cascara, calomile grains and what not) and have been in bed most of the time. I have been having a splendid time although my younger sister is my only playmate. Give my love to Mrs. Fay and remember me to Mr. Boyer, Mr. Staples, Mr. Sturgiss and Miss McFee. Rember [sic] me also to any boys you can get a hold of. I hope this will be a very succesful [sic] term. Good Bye, Your Friend and Pupil, Robert E. Sherwood."

The years at Fay were the green years of early sprouting. Those which followed at Milton Academy were the years of growing and maturing. Milton was a decisive factor in Sherwood's life, a place which he loved as he did Westport. One of the reasons that he loved it and that its influence proved molding and abiding was Albert Weeks Hunt, a courtly, civilized man, as human as he was fastidious, who before he became a member of the Milton faculty had entered the life of the Sherwoods at Skene Wood as Philip's tutor. It was Mr. Hunt, as Sherwood later wrote when inscribing a copy of *Roosevelt and Hopkins*, "who first taught me to tell time and then spent years trying to teach me to use it."

5

WILLINGLY TO SCHOOL

Sherwood's Annoyance at having to Study at a School He Loved—Ghastly Grades, Happy Years—The "Marks" System Made Ridiculous—Weekly Strappings—The Cherished Albert Weeks Hunt—Sherwood Champions a Cause—Fledgling Orator, Editor, and Author—No Diploma but Commencement Speaker

About the only thing wrong with Milton Academy from Sherwood's point of view was that at it he was required to take courses which he was expected to pass. From time immemorial this joint demand has been one of the unavoidable annoyances of schools and colleges. Sherwood did his valiant best to disregard it. Though unconventional as a student, he was conventional enough to be one of those who give aid and comfort to the enemies of education by succeeding in life after having failed in school.

His grades were ghastly; his indifference to them was monumental. His record was innocent of A's. In his four and a half years at Milton (illness forced him to miss the second half of his second year) he collected in the eleven subjects he studied a grubby harvest of two B's, eleven C's, thirteen D's, and two E's. The two B's were in English, and one of them, earned in his third year, was followed by a "plus." But as he ended his final, or First Class, year all his marks had dropped to D's with the exception of one C in Geography, and a B that he won in Conduct, an area in which, though nonacademic, he also needed improvement.

It was not that Sherwood was stupid, lazy, or incurious. On the contrary, he was bright, exceptionally bright; a driving force in student activities; and his interests were quilt-like in their variety. The trouble was that his resistance to the routine demands of education was massive. He worked hard at what interested him and little, if at all, at what did not, learning those things he wanted to learn and leaving blithely unlearned those things he ought to have learned. As a result, though in many ways ahead of his classmates, he was nearly always behind in his classes.

Shaw once observed that parents keep their dogs at home and send their children off to school. The school to which Sherwood was sent was one of the best of the Eastern preparatory schools. Milton was small, select, and expensive, its board and tuition rising from $850 (a large sum in those days) to $900 in Sherwood's last year. Although its students came from many states, the majority were from New England. Very near to Boston in every way, the Academy was no less close to Harvard to which most of its graduates then went almost as a matter of course.

Chartered in 1798, it had a long tradition. It had been coeducational until 1901. Then its six upper classes were divided into a Boys' School and a Girls' School, separately housed and instructed, and, except for a few commingling "Sociables" each year, clear-cut in their segregation of the sexes. The Boys' School, when Sherwood entered it, contained ninety-eight "scholars," as the catalogue optimistically referred to them, though Sherwood's presence reduced the number to ninety-seven. He was thirteen when, as the tallest, skinniest, and most gangling of youths, he faced the ordeal of being a new boy late in September, 1909. He was comforted by having Philip on hand in Forbes House, and four years ahead of him, to offer an older brother's guidance. And he was never to forget his joy on learning that he had been assigned to Wolcott House where his old friend and tutor at Westport, Albert Weeks Hunt, himself only a year at Milton, was housemaster.

With its sixty-five acres and its scattered Georgian buildings, the Milton that Sherwood came to gave the feeling of plenty of sky above plenty of ground. As academic oases do, it created the illusion of being an island surrounded by continent but entire of itself. The turmoils of adolescence were swamped by space until, outwardly at least, they seemed serene.

What space could not absorb, a rigorous routine did. Its purpose,

so to speak, was to gentle colts without breaking their spirits, and it
was wisely planned to empty long hours, to fill young heads, and to
build those healthy minds which tradition insists are to be found in
healthy bodies. The wide athletic fields, the quarter-mile track, the
gymnasium, and the squash courts were proofs that this tradition was
observed. The School-House, at the center of things, did not let the
boys forget why they were not at home. With its museum, its library,
its classrooms, and its large semicircular study hall, the School-
House was a strategically placed reminder of work to be done. Sherwood was among those for whom the clock in the study hall, even
when ticking, often seemed to stand still.

In Wolcott House, as in Forbes and Robbins, the younger boys
were tucked away in cubicles on the top floor. The older ones, sinking under the weight of their growing importance, were granted the
privacy of rooms on the floors below. All of them, the basses and the
trebles, lived on a schedule which put time into uniform. Each weekday morning a rising bell summoned them from their beds at seven.
Each weekday from 8:30 until 1:30 (with a break for a snack in the
middle of the morning) they attended classes. Each afternoon after
lunch, if not forced to catch up on their work, they were expected to
spend two hours exercising, preferably in the open air. Late each
afternoon came a short study period, each night a longer one, and
then lights out at nine for the younger boys and at ten for the older
ones.

Every Sunday afternoon services were conducted by a divine from
the Boston area. And every term some envoy from the outer world
came in Sherwood's time to present the different platforms of Taft,
Wilson, and Theodore Roosevelt; to give lectures, illustrated or
slideless, on "Norway," "Hunting in Alaska," "The Panama Canal,"
"Equestrian Statues," or the "Effect of Abnormal Postures Upon
Various Parts of the Body"; or to read his poems as Alfred Noyes
did.

As a routine, it was not lacking in a regularity which parents, who
had once faced, needed, and survived it or its equivalent, would have
found intolerable. Most of the young, however, including Sherwood,
were young enough not only to take it but to thrive on it. For them
each year was different, and each term apt to be so, because they
were different each year.

Sherwood arrived at Milton the gawkiest of youngsters, seemingly more bones than flesh, and already so tall that, in order to look down on him, condescending old boys had to look up. He was frail and ill-coordinated, awkward on a bike, and apt to damage himself at sports. His height bothered him and inevitably he developed a stoop to reduce those excessive inches which set him apart. From the school's point of view he slouched in other ways. Neatness, for example. He, who was to become one of the neatest of men and most fastidious of dressers, was one of the sloppiest of boys, and seemed the sloppier because there was so much of him to become sloppy.

Sherwood kept his body clean. He had to. The cold tub which was mandatory each day before breakfast and the one hot tub required every week saw to this as did showers after exercise. But his finger-nails, which he had a pathological dislike of cutting or having cut because of the acute pain the process caused him, were in his first years at Milton the longest, horniest, and dirtiest in the school and a constant trial to his masters and contemporaries. His hairbrush and comb were things he left to be washed by friends who could no longer bear the sight of them.

Then there was the matter of his general appearance. White shirts, neckties, khaki trousers, blue jackets, and old dancing pumps with flat bows (the precursors of "loafers") were in Sherwood's time almost a uniform on weekdays at Milton until dinnertime, when blue suits and stiff collars were in order. Milton boys, being boys, were not models of spruceness. Of all the shirts, however, that strayed from whiteness and the ties that went awry, of all the khaki trousers that became wrinkled and begrimed, and the blue jackets that accumulated stains, and the pumps that got scuffed and cracked, Sherwood's in his first years enjoyed an inglorious pre-eminence. There was also the problem of "conduct." As a new boy Sherwood was singularly careless about observing the simplest rules of behavior. He was not a rebel inciting others to revolt. He was a nonconformist bent upon going his own dogged and absent-minded way. As such he almost begged for discipline, and he was not denied.

Milton had long since abandoned "caning" as an un-American activity and in its place had substituted, as had many schools, a system of punishment known as "marks." Not "black marks" or "demerits." Simply "marks." A boy was allowed in a half week to

collect five of these. If he got six or more, he had to "serve" them,
ten minutes for each "mark" up to nine, by sitting in the schoolroom
Wednesday afternoon or Saturday morning. He did not have to
study. He had only to sit still enough not to acquire more "marks"
from the master who used the time to get papers corrected. More
than nine "marks" meant that a boy had to work them off on Saturday afternoon walking around the track, a lap to a "mark," under the
supervision of a bored teacher. Few boys had to do this, and to do it
at all was held to be the sign of a fairly low character.

That a boy could collect so many "marks" that he could not serve
them all on a Saturday afternoon had never occurred to anyone at
Milton until Sherwood arrived. With him, in his first two years,
collecting more "marks" than he could serve became a habit. He
acquired impossible totals with such metronomic regularity that he
became an embarrassment to the masters and the school.

Something had to be done, for the school's sake no less than
Sherwood's. And something was. It was Mr. Hunt, the gentlest of
men and devoted to Sherwood, who hit upon a solution which would
have horrified John Dewey. He asked two or three older boys to take
Sherwood in hand. Taking him in hand meant taking him to the
basement of Wolcott House just before changing for dinner every
Saturday night that he had had to serve "marks" in the afternoon.

There were warnings. "Bob, we're going to have to strap you," one
of the big boys told him, "if you get any more marks." Sherwood's
reply was, "You can go ahead and strap me all you want to but it
won't do any good." Thereafter, when the unwanted surplus of
"marks" came his way, he knew what to expect. He would go down
to the basement with the delegated older boys, slip down his pants,
and bend over, while two or three of them took turns belting him
sharply over his poor thin buttocks. By progressive standards, this
was approaching education from the wrong end. But it educated. At
the conclusion of the second year Sherwood was getting practically
no "marks."

Naturally, he never forgot the cure. Almost forty years later he
could name four of the strappers and still see "the beefy face" and
feel the "mighty wallop" of the fifth, a football player, whose name
he did not recall. "I richly deserved every whack," he wrote Philip,
"and I can truthfully say that I never held the slightest resentment

against the whackers any more than I did against our own mother and father who did their share with hairbrush and shingle." At Milton there was another kind of punishment known as "hot-ovens," which Sherwood was also to remember with tingling vividness. This was a form of running the gauntlet in which a boy would have to get on his hands and knees and crawl through two lines of other boys while they beat him. It was not fun, either. It, too, hurt, though not abidingly.

Sherwood's one major transgression was when he set fire to the schoolroom. The story has its wise and foolish versions. In the foolish one, Sherwood's only motive was diversion. In the rational one, he sought to destroy the bulging record of his offenses. To do this, he stole into the schoolroom and stuffed the damning evidence, along with some wastepaper, into a metal ventilator and lit a match. According to the first story, there were flames; according to the second, merely clouds of smoke. In the blazing version, Sherwood, whose responsibility for the fire was not known, is supposed to have said very casually, while being congratulated on his valiant aid in putting it out, "By the way, I started it." In the other version, though properly punished, he won the gratitude of his schoolmates by filling the schoolroom with so much smoke that no study period was held that afternoon.

That Sherwood had moments of feeling unwanted during these first two years was inevitable. When they were happily past and he was seventeen, he referred to them in a letter to Frank Edwin Lane, the then headmaster, as "a time when my presence in the world was lots more to [be] regretted than rejoiced at. During that period there were only four people in the world that, so far as I know, believed in me or held out hope that I could do anything to bring honor upon myself or my family. My mother was one, Miss Robinson [the matron at Wolcott House] was one, Mr. Hunt was one, and our talk last June, Mr. Lane, has convinced me that you were another. My father and other members of my family considered me as nothing much more than a rotten proposition, and, I must say, they were very near right then. But the encouragement of those four people has helped me to a higher standard more than anything else I could name, and, needless to say, I have an affection for them which only the love for my family can surpass."

This was young Sherwood being very young and having his youthful fun with facts, self-pity, and melodrama. He was accurate, however, in stating his closeness to his mother and his affection for three of the people at Milton who were among his many reasons for cherishing the school. His fondness for Milton was beyond the stab of doubts and loneliness, the reach of whackers, the indignity of serving "marks," the interruption of classrooms, and even the chill of College Board Exams.

Not all Miltonians could have matched his passion for the school, and certainly not all of those did who were literarily inclined. Edward Sheldon, who as a playwright was later to become Sherwood's close friend, found Milton too cliquey and conformist for comfort when, as something of an outsider, he went there between Hill and Harvard six years before Sherwood's time. More interested in Ibsen than football, he stuck it out for only one half of his intended senior year.

T. S. Eliot, though no better at football than Sheldon, grew closer to the school when he tarried there in 1905-6 for a maturing year on his way from St. Louis to Harvard before heading for London to become a famous English poet. He became fond enough of Milton to return to it to deliver, in Sherwood's fashion, a graduating address and a War Memorial Lecture. Yet in these his most specific memory of the school was as a place where he had always been three or four experiments behind in chemistry. "I never used to get anything to explode," he confessed. He was to get plenty to explode later.

To Sherwood, even when his "marks" were piling up and his grades were tumbling down and his rump was reddened with welts, Milton was "a slick school." For him it was not the cold print of its catalogue and curriculum. No school is, for anyone. The catalogue and the curriculum are the itinerary, not the journey; the passenger list without the passengers. In a school its teachers are more than the subjects taught, and the boys they happen to be teaching. It is a feeling both communal and individual. It is noses crimsoned in a fight, shaming complexions, first razors, outrageous thoughts, and noble ideals. It is bull sessions and cramming periods and days of dreamy deafness. It is nicknames bestowed with such accuracy that they refuse to die, and young friendships blooming or fading.

It is what is whispered in the dark of cubicles as much as what is said in classrooms. It is meetings, and clubs, and competitions, and dances. It is the ginger of gossip, anatomical jokes, ambitions shared, and the seasons told by sports. It is the sweaty smell of a gymnasium and the sealed odor of classrooms. It is a hunger for vacations, and strange, disturbing yearnings. It is packages from home and letters which must be sent there each Sunday night. It is weekend visits from the family and costly steak dinners with friends at nearby inns at the expense of parents. It is the pleasure of songs, the agony of recitations, the ordeal of exams, and the daily testing of character. It is nonsense as well as sense and being misunderstood no less than understanding. It is minds growing up along with bodies, sudden shifts in hobbies, and perhaps the awakening of abiding interests. It is youth knowing the pains of being alive. The joy, too. Youths in various stages of being tamed; youths lonely and crowded, shy and assertive, confident and withdrawn, learning more about themselves than books can tell them, yet learning about books, too, dead books which may just suddenly come to life. It is the same school for every boy, and a different school for each.

For Sherwood, Milton was a place at which among his many discoveries he could include the beginnings of his grown-up self. A quarter of a century after leaving he could write, "I don't believe there are many boys at any school who received so much in the way of tolerance, understanding, and superhuman forgiveness as I did at Milton." The school meant to his maturing what college means to most men, and he gave to it the affection that men usually give their college. His years there were among his happiest.

Although he never forgot how difficult he had been, he forgot his own difficulties. The early anguishes left no bruises, the "marks" became a joke, and the "hot-ovens" cooled into agreeably disagreeable memories. In fact, he enjoyed Milton so much that he forgave it for being a school, a forgiveness he achieved by ducking as far as possible the fact that it was one, and by busying himself with almost everything except his studies.

For him the center of Milton was Wolcott House, and, with him as with many another, the center of Wolcott House was Mr. Hunt, its housemaster. Mr. Hunt, Amherst '01 and a recent graduate student

at Harvard, was one of the most popular men ever to have been on
Milton's faculty. Irreverently nicknamed "Mike," he epitomized
urbanity, was the meticulously dressed squire, and even as a young
man had an Old World dignity reinforced by the many summers he
spent in Europe. He was what all the education courses in the world
cannot produce—a born teacher.

Short, pink-skinned, and with light-brown hair, he had blue eyes of
uncommon alertness and a smile as warm as his heart. One of his
favorite quotations was from William of Wykeham, the blameless
founder of Winchester School and Oxford's New College, who said,
"Manners makyth man." Mr. Hunt's manners were perfect, but there
was much more to him than his manners. Gentle yet firm, rigidly
respectable and not at all stuffy, he had a polarizing personality that
drew students to him when they were at Milton and when as graduates they returned there.

Though English, Latin, and French were among the subjects he
taught, he himself was the subject from which his pupils learned
most. None learned more than Sherwood. Mr. Hunt was *that* teacher.
There is always at least one that the fortunate young encounter, who
shapes their character, develops their gifts, and gives direction to their
living. Over the years Sherwood was to correspond with him, to
invite him to his Boston openings, and send him inscribed copies of
his books. "You will never know," Sherwood wrote him when he
asked Mr. Hunt to dine with him in Boston before his War Memorial
Foundation Lecture in 1954, "how much I owe to you for your
gentle wisdom and generosity and Olympian patience."

Twenty-four years after he left Milton he sent Mr. Hunt the kind
of letter which for a real teacher is as cherished as a diploma and
the justification of his labors. Said Sherwood, "I always feel close to
you and deeply grateful to you for the friendship that you gave to a
supremely difficult little boy. I think it was thirty-five years ago this
summer that you first came to Westport and started the apparently
hopeless task of trying to teach me some sense; but, although your
efforts in that direction met with repeated, discouraging failures, you
did give me a wonderful and unfailing demonstration of the power of
kindness and sympathy.

"I am almost totally devoid of the usual 'nostalgia for the old days.' The idea of ever attending a reunion of my class at college disgusts me, because I know that my two and a half years at Harvard were an utter waste of time. I have, however, the most tremendous feeling of sentimental attachment for Wolcott House. Under you, that was a really friendly and stimulating place for a boy to grow up in. Almost all the things in which I am most interested, and about which I have written (starting with Hannibal's crossing of the Alps), can be traced back to your room and to the atmosphere of cultivation and good humor which prevailed in it.

"Probably, the most important element of my enduring affection for you is the fact that I never think of you as a teacher or associate you with text-books or blackboards. My principal memory of five years in Wolcott House is of innumerable laughs." That memory, no doubt, also included the cache of candy which Mr. Hunt kept for him from which he fed Sherwood's ever-ravenous sweet tooth.

At Milton, according to another master, Sherwood showed "a most impressive faculty for friendship" and was "artlessly friendly with people of all ages." Among his schoolmates he was especially close to Winslow B. ("Babe") Felton, John W. ("Gus") Edwards, and Lewis H. Martin (known as "Tish" because his hair was Titian-red) who was later to appear in *The Road to Rome* and *Abe Lincoln in Illinois*. Sherwood's friendships, however, were not limited to his contemporaries. They ranged over the years because Sherwood was already wise and lucky enough to know that shared interests matter more than paired years. Already, too, he was unintimidated by age or position, and was a champion of causes.

It was with causes and friendship that he approached Mr. Lane, unawed by his being the headmaster and undeterred by the precariousness of his own academic status. Mr. Lane was an understanding man who made friendship easy and approach possible. Like every good headmaster, though forced to take the stern measures of a warden, he was also able to offer the solace of a chaplain. Officially, he was obliged to write Rosina at the end of Sherwood's first year telling her bluntly that her son had "done such wretched work in the past that I fear no improvement now could offset his previous failures. I hope you do not feel that we have lost patience with Robert, for I think we have exercised that virtue to a marked extent." Being Mr. Lane, however, he added, "I always hope that he will wake up and do better and I look forward to that some day."

Neither that day nor that improvement came the next year when, before leaving Milton in January for the second term because of illness, Sherwood collected one C, one D, two D—'s, and one E. He could scarcely have done worse had he tried to than he did by not trying at all. Nonetheless, an unfazed Sherwood, recovering from a nose operation in Washington at his brother Arthur's ranch by the Columbia River, did not hesitate to write Mr. Lane the kind of same-age letter that a graduate in secure possession of his diploma might have written, or, for that matter, a trustee. It was a request for Mr. Lane to meet a young Englishman who wanted to start a school like Milton in Milwaukee. "He is a very gentlemanly, nice, well-bred young chap," wrote the fifteen-year-old Sherwood, "and makes a very good teacher. . . . [He] is not the glibly spoken, slippery kind who make a 'hit' on first impression then fall in the estimation, in fact he is quite the opposite. You may communicate with him directly or through me."

Two summers later, while being tutored at Westport, Sherwood dashed off to Mr. Lane a long, long letter which came flaming from his heart. It was the same letter in which he named Miss Robinson, along with his mother, Mr. Hunt, and Mr. Lane himself, as one of the four people who had believed in him during his earlier, darker days at Milton, and Miss Robinson was very much its subject.

Edith Lines Robinson, known as "Bobby," was in her buxom twenties when she was in charge of the dining room, the kitchen, and the general welfare of the boys at Wolcott House. With her vigor, looks, and kindness, however, she seemed no "matron" to the boys. To them she was just old enough to be enviably beyond the uncertainties of growing up, and many of them, including Sherwood, developed crushes on her. She was feminine, gay, warmly understanding, and motherlike away from home, but much younger than their mothers.

Miss Robinson sensed that, long-legged as he was, Sherwood in his first years was very young, very lonely, and puppy-friendly. His solemn search for laughter amused her, and she was entertained by the intensity with which he would throw himself into a party, and, when called on for a stunt, would recite "Horatius at the Bridge" with windmill gestures. She was to remember him as an interesting, extremely mischievous boy who, when she helped him with his algebra, would draw pictures all around the edges of the page and at the lesson's end never know anything more about algebra than he did at the beginning. She once recalled his defensive warfare against algebra and his mischievousness when some twenty million people were listening. By then, Edith Robinson had become Edith Thompson, was in her slim sixties, and was being honored as "The Angel of Keystone" (Wyoming) on Ralph Edwards's radio program, "This Is Your Life," for her many public services as nurse, teacher, and resident in the Big Horn Mountains.

This was in 1950, thirty-seven years after Sherwood had written his letter about her to Mr. Lane. The letter was "unnecessarily fiery" as Sherwood came to realize when he had been shamed by Mr. Lane's patient answer which sympathized with his feelings but corrected his facts. Sherwood had to his sorrow known that summer of 1913 that Miss Robinson was not returning to the school the next year for reasons of health.

Her temporary ill-health was to prove the simple truth, confirmed by her doctors, as Mr. Lane later informed him, adding that her place had been held open for her as long as possible. But stories had begun to reach Sherwood at Westport, stories more and more upsetting and finally enraging. According to them, Miss Robinson had not been relieved; she had been dismissed. She was the victim of a conspiracy. A vengeful doctor was the villain. Mr. Lane had been taken in. Miss Robinson was being wronged. Justice had miscarried. That was enough for Sherwood; really, too much. He reached for his pen to do battle for the right and, no less prophetically, his contemporaries counted on him to do precisely this.

"Dear Mr. Lane," he wrote, "I have received letters, in some cases rather threatening, in regard to what they consider the shameful dismissal of Miss Robinson. Up to a short time ago, when the first of these letters came in, I had known nothing about the matter save that Miss Robinson could not return because, as I supposed, of ill health. I then received a rather brief letter from one of our younger graduates, in which he begged me to take some measures toward getting

Miss Robinson back, or, at least, doing my best towards getting her a
new position. Now of course this came like a bombshell to me. . . .
So I wrote various letters questioning various people about the subject and have received expert and conclusive testimony to the effect
that she is not only willing but perfectly able to resume her work at
school . . .

"Personally, I can only believe that the affair is all a little over-
estimated, but nevertheless, I want to beg you that, if reconsideration
is possible, you will reconsider. Miss Robinson is a very great deal
more to me than most of my near relatives. . . . The thought that
[she] is to be completely removed from my life is not only awful, it
is unbelievable. I think I have more cause to speak thus than most of
the fellows, as Miss Robinson has been more to me than to the rest,
but nevertheless I know for a certainty that every boy who has lived
in Wolcott House under her regime would do anything rather than
see her in difficulties, and make every sacrifice for her happiness, for
she has done that for them over and over again. . . . Mr. Lane, I
honestly believe that you are doing a very wrong thing, not only from
the stand point of the boys but from the point of view of the school,
in dismissing this wonderfully good and kind woman from the services of Milton Academy, and once more I beg that you reconsider
and take her back. It is not too late, is it?"

Although Sherwood's facts in this instance were wrong, his instincts were right and his reactions typical. With the same ardor that
he defended Miss Robinson (and cared for her) he hurled himself
into almost all activities at Milton—so long as they were extracur-
ricular. These activities loomed large in the life of the school, and he
loomed large in them. When it came to holding offices, he was a
veritable Pooh-Bah. From the little shrimp that is a New Boy (in his
case, a giant scampi from the start), he grew as an Old Boy into far
more than a physically "Big Man" in his class.

Was it the Glee Club? He was president. Was it the new Civics-
Literature Club? He was president. The Athletic Association? A
member of the Advisory Committee. A "Sociable"? Head usher. The
Dance Committee? A member. The Dramatic Club? A member and
the joke editor of one of its programs. Hockey? He starred for the
Blues and sustained injuries in a school game. Baseball? He, the

future friend of Joe DiMaggio, was a leading spirit in organizing "The Feds," who played for fun to jeers and cheers on the campus after supper in the spring. Football? He had his wrist broken on one of the worst teams in Milton's history, but he earned his "M," even if some claimed (he among them) that he did so only because of being so tall that he had merely to catch a pass, fall down, and stretch out his epically long arms to make a first down.

He did well, too, at public speaking, and at this period relished the mere act of spouting before an audience. A talk he gave on Leonardo da Vinci in his final year was praised by the *Orange and Blue* as "one of the very best given by any member of the First Class this year," because it "showed that the speaker was complete master of his subject." Sherwood was in truth on firmer ground with the *Orange and Blue*. Milton's monthly magazine was his special interest and release, and he its mainstay. No other contributor while he was at the school was more industrious, did more to raise its prep school standards, or fed as copiously in every department the recurrent hungers of its deadlines. His labors were rewarded. In his final year he became managing editor, a position he held happily until the April issue appeared, carrying an announcement which for him spelled gloom. "Because of the pressure of outside work," it read, "Robert E. Sherwood, '14, has been forced to give up his work as managing editor, although he will still remain a member of the Board. He has done a great deal of hard work in his position, and a glance at any one of his contributions is sufficient to show what an important factor they have always been."

Outside work. This is what his studies always were to Sherwood, and their pressure, unwillingly bowed to, removed him from the work that really mattered to him. But, though they could unseat him, they could not down him. The same April issue which carried the announcement of his forced resignation congratulated him on having been elected by his classmates to deliver the Valedictory address at Commencement that June.

Sherwood served the *Orange and Blue* as a Jack-of-all-trades, much as in later years he was to serve the *Lampoon, Vanity Fair,* and *Life.* Often he met his needs as an editor by supplying the materials he needed. Space was something to be filled and he enjoyed

filling it. He had his father's facility with verse, the easy command
of prose possessed by both his parents, and was enough of an Emmet
to try his hand at sketches. Though no artist, he was already an alert
doodler able to dash off recognizable impressions of people.

Writing was his real concern, and, in addition to short stories, he
dashed off editorials as hoarse with "school spirit" as a cheering
section, rejoiced in puns so magnificent in their awfulness that they
interchanged "innocent" and "in-a-cent," and ground out verses,
light, moral, or rhapsodic, to fit the season or occasion as automatically as a poet laureate and often with no more reliance upon
inspiration.

His verses, even in his last year, were not the stuff of "the boy
who's half a man/Or the man who's half a boy," in A. Conan Doyle's
phrase. They were the play, rather than the work, of a boy all boy,
and schoolboy at that. They bobbed along the surface like corks.
Written too early to be influenced by Pound or Eliot, they sounded at
times less like Kipling than they did Robert W. Service, and did a
disservice even to him. A gifted boy would not have written them
after 1920 because by then it would have been fashionable to borrow
from elders quite different in their attitudes and poetry.

Sherwood was not fooled about the merits of his verses. "O Muse
. . . ," wrote he, "we write most awful verse." Often he did, verse with
no hint of music in it. Most of his rhymes were doggerel of that kind
which becomes "a poem" only by candlelight at a birthday party.
Odes flowed from him; odes, mainly humorous, making fun of the
railroad's Mattapan division, odes to the returning alumni ("So to
our grads, the dear old lads"), to the hockey rink ("you will cough
and sneeze and all but freeze"), or to a lost love that turns out to be
a dead Jersey cow. He also had on tap very moral exhortations about
playing a man's part on the stage of life when "this schooltime drama
stops," or a mock epic about a success and a failure which was very
young in its grown-up cynicism.

Clearly the world was not as yet too much with him when in 1912
Sherwood wrote:

> I've read about
> The Turkish war,
> And how they shout,

And pile up gore;
But this falls flat,
And seems quite tame,
When you've been at—
A football game.

To the May issue of the *Orange and Blue* Sherwood contributed in his last year a parody in verse and prose of the "private style" of those who wrote most regularly for the magazine. His conclusion of this spoof was a *Notice:* "All those who feel they have been insulted above, and demand a verbal apology, will receive same over the long distance phone. Personally, we do not expect to be around these parts for some time to come."

His short stories were better than his verse, because even then prose came naturally to Sherwood. Being a boy, he wrote gleefully about horrors, but he was not of that later generation which was to write with joy about despair. His stories were tales of adventure about the ruses used by one famous British detective agency to outwit another in catching a dangerous criminal. Or how a worthless old toper from Lynmouth redeems himself and aids England by tossing into the ocean a lost torpedo for which the German navy is offering a large reward. Or a crazed old sailor in Ireland, a strong believer in a crystal ball, almost murders a stranger but at the last minute hurls himself into the sea. Or the trials of a young man who is working with an aged scientist to find a way of irrigating a desert in northeastern California.

Sherwood's stories were schoolboy writing. The calendar saw to that. And schoolboy writing must be judged by special standards. It is not meant to last. It is meant to be outgrown. Its hope may be to produce excellence, its author's momentary delusion the belief that he has produced it, but its point is to get the writing done. That, and in the process to come to learn the feel and value, the texture and color, and the challenge and invitation of words. It is no more than five-finger exercises or "chopsticks" to what can follow. It may flourish in one green season, and then wither permanently, the ease gone, the aptitude lost.

Young people, being young, are, if they are young and sheltered, bound to know more about life from books than from living. Except by betraying their youth in their reachings for age, their writing is apt to have less to say about themselves than it does about their reading. They do not have to play "the sedulous ape" and copy out pages by authors whose styles they hope to acquire. They imitate without copying. Their writing rings with echoes.

Young Sherwood's was no exception. His stories indulged in that ventriloquism which is a betrayal of youthful admiration. In them two voices could be heard antiphonally in the background—Robert Louis Stevenson's and A. Conan Doyle's. They were excellent models for writers, young or old, to take, and almost inevitable at that time for the young, even if Sherwood, being young, could never come close to approaching them. But his stories, youthful and amateurish as they were, did make it clear that Sherwood found joy in writing them, that he had a promising gift, and observant eyes for both places and people. They also showed, in spite of their awkward passages, that he was coming into possession of that clear, easy-flowing English which was to characterize his mature style.

The stories told their own slight story about Sherwood, and one direction in which he was heading. Yet they said no more about the wide range of his reading than his grades did, and these were accurate gauges only of what he did not know or care to know when he should have cared to know it. His stories did not, and could not, reflect the strength of his memory, his already burning interest in history, his passion for Shakespeare, or his extensive knowledge of the Bible from which he could quote at length. They did not reveal what Lincoln's speeches meant to him even when they were assignments, how abidingly stirred he was by Pericles's Oration when he came upon it in Thucydides, or the lasting impact made upon him by the Punic Wars when he started studying them "under compulsion," as he put it in the preface to *The Road to Rome*.

In only one of them did Sherwood make any mention of what was behind the headlines of the day. This was in his tale about the drunken idler who destroyed the lost German torpedo. "Now at the time of which we write," Sherwood paused to say, "international affairs were in a rather turbulent state. Despite the increased activities of the Hague Peacemakers, war between the great powers in Europe seemed imminent. The nations vied among each other to obtain the lead in the size and equipment of armies and navies. England, it is true, maintained her old supremacy at sea, but Germany's navy kept increasing at a rather startling rate, and Britannia was having a struggle to keep ahead of her competitors. Needless to say, every country was doing its utmost to obtain more deadly devices for the destruction of human life." But all that was in Europe. To most Americans in 1913 Europe's troubles seemed remote beyond belief, and almost as unreal as fiction written on another planet in another age.

Much more real to Sherwood, and of the utmost concern to him, were two things which happened to him at Milton as his final year approached and at its conclusion. In his usual dual role of natural encourager and obligatory disciplinarian, Mr. Lane figured in both as a bearer, first of good news, and then of bad. "I am glad to tell you," he wrote Mr. Sherwood, "that Robert has been elected by vote of the First and Second Classes, one of the four Monitors of the School for next year. This honor of being Monitor is one of the highest tributes the boys can pay to one of their fellows and shows the esteem in which he is held. It is a pleasure to add that the faculty approve of the choice." Rosina's note at the bottom of this letter was, "Think of this for my scapegrace!"

Mr. Lane's second letter, written on the first of the following June, was about Sherwood, "the scapegrace." It came after several last-minute appeals from Sherwood's desperate father and mother, and said, "I am very sorry that Bob has not done well enough in his work this year to warrant the granting of a diploma and I appreciate your regret and sympathize with it. However, it is not a surprise to us for as we look back over his record for the year, especially in Latin and Physics, we can see that this was bound to be the ultimate result of the work he has done for us."

Sherwood did not get a diploma but he did rise, towering and pale, to step forward to the podium and deliver the Valedictory address for his class in the crowded schoolroom at Commencement that June 13. He did manage, too, by tutoring and the gradual accretion of the needed credits, to squeeze his way into Harvard the next fall.

6

TEN O'CLOCK SCHOLAR

The Disadvantage of Harvard's Being a College—Running Battle with the Dean's Office—Fired Three Times, Twice Reinstated—Parading for Hughes—Real Work for the Lampoon *and the Hasty Pudding—Those Music Publishers, "Sherry and Powers"—Barnum Was Right—Plattsburg—Coming of War—Dislike of Germany since 1912—Prewar Britain—Lowell's Cambridge—Disapproval of Wilson's Neutrality—Joins The Canadian Black Watch—Outmaneuvers Harvard*

Milton's only drawback from Sherwood's point of view had been that it was an Academy. Harvard's more serious fault was that it was a College. Had it not been for the courses which must be taken, attended, and passed; the rhythmic menace of examinations; and the unblinking eye of the Dean's Office, he would have found it a pleasant place. But in 1914, the fifth year of A. Lawrence Lowell's presidency, an ever-expanding Harvard still took as seriously as it was to take thereafter the words written by its founders in the days of its small beginnings. Its purpose, those high-minded Puritans had said, was "to advance Learning and to perpetuate it to posterity." Official Harvard continued to believe this and to act accordingly.

Sherwood disagreed. Though Harvard was established by dissenters, he was a dissenter of a different breed. When it came to academic learning, he aligned himself, unchastened by his failure to get a diploma at Milton, with posterity's unwilling and allergic recipients. Sherwood refused to have his studies darken his otherwise bright college years. The pattern he followed in Cambridge was much the same he had followed at Milton, only more so. He enjoyed the Harvard that was not the College and ignored the Harvard that was.

76

The line he drew between the two was as clear-cut as Cotton Mather would have drawn between good and evil.

He did not formulate this division into a policy. He merely lived as if he had. As a code of behavior, his was superb in its simplicity. Its miscalculation, when carried to the lengths to which Sherwood carried it, was that it begged for trouble. He was so consistently successful in failing that Harvard the College could not ignore him. Neither could undergraduate Harvard which, by recognizing his gifts and offering nonacademic releases for his energies and talents, only added to his difficulties.

Except with his teachers, he was popular almost from the moment when, "as a heron in a field of sparrows" (a phrase used later by David McCord), he deposited his belongings in A-24 James Smith Hall, a member of the first class to occupy the new freshman dormitories away from the Yard and down by the winding Charles. Outside the classrooms then, and afterwards when he had moved to such a "Gold Coast" dormitory as Dunster, he did all of the "right" things in his two and a half years at Harvard. He went out for freshman football, made his house team, and was coached by the recently graduated Leverett Saltonstall who once, when Sherwood was cracked up, put him to bed. Socially he won the trophies of proper acceptance. He made the Institute, the D.K.E., the Signet Society (that haven of good talk), the Stylus Club, and the Hasty Pudding (which was especially dear to his heart), and he was elected president of the *Lampoon*, of which his father and his uncle Samuel had been two of the seven cofounders.

Popular as he was, it was clear from the outset that his textbooks were not his best friends. He was one of those who go to college without permitting it, when there, to come to him. In a day when C's were a gentleman's A's, he outdid fashion to the point of dandyism. Spiritually he was as a student a younger brother of Owen Wister's Billy and Bertie in *Philosophy 4*, those gilded youths of turn-of-the-century Cambridge whose indolence was their industry, though he never had their good fortune in bluffing his way through an examination.

His ultimate heresy was that his Harvard was Stover's slightly earlier Yale, with this important exception. Where Owen Johnson's

football hero grew into a reformer in the matter of sophomore soci-
eties, Sherwood never grew up to face his responsibilities as a student. As a type he was, in fact, less close to Stover than to Stover's
friend, McNab, who could frankly boast, "I'm here for a good time,
the best in life. It may be a short one, but it'll be a lulu." With
McNab he could have sung:

> Oh, father and mother pay all the bills,
> And we have all the fun,
> That's the way we do in college.
> Hooray!

Decades later, Sherwood was to serve as a "Most Reverend"
member of the Board of Overseers, and Harvard was with pride to
confer on him an honorary degree. After his death the University was
to hang James Fosburgh's painting of him as one of the two portraits
in the third-floor lounge of the Littauer School of Public Administration. The other was of Winston Churchill. No one, certainly not
Sherwood, would have guessed that an undergraduate, who in Cambridge was academically in constant disgrace, would ever achieve
there such a state of grace. The work he did not do caused a lot of
work to be done in his behalf.

Few files in Harvard's history could be more discouraging than the
Sherwood dossier preserved by the College in its catacomb of scholastic records, good and bad. With its short notes, its scribbled
memos, its exchange of letters three pages long, its tabulation of
melancholy marks, its summonses to the Dean's Office in University 4, its notices from the Library about books forgotten to be returned, and its warnings about proper security forgotten to be filed, it
bulges, in spite of some missing items, with eighty-eight exhibits.

These tell a sorry story of a student's good resolutions, halfheart-
edly made and wholeheartedly broken; of the distracted pleas of
anxious parents; the aid invoked of chastening older brothers; and a
steady rain of admonitions from deans as understandably threatening
as they were incomprehensibly forbearing. The wonder is not that the
toilers in University Hall or on the Administrative Board got put out
with Sherwood but that they got anything else done. Coping with him
became almost from the start less of a problem than a profession.

In Sherwood's file the phrase, as recurrent as the "Fate" motif in *Carmen*, was, "Unless you do this or that, your connection with the University will be severed." That ominous theme was not long in making itself heard. Sherwood's first November was scarcely over before he had been introduced to it. Then, it was the Bursar who had reported to Dean Henry A. Yeomans that Sherwood had not filed proper security, and the Dean who in turn warned Sherwood unless he did so, "I shall have to sever your connection with the University immediately." This was nothing more than carelessness in attending to a routine administrative matter. It was the beginning, however, of a deluge of graver warnings about conditions less easily corrected, of which the following are a mere sampling of the college year 1914-15.

(*December 14*) *Yeomans to Sherwood.* The Administrative Board has twice considered your unsatisfactory November record. At first it seemed to the members that they must put you on probation. Upon reconsideration, however, they decided, in view of all the circumstances, not to impose any censure on account of your standing before midyears.

(*March 25*) *Yeomans to Sherwood's father.* I am sorry to tell you that we have been compelled to exclude Robert from German A at the request of the instructor because of his unsatisfactory work in the course. He has also been placed on probation because of his low mid-year record. . . . Robert's situation is a precarious one, and I am sorry to see it is made the more difficult by his recent illnesses. Only the most careful work from now on will win him his promotion with his class, to say nothing of the possibility that his probation may be closed and his connection with the College severed in consequence.

(*March 27*) *Sherwood's father to Yeomans.* The young man has not been at all well and his extreme growth has, I think, retarded his power of concentration and ability to work. He is now in charge of his mother who will look after him and I hope and believe that he will do better when he returns to college. He is not lacking in ability and has given evidence of brilliant work in the past.

(*March 29*) *Yeomans to Sherwood.* You have been placed on probation by the Administrative Board because of your unsatisfactory midyear record. The grades in detail were as follows: *English A—D+, English 28—D, German A—E, Gov-*

ernment 1—E, *Physiography* 1—E. D is unsatisfactory and E denotes failure. In my judgment, your difficulty comes from gross neglect of your college engagements as well as from a failure to work diligently and with forethought in your courses. Your position is now rendered more serious, I am sorry to see, by illness. Nothing but the most faithful attention to business as well as perfect attendance can restore you to good standing. . . . Unless you (by April) have a minimum of two full grades of C and one of D, your probation may be closed and your connection with the University severed.

(*April* 2) *Sherwood's mother to Yeomans from Westport.* I am dreadfully distressed over Robert's poor work and have no excuses to offer, but I think I can feel assured that he will do his work faithfully in the future. . . . Bob felt he could do the work easily so gave himself up entirely too much to writing stories and drawing pictures. . . . He is a good boy and a clever one, but very careless and erratic about details. He is with me now and has been confined to the house with a very bad head cold. . . . Bob is my only really clever boy and he *must* do well. Anyone who looked into the matter would probably find that his mind had a very good grasp on the subjects he is studying and if he is faithful about his work I feel sure he will do well.

(*April* 14) *W. C. Lane, Librarian Harvard College, to Yeomans.* Can you bring some pressure to bear on R. E. Sherwood, '18 . . . to induce him to return to the Library four bound volumes of magazines which were due March 18th? We have sent him repeated notices but they have no effect. (*About April* 21) *Lane to Yeomans.* The books have been returned by the brother (Philip). Fine not yet paid.

(*May* 15) *Yeomans to Sherwood.* . . . Unless you win your promotion at the end of the year, your probation will be closed and your connection with the College severed.

(*June* 4) *Yeomans to Sherwood.* At the last meeting of the Administrative Board you were excluded from Government 1 because of your unsatisfactory record in that course. This exclusion means that you cannot possibly win your promotion to the Sophomore Class at the end of the current year. In consequence, your probation will be automatically closed and your connection with the College will be severed. As I wrote you not long ago, you cannot be readmitted except by special vote of the Administrative Board based upon a record of satisfactory work during the summer, preferably in the Summer School or at the Engineering Camp. . . . The Administrative Board is almost certain to refuse to consider a petition for readmission next fall unless you secure at the end of the current year at least one full satisfactory grade. Your exclusion from Government 1 leaves you only two and a half courses, in one of which— English A—there is no final examination. . . . You are in a position to make a desperate effort in English 28. I trust that you will make it.

(*June 7*) *Sherwood's father to Yeomans from Westport.* Mrs. Sherwood is recovering from a severe nervous attack which began last October. . . . I cannot tell Mrs. Sherwood about Bob at present: it would certainly cause a reaction.

(*July 22*) *Dean B. S. Hurlbut to Sherwood* (*copy to Sherwood's father*). You have passed in two and one-half courses with grades above D in a course and a half: ordinarily a student with such a record has his connection with the College severed, and technically, under the rules, yours is severed but . . . I find on your record card a note in Mr. George Washington Cram's handwriting saying that you are taking a half course in the Summer School. If you pass this with a good grade, you will be in a position where the Administrative Board, if it sees fit, may vote to combine the work of the summer with what you have hitherto done to give you Sophomore standing. . . . You did work at a great disadvantage last year owing to your anxiety concerning your mother's health, and your own unsatisfactory physical condition. I feel that you ought not to come back next year unless you are in a thoroughly good condition. . . . If you are at the Summer School, I shall be very glad indeed to give you a card to the Colonial Club which may perhaps make life in Cambridge a little easier during these weeks.

(*July 26*) *Sherwood's father to Hurlbut.* With respect to Bob I realize that early in the college year he was careless and lazy and did a lot of idiotic things but in the last few months he has come to his senses (so Phil tells me) and has worked hard and faithfully. I have talked to him most earnestly and made him promise that he would be attentive at the summer school. I feel quite sure that he will. It is indeed kind of you to offer him a card to the Colonial Club: he and I appreciate this most sincerely and gratefully.

(*October* 8) *Yeomans to Sherwood.* You have been readmitted to the Sophomore Class under the conditions as to a
satisfactory record which I indicated in my former letter.

That was the first year, at least in essence. The next two years—
both sophomore because he never made the junior class—were in
Sherwood's file merely continuations of a serial belligerent in its
monotony. The same resolutions were made by Sherwood with the
same regularity, the same promises given and broken. His marks,
after very mild improvements, plummeted to the usual depths, and he
continued to teeter undaunted on the tightrope of probation.

Instead of struggling with German A, he kept on fighting against
it. "Sherwood's case," wrote his outraged instructor in the middle of
the second year when urging that Sherwood be excluded from the
course, "happens to be a particularly flagrant one. He is a repeater,
and as such was warned that his work would be closely observed.
Nevertheless, he has repeatedly been unprepared, has failed to hand
in his blue-book when it was called for, and has often been absent.
At the November hour examination his grade was an E, his book
being the worst in the section. For two weeks past he has not attended class at all, and I have received no intimation from the college
office that he has been excused by illness. Last week I met him in the
Yard, apparently on his way to a lecture. He was absent from the
hour examination which I gave the section this morning." Sherwood's bad strategy succeeded. He was "excluded" from German A
again that year, and for the third time the next. This, though a poor
way of getting a degree, was an excellent, if unorthodox, way of not
taking an unwanted course.

Sherwood was absent his second year from other classes with his
first year's frequency, and once, in spite of warnings, was charged
with thirty-five "cuts," at least fifteen of which could not be attributed to illness. Occasionally, and without excuses, he also failed
to turn up for other examinations. The same pleas or reassurances
streamed into the Dean's Office from his distressed or hopeful parents, and different deans thundered identical threats, only to follow
these with the same sudden and unbelievable displays of tolerance.
That is, until just before or after the end of each college year. Then
the same severing action was taken, only to be rescinded the next

fall. The result was that Sherwood was fired from Harvard three times and readmitted twice, and the hope was even held out to him in 1917 that at the war's end he would be readmitted again.

There were slight variations in his dossier for the last two years. In 1916 Mr. Sherwood and Dean Hurlbut were able to break the monotony of their bleak parent-truant officer correspondence by writing pleasant, squirish pages about their country places which were opposite each other on Lake Champlain. In 1917 it was Mr. Sherwood who was so ill from a severe bout with pneumonia that he could not be told about Robert's difficulties and Mrs. Sherwood who took over. Twice Mr. Sherwood had to turn to his older Harvard sons, both of whom had had their own difficulties as students, to represent him at emergency conferences in the Dean's Office. In Sherwood's first sophomore year, it was Philip, '15, already in the Army, who was hurriedly dispatched as his father's delegate. In his second, it was Arthur, '10, temporarily in the East on business, who dashed up to Cambridge to "throw a scare" into Robert "face to face," confident that he would "listen" to him and change his ways. He did change them—by doing worse.

Sherwood had grown accustomed to spoiling his summers by having to devote them to academic rehabilitation. By the end of his first sophomore year, however, the pursuit of health became as important for him as the conquest of unpassed courses. Since he had been plagued with colds, was run down and very thin, his poor health was offered by both his parents and his deans as the explanation of his poor work. "It seems to me," Dean Yeomans had written with an unexpected toughness of logic, "that a man in his position who is not well enough to attend his classes is ill enough to be under a physician's care."

Sherwood was not that ill. Even so, in the spring of 1916, after he had had his connection severed with Harvard for the second time, a plan was hit upon to build him up physically during the summer so that he would be robust enough to study hard if readmitted to Harvard in the fall. Instead of having a tutor or going to summer school, he was given a hard physical workout at Skene Wood, and then sent to the newly opened student and senior military training camps at nearby Plattsburg on Lake Champlain.

At both of these Sherwood did well, to the understandable surprise and gratification of his parents. At the student camp he missed no drills and did not have a single demerit charged against him. At the senior camp, though ill for a few days, he was sufficiently diligent to be made corporal and designated a sergeant, even if his actual promotion never came through. His parents were jubilant. Once again they hoped, as did his deans, that he would do well when, and if, readmitted to Harvard in the fall.

He was given a physical examination at the beginning of the college term by a Harvard doctor who reported to Yeomans that, without shoes, Sherwood stood 6 feet 6½ inches (one-half inch less than the usual estimate), that his chest measured 33½ inches, and that stripped he weighed 166½ pounds. The doctor noted that Sherwood told him he had had several attacks of jaundice and that during the winter he had a cough which "made him feel used up and lose interest in his work." He had had no cough during the summer and the examination of his lungs and heart was negative. "The boy's strength and general development," concluded the doctor, "have not kept pace with his abnormal growth in height. But in spite of that he stood well the two months training at Plattsburg and gained nearly 10 lbs. during that period. . . . Everything considered I see no reason why he should fail to make a satisfactory record in his studies the coming year provided he takes good care of himself." Sherwood was readmitted and promptly proceeded to do the almost impossible. He did less well than before.

St. Theresa was uncomfortably represented in Gertrude Stein's *Four Saints in Three Acts* as being half indoors and half out of doors. Sherwood's academic position at Harvard was always equally uneasy, though far less of him contrived to remain indoors. That his precarious health, the toll of his height, affected his record was incontrovertible. It was the explanation supplied most often by his doctors, his parents, and the deans. Yet as an explanation his health could have been no more than partial, since among its uncertainties was its flexibility. It appeared to get worse whenever he approached a classroom and better whenever he left one. It made him lackadaisical as a student and yet enabled him to be active as an undergraduate.

In Cambridge it was such a drain on his energies by day that it kept him from attending classes and examinations, but by night it supplied him with sufficient energy to be a constant patron of movies, plays, and especially, musical comedies in Boston. It robbed him of the stamina to study but provided him with enough strength as a freshman to get into a fight with three townies, during the course of which one of them hit him across the face with a long stick and broke his nose. It did not stop him as a devout Republican from parading, torch in hand, down Boston's Tremont Street for Charles Evans Hughes on the night when he (and Hughes) thought that Hughes had been elected President. Or from celebrating that victory by getting "good and drunk at the Georgian" and spending the money he thought that he had won on bets. If it contributed to his flunking English A, the most elementary of freshman composition courses, it made it possible for him to be an editor of his freshman *Redbook* and later to write copiously and well for the *Lampoon*, of which he became president, and also for the Hasty Pudding.

Plainly Sherwood's frail health, though a reality, was a variable, and not the only reason for his woeful academic record. No less plainly his brother Arthur was seeing beyond what the doctors saw when, writing about Robert to Dean C. C. Little, he said, "I don't believe that his inattention to work comes from bad habits but simply from the fact that he is the most one-idea character I have ever known, and the *Lampoon* and the Pudding are so engrossing that his college work is a bad second. Since he was a small boy, he has been producing plays and acting, writing poetry, and such like activities, and this is the upshot."

To Arthur in the spring of 1917, these activities were "monkey business" at a time when the real business was getting through college, or at least staying in. Dean Yeomans and the Administrative Board agreed. Though they decided to postpone asking Sherwood to discontinue his work on the *Lampoon*, they forbade him to take any part in the acting or production of *Barnum Was Right*, the second play he had written for the Pudding. The first, *A White Elephant*, had been staged the year before, though out of prudence his name had not appeared on the program.

Mr. and Mrs. Sherwood were torn about the Dean's disciplinary decision. They knew all about Robert's obsessive interest in writing and the theatre and were sympathetic. With amused pride they had read his rhymes and stories, and looked at his drawings, and had been blissfully captive audiences at his theatrical ventures since the nursery days of *Tom Ruggles' Surprise* and *The Curse of Bacchus*. They had watched his productions grow in skill and elaborateness since the "Sea Breeze Fairs" had blossomed into annual Pop Concerts given at Westport's Casino with no less a person than Walter Damrosch collaborating.

At one of these, young Sherwood had outdone himself, as Gretchen Finletter recalled in *From the Top of the Stairs*, by his singing and staging of "When That Midnight Choo-Choo Leaves for Al-a-bam'!" Wearing white trousers, a checked jacket, a striped tie, and a stiff straw hat, he looked somewhat tortured of face as he paced up and down, twirling his cane, and singing Irving Berlin's lyrics with ever-mounting violence. But a great climax was ahead. It came when the street-scene curtain rose, and Sherwood swung aboard the back platform of a full-scale railroad coach which moved across the darkened stage with its windows streaming light created by flashlights held by the passengers who were crooning the chorus pianissimo. "I was not present," commented Mrs. Finletter, "at the premiere of *Aida* but I imagine it created the same furore. [The boys from] Camp Dudley recognized the touch of a master. This was Production. They gave it the great tribute—they pounded with their feet. Hot stuff. Oh, Boy!"

In other words, Mr. and Mrs. Sherwood had long had reason to realize that Robert lived with a will of his own in his own world, and they watched and nurtured his talents. After all, Rosina was an artist and Arthur, though a broker, had misplaced within him an artist's temperament. They, too, were book-struck and stage-struck. They had to admit Robert was a wretched student and that the deans were right in disciplining him. Yet, sensing in him something which was a continuation of themselves, they forgave him and pleaded for him, even when they had no other choice than to scold him.

Rosina faced the present but looked beyond it, when in Sherwood's behalf she dashed off a letter to Dean Yeomans in February, 1917. "[Bob] tells me," she wrote, "that you do not wish him to take part in the play [*Barnum Was Right*] and feels resigned about it, although of course deeply disappointed. But if his examination marks are satisfactory, I do hope he will be allowed to have credit as the author, and, always provided that his work is good, that he may be allowed to advise about the production. Mr. Sherwood read the play and thought it very good and, as he was very active in theatricals when he was in college, takes very keen interest in Robert's venture. I think it should be his last. . . . He will always be careless and odd, but he has lots of ability which will probably someday be turned to journalism or playwriting perhaps."

Mr. Sherwood was painfully and constantly aware of the awfulness of Robert's academic standing. He was upset, too, by his son's attitude to the University. Harvard indifference was one thing, an accepted tradition and almost a proof of loyalty. Indifference to Harvard was quite another matter and inconceivable to Mr. Sherwood. There was no question about it. Robert was indifferent to Harvard, and this distressed his father. Mr. Sherwood had never severed his connections with the College. The "arterial blood" of its Crimson (as the color was officially described) beat strongly in his veins. Cambridge was the scene of the beginnings of what he might have been, and the place in which he had spent some of his happiest years. He had been there the captain of his inclinations, as he could not be in business, and many of his unrealized dreams lurked beneath its elms.

Some of these dreams lived again in Robert, so perplexing in his brand of indifference and yet so like Mr. Sherwood in his interests. Forty years before, he, Arthur, had coadapted and acted in his Pudding show, *Fair Rosamond,* and served the *Lampoon* as its first president. Now, in a world fading from Charles Dana Gibson's into a predawning of John Held, Jr.'s, it was Robert who was the Pudding's librettist and the *Lampoon's* president. It was Robert who sang and danced and acted, as Mr. Sherwood had once delighted in doing. It was he who excelled at parodies and turned out lyrics with Arthur's facility. Yes, and it was Robert who intended to be a writer as Mr. Sherwood had planned to be. Accordingly, in spite of his upsetting correspondence with the deans, and Robert's excluding himself from Harvard the college almost as conclusively as some of his instructors "excluded" him from their classes, Mr. Sherwood had his compensations. As a father, he knew within his heart the pleasure of the repeated pattern, with its double sense of nostalgia and rebirth.

To be sure, Robert pushed his absorptions further than Mr. Sherwood had ever thought of doing. This was especially true when he went feverishly into business with his Milton friend Samuel P. Sears and opened a firm of music publishers known as "Sherry and Powers" (the "Sherry" for Sherwood, the "Powers" from Sears' middle name). Sears, a ruddy, cocky Bostonian from a Cape Cod seafaring family, was in time to become a well-known lawyer and make in 1952 an abortive bid for the Republican gubernatorial nomination against Christian Herter. Two years after that he was to be named the Mundt Committee's counsel to direct the Army-McCarthy investigation, and then be dropped precipitously when it was discovered that he had made previous statements favoring McCarthyism. He had come to Harvard from Milton a year before Sherwood, and their collaboration began by accident when he was a junior and Sherwood was in his first sophomore year.

Sears, a handy man at writing tunes, was banging out a melody at the piano in his room in Dunster Hall when Sherwood dropped in from his room next door. He listened for a few minutes. Then Sears turned to him and said, "All I need is a lyric." Without so much as a flicker Sherwood grabbed some paper and began drafting the rhythm on which to base his lines. "I have heard of rapid composers," Sears recalled, "but I doubt if any other American lyricist could equal the speed of Sherwood. . . . He was one of the most careless and shiftless men I ever knew. I became convinced that his capacity for creative writing so absorbed his life that nothing outside of that concentration was worth paying any attention to. His room, his desk, were in a perpetual state of confusion. But when a new lyric or a plot was called for, it came out clear and brilliant."

The writing of that first lyric was the beginning. Sherwood and Sears were soon both in partnership and in business. Having drawn up under seal a very embracing fifty-fifty ten-year contract, which was unbinding since they were both under twenty-one, and had it witnessed by a noted Boston lawyer, they proceeded to open their office on Harvard Square in a building where rents, appropriately, went for a song.

It was a small office but impressive. Against one wall was a battered old roll-top desk above which was an enlarged picture of Sherwood, surrounded by smaller photographs of such fellow versifiers as Shakespeare, Dante, Goethe, Keats, Longfellow, Gilbert, and Poe. At the opposite side of the room was a piano over which hung a huge picture of Sears, flanked by smaller photographs of such confreres as Mozart, Beethoven, Sullivan, Wagner, Bizet, and Liszt. True, none of these photographs was autographed, but visitors could not fail to notice that "Bert Sherry" and "S. Powers" moved in the best circles and knew of the right people.

Sherwood and Sears were bumptious pups who confidently expected to "put Widmark and New York's Tin Pan Alley out of business." Equipped with cigars (Sherwood's long enough to be in scale, Sears' short enough to be appropriate) and making the most defeated efforts to look like tough Broadway professionals as they concentrated on one of their songs, they were photographed by a Boston paper which reported, "Two Harvard gold coasters, sons of prominent Boston and New York families, are helping to earn their way through college by writing popular songs. . . . They are drawing checks from Broadway publishers that more than meet their cigarette expenditures. Sherry and Powers present a new phase of Harvard's contributions to the stage. While the students of the drama in Professor George Pierce Baker's course are furnishing plays for the stage, these two clever undergraduates are writing songs that are to be sung in the White Light territory of New York. . . . They employ a stenographer to check up the royalty receipts and answer the telephone calls while they are attending their college classes."

They did sell two songs to Ziegfeld. For these, according to Sears, they were paid one hundred dollars, of which only five dollars was left when Sherwood returned from seeing the fabulous Florenz in New York, because, in addition to his travel expenses, Robert had had to spend eighty dollars to get Ziegfeld in the proper state of mind. They also wrote two Pudding shows together, the second of which, *Barnum Was Right,* was canceled abruptly on March 23, 1917, shortly before it was scheduled to open. Sherwood was among the nine officers of the Pudding to sign the announcement in the daily *Crimson* which read, "We . . . have decided that, owing to the seriousness of the present national situation, it is unwise to give this year the annual play of the club, for which the list of rehearsals has been almost wholly completed. We feel that the time and energy involved in this production will in such a crisis be far better employed if devoted to patriotic purposes. We, therefore, announce that the play for this year is definitely cancelled." Two weeks later America was at war.

Oddly, the war was never mentioned in the bulky Harvard correspondence about Sherwood until the final letters. Even his summer at Plattsburg was discussed solely as a health measure or a demonstration of unexpected good behavior. The world stood still in those letters, with Sherwood's expulsion from college as its only threat. Yet the war in Europe, with all its threats to America, was very much on Sherwood's mind, and on Harvard's, too; in fact, it was more on Sherwood's mind than Harvard was, which could have been one source of his troubles.

When at Milton in 1940 he spoke of his Harvard years, he dismissed the "disgraceful" facts of his academic record in two lines and with a laugh, adding, "We needn't go into that." At the same time he felt the need of going into details about his military training as a sophomore with the ROTC, about his "trying to learn to be an officer" at those two summer camps at Plattsburg in 1916, and about his having further military training in what should have been his junior year. He also recalled returning to Plattsburg the next April, right after America's entry into the war, in the hope of getting a commission, being turned down, and then attempting to join the Navy or the Army, only to be rejected for being "too tall and thin." "The military authorities seemed to think it would be too much trouble to dig trenches deep enough for me" was his explanation. Had he wanted an "out," this was it. Most definitely, however, he wanted an "in." Nothing was going to keep him out of a war which he thought with shame was too tardily America's affair. Nothing did.

He had never liked Germany since, when sixteen, with his mother and Rosamond, he had visited the Baron and Baroness Munchausen at Bockstadt in Thuringia. He had hated the constriction and discipline of Prussianized life, the "hochs" and helmets, the heel-clicking and the goose-stepping. At the hunts on which he had been taken he had been horrified by the unsporting way in which the roe-deer became helpless targets when driven by beaters to the very fronts of the tree houses in which the hunters were hidden. He had been shocked to discover that, slim as they were, many of the young officers who called on the Baroness's daughters wore corsets under their uniforms to achieve an hourglass figure. Even the Kaiser, seen from the next box at a gigantic air show at Coburg, had left him unimpressed as, uniformed imperially, Wilhelm strutted about looking at a Zeppelin overhead while the ends of his mustache were putting on quite an air show of their own.

England, seen that same summer in the full assurance of its unshaken glory, had been different. He had loved it, and smiled at it, and responded to its greatness, and felt strangely at home in it, not withstanding his Emmet blood. As a young traveler he had seen London through the eyes of the usual American tourist. He had found it, as he recalled in his preface to *Waterloo Bridge*, "full of confident superiority, red coats and red beef," and a "dowdiness that transcended fashion."

To him it represented "power in effect and incalculably more power in reserve . . . a tradition that was more stalwart and less perishable than any reality." He had noticed blemishes on "its vast, placid, smug countenance, but even these, because they were seen through the mellowed glass of Dickens, appeared to be charmingly 'quaint' and 'picturesque.'" To him London seemed eternal. "It would know wars through the columns of its press," he had thought, "Kipling wars, involving millions of black men and a brigade or so of indomitable but essentially humorous Tommies. Such minor disturbances would not bother London. It would go on—'business as usual' —adding to its wealth and its girth, drinking its honest, unemotional beer and eating its tasteless Sunday joint, erecting unsightly monuments to the great men that it was capable of producing. The poor, said London, may always be with us—but so will the rich, the noble, the talented and the brave."

That was the England and the London which Sherwood took to his heart in the summer of 1912. He was scarcely neutral in his feelings when he arrived in Cambridge two Septembers later. For that matter, neither was Harvard. Outwardly, during his first month, it was a college going its traditional way in peace. It was Lowell's Harvard, no longer Eliot's, though the splendid old man, erect beyond the bending of the years, was still around, a walking column in his own honor. Lowell, stooped, with his head bent forward, his alert face crocheted by tiny wrinkles, his stalking eyes, his eloquence and wit, his impatient tolerance, and his dreams of a new Harvard, was, to be sure, a building president.

Proofs of this were plentiful. Down by the river, Gore, Standish, and the Smith Halls, the freshman dormitories which within three years would be used as barracks by the ROTC, were shiny in their Georgian newness. The Music Building was ready for occupancy. Widener Library, that proud, tumorous dowager of learning, corseted by its Corinthian columns, was nearing completion. Above the hammering, however, could be heard more and more clamorously each month the cannonading in Europe, even though at first the clock in the tower of Memorial Hall, America's endearingly ugly answer to the Albert Memorial, still tolled time for undergraduates who ambled or scurried instead of marched.

The marching was not far distant. The gates to the Yard could not be shut against the war, any more than could the minds of the young who, if the war came to America, would have to go to it. Wilson could issue a proclamation urging neutrality in thought and action, but he could not enforce it. The University seethed with the stir-craziness of potential soldiers who, though still expected to be concerned with the remote past, heard pounding in their ears the war drums of an uncomprehended but summoning present. It is not easy to concentrate on the best of books when a good fight is taking place outside the window. That was where it seemed the war was being fought more and more, especially after Germany's U-boats widened their activities. In an alarmed but unprepared America, "Preparedness" advanced little by little from the slogan of the zealous few to become a national concern.

From the beginning Lowell had encouraged students to go to such summer military camps as General Leonard Wood had established at Plattsburg. By 1916 General Wood, with two Regular Army officers, was at Harvard giving for academic credit a course in military science with 864 students enrolled. By then Harvard had its own battalion in which R. E. Sherwood, '18, served in Company C. The University's Dental and Medical Schools were sending ambulance and hospital units abroad. Undergraduates and recent graduates in ever-swelling numbers were enlisting in the British and Canadian forces or the Lafayette Escadrille. Early in 1915, on his return to Harvard from teaching in a Western college where the war at its coming had "seemed to the average student as unreal as the War of the Roses," Samuel Eliot Morison had the impression of being "on the outskirts of battle."

Among the aroused was Sherwood. He released his feelings in a thumping war song which the team of Sherry and Powers turned out in 1916 and was overjoyed to sell to a Boston music publisher. It was their answer to such a pacifist ditty as "I Didn't Raise My Boy to Be a Soldier," and was dedicated to J. Stuart Blackton "whose embassy of national preparedness" had inspired it by producing a propaganda film called *The Battle Cry of Peace,* a title which they borrowed. As poetry, Sherwood's lyrics must take their place among the war's atrocities, but the beliefs they tormented with their wording were unmistakable.

> In Europe they've taught us the mean-ing of war,
> Bat-tle with-out cease;
> The burst of the shrap-nel, the can-non's roar,
> Teach us the les-son of peace.
> We have seen the fire and pil-lage
> In ev'-ry Bel-gian vil-lage,
> We've heard the call for help a-cross the sea—
> But now that we have seen
> What war may real-ly mean
> Let us pre-pare to keep our na-tion free.

Chorus

> Put your gun on your should-er, be ready for war—
> That's the bat-tle cry of Peace
> For we can't stand back when the foes at-tack
> Striv-ing for our home and coun-try
> We need an arm-y to fight for our flag—
> And a larg-er nav-y too—
> With Peace for-ev-er
> We'll still be able to shout out
> The Bat-tle cry of Free—dom.   *(Repeat)*

An editorial in the *Lampoon* following America's declaration of war expressed (fortunately in happier fashion) the intensity of Sherwood's convictions. "The United States," it said, "has at last passed that brink upon which she has been hovering since the *Lusitania* disaster, and whatever she does now is done not as a cringing neutral but as an honorable co-worker in the cause of civilization. . . . She has regained her place among the nations of the world . . . waging glorious battle against an autocracy whose only doctrines are the doctrine of war and whose survival means unmitigated Hell on earth." Peace at the moment seemed delusively in sight. "But," continued the editorial, "whether or not we send any troops to Europe, we have at least vindicated our national honor and our right to membership in the brotherhood of man."

The next question raised was the course the government should take. "Our first move," urged Sherwood, "must be for universal service without regard for political or financial standing. The erstwhile pacifists and pro-Germans are urging a volunteer system with their dying gasp, but we should pay no more attention to this, their swan song, then we did to any other of their futile utterances." Sherwood had his own ideas about selective universal service, and the *Lampoon* being the *Lampoon* and Sherwood being Sherwood, these were not all stated in the phrases of a young man who had been stirred by Wilson. "Lampy," he added, "offers the following suggestions for those who should be conscripted first: Harvard Square students, Parlor snakes, The man who struck Lodge, All other pacifists, Movie heroes, Taxi drivers, Bill collectors, Cambridge cops. With such an army in action, we wouldn't care *how* many German shells took effect." As was to remain true of him, he was earnest and capable of smiling at one and the same time, and passionately serious even in his gaiety.

Sherwood was strongly for Hughes in 1916. So was Harvard which, in a straw ballot conducted by the *Crimson* a few weeks before the election, cast 1,140 votes for him and only 627 for Wilson. Youth, at the outset resistant to war, then caught with its fever and impatient for action, was in that ballot. Sherwood, if his age had permitted, would have cast his vote for Hughes and not merely because of the poor, echoing reason that his family was Republican. He had reasons of his own, the product of his nature. He was always to have little sympathy with, and less liking for, uncommitted people when moral decisions had to be made. Gentle and kind as he was, neutrality was alien to his nature. Later he was to remember with glee how he had used the editorial columns of the *Lampoon* to give the Harvard Union for American Neutrality "the 'razz' on every possible occasion," and how he, "together with several convivial souls, made a point of breaking up their meetings with eggs."

He scorned Wilson's hesitancy to act and the noble justifications he found for it. When Pershing led an inadequate expeditionary force into Mexico in pursuit of Pancho Villa, the *Lampoon's* comment on the headline, "Whole National Guard Can Be Rushed to Mexican Border in Week," was "Tumulty, reserve two lowers at once." Tumulty was Wilson's private secretary. The President's note-writing to Imperial Germany was highly irritating to Sherwood. He had little use for the Wilson who "kept us out of war" and much respect (mingled with some misgivings) for the Wilson who led us into it with a notable speech.

"Too proud to fight" and "peace without victory" (considering the enemy) were phrases which by temperament Sherwood could not accept. "The present German submarine warfare is a warfare against mankind"; "we will not choose the path of submission"; "the rights and liberties of small nations"; a League of Nations; "concert of peace"; "we have no selfish ends to serve"; and "the world must be made safe for democracy" were phrases he could not resist. They united a disunited nation and stated stirringly what he had been fumbling to formulate. For Sherwood the idealist, they codified his ideals. For him the crusader, they supplied him with the reasons for his crusade.

He did not wait for the draft which he had advocated. As soon as he could be, he was back at Plattsburg seeking to enlist. When he was turned down, his despondency was deep, his anger great. To his mother he railed against the "fat heads" there who had pronounced him "too weak to carry arms," and "chucked" him "into the discard as abnormal and overbalanced and disproportionate and unfit." Undeterred, he tried everything everywhere, and everywhere he was rejected for the same reason—his weight was not up to his height.

Neither, apparently, were the Armed Forces of the United States. But there were other Armed Forces.

By the middle of May he had resigned from the *Lampoon,* the board of which, though it consisted of twenty editors in March, was to dwindle to four by the next September.

On July 3, without telling his family what he planned to do, he stepped off a train in Montreal and headed for the Bleury Street Armory to enter the Canadian Expeditionary Force as a private. When his kilt was tossed to him, he learned he had been assigned to the 42nd Battalion of the 5th Royal Highlanders, famous as The Canadian Black Watch and with a record as illustrious as that of its Scottish counterpart.

Whatever dangers the war held for him, Harvard was safely behind him. Always closer to his disciplinary deans than to such of the faculty's "greats" as Kittredge, Bliss Perry, Briggs, and Baker, to whose lectures he had also failed to listen, he may not have picked up much learning at Harvard but he had acquired the wisdom to leave Harvard before Harvard could again ask him to leave it. He did not even bother to take the final examinations, given early for war reasons, in three of his courses.

A third of a century later when he was once again in Canada, this time to receive an honorary degree at Bishop's University, he told a youth who asked him for advice—any advice—that he had spent the rest of his life "regretting how stupidly and lazily" he had wasted his two and a half years in Cambridge. He also confessed how much time he had had to spend in the ensuing years educating himself and stressed the importance of considering a college education as a God-given opportunity rather than a tiresome chore. He knew his was "an obvious moral lecture." The young man had asked for it, and it was Sherwood's duty to oblige. Anyway it becomes the successful to speak of their failures.

He was weighted by no regrets when, with a feeling of high dedication, he left Cambridge. Sherwood was leaving far more than Cambridge and far more than he knew. During the spring when he was scurrying around trying to enlist, his father slowly recovered from pneumonia but was for the rest of his life to be a semi-invalid, with a heart condition which caused circulatory troubles in his legs. On the seventh of May, after Mr. Sherwood had been ill and incommunicado for some time, came the disastrous failure and suspension of his brokerage firm. This was to mean a dark variety of things—some snubs, many hardships, Rosina's brave mustering of her talents as a painter to help support the family, the closing of Mr. Sherwood's career and the crumpling of his spirit, the sale of Skene Wood and the Sherwood house in New York, and the dropping of the curtain on a charming and comfortable way of life.

In the midst of his misfortunes, Mr. Sherwood did have his satisfactions as a father in wartime. Arthur was building ships for the government at Portland, Oregon. Philip was serving as a lieutenant in the 17th U.S. Cavalry at Douglas, Arizona. And Robert, in spite of Harvard's thinking he was at Plattsburg, was in Montreal with the 5th Royal Highlanders. Mr. Sherwood reported all this proudly to the Dean, though his letter had another purpose. "I regret to advise you," he wrote, "that Robert has severed his connection with Harvard College at least for the present. I can not now afford to send him back and imagine that in any event he will be in active service for an indefinite period." The Dean's answer, after an expression of interest, was to inform Mr. Sherwood that Harvard had severed Robert's connection with the College. It was too late. At least this time Robert had made the first move.

7

SOLDIER OF THE KING

An Addition to Montreal's Skyline—His Friend, Corporal Child—The Canadian Black Watch—Canada at War—An Issue of the Lampoon *Recalled—Embarkation and Bramshott, Hampshire—London, 1917— Leaving for France*

Montreal has its many sights and for three months a kilted Sherwood was one of them. Taller than he wanted to be, taller than the United States Army and Navy thought that he should be, he seemed taller than ever in his Black Watch uniform. With a Glengarry slapped on his long head, the length of his neck underscored by the dark circle of his tunic's collar, his tunic buttoned tightly around the extensive stretches of his thin chest, a sporran dangling like a giantess's scalp from his waist, a kilt swinging from his lean hips, and his craggy knees plentifully exposed, he was from the time of his arrival an addition to the Montreal skyline.

Later, when the company organized a pipe band and chose Sherwood as its drum major, and he led his outfit as it paraded from Guy Street onto Bleury, and then up the mountain, swinging, with an expert's skill and a ham's relish, a baton six feet long, all the pride of The Canadian Black Watch was rhythmically released in the gyrations of a twenty-one-year-old giant, and a spectacle became a spectacular.

The quartermaster, Matt Hall, had rolled his eyes with disbelief up and down Sherwood when he turned up at the quartermaster's store on Guy Street to get his uniform. Hall, a veteran of the Boer War, had been around but now he was surveying the incredible. Here was a challenge to both his supplies and his ingenuity, a human campanile who stood 6 feet 6½ inches, or was it 7 inches, and whose shoe size was 17.

Hall called over F. Maurice Child, a corporal in his outfit, and together they pondered the problem of finding shoes, a tunic, and a kilt that would decently enclose the rookie. They might have added socks to their dilemmas, and doubtless would have, if Sherwood had not arrived with seven pairs, three more than the prescribed number. He had taken this precaution because he knew that he would have trouble replacing them. Rosina's solution had always been to buy the longest available woven woolen or wool and cotton socks, then cut off their tips, and pick up the stitches and knit new toes, thus making the socks fourteen inches long and allowing for shrinkage.

Sherwood's kilt proved a soluble problem. His shoes did not. He wore his own brown ones, reinforced with cardboard and tramped down to holes, through the wet of England and for several months in France before two new pairs could catch up with him. His tunic was a problem to which a solution was deliberately postponed by Sherwood and Child. The two of them had taken to each other at once, as will happen, especially in wartime when friendships are rushed by the sense that time may be curtailed.

In Corporal Child, who was seven years his senior, Sherwood found a jaunty, warmhearted, stoutly loyal, lifelong friend with the burr of Burns in his speech and an acquaintance with Sir Harry Lauder among his treasures. In Private Sherwood, Child discovered a friend, a constant correspondent, and a hero (in his words "one of God's noblemen") whose career he was always to follow and often to share in with proud absorption. They had humor, a delight in high times, generosity, and courage in common. As if these were not enough, they were both romantics exuberantly responsive to life.

Two things stood at first between their companionship: *K. R. and O.* (*King's Rules and Orders*) which, in those Georgian days that were still Edwardian, forbade a noncommissioned officer to fraternize with a common private, and the French Canadians who, by rioting in the streets of Montreal over conscription, made it all but impossible for a private to get a pass.

Sherwood's tunic came to the rescue of his friendship with Child. It provided them with a happy stratagem for circumventing authority and routing snobbery. They simply saw to it that the tunic did not fit. With the aid of an old sergeant major they fixed up a pass which they never gave up. With it they would get by the guard, Child explaining, "Corporal Child parading Private Sherwood to tailor, for military reasons." Then, heading for the regimental tailor two doors away from The Black Watch Armory, they would continue to the restaurant in the old Bonaventure Station where Sherwood, who had no fondness for army chow, would devour more food than Child had ever seen a man stow away.

Child's amiable disregard of *King's Rules and Orders* did not stop there. Often he sneaked Sherwood out to his apartment for dinner and a relaxed evening with his Swiss-born wife, Frida. When October came and Sherwood headed for overseas (Child followed in two weeks), it was Child, again more obedient to friendship than to regulations, who went down with Frida in the middle of the night to the Canadian Pacific depot to see him off. To show his gratitude for all these favors, Sherwood, as the train pulled out and people waved and fought back tears, stripped the green rosettes from his kilt and tossed them to Frida. From a Highlander, as Child knew, this was a compliment comparable only to a toreador's making a gift of the ears and tail of a bull he has slain.

In spite of its restraints, Sherwood fell gradually in love with The Black Watch, never afterwards to fall out of love with it. Years later when he was standing in a semicircle of Roosevelt's advisers at the White House during one of the President's radio addresses, the group came to attention as the Marine Band played the national anthem. After the music ended, an admiral turned to him to say, "Mr. Sherwood, one need not be a Sherlock Holmes to see that you once served in a Highland regiment."

"How is that, Admiral?"

"You stand at attention with your thumbs well back of the pleat of your kilt."

Sherwood's reply was, "I have been doing this unconsciously for more than twenty years, thanks to the good training of The Black Watch Regiment, sir."

The training was good, meaning good and hard, and good because

hard. "They lay it on pretty thick in the Canadian army," wrote
Sherwood to Mr. Hunt, explaining why he had not had time to
answer a letter. He was not complaining. He had come to understand
the need for indoctrination that was stiff.

At home Americans were marching as to war. The war had long
since invaded Canada. The States knew the exaltation of a war de-
clared but as yet unfought. Canada lived with the costs of a war
which had already been fought for three terrible years. Casualty lists,
on which the black ink was too often the herald of mourning, had
been the staple of her reading. Sherwood was living among the ini-
tiated, not the starry-eyed. The streets of Montreal were filled with
men "pretty well shot to pieces . . . boys minus various important
limbs, or with that sallow, hectic look that marks the gas victim."
Only the gravely wounded, he reported, were sent home. Those with
lesser wounds, although incapacitated for further service at the actual
front, were generally held in England for various reserve line duties.

Canada, wrote Sherwood to Mr. Hunt, had recruited seventy-five
percent of her eligible men by the volunteer system—a remarkable
record—and lost nearly seventy-five percent of these through casualties. The French Canadians were ingloriously different. For them at
that moment Sherwood had no use. They were parading nightly
around the city, shouting, "En bas, en bas la conscription! Nous ne
sommes pas français! Nous ne sommes pas canadiens! Nous sommes
CANADIENS-FRANÇAIS!" To Sherwood they were "a race gone to seed
. . . a good-for-nothing lot of slackers" who "repudiate France because she gave them up to England" and "hate England as an op-
pressor. . . . The feeling is so extreme that we are hissed and jeered
as we march through the streets, and regarded very much as the
Prussians are by Belgians. It is extremely unsafe for any man in
uniform to venture into the French districts."

Mr. Hunt read Sherwood's letter with its descriptions of Montreal,
the Canadian war effort, The Black Watch, and its advice to America
with such pride that he showed it to Edward Bacon, the editor of the
Lampoon, who liked it so much that he published it. Apparently,
however, neither Mr. Hunt nor the editors of the *Lampoon* read the

letter as carefully as they might have for international overtones. When it appeared, to the consternation of all a sentence was discovered near its end which caused the recall of the whole issue.

After the offending sentence had been inked out in gold, the issue was again released and considered safe for the Entente Cordiale, for Harvard, and for Sherwood, not to forget the *Lampoon*. The deleted sentence can still be read if the page is held up to the light. In a bunting mood Sherwood had written, "I never realized how patriotic I was to my own country, until I found myself serving under an alien flag, and doing obeisance to a little shrimp in Buckingham Palace."

Because of the French-Canadian riots and the threats of civil war, The Black Watch paraded through Montreal with bayonets fixed, and their sailing was delayed. During the waiting Sherwood had moments of despair. His knee, hurt in football at Milton, began under the stress of training to cause him such acute pain that he was sent to the hospital. There for a time he lived with the fear that, though the doctors would permit him to stay in some soft billet in the Army, they would declare him unfit for service overseas. This would have broken his heart, set, as it was, upon France.

Before he left, the rigorous days of preparation were brightened by some of those pleasant interludes which can ultimately erase the memories of hardship. A visit from his sister Cynthia who, in a carriage, followed the parade route of The Black Watch around Mount Royal. A short leave which allowed him, in full regalia, with his acres of knees exposed, to strut around Cambridge to the admiration of undergraduates and around Westport to the amused astonishment of old friends and neighbors. Then there were the new friendships made, or in the making, within the regiment, friendships with men for whom he developed that "we happy few, we band of brothers" feeling which cements those who have shared a fighting war.

Finally, there was the pleasure of having his mother come to see him off. She was on the platform with the Childs among those waving and fighting back tears the night his train pulled out.

"Mother," he said to her, "I want you to promise me something."

"Anything, my darling."

The promise he exacted was that, in writing to her sister Jane de Glehn or any of her other relations in England, she would never

mention his bad knee. He assured her that the knee would guarantee
him a bombproof job and that, therefore, she need never worry about
him because he would not be in any danger. This was a cheerful lie.
His real fear was that the knee might keep him out of action.

On October 4 his unit embarked at Halifax on the *Carpathia*
for Liverpool and proceeded to a camp at Bramshott in Hampshire
some fifty miles southwest of London. For Sherwood the months that
lay ahead were for the most part dreary. The camp was cheerless, located as it was on a gorse-covered moor over which chill winds blew
without mercy. The fogs were heavy even for an English fall and
winter. The nights were so damply dark that his whole heart was in it
when, in the evenings, he huddled by the stove in his hut, singing "If
the ocean was whisky and I was a duck, I'd dive to the bottom and
never come up." Furthermore, the intensive training involved working for hours in trenches filled up to his waist with mud and water.
This did not help his knee and resulted in his having a long siege of
influenza.

To make matters worse, someone on his arrival decided that Sherwood "looked like a most accomplished ditch digger, swill sifter, and
shifter of manure." Accordingly, as he wrote his mother, trying to
make light of it, he spent a large part of his time working the incinerator. "The latter occupation, as you may well imagine, calls for the
utmost delicacy and tact, and I hope to make a life work of it. Allow
me to explain, in case you don't know of this art, that the incinerator
is for the purpose of consuming the daily excretions. In other words,
it usurps the usual duties of a sewer, thereby releasing said sewer for
the front—it's all so romantic."

It is easier to be lonely than alone at an army camp. If at times
Sherwood was lonely as an American in a Canadian outfit in England, he did not say so. He kept quiet about his troubles except to
treat them as jokes. His letters home were good reading, and meant
to be just that. Written out of consideration rather than self-pity, they
said only what he thought his family wanted to hear—about him and
about the war. They were resolutely gay. So for the most part was he,
in his solemn way.

He was young. He was living with and on heightened wartime

emotions, the simplicity and intensity of which are swiftly forgotten and smiled at, once the dangers which have evoked them are past. He was where he wanted to be, preparing to go where he wanted to be sent, among men he liked in an outfit of which he, and they, were proud. Moreover, his months at Bramshott were not by any means all a matter of drilling and digging and mothering the incinerator. There were blessed hours off and, occasionally, still more blessed weekends when Sherwood and his friend Child went to Hindhead or the Isle of Wight.

Then there was London, where he would escape into the spacious elegance of the picture-strewn house of his aunt Jane de Glehn, the painter, and her artist husband, Wilfrid, and savor the ease and comfort of a home. He also enjoyed going to the theatre again, and gratefully saw Barrie's new play *Dear Brutus, The Better 'Ole, Chu Chin Chow* of course, and a small revue produced by Charlot in which "I'm going back to the shack Where the blackeyed Susans grow" was sung by a trim Canadian girl named Beatrice Lillie.

London looked as he had known it five years before. To be sure, there were craters in the Embankment and, here and there, buildings blasted by the Zeppelins and Gotha bombers which came over every clear, moonlit night. These were minor scars which did not alter a familiar face. Outwardly London was the same great spreading, stolid, and impressive city that Sherwood had seen in the days of its unchallenged assurance. The black paint daubed on the globes of the street lamps, the antiaircraft guns whose protecting shrapnel endangered civilians, the lack of coal, and the near-starvation diet were all insistent proofs that London had been very much at war for three appalling years.

The change which Sherwood observed in that dark November of 1917 cut far deeper. He remembered it vividly twelve years later when he wrote the preface to *Waterloo Bridge*. He recalled that on his leaves from Bramshott he would arrive at Waterloo Station, cross Waterloo Bridge, and enter the Strand "which was then a dark, sluggish river of khaki. Officers and men, from all those extensive areas that are colored pink on the map of the world, moved up and down the Strand, looking for something that wasn't there. On leave from France, Mesopotamia, the Channel patrol or the mine fields of the North Sea, thirsting for intoxicating hilarity, they resembled crowds of determined pleasure-seekers in an amusement park that has been closed for the winter."

In *Punch* Sherwood was delighted to see a burlesque of patriotic verse written in the "right," chin-up spirit. It ran:

> Though overhead the Gothas buzz,
> Stands London where it did? It does!

There was no question about the city's standing. But, as Sherwood saw it, "something tremendous" had gone out of it, and this "something was the insular complacency, the all-conquering pride which had made Britain universally great and, at the same time, universally unpopular."

That late fall marked the ebb tide in the spirit of her "tired, battered people. . . . There was no way of disguising the ugly truth that this war had not been a success. . . . Men and women still said, as a matter of course, that this or that would 'win the war'; but it was difficult to find anyone who believed, in his heart, that the war would ever be won; the utmost that could be hoped for it was that some day, somehow, it would be finished."

Londoners, in short, were giving "an incomparable performance" of what Alexander Woollcott was to call "the tragedy of the stiff upper lip," and Sherwood was moved by it during his months of waiting. With shame he noted the "growing suspicion that President Wilson's dramatic declaration of war was the pardon that came too late," since at that time the armies pouring into France were German, not American, and most of the Americans who appeared in the war zone were not soldiers but congressmen on journeys of inspection. Like his young American in the Royal Canadian Regiment in *Waterloo Bridge*, Sherwood was "one of the boys that couldn't wait."

He did not have long to do so. On a day toward the end of February he whispered to Child that he was leaving for France at midnight. That evening he and Child met outside the sergeants' mess and Child, because Private Sherwood could not be served at the bar, kept coming out with rounds of double Scotches which they downed on the parade ground. Then, for half of the six miles to the depot,

Child walked with him, helping carry his heavy load of equipment and grateful there was not an extra pair of shoes to tote. Sherwood was off in earnest to the war, proud to be one of those kilted soldiers for whom the Germans had a name:

> There's a toss of the sporran,
>   A swing of the kilt,
> And a screech frae the pipers
>   In blood-stirring lilt;
> They step out together,
>   As the pibroch notes swell—
> Oh, they're bonnie braw fighters,
>   The Ladies of Hell.
>
> As they charged at Culloden
>   Like fire o'er the brae,
> Their brothers are charging
>   In Flanders today,
> And one lesson in manners
>   The Boche has learned well:
> It's "Make way for the Ladies"—
>   The Ladies of Hell.

8

"THE LADIES OF HELL"

Every war creates its own vocabulary. This is not merely a matter
of new weapons or new types of combat demanding new terms. Even
when the contestants are the same, their names are different. Sherwood was heading for the war in which the Germans were "Boches,"
"Huns," "Heinies," and "Fritzes"; the British, "Tommies" and
"Jocks"; the French, poilus and "Frogs"; and the Americans, "dough-
boys," "Sammies," and "Yanks." It was the war in which enemies
faced each other from the patterned crisscross of trenches and sought
shelter in the smelly blackness of "dugouts." It was the war in which
men stood and watched, shivered or sweated in endless gravelike laby-
rinths. It was the war in which civilized men reverted with surprising
hardihood and ease to living like uniformed and disciplined animals
in the rigid cold or slimy warmth of the mud-mud-mud.

Men cut their way through "barbed wire" protecting their trenches
to go "over the top," "out there," into the "No Man's Land" which,
between enemies dug in, was the zone of open fighting. "Whizz-
bangs" and "minnies" were German shells. To "go west" was to die,
and "back to Blighty" meant for the English either a return home or
a wound that won a respite there. These phrases, now as quaint as if
they had not once been on everyone's tongue and the language of

survival, were the ones in which Sherwood, like his comrades, thought, talked, and wrote home.

He was one of the thousands who neared France in a dedicated mood. He was always to remember being "full of the spirit of high adventure" and feeling like "a Crusader." He was convinced that "the answer to all the grievous problems besetting mankind could be expressed in three words: 'Kill the Kaiser!' " Once that objective was achieved, he was sure they could all go home, those who survived, and live forever at peace. To most of the young who faced the possibility of sacrificing all, it seemed as simple as that.

Sherwood's mixed company of reinforcements landed at Boulogne and, after filtering through France rather rapidly, found itself in three days within ten miles of the front. On the way, during a day of waiting at Étaples on the Channel, the men fooled around playing games, and he, as an American in a Canadian Highland outfit, learned once again that the kilt, in spite of its picturesqueness and its handiness in alimentary emergencies, was "a poor kind of garment for baseball," since, as he put it, "when you slide into second base it flies up around your ears and you get your thighs scraped red." He was later to learn that it was "also a poor kind of garment when you have to go through barbed wire."

On the third night in France, Sherwood for the first time "heard guns being fired in anger." He went out of the barn in the village where he was billeted and looked eastward. There was "a heavy German barrage on and the night sky was punctuated with quick, piercing periods of light, and the stillness was shattered with thunderous echoes." For the moment, as he was to recall thirty-three years later at Bishop's University, his youthful enthusiasm was drained out of him. He was scared stiff.

He thought, "In a few days—or maybe, a few hours, how do I know?—I'll be up in that terror. How can any man live through that? Let's face it—I'm going to be killed in this war. And that's the end of me. And what have I done with my life? Who am I? Just another lousy (literally lousy) private in the Canadian Army. And all of these nice, decent guys who are here with me—guys from New Brunswick, Ontario, Alberta, British Columbia and the banks of the Saskatchewan—they're going to be killed, too. Maybe some of them have had lives that mean something—I haven't. But why should they have to die? Why should I have to die before I've realized some part of myself? Why? Why?"

Sherwood's spirits were not downed long, and his family was never allowed to know that they had been downed at all. Within a short time he had been assigned to the 42nd Canadian Battalion of The Black Watch. To say that it became a part of him is as true as to say he became a part of it. The skirl of its pipes was to remain for him sweet harmony. His feeling of pride in the association lasted for the duration—not of the war, but of his life.

His closeness to his companions was inevitably intensified by hardships and sprees shared under the threats of death. Within a month he had met up with Child again. From his experiences, too, came other enduring friendships. One was with his dashing young lieutenant, John Molson, of Montreal's famous ale clan. Another was with a sensitive, highborn Dane, Thomas Dinesen (younger brother of Isak Dinesen), who in *Merry Hell!* was to write graphically of his service in The Black Watch. Dinesen, to whom valor came as naturally as breathing, was the only member of the 42nd Battalion to win the Victoria Cross. He was awarded it for "most conspicuous and continuous bravery during ten hours of hand to hand fighting" in the course of which he five times in succession "rushed forward alone, and single handed put hostile machine guns out of action, accounting for twelve of the enemy with bomb and bayonet."

Sherwood first caught Dinesen's attention in Montreal during his strutting days as drum major. In France they became friends and had their friendly bouts behind the lines. In these the pop of champagne corks replaced gunfire, and the illumination came from good talk rather than from flares. Their minds clicked, their spirits, too, and Sherwood made a strong impression upon Dinesen, four years his senior, as "a rare personality—a man and a gentleman."

Sherwood was on active duty in France for five and a half months. The AEF under Pershing's command, when later it began to arrive in its swarming, tide-turning might, was to be in the line no longer. Is five and a half months a short or a long time? Compared to the four years that the British, the French, the Belgians, and the Italians (not to overlook the Germans) had endured the agonies of war, it was a very short time indeed. But who can measure time in terms of a nation or an individual at war? Each day, each month, each year of a war bleeds a nation irreparably. One minute at the front can be long enough to snuff out a man's life or to condemn him to that living death which the permanently disabled know. The fact that Sherwood was in a replacement unit was a reminder of how ravaged The Canadian Black Watch had been by its years of valiant combat.

He was twenty-one when he landed in France and was at Vimy Ridge some five weeks later when his twenty-second birthday came around. He was at once young and old, as he was always to be, the boy remaining in the man but the man maturing rapidly in ways and with the speed that war forced on him. His handwriting had already taken its adult form. It was clear and decided as it raced along in the straightest of lines with scarcely a correction, his hand keeping pace with his mind.

As war is to most men, Sherwood's was a good war and a bad one, a combination of danger and dullness with dullness also being a formidable foe. It was eye-opening and life-changing in the ways that wars, survived, are, and it had its unforgettable peaks of excitement and pleasure. Understandably, Sherwood could not relate the life he was living to the life he had lived at Harvard. "I hear a great deal from my old pals who are aviating somewhere along the front," he wrote. "They tell me that quite a number of the bunch from Cambridge have gone west already. It's the hardest thing for me to connect any of those boys with this war." Sherwood was facing the wartime obligation of discovering his new self as he was being changed by new challenges, including service in an army other than his country's.

He had definite opinions on almost every subject. Tanks, for instance: "Today I had a ride on a tank, and it was enough for me. I am glad I chose such a conservative, safe branch of the service as the infantry, and did not get mixed up in those crawling coffins. You can talk all you want about the daring, darling aviators; they certainly cut a great figure in the popular eye and appeal to all the romantic instincts—but I'll take off my hat to the boys who go into action encased in a tank. For sheer heroism and bravery and nerve, they can

give everyone else cards, spades, and the big casino, and still have a
sufficient margin left. The tank is the most typically British feature of
the war—slow, ponderous, cumbersome, portentous, but grim, tena-
cious and determined. They go on blindly, bumping along and spit-
ting hell, and they take what's coming to them without a whimper."

Sherwood in his moments of loneliness begged for mail, by saying,
"I would rather spend a month in the trenches than go a week
without a letter." From his family he sought more than mail. His
sweet tooth had always been in scale with his body, and war did not
diminish it. His letters home were studded with such pleas as, "I can
stand everything except the lack of candy," or "Don't forget the
S.O.S. (Send Over Sweets)." In one respect he surprised himself as
much as he would have surprised his teachers. This was when he
discovered that he possessed "a hitherto unsuspected knowledge of
French," could "gab quite volubly with the frog-eaters," and was
"constantly in demand as an interpreter."

Soldiers overseas are travelers as well as combatants. Like travelers, they carry a part of their normal life with them. Even in France,
when behind the lines for a rest period of nearly two months,
Sherwood managed to carry his theatrical interests with him. In a kilt
he remained the author of *The Curse of Bacchus*, the organizer of the
"Sea Breeze Fairs," and a Hasty Pudding librettist. "I am as usual,"
he confessed, "much in evidence at all theatrical performances and
comic dress parades and am maintaining the same standard as a
prime damn-fool that I established in the earliest days of infancy."
He played baseball, football, and took part in almost every event
when a grand field day was held by the entire division. He had some
apprehensions about the three-legged race, as the entries could not
select their partners and his fear was that the officials would probably, in a spirit of drollery, pair off his six feet seven with some runt
of four feet eight.

Sherwood's hope was that the Germans, from their observation
balloons which were clearly visible, could see the field day with its
Y.M.C.A. refreshment tents, its burlesque sideshows, grandstands,
and bales of bunting and flags everywhere. To him the exhibition
"had more the appearance and atmosphere of an old time country
fair than an assemblage of war weary fighting men within a few miles

of the front line." A glimpse of it, he was convinced, would have been to the Germans "a most enlightening demonstration of that morale and spirit which has prevented the Allies from throwing up the sponge."

As Sherwood reported to his mother, a feature of the show was a mammoth parade of floats and displays furnished by all the battalions and details of the division. "I was appointed to organize and stage manage the contribution from our unit, and I fixed up a float to represent the boat taking the troops home après La Guerre in 1950. The boat was built by the battalion pioneers (carpenters) who used a huge French farm wagon as a base. They made a beautiful job of it, and a smoke stack which exuded real smoke, furnished by some grenades—the kind we use when advancing to create a smoke barrage. The ship was drawn by six transport horses, and was laden with various trophies, including a Heinie prisoner chained, and the Kaiser's goat loaned by some French civilians. . . . It was all executed in a style of broad and very low comedy; but it got across in good shape, and we copped first prize, which was a large keg of swell beer."

One day after the big German offensive in March had started, Sherwood found himself confronted by a most unexpected caller, the short, bearded, reverenced man to whom he had referred so irreverently in the censored copy of the *Lampoon*, His Most Gracious Majesty, King George V. Sherwood's outfit had been relieved at the front and on the way back to base the transport system had broken down. Pressed into serving as quartermaster because the regular quartermaster sergeant had been "consigned to the cooler on a charge of grand larceny," Sherwood had stayed behind waiting for three days for transport which did not arrive. He had been "living high," billeted as he was at an exquisite Louis XIV château, with almost unlimited provisions at his disposal.

The King arrived with Sir Douglas Haig to inspect an Imperial Battalion (imperial meaning British as opposed to colonial) which had just come out of battle. According to Sherwood, he was standing to one side, watching the proceedings with a bunch of artillerymen. The battalion was lined up in the courtyard. As the King crossed over the drawbridge and passed through the gate, the band struck up "God Save the King," and all the officers, including the King, stood at salute while the anthem lasted. His Majesty then advanced, followed by Sir Douglas and innumerable staff officers, and "gave the troops the ole once over."

Suddenly Sherwood and the other stragglers realized that the King was coming their way. "We started to beat it into the château," he wrote his father, "as we were neither cleaned nor shaved nor shined up. One of the staff officers, however, came over and urged us to come out and show ourselves. Then the King came up and spotted me, of course. He just asked me how tall I was and I wised him up. He then said, 'You're a Canadian, aren't you?' To which I replied, 'No, sir, a Yank,' which moved the royal cortege to merriment."

Sherwood, in his impatience to have the Americans there, had begun to believe that they would never come and could scarcely believe it when they did. At last, one July night, he saw a regiment from Camp Upton as it moved forward through the darkness to relieve the British Guards Division which was holding the line on the right of the 42nd Highlanders.

He was sitting on the parapet of a communication trench as these green Americans, lighted occasionally by gun flashes and flares, filed through the mud to the front for the first time. They seemed to him "a bit nervous and tense" but were "certainly a splendid lot." They gaped at him in his kilt as if he were "just part of a Pathé News picture." Seeking to relieve the tension, Sherwood brought his "best Lexington Avenue lingo into play" and said, "Say, what is this outfit, anyway—the Bronxville Boy Scout Brigade going to storm Yonkers, or just a delegation of Elks bound for the annual clambake in Flushing?" Since the Americans had assumed Sherwood to be "a regular dyed-in-the-wool Scotchman" and thought that he "never did anything but look sour and maintain a death grip" on his bank roll, the result was an uproar which it took officers to quiet.

The time came when, with a heart volcanic with pride, Sherwood could report, "There are a million Yanks in France, and they are coming and coming and coming in tens and hundreds of thousands— which goes to show George M. Cohan was right. If you could only see the effect of this news on the magnificent boys who have been hanging on here for years! . . . They are like drowning men who grasped at a straw and found it to be a life-preserver thrown from the shore." Early in June came news even more stirring. The Americans were not only in France; they were decisively in action. At Château-Thierry, with the French, they had halted the German sweep on Paris and driven the enemy back twenty-five kilometers.

The war for Sherwood was by no means all training or rest periods, royal visits or joking salutes to arriving Americans. It was a tough war, as tough as trench warfare at its worst can be. After reaching France, he was with his outfit in the trenches for sixty-three days before being relieved. The 42nd was at Vimy Ridge which the Canadians had gloriously taken the year before; Vimy Ridge, that "long, undulating ridge," as Dinesen described it in *Merry Hell!*, "lying so desolate and empty . . . with neither tree nor house to be seen—grizzly, dead." Thereafter came a deserved "layoff," and then Sherwood returned with his battalion to the front south of Arras where he remained for a month and a half.

The life of trenchdwellers, as Sherwood called them, was "indolent but tense" and its discomforts were many. Lice, personally scratched as "cooties," were among them. These were mild compared to the huge, hungry rats (cursed at simply as rats because no one could think up a worse name), which nibbled at the living and the dead. To Sherwood, who was afraid even of a mouse, the rats were the one hardship of the war which he found unendurable. His was a more than ordinary hatred of them and a more than usual fear. When he was nine and Skene Wood was being built, he had caught a rat in a cage, lowered the cage into a rainbarrel, and watched the rat drown. His fear of rats from then on, he confessed in his diary thirty years later, was "the fear that they want to get revenge on me for that act of brutality."

If it was revenge the rats were after, they more than got it on Sherwood in France. Although he never looked back on his experiences at the front with horror, he wrote his Aunt Lydia that he shuddered and cringed every time he thought of those rats. No words could express his loathing and disgust for them. "They were the most forward and nerviest rats you ever saw—absolutely afraid of nothing. Besides running over us and frightening us out of our skins, they ate the rations, our candles, chewed the shoes on our feet and our leather equipment."

Later, when hospitalized in England, Sherwood was often to wake up at night "with a cold sweat and gooseflesh and offer up thanks to Providence" that he was free of rats. At the front he chose several nights to sleep on a muddy firestep in his trench, with only his rubber sheet to lie on, rather than seek the warmth of a bombproof dugout which was swarming with rats. Sherwood never forgot those rats. After the war, when his mother once asked him to do an errand for her and named the place, he said, "Mother, I can't walk down that side of Lexington Avenue." It turned out there was an animal store there which had a cage of rats in the window, and he just could not bring himself to look at them.

Decorations are not given for being brave about toothaches or putting up philosophically with the errors of dentists. If they were, Sherwood would have earned one at Vimy Ridge when one night he found himself in such agony from an abscessed tooth that he was permitted to leave the front and go to a first-aid station to be treated. This meant walking through six miles of trenches and over the top of Vimy Ridge, which at the time was being shelled. When he at last reached his destination, Sherwood found no dentist there, only a tough sergeant assistant. "What do you mean by coming here without brushing your teeth?" growled the sergeant. "Where I come from, there is no water and no toothbrushes. Pull out that tooth!" The sergeant, without the aid of an anesthetic, obliged by pulling out one wrong tooth and then another before he hit on the right one. Then, in pain, Sherwood trudged the six miles back under fire to his front-line trench and the rats.

He saw combat of the most fierce kind, and, though nonbelligerent by nature, in hand-to-hand fighting he did in self-defense what war demands of even the least bellicose of men. Asked once by Philip, when peace had come, if he had ever killed a man, he replied, "Hell, yes, I must have killed a good many. I wasn't much of a shot, but with all the firing I did I must have hit someone." Then, looking very troubled, he added, "I remember one time when I *know* I killed a man." It was when, having volunteered for a raiding party sent out to capture prisoners, he jumped into an enemy trench. A German officer, down on one knee, was pointing a revolver at him. Sherwood rushed him and shot him in the head. He did not like to talk about this, and almost never did.

This happened during his second stay at the front when he had been given his first opportunity, as he put it, "to utilize that area above the neck in which is billeted my limited reserves of gray matter." The censors, recognizing the lucidity and excellence of Sherwood's letters, recommended him for intelligence work which was ordinarily done by an officer, at that time absent. It was, observed Sherwood, just the sort of thing he had wanted to do in the U.S. Army.

It meant keeping track of the caliber and direction of enemy shells, identifying German regiments, noting enemy movements, and sending reports to headquarters. He minimized the dangers, which were real, though he admitted these raiding missions were "pretty stiff work." This work had its advantages other than its interest. It excused Sherwood from working parties and gave him better living quarters and rations. Also his proximity to officers put him "in line to receive occasional handouts of good cigarettes and cigars and even now and then a nip of the best Scotch."

One night late in July, Sherwood was gassed and taken to an emergency station. After being there a few days, he persuaded those in charge that he was all right and talked them into letting him rejoin his battalion. He had an urgent reason for doing this. Rumor had reached him that the big British offensive was about to start. Fit or unfit, he was determined to be a part of it. Burdened with heavy equipment, he walked the long way back at night, and the walk taxed his heart already affected, as it was, by the gas.

He got there in time. The British soon started marching to the east along the muddy roads. Every village through which they passed yielded its contingent until so many troops of all kinds converged that, to Dinesen, they seemed to swell "into one mighty stream, like a mountain torrent after rain." On the day before the attack The Black Watch rested after a night march, cooked and ate up their extra tins of food, and washed and shaved carefully "in order to look [their] best for Fritz." They had their gas masks, rifles, and ammunition inspected for the last time and before supper held their final parade. At 10 P.M. they were groping their way in tense silence along the sides of the crowded Amiens-Roye road, headed for their front-line trenches.

On the morning of the 8th the August sky was clear in the north-east and already reddening as zero hour approached. "Only once shall we live to see such a morning," wrote Dinesen, who was in the company next to Sherwood. The broad river valley below them was quiet and at peace. The scars of war were hidden by the long gray grass. Overhead the engine of a lonely plane droned. Occasionally a heavy gun boomed but in the distance. Though the ridges behind the German lines were sharply outlined, the bottom of the valley was a sea of mist. It seemed "a warm, smiling summer morning."

But two hundred thousand men, their numbers unsuspected by the Germans, were in position on the hills to the north, breathlessly awaiting the signal for the charge. Two thousand guns were massed behind the infantry lines. "The British lion itself was crouching without a sound, every quivering nerve and sinew ready for a spring," wrote Dinesen. When *forever* at last became *now* and the signal was given, "the whole of the western horizon burst into flame as if the earth had opened," with thousands of guns roaring at once and shells hissing and howling over the heads of men whose every sense was "drowned in the paralyzing roar of those first minutes."

Sherwood was to remember that, in spite of the tremendous concentration of troops, guns, and tanks at Amiens, the British attack on the Somme had completely surprised the Germans. He was delighted to write his family that he was not nearly so scared going over the top as he had expected to be. "We did not know when we were to go until the barrage opened and that lasted four minutes. It was short but Oh! how sweet! One cannot conceive the frightful intensity. The enemy's lines looked like a stormy sea of molten lead, the showers of red-hot shrapnel appearing like clouds of spray."

Contrary to popular belief, he insisted they were not drunk or doped. But he admitted that he could have stood a small shot of rum at the opening of the barrage, when the 42nd Battalion went over in the first wave, because he felt "a bit green around the gills." His was that odd wartime sense of disbelief, of feeling like an observer while being a participant. "As usual," said he, "I was disappointed in the affair as viewed from the dramatic standpoint. It doesn't live up to what the Liberty Loan advertisements say about it."

Writing to his mother, he pretended it was just an ordinary stroll through intensely interesting surroundings. It was much more than that, though much less than he had dreaded. True, "there was no charging at breakneck speed with bayonets fixed and concentrated hate and passion exuding from every nerve and fiber." The enemy, as he recalled, was "absolutely pulverized" at the start so that during that first day the 42nd Battalion gained twelve kilometers, seven of which (4½ miles) Sherwood himself walked behind enemy lines before he stopped walking for a while.

He encountered few dead ("stiffs" he called them) and very few wounded. At isolated intervals he could hear the crack of a rifle or a burst of machine-gun fire. Once they caught up with some of their own shellfire because of having reached an early objective over an hour ahead of time. Later, according to him, they were met by feeble resistance in spots—snipers and machine-gun crews in shell holes and pits, who fired until the Canadians came in sight and then "immediately threw up their hands and did the Kamerad act." Hordes of surrendering gray-clad figures were to him the chief reminders that he and his comrades were facing a foe.

"A very long way from the original front line," he admitted in a letter, "we finally ran up against a nest of machine guns and four of our men were wounded. But we extinguished the opposition in the same slow, methodical and complete manner." Almost immediately after this the war ended for Sherwood as a combatant.

He wrote home only the partial truth about what happened to him. He was accurate in saying that the Germans had dug a series of pits, about three feet deep and ten feet wide, which they lined with sharp stakes and tangled barbed wire and covered with sticks and twigs to camouflage them. Their object was to trap cavalry. No hussars, dragoons, or lancers passed that way but Sherwood did. This much he told his family.

He did not tell them that, before falling, he had been badly gassed or that, after falling, his protruding feet and legs, already scratched, were further lacerated by shrapnel. Nor did he tell them that he was carried unconscious from the trap by stretcher-bearers and did not come to until he was in a hospital in Amiens.

Instead, he wrote jokingly about looking down at his scratched legs and noticing that his hosetops "were suffused with a sample of New Rochelle's bluest blood." He explained his presence in a hospital by writing pleasantly fictionalized accounts of what had happened and expressing his delight at being kept out of action by a wound so slight that he "could easily have secured it at home at a minimum of trouble and expense." Although his intention was to spare his father and mother, their worries were only increased when, without his whereabouts being given, his family was officially notified that he had been wounded by gunshot.

During the next six months Sherwood made what amounted to a grand tour of hospitals. He was in eleven of them in France, England, and Canada. Early in September, still a stretcher case, he was taken to England and in October was transferred from Reading to Bushy Park, which he was to know twenty-five years later when it became the site of SHAEF, Eisenhower's headquarters in the outskirts of London. One English doctor thought Sherwood's heart would never recover; another was more hopeful. When in Canada he was finally discharged from The Black Watch, his disability was assessed at fifteen percent and at that rate he was granted a pension —he accepted it for only three years—for "dyspnoea [difficult or labored respiration] due to disordered action of the heart."

Sherwood learned a great deal about himself during these dragging months of being hospitalized and from his whole war experience. He gained this knowledge by learning about others and did not forget it. Years later he recalled in his preface to *There Shall Be No Night*, "I had been brought up to believe that because I was a 100 percent American—and a Harvard man, at that—I was superior." As a common soldier in the Canadian Army in training camps, in the line, and in clinks and hospitals, he mixed with men from all over the British Empire and the United States, and learned better.

He vividly remembered that in one hospital the occupant of the bed on one side of his was "an Australian who had been horribly burned by liquid fire in the crater at Loos three years before. In the bed on the other side . . . was a South African Jew; a machine gun bullet had lodged in the base of his spine and he knew he would never walk again." Sherwood confessed, "It was a great surprise to me to discover that these two men, and all other men whom I got to know well, thought and talked and acted and reacted just about as I did. What was so surprising about it was the revelation of the narrowness and shallowness of my own mind."

Beyond all the discipline, danger, pain, boredom, and loneliness which they had borne in common, Sherwood shared one dream with his fellow patients at Bushy Park. This was the hope of getting home.

Everyone could feel that peace was coming. By Christmas? A year away? No one knew exactly. But its dove wings were drumming in the air. There was a sudden lifting of hearts, a sudden certitude of hope, a sudden shaping of the pattern. Swiftly, rapturously, it became clear that the Allies were at last winning the long, hard, desperate war which again and again they had been on the verge of losing. This was October. March had been different, very different. Then the Germans had almost won. In April with their great offensive it looked again as if they might easily win. In June the decision was still within their grasp. By July it was plain, not that the Allies had won but that the Germans had lost. By August the Allied victory was in sight. By September and October it was at hand.

Within four months after the Germans had been conceded by experts in Paris and London to have an excellent chance of winning, they had surrendered. Few of history's spinnings of the wheel have been more rapid or dramatic. Because they won, many would forget how often and how long the Allies tottered on the brink of defeat. Sherwood was among those who knew better and never forgot. When victory at last came, he wrote his mother that he was "beginning to realize the extent of this miracle by which flesh and blood have triumphed over blood and iron. There is certainly no achievement in history so marvelous, so complete, or so inexplicable as this victory which, on the face of it, appears to be the natural result of four years of successful effort but which in reality represents the unexpected conclusion of a four year series of hair breadth escapes. . . . At least twice in the last two years it has seemed certain that we could never win and that we would be fortunate if we could stave off crushing defeat."

Hopes and rumors rose with the coming of the fall, and "the weary, fed up people" of England started trying to imagine what peace would be like. "They could no more envisage the circumstances of existence after the war than they could envisage life after death. It was a hazy, incredible blur, but it was infinitely pleasant to contemplate."

On the morning of November 11, Sherwood and his fellow "walking cases," wearing their regulation hospital uniforms of bright blue, were lined up in the stable yard at Bushy Park, waiting for their mail. "All of us," Sherwood recalled in his preface to *Waterloo Bridge*, "had been wondering whether the command to cease firing would be issued before we were given clean bills of health and sent back to the line.

"An Army Medical Corps sergeant appeared in the yard, blew his whistle, and instructed us to report to the Y.M.C.A. hut. . . . We went there, listlessly, and when we had assembled, the elderly chaplain (who had been invalided from France because he had organic heart disease) stepped up on the platform and asked us to join him in a prayer of thanks to God, because the war was over. So we said the prayer, and sang 'God Save the King,' and cheered Field-Marshal Haig and General Currie."

Then some of the patients, and among the first Sherwood, sneaked out through the barbed-wire fence about the hospital grounds, and climbed on a Hammersmith bus, and "rode into the insane bewilderment of London's celebration" in which he remained, absent without leave, for a week—or was it four days? He could never remember. On the way in, the bus passed a plowed field where some German prisoners were at work. "We shouted at them, 'Hey, Heinie —the war's over!' But they only grinned and waved at us amicably— not understanding, or not caring."

London this time was again a different London. The despair had vanished, and the city was reeling and riotous with victory. Flagless while the war was on, it was now aflame with flags. The Allied colors

suddenly blossomed forth on house after house. The Stars and
Stripes were everywhere, though usually upside down. Sherwood
wrote his mother, "The well known British phlegm went west. There
was a wild conglomeration of Tommies, Jocks, Australians, Yanks,
sailors, wounded men, Italians, Belgians, Indians, French, Portu-
guese, Land-girls, 'Waacs,' 'Wrens,' Munition Girls, and everyone
else in uniform parading and howling and hooting and dancing
through the streets and breaking things, and hurting each other. It
was much worse than New Year's Eve in New York."

Suffering as he was from the effects of being gassed, Sherwood
confessed he could not stick it for very long in the crowds. But he
went to shows every afternoon and evening where the fun was "particularly boisterous" and, though it was against the law to serve
liquor to anyone wearing a hospital blue uniform, he had no difficulty
in evading this prohibition.

Sherwood had what London was having, and that was "a swell
time." He was never to forget those days—and nights—when the
Strand and Trafalgar Square and all surrounding thoroughfares were
jammed with the wildest mob he had ever seen or ever hoped to see.
He was amused by the way in which Australians and Canadians
seized the captured cannon, placed in rows along the Mall, and with
them made a bonfire at the base of the Nelson Monument. The
flames enveloped the column and seriously threatened to cremate
Lord Nelson himself. "The London fire department," noted Sherwood, "fought manfully to check this destructive enthusiasm, but the
hilarious Colonials captured the hose and turned it on the firemen.

"Throughout the turmoil, the King and Queen and Princess Mary
drove through the crowds, in an open carriage with no attendants,
smiling and bowing and acknowledging salutes. Their Majesties
seemed to be particularly delighted to see soldiers climbing up on the
lamp-posts to scrape the black paint off the globes, exactly in the
manner of snake-dancers clambering up the goal-posts after the big
game." One of the paint scrapers was Sherwood.

He paid for his part in the celebration by being kept in bounds at
Bushy Park and put to work in the kitchen. On Thanksgiving Day he
was thankful that there were only three hundred patients to wash
dishes for. He did not complain. All that mattered was that it was

over, miraculously and at last over, and that in his letters to his
family he could begin to write of coming home.

Rosina was staying with Rosamond in New York at Lydia's
apartment at 535 Park Avenue. She was living impatiently with a
mother's hopes, having long lived with a mother's fears. Sherwood's
letters had told her again and again that, in spite of keeping his
fingers crossed, he had no idea when he would get home. Even the
letter she had from him a few days before repeated this, explaining
how crowded the ships were and that there were many troops to be
moved first.

Then one very rainy morning early in February the telephone rang
at seven. The treasured Delia, at this time Lydia's cook, answered it
and rushed to Rosina's room to waken her.

"Who can want me at this hour?" she asked.

Delia, her blue eyes large as lakes, said, "Mrs. Sherwood, I think
—I think it's Mr. Bobby."

Rosina flew to the phone, and "there," as she wrote, "was his
voice, saying, 'Hello, Mother.'" He was at Grand Central Terminal
and had just arrived from Montreal.

Rosina called Rosamond, and they dressed quickly and were at
the door to meet him. "He looked pathetic—gaunt & unkempt" after
the voyage on the *Scotian* during which, as he was too long for his
hammock, he had to sleep on the deck, sharing it with an intrusive
rat. He had a cold, and on the way down on the night train had had a
bad time with his heart. Rosina took all of him in at a glance. "He
had on an old khaki army blouse belonging to Wilfrid, much too
short in the sleeves and much too loose in the body, and a pair of
shabby khaki trousers, and a funny Scotch cap" with the feathered
Red Hackle at one side. He was carrying a great clumsy bundle on
his back.

Outwardly Rosina was calm, though inwardly she was as excited
as Rosamond and Delia. She thought that she and Delia gave Sherwood a good breakfast. She hoped so. Afterwards she could remember nothing about the meal, nothing except sitting by him on the sofa
when it was over, and looking at him, and hearing him talk, and
touching him occasionally, and making him lie down that afternoon

as he continued to talk. What he said, in those hours of catching up and rediscovery, was what he had not said in his letters home. It was the unvarnished and uncensored truth about his war, and Rosina was filled with pride and with the happiness of having that war over and him home.

9

"MR. BENCHLEY," "MRS. PARKER," "MR. SHERWOOD"

Return to New York—Meets Benchley and Is Hired by Vanity Fair—Fastidious "Crownie"—The Other Robert, Benchley—Dorothy Parker, The Stiletto Made of Sugar—"One Big Blur of Laughter"—Office Doings and the Axe

A war is not something that, deep within himself, a man leaves quickly or that quickly leaves a man. Wanting to forget it does not mean forgetting it. A war takes getting over. Remembered with dislike, excitement, or pride (or with elements of each), it becomes a part of the person it has changed.

In the bag which Sherwood carried home was his Black Watch uniform. Delighted as he was to be out of the service, humanly he could not resist dressing up in that uniform and showing himself off to his thrilled family and admiring friends, and to New Yorkers who, accustomed as they were to tall buildings, were somewhat startled by the sight of him. It was Rosamond who helped ready him for his public appearances in New York by scrubbing and starching his spats until, as Delia said approvingly, they were "as shtiff as Paddy's father, and him nine days dead." When he did emerge, with his Glengarry aslant, his khaki tunic immaculate, and his kilt and sporran swaying, Sherwood could have passed in review and was deliberately on parade.

He was twenty-two, a war-old twenty-two; looked, all seventy-nine inches of him, a Highlander, and seemed very jaunty in a morose way, with his sleek black hair, his trim nailbrush of a mustache, and his general spruceness. But neither the figure he cut nor his pleasure at being home in a uniform which was now a costume could hide the fact that he was far from well. His mouth and teeth were in poor condition. As a result of having been gassed, he was often short of breath and at times gasped distressingly. A doctor, fortunately no prophet, who prided himself on bluntness, warned the family that Sherwood's heart was so enlarged that he might die at any time. A rest, a change, and a period of being built up were urgently needed and strongly recommended.

Accordingly, Sherwood and Rosamond soon sailed for Savannah to join their father who, as a semi-invalid, was wintering there with a trained nurse, Mary Vincent, to look after him. Before leaving, Sherwood mustered enough strength to make a quick visit to Harvard, where in uniform he was interviewed at fitting length by the Boston *Herald* and enjoyed being the center of undergraduate attention.

Although the voyage south was pleasant, Rosina noted realistically that the reason her children took a boat was that it cost about half as much as the train. Money was scarce with the Sherwoods at that time. They did not discuss it or worry about it. They lived uncomplainingly with the economic changes which had overtaken them since Mr. Sherwood's failure. Lydia, as usual, helped. So did Uncle Bob, Rosina's colorful twin brother, a West Point graduate and an Indian fighter who had won the Congressional Medal of Honor. But the mainstay was the indomitable Rosina. At sixty-four she was painting profitably and happily, and much depended upon her skill and quick-moving brushes. After her children sailed, she stayed on in New York for a frenzied week during which she finished five portraits. A pleasant aspect of painting is that it is a portable profession. Rosina continued to paint sustainingly and with enjoyment in Savannah when she rejoined her family in the simple house which they had rented on a side street.

As for Sherwood, he for the moment felt young-man rich, with the back pay, the bonus, and the small pension paid him by the Canadian government. Money, at least during these weeks, was not his concern. Health was, and he took advantage of the peaceful ease of this Savannah interlude to regain his strength. Rosina described his stay there as "a long spell of quiet and inaction," adding "he never drinks a drop, never smokes, settles down to the stupidest humdrum existence . . . and is altogether an angel of a boy."

He was also a troubled and uprooted young man. He was not only convalescing physically, he was convalescing from a war. Like hundreds of thousands of other young men, he was a different man, come back to a different country to start a different life. With difficulty he was adjusting himself to the lower-keyed realities of peace. For the first time he was confronted with the full meaning, to him and to his family, of his father's failure and retirement. Skene Wood was gone. So was the Lexington Avenue house in which the Sherwoods had lived for thirteen years. So was the routine of going off to school or college which before the war had been part of his life. The question Sherwood faced, once he had recovered from his immediate past, was his future. He wanted to write and he needed a job.

By May he felt well enough to return to New York for a checkup and to look for a job that would allow him to do what he wanted to. The report on his health was encouraging. Dr. James Alexander Miller, a noted lung specialist, found him very much better and said that by the autumn he ought to be "nearly normal."

Long before then, Sherwood had gone to work under conditions and with people who were to give his career one of its decisive turns. On May 21 Robert Benchley, two days after he had taken over as managing editor of *Vanity Fair*, was writing in his diary about "meeting Bob Sherwood who presented his six feet five or ten in candidacy for a job he may get as Miss Bristed is leaving." The postscript, as expected, is that he got the job, and a week later was working at the office on a three-month trial basis at $25 a week.

The pay was bread but not butter, the doors thrown open were large and wide, and the fun (for the eight months that it lasted) was larger still. "No young writer ever had such luck in starting his professional career in such fast company," Sherwood wrote years later to Ilka Chase. *Vanity Fair* was the Gideon of the sophisticated. Frank Crowninshield was its boutonniere of an editor; Condé Nast, owner of the far more profitable but equally glossy *Vogue*, its ducal publisher; and Sherwood's two associates, in whose office he was given a desk, were Robert Benchley and Dorothy Parker with whom he at once formed an inseparable trio. The year was at the spring for

Sherwood, and the lark on the wing, even if morning was seldom at seven. He was walking into the twenties under the most smiling and knowing of auspices.

He had impressed Crowninshield, and the office of *Vanity Fair* before Benchley was working there, by turning up as a job seeker resplendently attired in his Black Watch uniform. Some may have thought his doing this poor taste; Sherwood thought it good sense. Today's heroes become tomorrow's bores all too quickly. But when a war is just over, uniforms can open doors—and hearts. Crowninshield was predictably responsive. His heart and Toscanini-bright eyes yielded to Sherwood. He knew the Sherwoods and knew of Robert from his work on the *Lampoon*, particularly the successful burlesque issue of *Vanity Fair* which had appeared under Sherwood's editorship on April 6, 1917, of all days.

"Crownie" might with accuracy have borne the name of Fastidious Brisk, Ben Jonson's character. Few of his contemporaries had such charm, and none such a flair for the modish. When he walked down a side street, it turned into a boulevard. War, labor troubles, and scowling issues were not what he might have referred to as his métier. He was shallow of mind and deep of heart, constant in his enthusiasms, and better at private pleasantries than at public crises. He was not a hard-boiled egg but a soufflé that could rise graciously to any occasion.

He wanted life to be charming, bubbly, and gay, and his magazine to be a cheerful and urbane, month by month "record of current achievements in all the arts and a mirror of the progress and promise of American life." He liked dinner talk in print. As Benchley observed, he would allow any entertaining writer to say practically anything in *Vanity Fair* so long as he said it in evening clothes.

Crownie belonged to the old school and yet anticipated the new. A traditionalist, he was also an innovator. Born in Paris and educated there and in Rome and London, he bootlegged artistic Europe with success into an aesthetically dry United States. He was one of those who helped open America's at first somewhat baffled eyes to the beauties of modern art. He had a hazel-wand genius for discovering new, young talents. Warmhearted and politely impish, he liked the young because of his own lasting youth and welcomed their restrained impieties. He admired their freshness and did not object, any more than Nast did, to their being inexpensive.

He compared himself to a literary lion tamer, a Clyde Beatty of the ink-stained, confessing that he had found it always the safest plan "to deal with such felines when they are still cubs; to snare them, in traps, before their teeth have sharpened and their claws grown long." High on the lengthy list of *Vanity Fair* lions that he could, and did, point to with pride at a safe later distance were "those amazing whelps"—Dorothy Parker, and Benchley, and Sherwood.

Sherwood had first seen, and heard, Benchley at Harvard in the fall of 1914. He had gone to a freshman smoker, "a sort of get-together, good-will, beer-and-tobacco pep rally," designed to create college spirit in those who might otherwise have been devoting their energies to developing "Harvard indifference." The platform sagged under the weight of such football "greats" as Charlie Brickley and Eddie Mahan and Lev Saltonstall (later governor and senator). Yet there, and this gave Sherwood "a particular thrill," costarred with them as if he were their equal, was Robert C. Benchley of the class of 1912, a mere writer, cartoonist, actor, and merry-andrew, already so formidable by reputation that the freshmen "started laughing at the very mention of his name."

All this meant a great deal to Sherwood at that time, on two counts. He was already going out for the *Lampoon* and memorizing all the jokes he heard in Broadway musicals for future use in the Hasty Pudding. He knew that Benchley had been the *Lampoon's* president in the golden days when Gluyas Williams, Frederick Lewis Allen, Paul Hollister, and Vinton Freedley were among his colleagues. He knew too that Benchley had appeared in and coauthored several Hasty Pudding shows. If Benchley, of the Pudding and the *Lampoon*, could be up there that night, a monarch among these crowned heads, there was hope for Sherwood. From then on, Benchley remained for him, though he did not meet him, "a shining objective towards which to strive as an undergraduate." Moreover, Sherwood determined to step into his boots.

Less than five years later he was doing more than that. He was stepping into Benchley's office to share it, to work under him as an editor and with him as a friend. Sherwood the month before had become a venerable twenty-three. Benchley was within four months of a tottering thirty. Before he found a seemingly cushioned berth at *Vanity Fair* at a hundred dollars a week, Benchley had had a varied time of it, consistent only in its financial insecurity and the widening ripples of his reputation as a wit and after-dinner speaker.

Benchley had translated French catalogues for the Boston Museum of Fine Arts; written advertising copy in New York for the Curtis Publishing Company; held a personnel job with a paper firm in Boston; worked with Franklin Pierce Adams at the New York *Tribune* where, in addition to getting to know F.P.A. well, he had become the friend of Heywood Broun and George S. Kaufman; briefly been a theatrical press agent for William A. Brady; and served as publicity secretary in Washington for the Aircraft Board. Since 1914 he had been contributing to *Vanity Fair* under his own name and later also as Brighton Perry. His pieces were *Lampoonish* trifles, matured in expertness and successfully topsy-turvy. Indicative of what was to come was Benchley's first article, for which he was paid a lordly forty dollars. It was a moon-struck disquisition on the difficulties of writing a novel, the abrupt title of which was *No Matter From What Angle You Look At It, Alice Brookhausen Was a Girl Whom You Would Hesitate to Invite into Your Own Home.*

Benchley was to become stout as his fame and the decades accumulated, and the writer in him seemed, to his distress, to be swallowed up in the actor celebrated for his humorous movie shorts. When he came to *Vanity Fair* he was, as Crowninshield remembered, a pale, slight young man who never had had a drink, was careful to wear long underwear and rubbers, and was given to biting his nails. To Sherwood at this time Benchley seemed "a methodical, teetotaling, non-smoking, galosh-wearing, penurious, homebound commuter, who didn't appear to have a worry or concern in the world beyond the precarious state of his bank account and the effect thereof on his family in Crestwood."

Sherwood soon came to know that this was only one character in the richly contrasted dramatis personae of Robert Benchley. The Benchley that Sherwood loved at once, and found "forever wonderful to be with, to read about, and to remember" even in the later years when they did not see each other often, was subject to some of the strangest reversals of mood and habits that Sherwood had ever seen in one human being. This was another bond between the two men because the antitheses in Sherwood's nature were also abundant.

A dark room seemed to brighten when Benchley came into it. No one was readier to laugh than he, and few have ever been blessed with such a laugh. His laughter was an explosion of good humor. It was that rare thing—total laughter, ungrudging and with no joy withheld. It wrinkled his face into a contour map of pleasure, caused him to squint his twinkling blue eyes, thrust his head back, and shook his shoulders. It was from the belly and the heart as well as the head, and hope was always in it—the hope for a good joke—and the grace to pretend that a bad one had been good. He was a wit who had no malice in him. Though he saw through fools, Benchley gladly made them tolerate themselves by reacting to what they said as if he had said it and as if they were not what they were.

His gift for gaiety came to distress him as much as it always delighted others, for at heart he was a Stephen Leacock who was also a Baden-Powell, a moralist who wore the motley, and a do-gooder who could not persuade himself that creating such laughter as he did was a form of doing more good than it is given most to do.

He was a humorous writer and wanted to be a serious one. He liked to accuse himself of knowing little when, as a matter of fact, his knowledge was prodigious. He read as seriously as he wrote uproariously, dashing off such pieces as "The Social Life of the Newt" by day while reading Nietzsche or Henry Adams by night—at least late at night. He devoured newspapers and magazines with a wolfing appetite and was uncommonly informed on the issues of the day, any day, and also on the trivia. He was a crusader for human rights, an earnest volunteer for the Urban League, a Puck who was to march in the picket lines for Sacco and Vanzetti, a dedicated pacifist, and, much to Sherwood's horror when he first knew him, an ardent prohibitionist tone-deaf to the music of a cocktail shaker, though in time he became amply responsive to its rhythms.

Benchley in those days was an ardent subscriber to two undertakers' magazines. One of these was unmincingly known as *The Casket*; the other more evasively was called *Sunnyside*. Both were often brightened with anatomical plates which showed at just what points the embalming fluid should be injected. It pleased Benchley to tear out these cheerful illustrations and present them to Dorothy Parker, and it delighted her to exhibit them in a row above her desk. Understandably, Crowninshield, with his drawing-room manners, would suggest that samples of the work, say, of Marie Laurencin would be less startling to visitors. Invariably, Mrs. Parker would meet such hints with a contempt equal to a declaration of war.

Dorothy Parker had come to *Vanity Fair* in 1915 after a brief and uncomfortable sojourn on *Vogue* as Dorothy Rothschild, an elfin young woman, slim, sleek, and tiny, with masses of dark hair which, if not battened down by a large mushroom of a hat, seemed quite appropriately to be tornado tossed. To Crowninshield she appeared reticent, self-effacing, and preternaturally shy.

Her smile was radiator warm; her manners perfect enough to have been suburban. But her tongue, which dripped honey, could also suddenly be asp-like in its sting. Her eyes, laughing, thoughtful, and fringed with exceptionally long, upturned lashes, were a curious mixture of hazel and green. When she read, they were encircled by horn-rimmed spectacles which she removed abruptly if anyone spoke to her without warning. Her walk, in flat-heeled shoes or pumps with black bows, was short-stepped and quick. Her mind was quicker still.

To those she did not like or who bored her, she was a stiletto made of sugar. Her malice came from the disappointment of a romantic rather than the cynicism of the disillusioned. Delightful as it was to be in her presence, it was dangerous to leave it. Her epitaphs for the dear departed were widely repeated. She was to become not only a legend, treasured and feared, but a dictionary of quotations, many of which, with her annihilating wit, she had said or written herself but all of which, if they were witty or annihilating, were automatically attributed to her. In spite of her japeries, she, like Benchley and Sherwood, had a conscience ready to erupt and the courage to back up what she fiercely felt.

The year before Sherwood turned up at *Vanity Fair* Miss Rothschild had become Mrs. Parker when she married Edwin Parker, a lifelong friend from Connecticut. If her apprenticeship writing captions for *Vogue* had been brief, it was because she chose to dash off for a page display of undergarments such a caption as "Brevity is the Soul of Lingerie, as the Petticoat said to the Chemise." Thereby she made it clear to those in authority that "fashion would never become a religion with her," and Crowninshield claimed her at a small salary for *Vanity Fair.* After the Armistice, as a bride waiting for her husband's return from France, she had become the magazine's dramatic editor, having already won a name for herself by baring her claws in "A Hate Song" she had addressed to Men. Of herself she said:

> But I, despite expert advice,
> Keep doing things I think are nice,
> And though to good I never come—
> Inseparable my nose and thumb.

Her nose and thumb were already in position when Sherwood became a triple pillar of that small, unconventional office at *Vanity Fair.* At first Benchley and Mrs. Parker may have thought, as Crowninshield believed they did, that Sherwood was "pretty fast." He wore his straw hat at a roguish angle. He made dates with the beautiful receptionist. He had lived a soldier's life in Canada, France, and England, and "had once, perhaps inadvertently, referred to a personal hangover."

In no time their acquaintanceship became a friendship, their friendship a federation. They were young. They wrote with youth's plunging facility. A conquerable thing called "life" lay not only ahead of them but all around them. They loved to laugh, and in one another's company found plenty to laugh about. Although serious too, they doted on pranks and planned them as solemnly as if they had been drafting State of the Union messages. Crowninshield's conviction was that at no period of their lives did they find "more enjoyment, make more friends, or work as hard or as easily."

On Sherwood's first day they addressed one another very formally as "Mrs. Parker," "Mr. Benchley," and "Mr. Sherwood." They continued to do so, almost invariably, throughout their long friendship. There were exceptions. The two Roberts often called each other "Rob," though no one else did. A month after Sherwood joined the staff, Benchley was referring to him in his diary as "Sherry." And, to make matters a little more complicated, Mrs. Parker sometimes addressed Benchley as "Fred."

To Sherwood his eight months on *Vanity Fair* were, at least until the very bitter end, "one big blur of laughter." Crowninshield was to remember him as a young man, stooping and gigantic, with dark-brown hair and cavernous brown eyes, who seemed markedly shy. This surface shyness was deceptive. Sherwood's self-confidence was real, and others responded to his strength by having confidence in him. If occasionally he appeared ill at ease, it was because he took his time in giving answers. He was not afraid of pauses. His words could seem railway stations apart.

Already Sherwood showed a gift for writing letters in which he could clarify involved situations and present both sides of a question. His other tasks were unpredictable. If Ina Claire was to be photographed by Baron de Meyer, Sherwood arranged the sitting. If an essay by Chesterton ran short, he added to it the needed Chestertonian lines. Should Grantland Rice's sports copy contain a paragraph that required a little fixing, Sherwood did the fixing. Assisting with captions and makeup also was his concern. At the end of his first three months he was hired for another trial period, and at the same $25 a week.

In a moment of rashness Crowninshield and Nast had sailed for Europe, leaving the publication of two issues of *Vanity Fair* to "Mr. Benchley" and his assistants, "Mrs. Parker" and "Mr. Sherwood." Not only was the High Command in Europe but the conductor of the "For the Well Dressed Man" department went on vacation, leaving behind a column only half written, which Sherwood was asked to complete. He set about the job gleefully, filling the page (which he was confident no one ever read) with such bizarre predictions for male fashions as "*On dit* that peg-topped pants and cloth-top shoes are coming back; also that the best-dressed man's next year's waistcoats will glitter darkly with cut jade." At least one person did read the column—its regular editor, and he was not amused. He came back raging.

It was also during the safe absence of Crowninshield and Nast that Benchley bought for seventy-five dollars the first of several pieces that Sherwood was to write for *Vanity Fair*. These ranged from a laughing survey of violent deaths in current plays ("The Blood Lust on Broadway") to a mocking contention that school children no longer needed to study geography, since they could learn from the motion pictures. For example, that "the Grand Canyon is that ditch which Douglas Fairbanks jumps across," or that "the Pacific Ocean is a body of water six paces due west of the Mack Sennett Bathing Girls." Sherwood's pieces were like his *Lampoon* stuff. They were trivia which huffed and puffed to be gay. They were important only to him. For Sherwood they served their purpose. They brought in welcome money, established him in print as a member of the threesome, and introduced his name to a sophisticated public.

When Crowninshield and Nast returned from Europe at the end of August, the "cat's away" trio were sorry to have their holiday of work over but glad to see Crownie. They spent some time scurrying around town to get the most garish decorations they could find, including banners and crepe paper, to welcome him home to his office.

Mrs. Parker, Benchley, and Sherwood bought nothing for Nast. Little by little, it was becoming clear that they were misfits in the hothouse atmosphere of his organization. Although they were zealous workers when they got to work, they did not believe in having to be at their desks at nine. Nast did, as firmly as he believed in salaries constant in their smallness. He was a routineer; they were last-minute inspirationists. As an executive, he had ideas about efficiency which were baffling to them. The frequent ukases issued by his office manager, Francis Lewis Wurzburg, were not for them edicts but invitations to revolt.

There was, for instance, the *Policy Memorandum* requiring tardy employees to explain their lateness on cards. It delighted Sherwood to recall the annihilating conscientiousness with which Benchley one morning complied with this regulation. His explanation, which covered the card, its margins, and its back with the most minute writing, concerned his having had to help round up a herd of elephants that had escaped from the Hippodrome, with the result that he was eleven minutes late getting to the office. This was his last tardy slip.

There was that other *Policy Memorandum* "forbidding discussion among employees of salary received." This was answered by Sher-

wood, Benchley, and Mrs. Parker with prompt and deserved contempt. Not limiting themselves to a hotly worded written protest,
they made placards, on which their salaries were printed large, and
paraded through the office wearing them. That, according to Nathaniel Benchley's biography of his father, put an abrupt end to another commandment.

Where there had been happiness, there came friction, apprehension, and anger. The sound of a snickersnee being sharpened was in
the air. By early January in 1920 the lighthearted threesome was,
according to Benchley's diary, "waxing very low." They suspected
that Sherwood was "on the verge of being canned" and knew that
Mrs. Parker's pittance had not been upped at the first of the year.
The spirits of the three so drooped that, before Sherwood and Mrs.
Parker learned their fates, they had at a little tea at Henri's "all but
decided to tell the Nast Co. to do what it could with itself." Even the
ebullient Benchley was in a "to hell with everything" mood.

The axe fell on Sherwood the next day. Having asked for a raise, he
had a long conference with Crowninshield during which he was politely told, "in exquisite pussy-footing" according to Benchley, why
his salary could not be increased and why he really ought to get out
and do something else inasmuch as the music teacher of Condé
Nast's daughter was coming in to take over his work. When this
terminating interview was reported to Mrs. Parker and Benchley, the
latter noted that the day "degenerated into a hate-feast" which began
at luncheon and continued through dinner and the theatre and until
Sherwood saw Benchley off on the 11:36 for Crestwood.

Mrs. Parker's was the next head to roll. Three days later, a Sunday, she was asked by Crowninshield to talk over her work with him.
At a pleasantly decorated tea table at the Plaza she was informed
that she was no longer to be *Vanity Fair*'s drama critic but that
"she could write little things at home, etc." Inevitably, she rejected
the offer and resigned.

There was a reason for Crownie's velvet-glove move which he had
already admitted to Benchley. Mrs. Parker's reviews had wounded
some of the staunch advertisers who had come within her notices.
Florenz Ziegfeld was one of these. Mrs. Parker displeased him by
saying of his wife, Billie Burke, in a Maugham comedy, that "in her

desire to convey the girlishness of the character, she plays her lighter scenes rather as if she were giving an impersonation of Eva Tanguay."

In the year of the vast success of Samuel Shipman's *East Is West*, when Chinese dramas were as plentiful as rice in chop suey, Mrs. Parker also failed to beguile David Belasco by saluting *The Son-Daughter*, which he had written with George Scarborough, in these terms: "If Mr. Samuel Shipman is in the house, I should be glad to have him observe me get down and crawl abjectly along the ground for anything I may have said about his brain-child, *East Is West*. Last season, in the exuberance of youth, I used to think that no play along the same lines could possibly be worse; that was before the dying year brought *The Son-Daughter*." As dispraise, this was mild compared to *"The House Beautiful* is the play lousy," which Mrs. Parker in the years to come would toss off for *The New Yorker*. But since it was harsh enough to inflame advertisers, it alarmed Nast.

Benchley had been telephoned in Crestwood by Mrs. Parker immediately after her talk with Crowninshield. He had been waiting for the call and, though it did not come until 7:30, he took the next train to New York and at a meeting with the Parkers decided to resign. Early the next morning he was back in town and at *Vanity Fair*, where he wrote out his resignation which Crowninshield read "very quiet and grieved," supposing that it was the best thing for him to do and assuring him that he would become very famous. In his resignation Benchley stated, as he noted in his diary, that wholly aside from the merits of the management's "stupid and insincere action in Mrs. Parker's case, the office wouldn't be any place to work in without her and Sherwood."

Benchley's action was characteristic, spirited, generous, and quixotic, and it was accepted by his wife Gertrude with equal spirit. He had a family to support, too little money, too many debts, and now not even a regular job. That same day Sherwood, though in effect already fired, sent in his resignation too. The black morning over, the two men and Mrs. Parker lunched together, feeling the excitement of rebels, the pleasure of martyrs, and the misgivings of the unemployed. They returned to the office, where they busied themselves on the telephone, announcing their availability, and betrayed their depression by laughing a little too loudly. The next day, another long and happy "hate-feast" was enlivened for them by an article in the *Times* reporting their walkout. It was written, though not signed, by Alexander Woollcott who, with his gift for being the eye of a hurricane, had just chanced to join them at dinner the previous night when they were laying their plans.

During the next two weeks Mrs. Parker and Sherwood finished up their jobs and on Saturday afternoon, when they had cleaned out their desks, headed for Mamaroneck to see about writing subtitles for D. W. Griffith. The interview proved nothing except Sherwood's already strong interest in the movies. As for Benchley, who was getting various nibbles from newspapers and magazines, he stayed at *Vanity Fair* for the sixty days required by his contract. They were out, the three of them, and very much on their own. Sherwood went his way alone. Mrs. Parker and Benchley took a cubbyhole of an office in the Metropolitan Opera House and planned grandly to write a play, which of course they never did. Benchley, pondering the whole experience, came to the conclusion, "It would have been nice to have had it last as it was, but it probably is better for all of us to do things for ourselves." He proved to be right.

10

THE ALGONQUIN GROUP

Barnum Was Right *Done by the Hasty Pudding—Briefly on the Boston Post—The Midgets and the Giant—Special Flavor of the Algonquin—Frank Case as Host—Glittering Round Tablers—Insults and Puns—Edna Ferber Describes the Group—Pets and Patsies*

The Cambridge elms cast their protecting shade. First, the Hasty Pudding, then the *Lampoon* came to Sherwood's relief; the former by supplying him with something to do for the time being, the latter by easing his way into a job. The Pudding, back to normal in a Harvard once again at peace, needed a spring show and realized that it had one in *Barnum Was Right*. This was the musical, written by Sherwood and S. P. Sears three years earlier, which had been canceled shortly before its opening because of the war. Almost all of the forty members of that previous cast had exchanged their costumes for uniforms, many were wounded, and seven lost their lives. Among the others who enlisted was Sears who, as a lieutenant (jg) in the Navy, had won the Distinguished Service Medal.

The Pudding got in touch with Sherwood who, about to be unemployed, was receptive. Early in February, after lunching with Benchley, Woollcott, Heywood Broun, and Murdock Pemberton, he set off for Boston for two and a half months during which he rewrote his book and nursed it through rehearsals and performances. There were some weekend breaks in New York when, with Benchley and the Parkers, he went to see young John Barrymore malignly lumped and humped as a dazzling Richard III. Or sat before the plumed and spangled wonders of the new Ziegfeld *Follies*, enlivened that year by

Fanny Brice and W. C. Fields. Or talked about F. Scott Fitzgerald's *This Side of Paradise* in which Sherwood's generation found its voice in print. Or discussed until the smaller hours the even now unsolved mysteries of the Elwell murder case.

This time Sherwood was glad to be in the Cambridge he had been glad to leave. Cash was scarce, and food a problem which he solved by exhausting his credit at his clubs, eating at one of them until posted and then moving over to another. Even so, to undergraduates he was an impressive figure. More than having been prominent in the Pudding and the *Lampoon,* he was a professional writer, as *Vanity Fair* had proved, who just happened to be between jobs. He had about him the glamour of a war veteran, set apart from other re- turned veterans because of his service in The Black Watch. Further- more, since he was now undisturbed by studies, he was not a failure at Harvard. The Pudding was his dish.

It is not everyone's. To get the fullest enjoyment from a Pudding show, or shows of a similar kind staged by the Princeton Triangle or the University of Pennsylvania's Mask and Wig, there are certain things which help. To be in them is one. To be of college age or under is another. Nor does it hurt to be a relative of someone con- nected with the production, the fiancée of one of the bewigged and skirted huskies in the cast, or a graduate, still an undergraduate at heart, who has drunk deep of more than the Pierian spring.

In the original version of *Barnum Was Right* Sherwood and Sears had written an intricate allegory about the efforts of a character named the "Spirit of the Movies" to win recognition from Jupiter for the motion pictures as an art form on Mount Olympus. The new version had the Valley of the Nile as its scene and, in spite of such sudden musical flights out of Egypt as "In Havana" and "When They Played Little Buttercup Up and Down Broadway," remained more or less geographically fixed. It was an extravaganza about the misadven- tures of an American movie company on location during the shooting of a foreign film. By the time the cameras roll, a Yankee bounder, Barnum O'Brien, has substituted himself for young Rameses XII whose return to life has been foretold. The book's point, as sum- marized in its finale, was:

Robert Emmet Sherwood, 1940

Sherwood's mother, Rosina

*The three Emmet sisters, Lydia, Rosina, and Jane
(later Mrs. Wilfrid de Glehn)*

Mrs. John Sherwood, Robert Sherwood's grandmother M.E.W.S.,
painted by Rosina

Arthur M. Sherwood, his father, painted by Rosina

*Bobby at fifteen months, painted by
Lydia Field Emmet*

At two, beside Lake Champlain

Skene Wood, the Sherwood house at Westport, New York

Bobby at camp, 1910

An addition to The Canadian Black Watch, 1917

Luncheon at the Algonquin, as drawn by Al Hirschfeld for Horizon. *Clockwise: Robert E. Sherwood, Dorothy Parker, the Lunts, Robert Benchley, Frank Crowninshield, Alexander Woollcott, Heywood Broun, Marc Connelly, Frank Case, F.P.A., Edna Ferber, George S. Kaufman*

All-star chorus for No Sirree!, 1922. From left to right: June Walker, Helen Hayes, Winifred Lenihan, R.E.S., Ruth Gillmore, and Lenore Ulric

After their wedding in October, 1922: Sherwood and Mary Brandon Sherwood with Booth Tarkington, Mrs. Tarkington, Douglas Fairbanks, and Mary Pickford

Philip Merivale, Jane Cowl, Joyce Carey, and Fairfax Burgher in The Road to Rome, *1927* (Courtesy of the Museum of the City of New York)

Little Mary Sherwood in 1927, painted by Rosina

The beginning of "The Red, Red Robin' —Sherwood and his nephew James Townsend, 1926

Mary about twelve

Alfred Lunt, Lynn Fontanne, and Henry Travers in Reunion in Vienna, *1931* (Vandamm Collection, New York Public Library)

The Lunts in Idiot's Delight, *1936* (Vandamm Collection, New York Public Library)

Madeline Sherwood, by Neysa McMein

Madeline Hurlock (Sherwood) in a scene from an old Mack Sennett comedy

The Sherwoods' house at Great Enton, Surrey, England
(Photographs by Chaplin Jones)

*The Sherwoods
at Great Enton*

Acropolis

Sherwood crowned Duke of Enton
(Snapshot by Geoffrey Kerr)

The O.S.C.C. (Old Savoy Croquet Club). Left to right, front row: Geoffrey Kerr, Richard Bird, Geoffrey Massey, Henry Hunloke, Raymond Massey; second row: Madeline Sherwood, Adrianne Allen, Sherwood, Lady Anne Hunloke, Joyce Barbour, Mary Sherwood (Photograph by Geoffrey Kerr)

Leslie Howard and Humphrey Bogart in The Petrified Forest, 1935 (Vandamm Collection, New York Public Library)

Muriel Kirkland and Raymond Massey in Abe Lincoln in Illinois, 1938 (Courtesy of the Museum of the City of New York)

If you dine on the public
You're sure of a feast,
They are innocent lambs
And they long to be fleeced.
For they are fools, gosh darn 'em,
Said P. T. Barnum,
And Mister Barnum Was Right.

The jokes were—jokes; wax plums superimposed on the pudding; proving that at least while listening to Broadway's run-of-the-mill musicals Sherwood had done his homework. *To a young lady:* "How old are you?" "Oh, I'm shy about my age." "How many years shy?" *Of Rameses:* "It seems he was a ruler and a crook at the same time." *Vamp:* "I've never heard of a square ruler." *Or for diners in Cairo:* "How about a nice second joint for an entree?" "Never mind, we have the entree to all the first joints in the town."

Notwithstanding, *Barnum Was Right* was a triumph by Hasty Pudding standards. It was the first of the club's shows to be produced on a $12,000 rather than a $2,500 budget. At nine performances in Cambridge, Boston, Philadelphia, and New York it played to packed houses. From New York the British actress Alexandra Carlisle, strangely equipped for the task by having just appeared in special matinees of John Masefield's *The Tragedy of Nan,* was imported to direct, and two people who worked in *Chu Chin Chow* were brought in to train the dancers.

The heroine, a parody of a Theda Bara vamp, was played with allure by Edgar Scott, future president of the Philadelphia Stock Exchange. Among the shorter, hard-dancing "ponies" in the chorus, as opposed to the taller athletes cast as "show girls," was young Thomas S. Lamont, a future partner of the House of Morgan, whose distinguished father, Thomas W. Lamont, twenty-eight years earlier in the Pudding had played "a school girl" in *The Sphinx, or Love at Random,* along with B. L. Hand, later famous as Judge Learned Hand.

The reviews danced with superlatives. The *Crimson* was typical. In it J. W. D. Seymour, who had been scheduled to appear in the 1917 production, wrote with an enthusiasm which went beyond the demands of club or college loyalty. "The best ever," said he, "a perfectly rounded evening's entertainment . . . far above the average musical comedy." Among the other papers that agreed were the Boston *Transcript* and the *Post*, the latter saluting *Barnum* as "tuneful, colorful and far from the jejune trade stuff of the average professional extravaganza."

Everyone concerned with the production came in for his double scoop of approval. The show as a whole was saluted for "its sureness of touch"; Sherwood for the wit of his lyrics and the "humorous twists of his plot"; and Sears for his tuneful and lively score with its "gems of popularity."

During the run, well-timed stories appeared in the *Crimson*, not only announcing that the book had been bought by John Craig in conjunction with the Shuberts for professional production in America, but also that Miss Carlisle had purchased it for London and that she, Sherwood, and Sears were to sail for England immediately after the last performance in Boston. These press releases may have been authentic, or they may have been puffery. At any rate, there was in them realistic talk of needed revisions, however slight. As calculated, the rumors did not hurt the box office.

Good or bad by professional standards, *Barnum* as a Pudding show was exceptional. Those who saw it or participated in it did not forget it. In the years to come, they huddled around pianos, drinks in hand, to sing its songs and its praises. Its success had its effect upon Sherwood. For the first time he enjoyed the exhilaration of having a work of his greeted by reviewers and audiences and acted in playhouses where S.R.O. was a fact. For Sherwood the experience was a bridge between what he had played at as a child and was to work at as a man.

While having his fun in Cambridge, he did scurry around Boston searching for a paying job, and found one. It was as a reporter on the *Post*, and it lasted three days. Some educator in an interview had said that marriages were apt to be more successful when the participants had had previous sexual experience. The *Post*'s editor, thinking a woman's point of view would be interesting, sent Sherwood to question the Dean of Women at Boston University. The Dean was conventional, curt, and noncommittal. To save her from her dull propriety, Sherwood, when he came to write the story, magnanimously put into her mouth the progressive views which were his own. The editor, at first excited by the frankness and novelty of the Dean's statement, came to doubt its authenticity and in the nick of time sent galleys to her. She, it turned out, as S. N. Behrman related the incident in "Old Monotonous," his *New Yorker* Profile, was "definitely ungrateful for the liberality of outlook imputed to her by the visionary Sherwood." From her there was a quick denial; from the *Post*, the swift removal of Sherwood.

It was in New York, not London, that he found himself that May, the New York which was already taking on the shape of the twenties. It was the New York of "Mrs. Parker," "Mr. Benchley," and "Mr. Sherwood," only this time they were without *Vanity Fair*. In their months on the magazine they had grown accustomed to lunching and dining together so as not to interrupt the serial which was their conversation. Naturally, they had sought some welcoming and agreeable place nearby. *Vanity Fair* was at 19 West 44th Street. Had men's clubs in those days augmented their income by admitting women, the three might have gone to the Harvard Club a few doors away, as Benchley and Sherwood did when Mrs. Parker was not with them. Since she generally was, they got in the habit of going a little farther down the block to the Algonquin.

Their stroll from the office was not always as agreeable as it might have been. For a time Sherwood's height presented a problem. It drew to him, as inevitably as Hillary was to be attracted to Mount Everest, a troupe of midgets who were appearing at the Hippodrome across the street. On these embarrassing occasions, Sherwood depended upon tiny "Mrs. Parker" and medium-sized "Mr. Benchley" to convoy him. Their assorted sizes made them look, in Nathaniel Benchley's phrase, like a "walking pipe organ." The protection they offered, however, was only partial, because the midgets, an odious lot, would run after Sherwood and surround him, screaming up at him and taunting him with the familiar "How's the weather up there?"

The trio were not alone in finding the Algonquin a beckoning place, nor did they by any means discover it. Since its opening in 1902 it had had a magnet's tug for writers, theatre people, and the stage-struck. Richard Harding Davis had been one of its devoted patrons, and among the others were Gertrude Atherton, Lady Gregory, Alfred Noyes, Charles Hanson Towne, and Booth Tarkington. Eugene Walter had written there *The Easiest Way*, and Paul Armstrong *Alias Jimmy Valentine*. John Drew, Raymond Hitchcock, Elsie Janis, Fred Stone, Frank Craven, Constance Collier, the Barrymores, and Ina Claire were some of the actors who made it their working headquarters. Douglas Fairbanks, who took his exercise skipping rope on the roof, should not be forgotten. Nor his son, Douglas Jr., who as a fat little boy used to steal into the Vinton Freedleys' front corner suite to take successful pot shots with an air rifle at the electric bulbs in the Hippodrome sign across the way.

Though a hotel, the Algonquin had come to have all the endearing attributes of an inn. Always too small, with its one elevator for passengers rising and descending as sleepily as if awakened from a nap, it was an Edwardian reminder that certain fundamentals of comfort are beyond the whims of decorators. When Sherwood, Benchley, and Mrs. Parker found themselves among its new habitués, the Algonquin was not so much an old-fashioned place as a place settled, long lived in, and loved. Some likened it to Brown's Hotel in London, Louis Bromfield to old Frau Sacher's in Vienna, about which Sherwood was to write. It did not need a "Welcome" mat. Welcome was in the air.

There were plenty of other hotels and restaurants in the Broadway neighborhood that might have won the theatre's trade and the legendary name which came to the Algonquin in the twenties. But none of these had Frank Case as master of the inn. He was the one who persuaded his boss, its builder and first proprietor, not to call the hotel the Puritan but the Algonquin, because a visit to the Public Library had revealed to him that the Algonquins were the first and strongest people in the neighborhood. Some argued that the new tribe, which moved in with the establishment of the Round Table, used tomahawks with inherited skill and were also master scalpers.

Case was as stage-struck as they come, and those who came to the Algonquin in Sherwood's time could not have been more so. They were all writing plays or planning to write them, conducting columns, acting, working for magazines, turning out novels, or reviewing the theatre, the movies, music, or books. Case's induction into the theatre had been early and proved abiding. As a high school boy in Buffalo, while serving as an usher, he saw all the touring stars and had his life changed when, one evening at the stage door, Julia Marlowe said "Good night" to him as melodiously as if she had been playing the Balcony Scene.

Case was the ideal Boniface for a hotel that catered to actors and writers. A lean, spruce man, pale of face but warm of heart, he had a somewhat beakish nose, a thin mustache over thin smiling lips, and twinkling eyes that radar-swept a room, spotting at once the important persons who were present. His *Social Register* was *Who's Who in the Theatre*. Big businessmen, social leaders, and politicians did not impress him. Writers, musicians, painters, and particularly people of the theatre did. They were different, set apart, special. From the outset he was determined to attract them. What is more, he did.

He supplied the kind of eating and staying place which was liked by the kind of people he liked. He enjoyed them as thoroughly as they did themselves, and he understood their needs and temperaments. He provided good food at reasonable prices in a friendly setting and, having known hard times himself, was generous in extending credit to those whose hard times were part of their glamour. His firm belief was that gifted people, more than being tolerated, should be encouraged "in their strange and temperamental antics."

This belief was his policy at the Algonquin. He had the listener's gift and, as a measure of his patience, tact, and absorption, was as truly interested in hearing a performer talk about his performance as the actor was. He coddled egos with the skill of his chef coddling eggs. He welcomed individuality, an invitation which his patrons accepted, and none more willingly than those men and women who in 1919 began to assemble at what came to be known as the Round Table.

The Round Table was an improvisation which turned into a habit and, in the process, became a force and then a myth. Always blessedly free of officers, by-laws, attendance requirements, dues, and a gavel, it stumbled into being when a number of individuals, many of whom were accustomed to eating at the Algonquin, started lunch-

ing there more or less as a group day after day, and continued to do
so for about a decade.

The initial impromptu gatherings were in the long side room, now
called the Oak Room but then known as the Pergola. Case, a shrewd
publican, was quick to realize the value of having so many publicists
at his inn, mentioning it in their columns while mentioning each
other. He moved them into the Rose Room, his main dining room at
the back of the lobby, placing them at a table near the entrance. As
the attendance increased, he moved them again in the same room,
this time to a large circular table upstage center. At it, and at neigh-
boring tables if there was an overflow, these "celebrities"—real,
small, large, or self-imagined—were on exhibition, and as they grew
in fame more and more people came daily to stare at them at their
round table.

Pleasant rather than pretty, this pink and white dining room was
public, a fact which did not bother most of the regulars at all. Moreover, it was brightly lighted. Case, who claimed to have invented the
term "café society," found himself catering to the society he admired.
Without his having to hire one, he had acquired a floor show, literary
and theatrical, which attracted a sizable public and an even more
sizable press.

At first the group was as nameless as a foundling. Then some of its
members began to refer to it jokingly as "The Board." When a waiter
named Luigi was assigned to them, this inevitably became "The
Luigi Board." From that they proceeded with delight to "The Vicious Circle." In *Black Oxen* Gertrude Atherton within a few years
referred to them as "The Sophisticates." Their enemies, in whom
they were rich, were from the beginning less kind. They called them,
among other things, "The Log Rollers." To many they were, and
remained, "The Algonquin Group." To more they were known as
"The Round Table," because of the cartoon Edmund Duffy of the
Brooklyn *Eagle* drew of them as knights in armor sitting at their
round table. They would have been the first to admit that there was
nothing Arthurian about them except the shape of the table which
Case reserved for them.

They were a glittering lot, these men and women with whom
Sherwood began to lunch almost daily. All of them were young in

spirit, and most of them in fact. Sherwood, twenty-three, was within months of being the youngest, and the next to oldest by a year was Franklin Pierce Adams, thirty-eight, better known because of his *Tribune* column, "The Conning Tower," as F.P.A. Those who already had reputations were on the verge of adding to them. The majority of those who did not were about to make them. In or out of print, in the theatre or in the glare of columns, they were to move increasingly into the spotlight as the twenties progressed. The journalists among them, by quoting their cronies or mentioning them in print, saw to it that they were not dogged by obscurity. To the delight not of all but of many, including themselves, they became the town's ruling wits, and theirs was a lively rule.

Among the faithful or fitful in their Round Table attendance, in addition to Sherwood and F.P.A., were Woollcott, Heywood Broun, Benchley, Marc Connelly, George S. Kaufman, Frank Sullivan, Donald Ogden Stewart, Deems Taylor, Howard Dietz, Harold Ross, Laurence Stallings, John V. A. Weaver, John T. Winterich, John Peter Toohey, David Wallace, Hawley Truax, and the two Pembertons, Brock and Murdock. The women included Edna Ferber (when she was willing to take time off from her writing), Margaret Leech (a regular because she had an office next door), Alice Duer Miller (an intermittent visitor), Ruth Hale, Beatrice Kaufman, Jane Grant, Neysa McMein (very rarely present), Alison Smith, Mary Brandon (who was to figure in Sherwood's life), Ruth Gordon, Peggy Wood, Margalo Gillmore, and, of course, Mrs. Parker. Actually about ten people were apt to lunch each day at the Round Table. Guests who accepted an invitation to join them ran a risk not covered by insurance. To survive in this company, outsiders had to be armed and armored.

To say what a thing is not is an approach to saying what it is. Among those who were not members of the Round Table were Ernest Hemingway, Stephen Vincent Benét, Willa Cather, Eugene O'Neill, Edna St. Vincent Millay, Sinclair Lewis, Elinor Wylie, Theodore Dreiser, Sherwood Anderson, F. Scott Fitzgerald, Thornton Wilder, John Marquand, Thomas Wolfe, Don Marquis, Christopher Morley, Walter Lippmann, Mencken and Nathan, Lewis Mumford, Stark Young, Joseph Wood Krutch, Edmund Wilson,

Malcolm Cowley, Carl and Mark Van Doren, Gilbert Seldes, Percy Hammond, Norman Bel Geddes, and Robert Edmond Jones. These, by their absence, help to define the nature and concerns of those present. Some of the unincluded were occasional visitors; others were greatly admired by the group; still others, by temperament and cast of mind, were utterly alien to it.

The Tablers did not meet as candidates for the Poets' Corner, political pundits, members of a Faculty Club, or as lily-claspers made grave by beauty. Among them Benchley no more discussed the notes he was making for a serious study of the humorists of Queen Anne's day than F.P.A. recited Horace in Latin or than Sherwood thought of mentioning his reading of Livy, Juvenal, and Mommsen. They did not meet in public to be solemn.

They met as what they were—men and women the majority of whom had shiny and capering minds. Most of them at the outset were beginners, like Sherwood, bubbling over with the yeast of youth, and all of them remained coltish even when they had made their names, which, in Sherwood's fashion, many of them proceeded to do with incredible speed.

The craftsmen among them were more plentiful than the artists, the journalists than the authors, the reviewers than the critics, the wags than the philosophers, the playwrights than the dramatists, and the strong feelers than the deep thinkers. Their luncheon meetings were their way of adding to a fruitful day by interrupting it.

Fun was what they sought, and fun was what they had—and gave—a kind of fun that has all but vanished. While nourishing themselves, they fed their minds and sharpened their wits on the stimulation and challenge they presented to each other. Meeting during the Prohibition years, they had no need for liquor to keep their spirits high. They had sufficient energy to work as earnestly at their play as they did to make their work seem like play. Their jokes and pranks were among their productions, and their productivity was dazzling. They were earnest in their ambitions but lighthearted in their talk.

Abstract ideas did not interest them; their times—and Times Square—did. Gathered around their table at "Château Case," as Sherwood called it, they found large pleasure in small things. This would not have set them apart, because after all others lunched and talked together even then, if their wit however intramural had not also been large. Actually, they could be as parochial in their talk as the guests at a clergyman's tea party in Trollope. F.P.A.'s two-volume *Diary of Our Own Samuel Pepys*, so fascinating to would-be sophisticates when its entries appeared each Saturday in Adams's changing newspapers, and now, except to the included, so monumental in the boredom of its mannered trivia, makes this all too clear. But the Round Tablers' parish included the world of books and plays and tennis matches, and all the people then most glamorously in the news. That, during the twenties, made the difference.

The respect of these men and women for writing was genuine, and often they plunged into discussions of it, or the theatre, or any other subject that came to tongue, with muscular vivacity and perception. They hated bores and being bored, and were the highly vocal foes of the affected, the long-winded, or the self-important. All of them were aware, as their guests sometimes were not, that every time they spoke they ran the risk of turning themselves into targets. Hence, while not guarded in their speech, they had to be on guard.

To their delight and the delight of those who could hear them only when their sallies were reported in print, theirs was frequently the comedy of bad manners. They were wisecrackers, more apt to use the bludgeon than the rapier, who often spoke not to encourage further talk but to silence what had gone before. Their malice could be greater than their mercy. What they were able to give, they expected others to be prepared to take.

They knew a good line when they heard—or said—one, and were as warm in their respect for the mots of others as for their own. Conversationally, they stalked each other waiting for the chance to fire the topping gag. This required, as Case's daughter, Margaret Case Harriman, noted in her charmingly evocative *The Vicious Circle*, "a miraculous sense of timing" because "with them a joke had one chance, and only one." "A Round Tabler," she pointed out, "might treasure for a half an hour a remark he had thought up, chatting amiably meanwhile, and then, in the space of an indrawn breath, expel it into precisely the right moment of silence." Although, according to her, "all of them were hams, in the most lovable sense of the word," the writers oddly enough were more expert at this split-timing than the actors.

If insults were their favorite weapons for demolishing adversaries, or even those guilty only of inanity, nonsense was one of the ways in which they made sense. To the charge sometimes brought against them that they worked too hard at trying to be wits, they could have answered, as Charles Lamb did, that trying to be witty is at least as good as aiming at dullness.

With that ginny, smoky, delectable little man, they had another thing in common. They loved puns. They loved them as much as all people dislike them who cannot make them. They were not among the witless who dismiss them as the lowest form of wit. They knew that there is no such thing as stooping to a pun. There is the challenge of rising to a good one or appreciating a bad one, if only it is bad enough and meant to be so.

Their puns, such as Kaufman's "One man's Mede is another man's Persian," Peggy Wood's "Well, back to the mimes" when returning to a rehearsal, Woollcott's saying at cards "I'll fold up my tens and silently steal away," Sherwood's "None but the brave *chemin de fer*," Frank Adams's solving the problem of building a sentence around "meretricious" with "Meretricious 'n a Happy New Year," and Mrs. Parker's solving the same problem with "horticulture" by coming up with "You may lead a whore to culture but you can't make her think"—these and a hundred others of their kind may by now have become enfeebled by familiarity. But they were born of a moment, and meant for that moment, and at that moment they were triumphant. Rob a pun of the moment of its first being made, and, no matter how good it may remain, it has already lost something. As Lamb knew, "a pun has a hearty kind of ear-kissing smack in it; you can no more transmit it than you can send a kiss."

The Round Tablers' brightness was of a kind that caused many to squint, some to view them through the darkest of dark glasses, and others to turn away entirely. Being gay, they seemed frivolous to the serious, and, having the power that came from print and success, they irritated those who resented their influence. Too special in their tastes for all, they were too strong in their dislikes and enthusiasms not to invite enthusiastic dislike. They did not have to wait for their detractors and in time were to have their unexpected defectors.

George M. Cohan, upon whose Broadway they poached, described them as "A Round Table without a square man at it." Then, there were those who dismissed them, or tried to do so, as a coterie of exhibitionists and back-scratchers, and deplored their manners (as if they all shared Woollcott's), and ridiculed their tastes. Decades later the very memory of them in their heyday stuck in the craw of John Marquand. With a fine mustering of spleen, some of it unfeigned, he recalled them as "a lot of conceited second-raters" whose pranks were as intolerable as their assumptions of intellectual superiority.

As late as January, 1959, Ben Hecht and, of all people, Mrs. Parker were attacking them on a television show. Hecht damned them as "a remarkable unit of illiteracy"; Mrs. Parker, the most quoted of their jesters, complained of "their little jokes all about themselves," and contended, her memory playing odd tricks upon her, that "none of them had read anything written before 1920." "Most of them," she said, "are dead now, but they weren't too alive then." They were, however, alive enough to make New York for a decade a far livelier place than it was before or has been since by what they wrote and did and because of what they were.

On the same television program Mrs. Parker also insisted that the Round Table was not a bit like the Mermaid Tavern. Maybe so. But many of us who were never present at either, much less at both, were eager to believe, as stage-struck, print-bedazzled newcomers to New York in the mid-twenties, that the Round Table was a straphanger's version of the Mermaid Tavern, Will's Coffee House, and a Thursday evening at the Lambs' all rolled into one.

On those occasions, and for us they *were* occasions, when we went to the Rose Room, we could not at our side tables hear what was being said by those men and women whose plays and performances we were seeing, whose books, columns, and reviews we devoured, and who seemed to us the embodiment of Times Square sophistication, gaiety, and success. We could only gape at them, and hear their distant laughter, and be hopefully certain that what they laughed at was the ultimate in wit and drollery. We, the younger ones, were not alone in feeling this. Countless older New Yorkers, also avid readers of "the page opposite" in the *World* on which the columns of Broun,

Woollcott, Deems Taylor, and Stallings appeared, felt as we did, and so did out-of-towners beyond numbering who flocked to the Algonquin as part of their Broadway pilgrimage.

Some of us in the years ahead, when they no longer met, came to know the Tablers slightly, with fair intimacy, or well, and by what they were and had become were able to guess at what they had been. They, the spirit of their meetings, and the thrust of their interchanges have been vividly captured in their own writings or evoked in their spoken reminscences, and in such books about them as Frank Case's *Tales of a Wayward Inn*, Mrs. Harriman's *The Vicious Circle*, or Samuel Hopkins Adams's biography, *A. Woollcott*.

No one to my knowledge has more incisively appraised their quality or their contributions than Miss Ferber in her autobiography, *A Peculiar Treasure*. She knew them all intimately and was one of them whenever she chose to be. Miss Ferber also knew, as they did, that because they met as a group they were often accused, in spite of their abrasive references to one another in and out of print, of meeting as a cabal to promote each other. Her answer to this was that "Far from boosting one another they were actually merciless if they disapproved. I have never encountered a more hard-bitten crew. But if they liked what you had done they did say so, publicly and wholeheartedly. Their standards were high, their vocabulary fluent, fresh, astringent, and very, very tough. Theirs was a tonic influence, one on the other, and all on the world of American letters. . . . They were ruthless toward charlatans, toward the pompous, and the mentally and artistically dishonest. Casual, incisive, they had a terrible integrity about their work and a boundless ambition."

Had the Round Tablers no more than lunched together for a decade, they would inevitably have been identified as a group. But their meetings did not stop there. They were gamblers as well as talkers and had a passion for games of nearly any kind. Most of the men among them, including Sherwood, on Saturday nights disrupted their finances and the upstairs room which Case set aside for them at the Algonquin by gathering at the Thanatopsis, a circle which under that name was to become almost as well known as the Round Table itself, although it was more intimately and accurately referred to as the Young Man's Upper West Side Thanatopsis Literary and Inside

Straight Club. There, sometimes until noon on a Sunday, they played poker for dizzying stakes ($500 was a normal table stake), imperiling their salaries or a week's fat royalties, but with the losers partially consoling themselves by getting off some of the puns and insults which they cherished most.

Their comrades in recklessness were apt to be Jerome Kern; the *World's* brilliant, gravel-voiced executive editor, Herbert Bayard Swope, a Roman emperor of a man, red-haired and red-faced, whose speech was so volubly encyclopedic that someone once wished that "he would not Swope until he was Swopen to"; F. Scott Fitzgerald, of whom Sherwood saw much at the time and whom he was to remember thirty-five years later as "the supreme glamour boy of the literary world"; Woollcott's pet, Harpo Marx without harp but with voice; the shy and silent Ring Lardner, revered and loved by all of them and one of Sherwood's gods; Raoul Fleischmann, *The New Yorker's* suave and friendly backer; Emanuel Haldeman-Julius, who was forever publishing short classics for a nickel; Donald Ogden Stewart, whose poker was described by Woollcott as being even more hilarious than such of his books as *Mr. and Mrs. Haddock Abroad* or *A Parody Outline of History*; the Romanian Prince Antoine Bibesco, with whom it was possible to get even when he won by saying that his game was "funny without being Bulgar"; Henry Wise Miller, seemingly a refugee from the Union Club but actually, as Alice Duer Miller's husband, her delegate at the game; John V. A. Weaver, who on one occasion was relieved of all the royalties for the preceding six months from his book of poems, *In American*; and such a literarily inclined representative of Wall Street as Gerald Brooks.

Whenever any of them made a foolish play, all the others rose by tradition as a body to sing "He Remains a God-Damned Fo-o-ool," their adaptation of the "Englishman" song in *Pinafore*. The only women admitted to the game were Neysa McMein, Ruth Fleischmann, Jane Grant, and Beatrice Kaufman, but they sat in occasionally and only for a little while, as Mrs. Harriman wrote, "the way you let a child have *one* piece of candy before dinner." From time to time such players as Ina Claire, Lynn Fontanne, Alfred Lunt, Beatrice Lillie, and Roland Young, their week's work done, were permitted to drop in, though merely to ornament and kibitz.

These draining all-night sessions did not exhaust the energies of
the hard-working Round Tablers. By the fall of 1923 three of them
—Broun, Connelly, and Woollcott—had resigned from the Thanatopsis. This was not because they were tired or piqued by their
losses. It was because they were convinced, in Woollcott's words,
that "poker (with just three final rounds of jackpots, everybody up, at
nine o'clock in the morning) is a preposterous waste of time." Sherwood was not among the convinced.

The Round Tablers had their other diversions as the decade advanced, and these were plentiful. Some of them were fond of dashing
up to Central Park to play croquet together at $10 a wicket, and
none of them, mallet in hand, was more furious in his earnestness
than Sherwood. Many of them, with Sherwood's relish, went to the
Swopes' on Long Island for lively weekends of tennis and talk and
parlor games and cards, or across the Hudson up to Averell Harriman's Arden for the same releases. Or, on nights when there were no
Broadway openings, they often met for parties at Miss Ferber's, the
Kaufmans', the Millers', or Miss Leech's. (In 1928 she married
Ralph Pulitzer, the owner of the *World*.)

One of their favorite playgrounds was Neysa McMein's studio
over which, all charm and wonder and vagueness, she presided.
Often she wore a paint-dappled smock and sat at her easel finishing a
magazine cover. Other guests, such as George Gershwin, Irving Berlin, Jascha Heifetz, Charles MacArthur, Helen Hayes, and Noel
Coward, were often also present to delight in a turmoil of conversation, cribbage, music, anagrams, guessing games such as "Who Am
I?" and charades which in time evolved into the intricacies of "The
Game."

The Tablers had their pets and their patsies, their disagreements
and their feuds. They were bound to, not only because they were
human but because they were such humans as they were. A spoken
word with them could be a machete, letters such as Miss Ferber once
fired at Woollcott and Woollcott at Ross the equivalent of bombs.
The wonder was that the flare-ups were not more frequent; the
greater wonder that so many prima donnas were able to sing together
in fair harmony for so long a time.

11

ROUND TABLERS ALL

Sherwood and the Algonquin—The Dynamite of Stimulation—The "Improbable" Alexander Woollcott—F.P.A., Curator of Taste—Heywood Broun, Untidy Titan—Connelly and Kaufman—The Distaff Side— Sherwood in the "Society" That He Liked—The Challenge of Their Example

Sherwood took to these men and women, and they to him, just as he took to the world to which they introduced him. They were molding influences and examples. In them he found the echoes of his hopes and needs, and reflections of himself, or diversion and companionship. They were not like him but like enough to be near to him or sufficiently different to amuse him.

In their dissimilar ways they fitted into the intricate cloisonné of his character, and most of them were to remain his friends even when he and they, in Alice's fashion, had moved on to different squares. Had they been Bohemians in the Greenwich Village sense, he would have shunned them as scrupulously as he, very much a "gent" (to use an old-fashioned word which in its fullest meaning was with him the final accolade), avoided the stodgily genteel.

He liked these people because they were anything but stodgy and bright rather than genteel. He liked them because, instead of belonging to that part of their generation which was happily "lost," they were, in spite of the disillusionment which had come with the peace, gleefully finding themselves. He liked them because they were professionals, not dilettantes, who wanted to succeed and were not ashamed when they did. He liked them because they took their work rather than themselves seriously. A worldling himself, but always more than that, he liked them because they, too, were more than worldlings. He liked them because the thought of money gave them no offense and they enjoyed comfort even when they could push it to luxury. He liked them because they liked a good time and were good to themselves and others while championing good causes and writing good things. He liked them because they had the dynamite of stimulation in them, because they laughed and made him laugh, and because, in addition to being different from humdrum people, they were markedly different from one another.

Woollcott, for example, of whom Sherwood was fond and who was fond of Sherwood, was, to the relief of some, like no one else. He sported his personality like a blazer and rejoiced in being un-muffled by those restraints to which most submit. The man who came to lunch was in many respects already the man who was to come to dinner. Even then he was sitting for a preliminary sketch of Sheridan Whiteside. Portly as a matron, he was inevitably caricatured as an owl because of the roundness of his face, the swoop of his small nose, and the thick, large glasses through which he stared unblink-ingly.

Kaufman, once asked to summarize him in a word, thought hard and said, "Improbable." That was what Woollcott was in his appear-ance, gifts, and contradictions. A sizzling mixture of arsenic and treacle, he was as warm in his resentments as in his enthusiasms. He was an actor who was forever playing one or the other of his two favorite parts—"a much uplifted onlooker" or "an old meanie." When Sherwood first knew him, his daily reviews for the *Times*, next the *Herald*, then the *World*, may not have been criticism but they were performances, Woollcott performing so that the emotions of a first night were captured in print with an immediacy unmatched in our times.

Phalanx, New Jersey, where he was born, Hamilton College to which he went, the mumps which came to him when he was a young man, and the First World War, during which he served overseas on *Stars and Stripes* with Adams, Ross, and Winterich, were among the ⸱ding influences on Woollcott—these and the theatre in terms of ⸱⸱he was always to see life. A "perhapsless" man, he could be ⸱⸱in sentimentality of Barrie's McConnachie or feline in the swiftness of his scratch. He loved wonder, coincidence, murders, anecdotes, rags-to-riches yarns, trivia, and suspense, and was able in his talk and writing to convey his infatuation with them.

Naturally he had his enemies, but he rejoiced in them even as he did in his no less numerous friends whom, as the years progressed and he became a part of the public domain, he sometimes seemed to choose as much for his reader's enjoyment as his own. He was a "curmudgeon," though not the "bogus" one he liked to describe himself as being. He had the courage of his eccentricities, his whims, his indifferent taste, and his misbehavior, and, though he gave pain, he gave pleasure, and much of it to Sherwood. The two of them were to watch one another's changing careers with interest and admiration.

Franklin Pierce Adams, with whom Sherwood also enjoyed talk and cards and companionship, was not so noisy a bully as Woollcott but he, too, was intimidating, and even Woollcott deferred to him. His was a scowling, prowling, dusklike Armenian face which suddenly became noontime in the brightness of its smiles. A dead pan at one moment, it radiated life at the next, and was made winning by the fullness of its participation. F.P.A.'s cone-shaped head was topped by black hair that had the look of steel wool, used, scratchy, and rusty. His nose was a promontory, his mustache a shaded cove, and his chin somewhat in retreat from his lower lip which had a gargoyle's outward thrust. His ugliness was readily forgotten, however, because of the wrinkles of recognition which without warning would animate his features and the unpredictable blaze of his small, dark, closely spaced eyes as they came on to light his witticisms on their way. He was a curator of taste, passionate in his concern for the purities of the language, blessed or cursed with a proofreader's eye for correction. Though he delighted in seeming grumpy or gruff, he was essentially kind and could be beguiling.

Heywood Broun, more than seven years older than Sherwood, came to be involved sooner than he did in serious causes, but in what was to be Sherwood's fashion he combined ardent commitment with the gift for gaiety. Widely loved and widely loving, Broun was feared for his indignation and treasured for his humor. On the undulant acreage which was his face, his precise, pointed nose struggled to recognized. His hands were balloon-large, and among his ample curves were his thumbs which bent wristward as if weighted down by prodigality. His small, dark eyes fought against the flesh which encircled them but never against the laughter within them or the kindness. His body was mountainous like his inner abundance, his clothes always a range of wrinkles. Finding images for his sloppiness was an easy and popular sport. Someone likened him to "an unmade bed," another to "a one-man slum," and Peggy Bacon to "a stage elephant made of two men."

A sentimentalist (in his phrase "an easy weeper") and a wit, Broun was also an extravagant champion, a formidable foe, and a crusader whose indignation, when aroused as in his defense of Sacco and Vanzetti, blazed forth with passion and without restraint. He had the facility of the naturally humorous and the eloquence of strong feelings. An able sports writer when Sherwood first knew him, Broun soon became a diverting theatrical reviewer, and then a powerful freewheeling columnist. Untidy in his turbulence, he tried painting, novel-writing, and biography too, and in time helped organize the Newspaper Guild. Although he hated to approach a typewriter, he was miraculously swift when at the last moment he sat down before one. He had only contempt for commentators whose search was for the right word rather than the just cause. He never had to search for either. There was nothing lazy about his conscience. In print or in conversation it was articulate. Years later, in 1939 some months before Broun's death, Sherwood was to refer to Broun in his diary as "one of the world's best talkers." The others he named were Booth Tarkington, Will Rogers, Swope, Charlie Chaplin, and George Bernard Shaw.

The theatre, a fever in the bloodstream of the twenties, was an epidemic among the Round Tablers. Most of them were seized with the desire to write plays, and sooner or later, in Sherwood's fashion, most of them did with sweet-moneyed and garlanded success. Chief among the carriers were two of their own number, George S. Kaufman and Marc Connelly, who spread the contagion by turning to writing early and making it seem easy by the series of hits they ᵛ From 1921 to 1924, from *Dulcy* and *To the Ladies* to ᵗʰe *Movies* and *The Beggar on Horseback*, Kaufman and

Connelly were Broadway's favored Siamese twins, collaborators as linked in the public mind as Gilbert and Sullivan or, for that matter, Kaufman and Hart were to be in the thirties. Although thought of during these budding years as if they were one person because of the deceptive blend their comedies seemed to be, they were glaringly dissimilar.

"Marcus," or even "Marcus Parcus" as he was sometimes called affectionately by those whose lives and living rooms he brightened, was a plump, Pickwickian man, already bald, whose nose rose from his face like the pointer on a sundial. He was a Winnie-the-Pooh grown up, protean within himself and protean in what he could become. Inhibitions did not shackle him nor audiences large or small dismay him. An author who contained an actor, he was an actor who enclosed a professor.

Radiantly gifted as a mimic, as good at improvising as at remembering, he could, without bothering about props or costumes, be Spartacus at one moment or at the next either Barbara Frietchie waving her Rebel flag or Ruth Draper serving coffee at a railway lunch counter on the Western plains. He could lift a party as few could, and drop it only when the Herr Doktor in him took over or he arrived too fresh from a reading of the encyclopedia. He worked rapidly and well, once he got started, but his imagination was such that he could mistake the intention to work for work already done. Woollcott, who came to respect him hugely, called him an "infuriating blend of poet, peacock, and procrastinator." He was more than that, far more, as Sherwood realized when once he defended him against Woollcott's charge that he would never get anything done after the Kaufman-Connelly partnership dissolved. *The Green Pastures* lay ahead. Sherwood not only admired Connelly but counted him a close friend until their break in 1934.

Kaufman was in many respects Connelly's antonym. All nerves and concentration, he was as lean and tense as an exclamation point. His face was long, his patience short. His black hair rose like a cliff from his expansive forehead, his chin had cement in it, his nose was large and imperious, his cheekbones were as high as an Indian chief's, and his dark eyes burned behind his tortoise-shell glasses like coals banked deeply in a grate. A tireless worker, he was a craftsman who labored over the fashioning of a line or scene until both functioned with the accuracy of precision instruments.

Shyness was at the core of Kaufman's being. Friendship with him was not easy, though many, in Sherwood's fashion, found it well worth the difficulties. He could—and did—write letters in which he expressed the kind of warm appreciation of people that he was incapable of stating face to face. He writhed when complimented and cringed at betrayals of emotion. He himself was often seized and touched emotionally, as Moss Hart came to know and said in *Act One*, that most successful of theatrical success stories, and was as susceptible as the next fellow "to the dark doubts which licked other men's souls." But he fought a winning battle to keep his stronger feelings hidden. As Hart observed, "he was not driven by a savage necessity to be liked." He had his own standards, was indifferent to the good opinions of others, kowtowed to no one, and could be dispatchingly abrupt. His wit which won him wide respect also caused him to be widely feared, and made even Woollcott uneasy in his presence. More than putting up with Kaufman, his friends shared Sherwood's fondness for him, knew that his heart was warm, cold as his manner could be, and delighted in countless sessions with him such as the one at which Sherwood noted in his diary, "George steadily comical."

Sherwood, the gregarious man who could seem lonely in a crowd, was close to many of the other men in the Round Table, such as Deems Taylor, Frank Sullivan, and Harold Ross. He liked the women, too. Edna Ferber with her fine lioness's head, her alert black eyes, her expertly mobilized gifts, her tenderness and sensitivity, and her anger which could erupt so that some wondered if she should not have been named Etna. Margaret Leech, with her strawberry and cream complexion, her blonde hair, her china-blue eyes, and her mind so witty and muscular that she was dotingly nicknamed "Vinegar Nell." The patrician Alice Duer Miller, with her warming graciousness and her love of poetry, mathematics, and fiction. Ruth Gordon, bantam in her person and large in her magic, with her wide smile and her winning eagerness. And Margalo Gillmore, with her huge, soft dark eyes, and radiant in her youthfulness and the glow of sensational first successes.

Among these Round Tablers Sherwood stood out like a grandfather's clock. The tick of his talk was measured, his words seeming to be spaced by minutes, but when he chimed he struck gaily. What was deepest in him had, except when he wrote, a hard time getting out. Although his likes and dislikes were strong and he could say sharp things, he took no pleasure in wounding and was not among the scrappers. The slowness of his speech was his tongue's guardian in such fast-talking company. His silences were often his retorts, his somewhat tortured smiles his signals of enjoyment, and his look of incredulity the register of his mustering disapproval.

Paul Hyde Bonner, the diplomat and novelist, remembered Sherwood at the Algonquin as being the kind of conversationalist who let others speak first, and then came in with a droll tag line. He recalled Sherwood's curious, slightly adenoidal speech, which was not quite Cambridge, not quite New York, nor for that matter quite Middle West, but which for no reason had a slightly Midwestern overtone. In particular, Bonner remembered how he would drawl out, "A-b-s-o-l-u-t-e-l-y m-a-r-v-e-l-o-u-s," until the two words seemed a paragraph.

Through the years Sherwood's drawl was to become accentuated, a habit which grew into a mannerism, and a mannerism which as an aid to a droll comment could be as helpful as Charles Lamb's stutter. Sherwood's points had to be waited for. They came as victories of the tortoise over the hares. They gained in humor because the ease of their phrasing was at odds with the seeming pain of their delivery and their gaiety in strange contrast to the gravity of Sherwood's face.

He had much of Benchley's gentleness and not a little of Kaufman's shyness. At times he had a disquieting way of being absent, though present, and at other times of suddenly joining in as a jubilant participant. He was not at all shy when it came to the parlor games at which the group excelled, nor to public speaking, radio appearances, acting, singing, or dancing. In spite of the misery on his face while performing, he reveled in all these displays, being, as he confessed, "just a frustrated actor, exercising vicariously an exhibition complex."

Sherwood, who seldom forgot anything whether it was history, a book, a newspaper story, a place, a play, a performance, or a chance remark made during dinner, had a memory of old songs and the

lyrics of mildewed musicals which was staggering. Nor did he mind
sharing this knowledge. He sang and danced these numbers as if he
were composing the Gettysburg Address, but he loved doing them.
From the mid-twenties on, when first at a family party, with his
young nephew James Townsend, he strutted and sang his way in
blackface through "When the Red, Red Robin Comes Bob, Bob,
Bobbin' Along," he took over this Jolson song until it became his
signature. In his later and last years a party was not a party for him,
and therefore for his friends, until he, this brooding man, was happy
enough (the blackface long since omitted) to reach for a hat and
cane and plunge into this routine, his long arms and legs twirling like
the sails of a windmill in a hurricane.

Due to his gravity, Sherwood appeared to be older than he was.
The pain he had known in the war was on his face, and so was the
distress that the peace had brought him. He approached the Round
Table welcoming the armistice of laughter which its members and
their friends gave him but not forgetting the troubled world beyond
this special one. There was something about this older-young man
which even at twenty-four inspired confidence and confidences.

Among the many who felt this was a young Milwaukee-born actor
named Alfred Lunt, who had just captured New York by his comic
excellence in Booth Tarkington's *Clarence*. Lunt was convinced on
meeting him that season that Sherwood was three years his senior
when, as a matter of fact, he was three years Lunt's junior. At their
first lunch together Lunt found himself telling Sherwood, as most
decidedly he had not intended to, that he was very much in love with
an English actress, Lynn Fontanne. She was then making her name
in Laurette Taylor's company and would soon establish herself in
Dulcy, the merry comedy which Kaufman and Connelly were to
build around Dulcinea, that queen of bromides in F.P.A.'s column.

Sherwood had found his place in the literary and theatrical world
of his liking and dreaming. It was not a world in which M.E.W.S.
would have been happy since it failed to include royalty, statesmen,
cotillion leaders, and "the four hundred." It was Sherwood's revolt,
and the revolt of the times, against that other world. His father, had
he followed his instincts rather than becoming a prisoner of the
genteel tradition, would have enjoyed this new world even as Rosina
did, and as Sherwood's friends came to enjoy her.

The twenties and the thirties were, in New York, Hollywood, and London, to bring new friends of the same kind, such as Moss Hart when he began collaborating with Kaufman. But they brought no change in Sherwood's feelings. In the spring of 1938, after a weekend at Moss Hart's place in Bucks County during which he had lunched at the Kaufmans' with Woollcott, Ruth Gordon, and Oscar Levant, he wrote in his diary, "Moss's home is very comfortable, cheerful, companionable, and this is the kind of American society I like best— I could come pretty close to saying it's the only kind that I like at all."

Naturally, in such a world Sherwood was bound to try his hand at writing a play. He had been writing plays since childhood and had come to the Round Table fresh from the deceptive amateur success of *Barnum Was Right*. What the others could do, and were doing, he would do. The doing was not to be as easy as he thought. By 1922 he had dashed off a happily lost and forgotten script, *The Dawn Man*, "actually my first play," he was to say, meaning for professional production, but it was "so dreadful" that it caused him to abandon playwriting as a career.

Not for long, however. The Tablers continued to tempt him by example; in particular, Laurence Stallings, that exuberant ex-Marine captain who had lost a leg at Belleau Wood. Two years after Sherwood's abortive attempt, Stallings with Maxwell Anderson, an editorial writer for the *World*, had written *What Price Glory?* With rapture Sherwood listened to the applause and cheers, loud as a bombardment, that greeted this lusty play which, as Woollcott recognized, said more without editorializing about "the war, its immensity, and its crushing evidence of human failure" than all the editorials on the subject. Listening to those cheers and that applause, Sherwood decided then and there "it would be a wonderful thing to be a playwright."

Actually, it was three years after *What Price Glory?* that in 1927 in *The Road to Rome* he turned successfully to playwriting, and that was seven years after *Barnum Was Right*. The years in between were full.

12

LIFE AND MARRIAGE

"The Silent Drama"—Charles Dana Gibson as Editor of the Old Life—
*Changes in the Magazine World—Edward S. Martin as a Champion
—Sherwood's Swift Progress as* Life's *Movie Critic—Enter Mary Bran-
don—No Sirree!* and a Chorus Ziegfeld Could Not Afford—Douglas
Fairbanks, Sr., Reduced to an Usher—"The Land of Ice and Snow?"

"To all movie fans: LIFE begs to announce that a new department,
THE SILENT DRAMA, conducted by Robert E. Sherwood, will begin in
the next issue. In this department there will be reviews of the latest
films and a Confidential Guide."

That was on January 20, 1921, and *Life*, of course, was not the
huge, bustling newspicture magazine it became in 1936 when Time,
Inc., bought its name. It was the old humorous weekly now as invariably referred to as *The Old Life* as if it had been called that.
Pleasant, civilized, and leisurely, at once sentimental and mocking, it
was America's *Punch*, indeed too much so in the early twenties for
its own enduring good.

It still had its excellent drawings and features, and its lively and
illustrious contributors, but with its "he-she" jokes and somewhat
labored humorous pieces it was cherished out of habit in new times
when habits were changing. *Puck*, once its competitor but never its
equal, had died of these times as an independent magazine three
years before, and *Judge*, though it was to outlast *Life* briefly, was
also to die of them after fighting a fluttery, losing battle.

Life seemed hale enough in 1921. Its circulation reached that year
an all-time high of 238,813. Good years lay ahead, too, under its old
contributor and new owner and publisher, Charles Dana Gibson. His
lovely, haughty, and aristocratic "Gibson Girls," with their sailor

hats, puffed sleeves, and wasp waists, and their lifted eyebrows and ballooning pompadours, had in the nineties been its most treasured feature.

Gibson was still drawing for it, though only occasionally with his old flair. He remained an impressive figure, this handsome, jovial, barrel-chested man, with his cliff-like stiff collars, and a jut of jaw and bulge of forehead suggestive of a benevolent Mussolini. Gallantly he had risen to an emergency and taken over the running of *Life* after the recent deaths of Mitchell and Masson, the two older men who had guided it through its great days. But Gibson, though only fifty-three, was a tired fifty-three.

His career had reached the stage of being a résumé of what had gone before. The past was becoming his present. He was harassed by his new chores, and as unequipped for them as he was for the coming decade. In Fairfax Downey's words, he was "weary of his pen and his work showed it." As for *Life*, the years were catching up with it, too. It was a venerable thirty-eight and beginning to show its age, even if it did not as yet feel it. The war had changed its public without changing it. It had changed humor, too, toughening and sharpening it, and made *Life's* readers more sophisticated. Without knowing it, they were ready for what the magazine did not give them. The success of *Vanity Fair* had been a storm warning. That of *Time* in 1923 was to be another. So, the next year, was the *American Mercury's*. *The New Yorker*, when it did succeed in the later twenties after a wavering start in 1925, was to prove the storm itself.

Life's editors wisely tried to meet the new demands of the new decade by turning to younger writers and artists. Among these younger men was Benchley, who in 1920 had already taken over the job as dramatic critic which the wise and fiercely independent James S. Metcalfe had held for thirty-one years. Another was Sherwood. When, however, at twenty-four he became *Life's* motion-picture critic, he followed no one. There was no one to follow.

By opening its pages to a critical department devoted to the motion pictures, *Life* was making a resolute effort to join the new day and Sherwood was establishing a precedent. No regular reviewer for a national magazine had approached the movies with his standards or his belief in their possibilities. This is what Kaufman had in mind when years later, at a dinner at which Sherwood was present, he suddenly asked, "Do you realize that there sits at this table the founder of a new form of journalism?"

Sherwood was not a stranger to the pages of *Life* when he began "The Silent Drama." From France in 1918 he had written his mother a long letter which ended, "By the way, I see *Life* is paying $10. for letters from the front, and if you could piece together any of my disjointed utterances into a fairly coherent mass, you might make a try for the money." Several of his letters, so pieced together, were forwarded to *Life*, and in their combined form two of them were published there, the first in October signed "Your loving Bob," the second in November signed "R.E.S.," those initials which in the years ahead were to become so familiar to *Life*'s readers.

When hospitalized in England, Sherwood had gone one late October day to London and there had had the author's satisfaction and panic of seeing himself in print. At a newsstand in Waterloo Station he spotted a copy of the magazine and bought it without looking at the date. "On the cover was an excellent Gibson drawing representing Liberty making an appeal, with the caption, 'Yes' or 'No'? 'Can you look her in the eyes?' "

Though in uniform and wounded, Sherwood had "an immediate accession of that 'guilty feeling,' and opened the paper at random, and there, lo and behold! was one of my letters." It was his hat-doffing tribute to the tank and he confessed to his mother, "I read it through and thought it was swell. As far as I can make out I have copped $75 from *Life*. Your allusions to the *North American Review* made me give vent to a horse laugh; say, my line of stuff would be about as appropriate in that publication as a 'God Bless Our Home' sign in Sing Sing, in the death house."

Life's editor, Edward S. Martin, had reasons of his own for being interested in Sherwood before and after his wartime letters. He was an old friend of Sherwood's father and with him at Harvard had been a cofounder of the *Lampoon*. In 1920 when Sherwood first came to know him well, and respect him to the point of reverence, Martin was a fragile sixty-four, slight, slant-shouldered, bald, bespectacled, deaf, and a little quavery. Outwardly he may have seemed tired but, unlike Gibson of whom the reverse was true, inside he was not.

His mind remained lively, his charm ensnaring. He had realized in *Life*, since its first number, the dream which he had had at college of becoming later the editor of a humorous weekly similar to the *Lampoon*, only brought out by professionals. As a matter of fact, *Life* was the name which Sherwood's grandmother, the redoubtable M.E.W.S., had suggested for the *Lampoon*.

That Sherwood, like Benchley before him, had edited the *Lampoon* did not count against him with Martin, any more than did the *Lampoonish* pieces which he, again like Benchley, had been writing for Crowninshield. It was not surprising, therefore, to find free-lance articles by Sherwood appearing in *Life* soon after he and *Vanity Fair* had parted company, or to have him within three months become, in Benchley's fashion, a regular contributor. A few days after the arrival of "Mr. Sherwood" and "Mr. Benchley," "Mrs. Parker" also was working for *Life*. The threesome was reunited.

What was surprising was the speed of Sherwood's progress at the magazine. Less than a year after the first of his occasional pieces appeared he was entrusted with the new movie department. A little more than three years later he was asked, at twenty-eight, to become *Life*'s editor, following Louis Evan Shipman who had meanwhile followed Martin.

"My Bobby," wrote Rosina to Jane de Glehn in London on May 1, 1924, "has been made editor of *Life* with Bob Benchley. . . . I hope they will make it more entertaining. Bobby's salary is $10,000. Dana Gibson proposed giving Bobby a larger share because he did so much more, but Bobby insisted on sharing equally." Sherwood's name did not appear on the masthead until the next year; Benchley's was included for only a few months three years later. Benchley's commitments were such that, though he wrote pieces and helped with ideas, his chief and very real contribution was his weekly drama page.

As *Life*'s movie critic, Sherwood made his mark so swiftly that he soon had the dubious, because aging, pleasure of finding himself referred to as "the dean" of his profession. To Lillian Gish he was "the only one reviewing pictures that Griffith, or any of us, looked forward to reading and took seriously everything he wrote." A measure of the recognition he had won came within a year and a half of his taking over his reviewing job. It was then that V*anity Fair* enshrined him, along with Benchley, in a double-page cartoon by Ralph Barton of "celebrities" apt to be on view at a Broadway opening. The others included the Gish sisters, David Belasco, Otto Kahn, Samuel Goldwyn, George F. Baker, Florenz Ziegfeld, Jr., Irving Berlin, John Barrymore, Kaufman and Connelly, Ring Lardner, John Drew, Irvin S. Cobb, Woollcott and Broun, Irene Castle, Efrem Zimbalist, Gilda Gray, Geraldine Farrar, and George Jean Nathan, he, of course, overcoat on and leaving the theatre in the middle of the second act. Sherwood had gone far fast.

In addition to writing for *Life*, he was soon doing movie reviews for a newspaper syndicate, for *Photoplay, Movie Weekly*, and *McCall's*, and from 1922 until 1924, when Ogden Reid merged it with the *Tribune* and dropped him, he was motion-picture editor of the New York *Herald*. Fortunately, he had a sturdy talent for finding fresh phrases for identical opinions because he sometimes had to review the same picture five times.

Following the example of Burns Mantle and Edward J. O'Brien with their yearbooks, *The Best Plays* and *The Best Short Stories*, he also edited *The Best Motion Pictures of 1922-1923*, a book of appraisal, personal experiences in Hollywood, and statistics which he hoped would be an annual but which died after the first year. His movie anthology, like his reviewing, was innovational. In his introduction he described the rigors of his professional life. "I am compelled," said he, "to see about two hundred feature films a year, and a great many shorter pictures, such as comedies, scenics, educational films and news weeklies. It all adds up to something like twenty-five hundred reels, which, when resolved into terms of linear measure, amounts to two million, five hundred thousand feet, or over four hundred miles."

It added up to more than that. Since *McCall's* is said to have given him $250 to $300 a review and the other publications paid acceptably, it added up to money. And money was something which Sherwood needed more than ever, after, late in the afternoon of Sunday, October 29, 1922, he was married to Mary Judah Brandon at the Church of the Transfiguration, better known to the world and to "The Profession" (which crowded it that twilight to overflowing) as The Little Church Around the Corner.

It was as a member of The Profession that Mary Brandon then hopefully thought of herself. According to the *Herald* when her engagement was announced early in October, she was "one of those young women who have left a social career in order to follow their bent for the stage." The daughter of Henry J. Brandon, a lawyer and businessman of Indianapolis, she had, after going to school there, come to New York to enter the theatre.

Some newspapers reported that she was Mrs. Booth Tarkington's niece; others that she was Tarkington's. Actually she was related to neither and her family connection with Tarkington was of a most remote kind. She was, however, close enough to him to call him "Uncle Booth" out of affection. This gave her an entree to the Round Table, ringed as it was with Tarkington admirers (among them Sherwood), which, though an attractive young theatrical aspirant, Mary Brandon might not otherwise have had.

It should have supplied her with sufficient peripheral glamour to satisfy even Woollcott's glamour-hungry eyes. But Woollcott, being Woollcott, sought for more and deluded himself into believing that he had found it. Because Mary's middle name was Judah, he leapt to the conclusion that she was related to Judah P. Benjamin, Jefferson Davis's brilliant Attorney General, then Secretary of War, and finally Chief Secretary of State. Woollcott's self-mesmerizing pleasure was always to make his own life more glamorous by adding to the glamour of his friends even if fiction had to be called in to rouge facts.

Mary Brandon's claims to fame in her own right were incipient rather than real, and fragile at best. She had made her Broadway debut in 1920 (without being mentioned by Woollcott) in a frail comedy, *Welcome Stranger,* and the next season had appeared as an ultramodern flapper in something called *Up the Ladder,* and with Louis Mann in *Nature's Nobleman,* a play which was said to range "from negligible to worse." She had also been seen, by those with alert eyes, in one motion picture, *The Bashful Suitor.* Her knockings at the gates of Broadway and Hollywood had, in other words, been at best faint tappings. They scarcely merited the unloving item which the *Herald* printed the day after her engagement was announced. After noting her brief stage career and pointing out that she had "finally attained the motion pictures," it added, "Miss Mary Brandon . . . evidently feels that she owes herself some recognition for achiev-

ing this plane. So the other day she went and had herself christened."
She had to. When she confessed to Dr. Ray that she had never been
baptized, he said that she would have to be before he married them.

Although Sherwood was susceptible to blondes, the dizzier and
more brainless the better, Mary Brandon was a brunette. She was as
tiny as he was tall, and could walk under his arms when he stretched
them out. Trim, chic, and very pretty, she had fine teeth, beguiling
dimples, a lovely complexion, and dark flashing eyes. With the ease
with which a thermostat is turned up, she could turn on a warmth
which, though it seemed true enough to be conquering, was deceptive. Her mind when applied to her own interests, as it usually was,
was sharper and more practical than seemed possible in one who at
that time had, and traded on, such a little-girlish look. She was one
of those people, as Sherwood was to discover, who look one way and
are another. She appeared soft and was tough, seemed yielding and
was demanding. She was self-absorbed to the point of egomania, self-
deluding to the verge of pathos, and bantam in everything except her
faults. Sherwood, not then knowing this, thought, as a bridegroom
should, that he was lucky and knew he was very much in love.

He had met Mary at the Algonquin and had come to know her
well at rehearsals when the Round Tablers, in an invincibly collegiate
mood, had, on the last Sunday night in April, 1922, put on at the
49th Street Theatre for one performance a revue, *No Sirree!*, the title
of which was a pun on the Russian *Chauve Souris*. Broun was the
Balieff of the occasion, and Woollcott, Benchley, Kaufman, Connelly
and F.P.A. were among the inevitable participants.

The numbers ranged from spoofs of Eugene O'Neill, Zoë Akins,
and A. A. Milne to Benchley's *Treasurer's Report*. Sherwood was
seen as the Governor of New York in a parody of any Samuel
Shipman melodrama, Mary Brandon in *The Editor Regrets*, a skit
laid in the office of a Renaissance twice-a-month magazine, *Droll
Stories*, and the two of them took part in a number called, with a
bow to Andreyev, *He Who Gets Flapped*. In this Sherwood, wearing
white flannels, a blazer, and a boater, was discovered leaning non-
chalantly against the proscenium, surrounded by some rompered
chorus girls who would later have been too expensive to hire since
they included June Walker, Winifred Lenihan, Tallulah Bankhead,

Mary Kennedy, Lenore Ulric, Helen Hayes, and Mary Brandon.
They all sang and danced their way through Mrs. Parker's "The
Everlastin' Ingenue Blues":

> We've got the blues, we've got the blues, we
>   believe we said before we've got the blues.
> We are little flappers, never growing up,
> And we've all of us been flapping since Belasco
>   was a pup. . . .

The Brandon-Sherwood wedding was quite a show, as star-
studded as the flag. In addition to being a news story in its own right,
it told a story which, though it said little except indirectly about
Mary, said much about Sherwood, his new friends, and his immersion
in his new life. Mr. Brandon, of course, gave Mary away. Roberta
Arnold, Frank Craven's leading lady in *The First Year*, was the
matron of honor. Margalo Gillmore, fresh from her success in *He
Who Gets Slapped*, was the maid of honor. The flower girls were
Sherwood's nieces, Elizabeth and Julia Townsend.

The best man was Sherwood's brother Philip. Only two of his
ushers, James Lee and Louis Perkins, represented his prewar life.
The rest of them, all proudly recruited from the Round Table,
Broadway, and Hollywood, were Connelly, Benchley, Grant Mitchell, Sidney Howard, Woollcott, John Emerson (Anita Loos's
husband), and Frank Case. These were stellar enough but they did
not steal the show. Nor, for that matter, did the bride and groom. If
the street outside The Little Church Around the Corner was lined
that Sunday afternoon and many of those who had come to Vespers
stayed on after the service, the reason was still another usher—
Douglas Fairbanks. Word had got around that he was to be in the
wedding party and that his wife, Mary Pickford, would be present. It
would be impossible nowadays to think of a movie couple with
names as magical as theirs then were. The two of them were at the
height of their world-wide popularity. When Fairbanks asked those
sitting up front to move back in order to make room for Rosina,
Rosamond, and the waiting families, their first response was to ask
him for his autograph.

After the ceremony a supper was given at their home by the Emer-
sons. Among the guests were the Booth Tarkingtons, Mary Pickford,

Clare Eames, the Louis Evan Shipmans, Tallulah Bankhead, Peggy Wood, John V. A. Weaver, Ina Claire, the F. Scott Fitzgeralds, the Morris Gests, the Henry Wise Millers, the Richard Barthelmesses, the Frank Gillmores, Mrs. Benchley, Frank Crowninshield, the Rex Ingrams, the Charles Dana Gibsons, Roger Burlingame, and Theodore Shane. To Sherwood's delight, and Mary's, it was all glitteringly *Who's Who*.

Perhaps the most spectacular figure at the wedding and the reception was Maurice Child, Sherwood's old friend and sergeant from The Black Watch. Sherwood had run into him on Madison Avenue the week before and said, "Maurice, I'm getting married at The Little Church Around the Corner next week. Put on your kilt and come down, won't you?" And in his kilt Child appeared, as pleased to see Sherwood again as Sherwood was to see him, and no less delighted to be mingling with Doug and Mary.

On the way up the aisle Benchley and Connelly walked together, singing softly to each other, "Will she come from the east where the Broadway peaches grow? Will she come from the north, the land of ice and snow?" That temperamentally was the real question.

13

THE GALLOPING DAGUERREOTYPES

Critic of a New, Still Dubious Medium—The Silent Movies at Their Peak—Sherwood Visits Hollywood and Lectures on It—From Passion to The Singing Fool—Pioneering as a Critic—Capsule Comments— Heroes: Fairbanks, Harry Landon, Buster Keaton, Harold Lloyd, Charlie Chaplin, and Jackie Coogan—"The Hollywood Zeus," Cecil B. De Mille —Heroines: Lillian Gish, Mabel Normand, Norma Shearer, Greta Garbo —Mussolini as a Ham—The Coming of the Talkies

Reducing Douglas Fairbanks to an usher was an indication of the place Sherwood had rapidly won for himself as a movie critic. Why he wanted to become one was another matter. In the early twenties it was fashionable for those who fancied themselves among the knowing to look down on the movies, even as later their like would look down on radio and television and for the same reason. All three were designed to be enjoyed and, worse still, understood by mass audiences. This meant that, for the many who thought of themselves as the discriminating few, what was good enough for most could not be good enough for them.

Among those who could not understand Sherwood's enthusiasm was *Life*'s Louis Evan Shipman. When writing in the magazine about the headliners on its staff, he did not question Benchley "who loves the theatre, and guys and guides the drama." But Sherwood perplexed him by being "for some strange reason enamored of the movies." Enamored of them Sherwood was, in spite of their formidable faults.

His attacks on them were constant and unsparing. He admitted that most of them were stupid and obvious and made little appeal to the intelligence. He conceded that they were the Peter Pan of the arts and, seemingly, as resolved as Peter not to grow up. He granted that too often they were put together in a careless, haphazard way, and had as their promoters those who believed the box office to be the ultimate goal of all human endeavor. He rejoiced in their popularity but resented those producers who thought that, to insure it, they must treat the public as if it had a child's mentality.

Notwithstanding all this and more, Sherwood's respect for the movies was deep and his faith in their possibilities abiding. His contention was that, though a lot was wrong with them, a great deal was right with them, too. What they most often were did not blind him to what they occasionally proved they could be.

His attitude was completely in character. By nature he did not belong among the long-haired and abhorred the "arty." He, who was to spend his life seeking in various forms to reach as large an audience as possible, had only contempt for the intelligentsia who belittled the movies because of the size of the public to which they had to appeal. He had no patience then, and never was to have any, with "those who like to believe that art is their own exclusive esoteric property" and that "nothing can be popular and be art." With Alice Duer Miller he agreed that one trouble with the movies was that the people who went to them did not criticize them and the people who criticized them did not go to them. He did go to them, week after week, for eight long years, enduring the drudgery and knowing the despairs and pleasures of that servitude which is professional reviewing.

Those eight years were the peak years for the silent films, and never in all history has silence proved so golden. The early days seemed distant when in penny arcades viewers had been tantalized— for a minute—by looking into a machine, turning a crank, and peeking at such juicy morsels as *What the Bootblack Saw* or *How Bridget Served the Salad Undressed*. Since then the "galloping daguerreotypes," as Sherwood termed them affectionately, had galloped fast and far indeed. A peep show had become a recognized amusement, that amusement a multimillion-dollar industry, and that industry on rare occasions an art. By the time he left *Life* at the end of 1928 the "daguerreotypes" had galloped even farther, so far in fact that, to keep up with their progress, he was forced to change the name of his department from "The Silent Drama" to "The Movies." The talkies had arrived.

After a little more than a year of reviewing, Sherwood decided that seeing movies was not enough. He must see Hollywood, too. A field expedition was needed. Accordingly, in the spring of 1922 he persuaded *Life* and the movie magazines for which he wrote to send him across a country officially parched by Prohibition "to learn the truth about this sink of iniquity, this twentieth century Babylon, this celluloid Sodom."

Hollywood at the time was blanketed with a smog of scandals. Filthy details of the "Fatty" Arbuckle case, ugly suspicions about the unsolved murder of director William Desmond Taylor, and succulent stories about dope addicts and sex orgies hung so thickly in the air that films, good and bad, were being banned, and Will H. Hays, fresh from the cleanliness of the Harding Cabinet, had been appointed by an alarmed motion-picture industry to function as its morals "czar."

If Sherwood hoped for the worst when he headed west, he was disappointed when he got there. He did not see, as he pretended to expect to, "actors and directors striding around the streets with both hips bulging—a six-shooter in one and a flask on the other." Nor did he find that "the municipal pipe lines carried supplies of liquid cocaine and morphine to the various residences."

With Adela Rogers St. Johns of *Photoplay* as his guide, he toured the studios and met many of the prominent actors and directors. On his own he visited the homes of several stars and went out on the town. After his first ten days he had to confess ruefully, "I have attended no orgies (and as heaven is my witness I have spared no effort in trying to locate them), I have seen no murders and I have been offered no cocaine, hasheesh or bhang." The sole hint of lawlessness he encountered was when someone told him he knew a man who made fairly good beer in his kitchen. Sherwood was still hoping to find that man. At a ball crowded with Hollywood's elite he observed only two people degraded enough to carry flasks, adding, "The other one was Mr. Arthur James, who is also in the magazine business in New York."

The Hollywood he saw was a sad letdown. It was "a normal community inhabited by regular people who go about their business in much the same manner as do the people in Emporia, Pawtucket, Little Rock, and Medicine Hat." Quiet as a small college town, it was in his eyes a place where everything was spick-and-span and brand-new. The glistening white buildings glared excessively in the light of the California sun, and the taste in architecture was as terrible as it appeared to be in the films. The trouble was that it was just the opposite of what the yellow journals said. It was "foolishly respectable," "positively puritanical," "abnormally virtuous," and the dullest place (as far as orgies went) that he had ever seen.

Sherwood incorporated his sensationally unsensational findings into a humorous lecture which he illustrated with a thirty-minute burlesque film that he somehow found time to make and appear in during his crowded weeks of sin-seeking in Hollywood. With a bow to Benchley's very popular talk "Through the Alimentary Canal with Gun and Camera," Sherwood called his lecture "Through Darkest Hollywood with Gun and Camera." He tried it out at the theatre in the Beverly Hills Hotel before what the Los Angeles *Times* described as being a goodly percentage of the socially and cinematically select of the film colony, and repeated the lecture to full houses and shouts of laughter in St. Louis and New York, finding in James B. Pond a manager eager to handle it. Pond headed his announcement: "AT LAST! THE TRUTH ABOUT HOLLYWOOD!" He advertised the talk as "screamingly funny," described its accompanying pictures as depicting "your wildest imaginings—dance halls, opium dens, midnight orgies, life in the studios," and heralded the program as "a spring tonic for any entertainment course."

The truth about Hollywood, at least as he saw it, was what Sherwood was writing as a reviewer. The first picture he covered for *Life* was *Passion* (1920) with Pola Negri, a film to which some flag-wavers objected in those postwar days because it was made in Germany. Among the last was *The Singing Fool* (1928) in which Al Jolson spoke and sang. The years between were the years when the movies were slowly being cured of that St. Vitus's dance with which Vachel Lindsay had accused them of twitching. If even the best pictures then produced now seem quaint, it is because, in spite of their virtues, they could be technically no better than the machines which recorded them. What mattered to Sherwood and his readers, and to moviegoers everywhere, was that they did not then seem quaint, regardless of their jerkiness, the exaggerations of their pantomime, or the subtitles which all too frequently interrupted them. They were making impressive advances and the merits of the better ones were such that, though silent, they often spoke eloquently for themselves.

Sherwood had his own approach both to the movies and to the job of reviewing them. His, like Benchley's, was the winning talent of being exceptional and sounding average. He did not pontificate; he reacted. Abstractions were not his concern; particulars were. His tone was down to earth, his point of view personal, and his style conversational in its ease. Although he had the self-assurance of anyone who thinks his opinions are worthy of print, he was almost belligerently without aesthetic pretensions.

Anxious as he was to have the movies take their place among the arts, he avoided when possible the word "art," because to him it was the most flexible term in the English language. "There is no one," he insisted, "who can definitely and authoritatively say what 'Art' is. That which exalts one may nauseate another. One man's art is another man's hokum. There are those who believe Picasso is a greater artist than Velásquez, and those who rate the poetry of Gertrude Stein above that of John Keats. Every statement on this subject is qualified with the clause, uttered or implied, 'it seems to me.' "

He stated his credo as a reviewer frequently, and never more clearly than when he said, "This department is not devoted to the cause of intelligent criticism; it is merely a page upon which the violent opinions of one solitary individual may find expresssion. I am not conducting a service for movie exhibitors—telling them what pictures will make money and what will flop—nor am I engaged in the great profitable profession of uplift. I am here to say what I think (on the catch-as-catch-can, take-it-or-leave-it, Marquis-of-Queensberry-be-damned basis), and no one can tell whether I am right or wrong—including myself; in matters of opinions, right and wrong simply don't exist."

To many in and out of Hollywood, Sherwood seemed tough, which he was. To Woollcott he appeared "embittered," which he was not. There was never any question about what he thought. His own image of himself was as "the silent drama's best pal and severest critic." He was both. He could say a lot in a few words, and did so in his capsule comments on current movies which he ran as a guide each week after his reviews of new films. Typical of these when he was in a dismissive mood were: (*Madame Sans-Gêne*, 1925) "Gloria Swanson came back from France with a husband and this picture. The husband seems like an awfully decent sort of chap"; (*Brown of Harvard*, 1926) "No Yale man should miss this one"; (*Man and Maid*, 1925) "Just to prove this is really a story, the producers show you a close-up of Mme. Glyn in the act of writing it."

Although he was never faced, as Benchley was in the case of *Abie's Irish Rose*, with the problem of finding new ways each week for five years of commenting on something he had seen, Sherwood did again and again have to recast his opinions of long-run movies. *Don Juan* (1926) was one of these, *Ben Hur*, during the same season, another. The former he variously described as "John Barrymore gets a half-nelson on Lucrezia Borgia"; "Ten reels of John Barrymore's famous profile"; or "John Barrymore makes love but not sense." *Ben Hur* presented a more trying challenge which he met in such terms as: "Let's get together, boys, and put Christianity over with a BANG"; "One of these days Messala is going to surprise the public and win that chariot race"; or "The birth of Christianity and Marcus Loew's bank roll."

Sherwood knew, of course, his moments of despair as a critic when, downed by the mediocrity of much of what he had to see, he could write, "There is only one thing less pleasant than attending the movies—and that is reviewing them." Actually, he enjoyed doing both. A reviewer lives on hopes and would have neither standards nor respect for what he is reviewing if disappointment were not a staple in his diet. Although most frequently forced to damn, Sherwood really liked to like, and when he did so, which was often, he liked with all the ardor of his nature. The weeks which by his own admission depressed him were those when he was compelled to litter his reviews with "buts."

Most humorists (and he was one, writing for a humorous magazine) become embarrassed when they have to praise. Making fun is by profession their way of giving it. Even Benchley, with all his generosity and warmth, seemed to blush slightly when he had to admire, because there is little laughter in surrender. Sherwood was different. All panning and no praise, said he, makes for a dull column. His major complaint against the movie producers was that they did not enable him to praise their work more frequently. When they did, he praised it with such enthusiasm that with him having the strength of his convictions often meant having the courage of his superlatives. "Great" was an adjective which he used with conviction but no caution.

As the years passed, Sherwood had his lengthening list of those who could not do wrong (but sometimes did) and those who could not do right (but sometimes did). One of his idols that toppled was D. W. Griffith, once supreme for his technical innovations and as an "instigator of tears." With one bad picture after another he had become a shrunken giant. Such a film as *Sally of the Sawdust* (1925) seemed to Sherwood "the work of a man who has become so completely soaked with theatrical trumpery that he wouldn't recognize reality if it stepped up and slapped him in the face."

In his earlier productions (*The Birth of a Nation*, 1915, *Broken Blossoms*, 1919, and *Orphans of the Storm*, 1920) Griffith had "demonstrated an amazing degree of imagination and admirable courage." To Sherwood the decay that followed was "among the major tragedies of movie history" and a "cause for lamentation." He never forgot that "Griffith was the first heroic figure in the movies, the first to boost them from the nickelodeon class, and the first to establish their permanence," and insisted that he be given full credit for what he had been, in spite of what he had become.

Then there were Sherwood's heroes. About each of them he was so enthusiastic that he sometimes had difficulty remembering which one he admired most. When he wrote about them, the sky was the limit. He did not praise; he raved. A press agent could not have been more rhapsodic.

Among his favorites from the very start was his future usher, the elder Douglas Fairbanks. Everything that was lastingly boyish in

Sherwood, everything that always responded to Dumas and Robert Louis Stevenson, everything that his height and lack of coordination had denied him as a would-be athlete combined to make him cherish Fairbanks. When Sherwood went to Hollywood in the spring of 1922, he visited Fairbanks at his studio where he was working on *Robin Hood.* Although "Doug" was wearing a pair of shabby flannel trousers, ancient tennis shoes, and a T-shirt, he seemed to Sherwood to be in costume and in character since, while he talked, he was thrusting furiously right and left with a wooden sword and felling imaginary enemies.

With him praise for Fairbanks was a runaway horse. At the time of his Hollywood visit he had already saluted *The Mark of Zorro* (1920) as a film which was "the all-around champion of the world." He had also maintained that Alexandre Dumas, when he sat down at his desk, smoothed his hair back, chewed the end of his quill pen, and began to write *The Three Musketeers,* had but one purpose in mind, and that was "to provide a suitable story for Douglas Fairbanks to act in the movies."

The completed *Robin Hood* (1922) was to Sherwood "magnificent . . . the best picture of the year." In a "swooning review" of *The Thief of Bagdad* (1924) he claimed Fairbanks had surpassed his D'Artagnan and his Robin Hood. "He is a genuinely great man. . . . Had I an entire volume of *Life* at my command, I should still fail to convey so much as a glimmering suggestion of the miracle that has been wrought in this Arabian Nights' Entertainment."

At the top of Sherwood's list of heroes were such graduates of the Mack Sennett lot as Harry Langdon, Buster Keaton, Harold Lloyd, and, of course as the Abou Ben Adhem, Charlie Chaplin. He was convinced that "one can always look to the low-brow slap-stickers for honesty and artistic integrity." In addition, he found delight. He did not approach these comedians as a highbrow slumming or discuss prattfalls and thrown pies in Walter Pater terms. He never read elaborate symbolism into their antics, never pretended to discover in them qualities which the public had not long since recognized, nor when writing of them indulged in humorless dissertations about comedy which killed the Comic Spirit while dissecting it. Something of a dead-pan comic himself, he took these comedians on their own terms, loving them because they fed his huge appetite for laughter. He felt utterly at home with their rowdiness and irreverence and also with the loneliness of the characters they created.

He prized the frozen-faced Harry Langdon who in *Tramp, Tramp, Tramp* (1926) looked "out at the world through large saucer eyes, trying desperately hard to comprehend and never quite succeeding." He found his appeal "utterly irresistible," and liked the way in which he seemed "ever at a loss for something to do." Sherwood had a special place in his roomy heart, too, for Buster Keaton whose crisp comedy smacked "of the London 'alls." He knew the "sniffers" might say that some of Keaton's gags were "mechanical," but they could not, he contended, "dampen the merriment" these gags provoked. As for the Walter Mitty moments in *The Camera Man* (1928) when Keaton went to the Yankee Stadium to photograph Babe Ruth, found the game called off, and stepped up on an empty diamond to deliver some imaginary pitches himself, wither an imaginary umpire in an argument, hit an imaginary home run, and acknowledge the cheers of an imaginary crowd, Sherwood, an old baseball fan himself, thought the scene "beautiful and true and infinitely touching," and typical of Buster Keaton at his best.

Even higher on his list of idols was Harold Lloyd, whose intelligence in criticizing his work Sherwood had observed during his first trip to Hollywood when he accompanied Lloyd to see a preview of *Grandma's Boy* in Long Beach. To Sherwood, Lloyd, with his pinch-back suit, straw hat, and horn-rimmed spectacles, was "as fresh as an Oregon breeze" and as American in his humor as George Ade. He was "clean and wholesome, but not to an offensive degree." Like Chaplin, he knew what was "the most vulnerable and laughable portion of a policeman's anatomy" and was "not afraid to exploit it." So great was Sherwood's enjoyment of *Grandma's Boy, Safety Last* (both in 1923), and most of *The Freshman* (1925) that he could write, "If Harold Lloyd ever should make a really bad picture, the effect on my work would be positively devastating." In the case of *Girl Shy* (1924), it was the merits of Lloyd's work which devastated Sherwood. Of it he wrote, "One might well say that it is the most furiously funny comedy in history; in fact, I think I'll be the one to say it."

Much as he respected him, Sherwood did not fail to observe "the vast gulf which divides the superlative cleverness of Harold Lloyd from the genuine genius of Chaplin." In those years, unclouded by politics, Chaplin was Charlie, not Charles. With his tattered derby and bamboo cane, his nailbrush mustache and pinched coat, his slight shoulders with their eloquent shrugs, his baggy pants which he kept hitching up with hornpipe gestures, his tramp's shoes headed in contrary directions, his shuffle, and his way of teetering around corners with one foot uplifted for balance, Charlie was the pathetic little misfit and poem unlimited who around the world created huge laughs.

The underdog was at his most resilient in him. He was a Sennett comedy made sensitive, the fugitive in mad chases, the butt of pies, the obstacle in swinging doors, the rough-and-tumble low comedian, long loved by millions, who was coming to be recognized by intellectuals as an artist. Like all great clowns, he was on speaking terms with tragedy, and for him Sherwood felt an admiration so exuberant that having to reduce it to reasoned words was a trial, if not an impossibility. He did not want to interrupt his laughter or his happy crying by asking himself why he was doing either.

The Gold Rush (1925) was a case in point. In a brief and breathless first notice Sherwood wrote, "I shall not try to review it until I have seen it seven or eight more times and regained some measure of critical balance. Just at present having seen it but once, I am rendered practically speechless." Sherwood knew that technically the picture was no more advanced than "the earliest Sennett two-reelers," that the photography was "primitive," the scenery "ridiculously artificial," and the incidental acting "ham." Still, for some reason which he could not explain, he found all these blemishes "singularly appropriate." Such was his enjoyment of the film, he confided, that "I forgot I was supposed to record my impressions in print. Indeed, when I thought the matter over, I could not say that I had any impressions to offer."

The "certain glamour" in the person of Chaplin, "the glow of immortality," and "the effulgence that has been generated by a few lonely figures in history" could not "be explained away in any fine phrases." He did not attempt to find those phrases. He merely tried to convey the suggestion that the picture was one the reader should see for himself. Sherwood perhaps came closest to capturing Chaplin's screen character when, writing of *The Pilgrim* (1923), he said, "He is the supreme gamin, strutting about in the mantle of genius and thumbing his nose at all institutions that suggest dignity, importance, and fat-headed pomposity. Nothing is sacred to him—except humanity."

The true heat of his regard for Chaplin was released in his review of *A Woman of Paris* (1923), which Chaplin wrote and directed though he did not appear in it. It blazed in, "That Charlie Chaplin is the greatest man of his time is a subject for debate, but not on this page. There is no room here for argument on that score, and those who want to dispute with me about it will have to look elsewhere for an arena."

Jackie Coogan was another reason for his gratitude to Chaplin. Coogan was five when *The Kid* (1920) was made and when, because of his "highly developed power of emotional appeal" and his "genius for the droll," he held his own with "the great Charlot himself." He walked then into Sherwood's heart at the very beginning of his reviewing days, and there "this amazing child" remained for the next four years. Sherwood made fun of himself for what he called his "ridiculous fondness" for the boy. "I am just a sentimental, maudlin, old fool on the subject," he admitted, adding, "My admiration for Jackie Coogan is as rabid as that of any high school girl for Rudolph Valentino."

On his trip to Hollywood, he went to the Coogan home hoping to find Jackie a fresh, spoiled brat. Instead, he found him singularly natural and altogether lovable. He also visited the studio where the boy was making *Oliver Twist* and, during the filming of the "Please, sir, I want some more" scene, was impressed by discovering that the child, then nine, was as quick to take direction as, between scenes, he was alert in the schoolwork he was doing with a governess.

The problem which Jackie Coogan presented to Sherwood was finding superlatives which were superlative enough. Of those who claimed that Jackie must be no more of a genius than a trained dog in an animal act, Sherwood made mincemeat. He insisted that, as an individual, the boy was possessed of "an unaccountable power of

dramatic expression," and in his honor indulged in the most sincere
and constant of "verbal genuflections."

Sherwood maintained that the silent drama could claim at least
one great distinction. It had "provided the only possible medium of
expression for Jackie Coogan's altogether inexplicable genius." He
did not pretend to know what would happen to that genius when
Jackie reached maturity. "He may turn out to be a ham actor, wearing pinch-back suits in De Mille society dramas." But of this Sherwood was confident, "whatever becomes of him in the future, to
whatever dim depths of mediocrity he may descend, he has at least
been an artist, a great artist, in his time. Which, in the words of the
prophet, is something."

The passing reference to De Mille in Sherwood's forebodings
about Coogan's future might seem innocent enough to casual readers.
For *Life*'s regulars it would have had sulphurous overtones. From
long experience they would have known that in his demonology a
special furnace was reserved for Cecil B. De Mille. For his brother
William (who, as Sherwood noted, was content to spell his name
with an unemphatic little "d") he had respect. For the big "D"
Cecil he had mainly contempt and clobbered nearly all his films with
the regularity with which Big Ben strikes.

"The Hollywood Zeus," Sherwood called him in a profile written
for *The New Yorker* in the mid-twenties, boasting in it that as a critic
he had used every unkind word about him that his vocabulary would
permit. One contribution, Sherwood conceded, De Mille had made to
mythology. He had given the world a type. As surely as John Bull
was the embodiment of England, Lord Byron the personification of a
poet, or George F. Babbitt the symbol of the American businessman,
Cecil B. De Mille was the movie director incarnate. He was "a
composite photograph of all the Olympian gods who have descended
from Mount Hollywood to dominate the earth."

It was De Mille who "invented the correct directorial garb—sport
shirt, riding breeches, puttees and megaphone." It was he who "perfected the most moviesque of all movies, the society drama, with
orgies at which young ladies and gentlemen, wearing paper caps and
throwing confetti, dive *en masse* into swimming pools"; he who produced films in which "most of the action is limited to beds, con-

structed of the classiest Carrara marble and equipped with patent leather sheets"; and he who "converted" *The Admirable Crichton* into *Male and Female* (1919), because "an exhibitor had complained that Barrie's original title suggested a naval theme."

Sherwood did not dally in starting his attacks on De Mille. Two weeks after becoming *Life's* critic, having just seen *Forbidden Fruit* (1921), he shot for the first time. That review hit at "gross" in other than box-office terms. In intensity it was a popgun compared to the artillery that he was to bring up.

Sherwood's barrage against De Mille throughout the years that followed was heavy and almost continuous. Its "Big Bertha" was his notice of *Fool's Paradise* (1922). In it, at twenty-five, he blazed forth with the muscularity of youth and with its lack of mercy. "Leonard Merrick's story, *Laurels and the Lady*," he thundered, "has been mutilated, deformed, truncated, disfigured and beaten to a pulp. In other words, it has been made into a motion picture by Cecil B. De Mille. Mr. De Mille has been growing weirder and weirder and more and more absurd with each successive production. But *Fool's Paradise* is the farthest point south. Beyond this, progress is impossible."

Although Sherwood had met De Mille once and thought he "seemed like *such* a nice man!" the lulls in his cannonading of him were brief. One came with *The Ten Commandments* (1924). Of it Sherwood wrote, "There is an end to the world and to all things associated with it. . . . The day would come, I knew, when I should have to utter praise for a Cecil B. De Mille production." He commended De Mille for his "directorial genius" and the film for being "profoundly stirring." But his praise, though genuine, was on the stinting side. He did not fail to point out that "Mr. De Mille, in his time, has mutilated the works of many writers—from James Matthew Barrie to Alice Duer Miller. But when, in *The Ten Commandments*, he approached the words of God, he became suddenly overwhelmed with the idea that it would be better to set them forth unchanged."

Inevitably, as reviewers must, Sherwood somehow survived the many bad pictures which he had to see and did his best to make the better ones survive. Inevitably, too, he saw during the eight years an immature art race forward to maturity and motion-picture history being made. Although he did not pretend to write of it as an historian, its history and development can be followed in those weekly columns of his in which he functioned frankly, gaily, and sometimes passionately as the diarist of his own responses.

It was the period of the great comedians and of Fairbanks and Jackie Coogan; the period of such stars as Mary Pickford, Norma Talmadge, Richard Barthelmess, Wallace Reid, Rudolph Valentino, John Gilbert, William Powell, Ronald Colman, Blanche Sweet, Lon Chaney, John Barrymore, Dolores Costello, Ramon Novarro, Adolphe Menjou, Marion Davies, Gloria Swanson, Thomas Meighan, Victor McLaglen, Conrad Nagel, Emil Jannings, Nazimova, and a whole planetarium of others. Sherwood watched them twinkle and shine, then often twinkle again and vanish. Many of them he had met and some he knew well, but being a friend in person did not mean that he was a friend in print. With singular impartiality he judged by specific instances, often having to cudgel those he had previously complimented.

Take his heroines, for example. No man ever objected less than Sherwood to beautiful women, although he once complained because there were so many of them and so few good pictures. When he did see a woman who was beautiful, could act, and was allowed to do so in a good picture, his surrender was complete. He was constantly finding new favorites. One of the earliest and most abiding of these was Lillian Gish, "that lovely lady . . . with the fragile charm of a tender bluebell." He lived in the hope that someday producers would learn that she "possesses greater emotional force in her left eyebrow than all the fake thrills that the silent drama has perfected."

Another early favorite was Mabel Normand. When scandal touched her and her pictures were being banned, he rose to her defense, insisting that she was still "the first comedienne of the screen. They can ostracize her in Kansas and view her with alarm; they can submerge her in a vat of righteous indignation. But they can't seem to suppress her enormous talent."

Later there was Norma Shearer. "It becomes more and more evident," he wrote of her when reviewing *His Secretary* (1926), "that

Miss Shearer is my favorite little lady of filmdom, and one of these days I'm going to write her a fan letter and ask for a portrait of herself, handsomely autographed in white ink by her press agent." Then there was Garbo. In *The Temptress* (1926) he crowned her as "the Dream Princess of the Silent Drama Department of *Life*." He went further. "Anyone who says that Greta Garbo isn't the most ravishing, alluring, enthralling, etc., etc., has me to fight."

Sherwood liked to pretend he had praised so many films which had failed at the box office that producers read his pannings with relief. Even so, they cannot have read his "raves" without pleasure because he was as exuberant a champion of the pictures he liked as he was of the actors and actresses he admired. High among his favorites were *The Four Horsemen of the Apocalypse* (1921), *Tol'able David* (1921), *Nanook of the North* (1922), *The Dramatic Life of Abraham Lincoln* (1924), *The Big Parade* (1925), *Grass* (1925), *Moana of the South Seas* (1926), such German films as *The Last Laugh* (1925) and *Variety* (1926), and, from the Soviets, *The End of St. Petersburg* (1928). These, he insisted, were in their various ways what the silent drama was meant to be. These were moving pictures really worthy of the name. These were "fine," "superior," "marvelous," "excellent," "outstanding," and, more often than not, "great." Sherwood was no mincer.

When, as was most frequently the case, there was constabulary duty to be done, he did it, flailing with muscularity. He did not limit his onslaughts to his reviews and weekly summaries. He had a pet device for exposing the inanities of most movies. This was to print (sometimes with the aid of contributors) episodes from "The Great American Movie" which over the years he claimed to be preparing. In these his practice was to write a scene as it would have occurred in life which was, of course, just the opposite from the way it would have occurred in Hollywood.

During his eight years of reviewing movies Sherwood followed, among many changes, the decline of D. W. Griffith and the rise of such a race of new directors as Rex Ingram (*The Four Horsemen*), Henry King (*Tol'able David*), Robert J. Flaherty (*Nanook* and *Moana*), King Vidor (*The Big Parade*), James Cruze (*The Covered Wagon*, 1923), F. W. Murnau (*The Last Laugh*), Sergei Eisenstein

(*Potemkin*, 1926), and V. I. Pudovkin (*The End of St. Petersburg*).
He watched with amusement movie theatres as in the larger cities
they distended to become "cathedrals of the screen" as elaborate as
New York's Paramount, in which the untraveled could persuade
themselves they were royal transients at Versailles, or such a giant
grotto for lotus-eaters as Roxy's. Once he wondered if these buildings were not such shows in themselves that their owners too often
overlooked the need of putting on in them any others as good.

Among the thousands of players, admirable, competent, indiffer-
ent, or terrible, remembered or forgotten, that he reviewed was one
Italian strutter who turned out to be a bad actor on a larger screen.
In February, 1924, he appeared with Lionel Barrymore and Barbara
La Marr in some "nonsense on a heroic scale" produced in Rome by
Samuel Goldwyn, and his name was Benito Mussolini. "Yes," wrote
Sherwood, "the Fascist Napoleon appears in *The Eternal City*, sup-
ported by his legions of black-shirted followers and his tidal waves of
sonorous propaganda. His deportment on the screen lends weight to
the theory that this is just where he belongs."

That same year Sherwood also saw an early example of successful
color photography. It was Zane Grey's *Wanderer of the Wasteland*
(1924), shown at a time when many people thought that color photography would never be popular because so many previous experiments had looked like badly printed colored comics in a Sunday
supplement. Aesthetically these objectors had raised the point that
color destroyed everything in the movies that was stimulating to the
imagination by increasing their realism to such an extent that the
screen became nothing more than a mirror. Sherwood, always on
speaking terms with the future, denied this. "In my non-professional
opinion," said he, "there can be no doubt that colored movies will be
universally accepted within the next few years. The Technicolor process, which is the best at this time, is necessarily deficient. But invention in this field is progressing, and the old blacks and whites are
bound to be discarded before long. Movie stars will do well to start
studying the art of make-up now."

They would have done better to take voice lessons because the
talkies were just around the corner. He recognized their nearness
when in the fall of 1927 he saw *The Jazz Singer*. "There is one mo-

ment in *The Jazz Singer* that is fraught with tremendous significance. Al Jolson, appearing as a Jewish youth, returns to his old home after years of wandering around the Pantages circuit. His strictly orthodox father has disowned him because he chose to sing mammy songs in music halls rather than chants in the synagogue; his mother, however, welcomes the prodigal with open arms. Al sits down at the piano and sings 'Blue Sky' for his mother. Thanks to the Vitaphone attachment, his marvelous voice rings out from the screen, the sound agreeing perfectly with the movements of his mobile lips, the wriggling of his shoulders, the nervous tapping of his feet.

"After the song, there is a brief bit of spoken dialogue and then Al bursts into 'Blue Sky' again. When he is half-way through the chorus, his father enters the room, realizes that his house is being profaned with jazz, and shouts, 'Stop!' At this point, the Vitaphone withdraws and *The Jazz Singer* returns to a routine pantomime punctuated with subtitles." But the brief interlude of sound had been enough to convince Sherwood. "There is no question of doubt that the Vitaphone justifies itself in *The Jazz Singer*. Furthermore, it proves that talking movies are considerably more than a lively possibility: they are close to an accomplished fact."

A year later he admitted that the fact was accomplished by writing, "Well, the silent drama is now expiring (the talkie is its death rattle) and I am compelled to abandon it as a label for these weekly comments. Shed no tears for the passing of the noiseless films; their time had come, and they were unable to live beyond it. The talking movie may be crude, and offensive to the finer tastes, but it has great possibilities, and these eventually will be realized. It is still an experiment—and, what is more, it is noble in motive. Anything that aims to abolish subtitles and subtitle writers deserves to be encouraged."

That year his career as *Life*'s movie critic was also over. On December 28, 1928, his last column appeared. "For the benefit of those who have followed the Great American Movie in this department, I beg to issue one final bulletin: this colossal picture is never to be released. Just as I had completed the two-thousandth reel, the talkies came in, and I have obstinately refused to equip my masterpiece with a sound accompaniment. So—with a sigh for the vanished youth of Jackie Coogan; a last, wistful wave to Greta Garbo, and a prayer that Cecil B. De Mille, Rupert Hughes and Will H. Hays will forgive and forget—I depart from this department for good, and all. In case any of my loyal readers (by the way, what ever became of that fellow?) should care to send floral tributes, I beg to state that my favorite flower is still the raspberry."

It never was, though at the moment he had good reason to feel bitter. Some two weeks earlier he had been fired abruptly, not because of his opinions as a reviewer but because of his differences with *Life*'s management as its editor. The loss of both jobs simultaneously was serious and would have been more than that had he not, two years before, found a new and lucrative profession. With *The Road to Rome* he had become a successful playwright.

14

EDITOR AND EARLY GHOST-WRITER

As Editor of Life—Harold Ross Offers Damaging Competition with The New Yorker—Life's *Parody Issues—Sherwood's Contributions—First Public Mention of F.D.R.—Dabblings in Politics—Runs Will Rogers for President—"He Chews to Run" on the Anti-Bunk Platform—Ghostwrites Copy for Rogers—Glad to Be Fired*

Sherwood, who was already interested in writing for the movies, was not quite through with writing about them when *Life* discharged him. During the next three years he was to cover them for other publications and to grind out with diminishing enthusiasm a general weekly newspaper column called "The Moving Picture Album." He was, however, through with editing, and glad to be rid of it. By his own admission he was miscast as an editor and came to look back with gratitude to the day he was fired, saying, "Thank God, it marked the end of my editorial career."

Even so, he enjoyed the job while he had it and was better at it than he said, being neither spectacular nor dedicated, but amiably competent. According to Fairfax Downey, a member of the staff and Charles Dana Gibson's clear-eyed biographer, Sherwood came closer to making the magazine click than any of its editors after Mitchell— that is, until he was "seduced by his new-found ability as a playwright." Under him the circulation, which had fallen by 100,000, fluctuated but rose one year by a comforting, if slight, 21,000. Although this was gratifying, there were other satisfactions which were richer.

Benchley and Mrs. Parker, when Sherwood took over, were old and close friends. So were such other Round Tablers as Connelly,

Kaufman, F.P.A., and Frank Sullivan. With them he enjoyed the
comradeship of liking to laugh and finding the same things funny. He
also enjoyed this same comradeship with such writers as George S.
Chappell, Morris Bishop, Newman Levy, and Corey Ford, and with
such cartoonists as John Held, Jr., Gluyas Williams, and H. T.
Webster.

At the office at 598 Madison Avenue the atmosphere was be-
calmed, compared to that which was soon to exist at *The New
Yorker* under Harold Ross. It was agreeably relaxed, even playful.
There were some frictions, of course. Sherwood had no fondness for
the business manager Clair Maxwell, disagreeing with him over policy
and finding him pompous under a frayed disguise of good-fellowship.
He was scarcely more compatible with Gibson's son Langhorne, a
handsome young man who preferred foxhunting to publishing and
was a misfit on a humorous paper.

By and large, Sherwood was happy as *Life*'s editor. It was a
task which he could take at a trot rather than a gallop. It paid him
extremely well (for those days), though not enough to meet his
mounting debts. It increased his prestige, permitted him to continue
his page "The Silent Drama," and left him time for other activities.

A family reason added to Sherwood's pleasures. He had talked his
brother Arthur in 1926 into moving to New York from Oregon and
joining the editorial staff. Arthur, his elder by eight years, was the
brother who had "beaten the pants off" him when he was an "objectionable little egomaniac," and thus won his intense dislike as a boy.
These beatings had long since been forgiven and, in Arthur, Sherwood had found the "perfect elder brother . . . sympathetic, understanding, and encouraging," who helped him "enormously in the
tough process of maturing." With his strong Emmet clannishness
Sherwood was delighted to have Arthur working with him. He knew
Arthur's talents were stronger than his energy or will, and that in
several businesses he had been one of the luckless who are misfor-
tune's friends. Yet he was confident that, as a writer, Arthur would
be "a great success."

James Thurber insisted that no one would ever have picked
Harold Ross out of a police line-up as the editor of so sophisticated a
magazine as *The New Yorker*. No more would Sherwood have been

spotted as the editor of *Life*. As surely as in appearance Ross was the denial of Eustace Tilley's elegance, Sherwood at first glance bore no resemblance to "Laughter holding both his sides." To Thurber, Ross, with his gruff manner, his low receding brow, his outreaching under-lip, his usually crumpled clothes and defiant shock of hair, appeared, even in a dinner jacket, "loosely informal, like a carelessly carried umbrella."

Sherwood, especially in his long, black winter overcoat, looked to his secretary, Lois Whitcomb, "like a walking coffin." To her eye and ear he contradicted what she knew him to be. His speech was slow, his thinking fast; his voice lugubrious, his tongue quipful. Though he was gay at heart, his expression was often "hound-dog mournful." A reason for this was that he was in pain, suffering already from sinusitis, a malady which was to plague him with increasing severity.

As a rule, Sherwood arrived at his fifteenth-floor office shortly after eleven. He found coming in earlier a waste of time, because his sinusitis did not clear up until then and he could not function before it did. He would park his hat on the top of the partition, this being handier for him than stooping over to hang it on the rack, and then settle down to go through his mail. Almost every day he left at about 12:30 for lunch at the Algonquin and returned in two hours, or even later if the talk at the Round Table had taken fire.

With Ross, editing *The New Yorker* was an obsession. To Sherwood, editing *Life* was an amusing way of earning needed money and a pleasant position. It was a job which took him back, in grown-up terms, to the kind of work he had done on the *Lampoon*. Ross was captaining a brand-new vessel of his own designing, Sherwood steering a ship not only outmoded but sinking, the kind of ship which Ross had piloted when he served briefly as *Judge's* editor. What is more, Sherwood steered it with one hand. His movie reviewing remained his major interest in the magazine and his most mature contribution to it. Because of it, he spent more time in motion-picture theatres than in his office. According to Miss Whitcomb, when he did buckle down to his job he was very quick and sure, and could go through a whole mass of manuscripts in an afternoon. As his friend Paul Hollister observed, he had a turtle's gift for withdrawing into his shell and shutting out the world.

Unlike *The New Yorker* when it came along in 1925, *Life* WAS edited for the old lady in Dubuque. Its appeal was to the young and old, and to the undergraduate in graduates. Its grim business was to be funny, and styles in humor, like other styles, are the products of a period. Many of the jokes and humorous pieces in *Life*, including Sherwood's, now read as if they had been written in another language. During the years Sherwood was on it, however, the weekly still had its devotees who eagerly awaited its coming. They chuckled over it, unshocked by its insensitive Irish, Italian, Jewish, and Negro jokes. To them it was warmhearted, and they prized it the more because of its innocuous crusades.

In earlier years the editors had said among themselves, "We need a good hate." Gibson, a smiling rather than splenetic man, seemed to have run out of hates once the Kaiser was safely cooped up at Doorn. Although, when he was editor. Sherwood did not come up with any galvanizing new hates, he did his best, in a lighthearted way, to salvage the magazine. For one thing, he sought to brighten its appearance by turning to William Dwiggins, a master at such things, to redesign the format and typography. For another, he continued to try to boost the circulation and the advertising by those old reliables, letter contests and "Special Issues."

Under him these multiplied with a frequency which was almost a confession of alarm. When one contest ended, another began, and "Special Numbers" appeared nearly every other week. They grasped hopefully for any subject which might prove popular—Radio, Big Business, Football, Political Conventions, Automobiles, Dixie, Boobs, Broadway, or "Vawdvil." When a winner, such as St. Patrick's Day or Old Home Week, was stumbled on, it was certain to be repeated the next year.

Among the Special Numbers Sherwood most enjoyed working on were the occasional Burlesque Issues, slapdash parodies that were echoes of the *Lampoon*. In them samplings were offered, printed in their type and written in their manner, of such magazines as the *Saturday Evening Post, American Mercury, True Story, College Humor, The New Masses, Physical Culture, Photoplay, The National Geographic, The Literary Digest,* and *Time.* Benchley and Connelly, who collaborated on them, shared Sherwood's fun in getting them out, and the fun they had in doing so was shared by readers.

When he was on *Life*, its editorials by tradition were in sober counterpoint to the obligatory lightness of the weekly's over-all tone. Until the middle of his last year they were written with mellow wisdom and resolute earnestness by Martin (though Martin could be humorous even when writing about humor). After Martin's retirement at seventy-two, Sherwood replaced him with the thirty-eight-year-old Elmer Davis, that brilliant classicist and reporter who somehow brought to print the cool sanity of his Hoosier twang. Thus it was Martin and Davis, rather than Sherwood, who had their earnest, if gibing, say on subjects of national interest. It was Martin who assailed Prohibition, the Ku Klux Klan, the Harding Cabinet, the Teapot Dome, Coolidge prosperity, and the Scopes trial; and Davis who dryly kidded the unplanned obsolescence of the D.A.R., laughed at those White Cliffs which were Hoover's collars, and uttered such heresies against installment buying that advertisers began to cancel their contracts.

As for Sherwood, before and while he was its editor, he limited his political observations in *Life* to gags, doggerel, humorous pieces, and sudden deflating comments tucked away in his movie reviews. Although he lamented the twenties as the "age of bluster, ballyhoo, and bunk" and touched upon the headline subjects dealt with by Martin and Davis, he approached the news wearing motley or, if not that, a raccoon coat. His stray contributions were for the most part tethered in spirit and method to his collegiate past. From them one would have guessed—and wrongly—that, though he took Hollywood seriously when it permitted him to do so, he took the country and the world lightly. The fervor of which he was capable showed through only when he denounced war with passion in his notices of war films.

His first mention of Franklin D. Roosevelt in 1920 was in his more usual old-grad mood. The election which swept Harding and Coolidge into office (the returns were the first to be broadcast) was three weeks past. The month, however, was still November and Sherwood felt it his seasonal duty as *Life*'s "Football Inexpert" to name the "All-American Political Team." After admitting that "it is not easy to pick an all-star team when there are so few stars to pick from," he said he had "done his best with the mediocre material at hand."

The line-up included Harding and Cox as halfbacks, the elder Lodge ("the gridiron ace of the season") as quarterback, the commodious William Howard Taft as center, Coolidge as right end, and Roosevelt as left. Roosevelt, the defeated candidate for the vice-presidency, was then the tall, slender, handsome young man who, as Frances Perkins remembered, at the San Francisco convention displayed his athletic ability by vaulting over rows of chairs to get to the platform in a hurry.

Of the ends Sherwood had this to say: "Calvin Coolidge, who wore the purple at Amherst and has since worn the purple on Beacon Hill, and Franklin D. Roosevelt, of Harvard and the Navy, seem to be the logical candidates for the wing positions. Both young men are nimble and alert, and ready to tackle anything that may come their way. During the past season they have demonstrated that they can handle any forward passes that are thrown to them from the back-field—no matter how weakly or inaccurately they may have been hurled—and they have both been adept in recovering fumbles."

Denied politicians as a subject, American humor would not be the same. They have always been fair game, and in *Life* it was only as a game that Sherwood dealt with them. He had his greatest fun with them in *Life* when, as its editor, he indulged in 1928 in his culminating and most protracted joke. On May 31, two weeks before the Republicans nominated Herbert Hoover in Kansas City, and four weeks before the Democrats, sweating it out in the heat of Houston, selected Al Smith, he announced that, as a protest against the bunk and hypocrisy in both major parties, *Life* was sponsoring a new party, the Anti-Bunk or Bunkless party, with Will Rogers as its candidate.

On the cover was a portrait in color of Will with his unruly forelock spilling down, his mouth stretched wide in a grin, his cheek wadded with gum, and his pale-blue eyes almost audible in their laughter. At the front of the magazine, after a preliminary statement by Sherwood about the new party and its candidate, Will began his speech of acceptance by saying *Life*'s offer had left him dazed and adding, "If I can stay dazed, I ought to make a splendid candidate." He went on to insist that his acceptance was based on one and only one thing, "If elected I absolutely and positively agree to resign." This was his sole campaign pledge, and he was beyond challenge when he claimed, "That's offering the Country more than any Candidate ever offered it in the history of its entire existence." From then on until after the election in November, the first pages of *Life* were given over each week to a speech, allegedly written by Rogers, which was followed by a column of "Anti-Bunk Bulletins" conducted by Sherwood.

There was no vice-presidential nominee, Lindbergh having been suggested and rejected on the ground that the Colonel "has done too much for this country to be rewarded with a sentence of four years in the United States Senate." There were no rallies. There were no campaign funds. There was no platform, except "whatever the other fellow don't do, we will," and the assurance that "no matter what's on our Platform, on November the fifth we will have a bonfire and burn the Platform."

There were no planks except those that could be carried in by voters. "If we get to a State that wants a wet plank," said Will, "why we just stop and put it in for 'em, and if we get to a State where the farmers want relief, why we just stop and sell their farms for 'em, and give 'em relief. . . . If somebody wants flood relief, we move 'em to higher ground. . . . We want every part of the Country to do what they want to do regardless of some other part."

There were no commitments because, as Will put it, "We want the wet vote, and we want the dry vote. We are honest about it . . . so our Plank will run something about as follows: 'Wine for the rich, beer for the poor, and moonshine liquor for the prohibitionist.'"

There was only Will Rogers, and his picture was distributed on thousands of buttons on which, as an answer to Coolidge's recent "I do not choose to run," Sherwood printed "He chews to run." There was only Will who, though he went to Kansas City and Houston to comment on the Republican and Democratic antics, avoided the wear and tear, the backslapping and handshaking of a campaign by campaigning for himself only in his speeches that appeared in *Life* each week.

For many people Will Rogers was enough, the welcome guarantee of a campaign which would be different. This gum-chewing, lariat-twirling philosopher from Oklahoma with his Cherokee blood was, as Sherwood stressed and he frequently claimed, indisputably a genuine pre-Mayflower American. Furthermore, he was the first presidential candidate in years who was intentionally funny. He saw through shams, was unawed by anyone, afraid of nothing, and earned a fortune by using bad grammar to make good sense. When asked once what his business was, his reply was "Everybody's." He was fond of saying that all he knew was what he read in the papers, but he read them to see through them and, in or out of print, in his comments on them could lasso the laughing truth as accurately as he could rope a running horse.

People smiled when they mentioned his name and laughed out loud when they read him, and roared at his thrusts when they saw him. He was a person to brighten eyes, clear minds, and blow away fogs. "I never yet met a man I didn't like," he said in a widely quoted and misunderstood sentence. There were many men and more things he did not like. When he hit hard, he meant to do so, as Sherwood insisted, though his smiling manner softened the blow.

The public men he did not bother to go after were the ones whose vanity he hurt most. A gag about them from him was a proof of their importance. But he was more than a funny man. In him there was something large. Everyone sensed this. The country felt an admiration as well as an affection for him which ensured him his privileged position as court jester to the nation. To Damon Runyon and most others, "he reflected in many ways the heartbeat of America." When with Wiley Post he was killed in Alaska in a plane crash in 1935, two Lincolnians thought at once of Lincoln. One was Carl Sandburg, the other Sherwood who said, "The impact upon the people of America at the death of Will Rogers was similar to that produced by the death of Abraham Lincoln."

Rogers, an old friend of Sherwood, had been an intermittent contributor to *Life* six years earlier. Sherwood's admiration for Will went back to the *Frolics* and the *Follies*. In reviewing his two-reelers, he had saluted him as "the divine Will" and insisted that, "in addition to his established talents as a paragraphic cowboy," Rogers was "a first-rate actor."

Running Will Rogers for President was something Sherwood thought up with Fred Cooper, the artist. The idea was not entirely new, since in 1924 Rogers received a scattering of votes in that "gruesome" marathon of balloting which had been the Democratic convention, and some people took the trouble to write in his name at the polls. More than a man, he had become an institution, a proof and ventilation of the average American's down-to-earth common sense, a wise man who chose humor as the expression of his sanity.

Although Sherwood's launching of Will as a candidate was a joke, many people took it seriously, or pretended to. Among these was Henry Ford who, in a letter to Sherwood, said, "The joke of Will Rogers' candidacy for President is that it is no joke. It is a serious attempt to restore American common sense to American politics." Elated, Sherwood wrote his mother in the playful mood of the whole Anti-Bunk campaign, "We'll get Will in the White House yet, and then it's the Court of St. James for me."

The campaign was for him not all play and no work. The reason was Rogers. Everything seemed set after Sherwood had gone to see Rogers in his room at the Hotel Astor, as he remembered, and talked him into accepting the nomination. It was Rogers, according to Sherwood, who gave the Anti-Bunk party its name. Almost a quarter of a century later when reminiscing for Homer Croy, one of Rogers' biographers, Sherwood recalled that Will agreed to write several hundred words a week giving his platform and campaign speeches. "It is my recollection, possibly fallible," said he, "that we paid him $500.00 a week, which was a lot of money for *Life*, but peanuts to Will. . . . We were given time on a local radio station for weekly broadcasts and had a lot of fun with this getting such guest stars as Eddie Cantor, Leon Errol, Bob Benchley and Amelia Earhart. Will himself never appeared on this program as he had other radio commitments."

"As a matter of fact," Sherwood confessed, "I don't think Will ever took much interest in the campaign and we had one hell of a time getting copy out of him. When he did get it in it was very

sketchy and never nearly enough of it to fill the necessary space. So I
filled it out, imitating Will's style as best I could. This had the unfortunate effect of convincing Bill that he need write practically nothing
and I think there were one or two weeks when he did supply nothing
and I had to write the whole piece. He never complained about my
work. The only allusion he ever made to it was that now and then he
would say to me, with a slight grin, 'That was a pretty good piece I
wrote for you folks last week. If this quality keeps up I'll have to be
asking for a raise.' "

The Anti-Bunk campaign was the first time Sherwood served a
presidential candidate as a ghost-writer. When next he did so in
1940, the campaign, the candidate, and the times would be different,
very different. It also marked the approaching end of his editorship
of *Life*. A little more than a month after the election an embarrassed
Clair Maxwell made a cold day the colder for him by dropping by
his office late in the afternoon to tell him that things at the magazine
were in a bad way and that he was fired.

For Sherwood, who had been married six years and had a five-year-
old daughter, this was bad news financially. But the interview, which
dragged on into the twilight, was in part redeemed by being turned
unexpectedly into the kind of theatre which appealed greatly, as Paul
Hollister put it, to Sherwood's "sense of pure Indian corn." The door
opened and who should prance into the room but his chubby little
daughter Mary. She flung herself into her father's lap and with her
arms about his neck cried, "Oh, dear Daddy, you're the dearest daddy
in the world!" There was no snow falling, at least not inside the
office, but it was a scene worthy of *East Lynne*.

A general reorganization of the magazine followed. Sherwood was
not the only one to leave. Out of loyalty to him his brother Arthur,
Elmer Davis, and three other members of the staff resigned. Benchley continued as dramatic critic until the spring, moving over to *The
New Yorker* the next season.

Life had made for Sherwood a decision which later he wished he
had made for himself—and earlier. One of his troubles as an editor,
he admitted to Lou Cowan years after he had ceased to be one, was
that when he read something which he knew was not quite right or
thought too long, instead of dropping it or cutting it, he had one

desire and that was to rewrite it in his own way. Looking back in 1931 on his literary beginnings, he felt that at *Life* through a combination of lucky circumstances he had got off to a fast start, which was too fast and in the wrong direction. He had found himself the editor of a national magazine at twenty-eight when, as he told an interviewer, "I was never meant by the gods to be an executive, and I now wish I had spent those early years writing the sort of things I wanted to write instead of wasting my time editing other people's writings."

15

AUTHOR IN SEARCH OF HIMSELF

A Young Man Up to His Neck in High Living—Mary Brandon as a Wife—Turns to Movie Writing—Tries Short Stories—Scribner's Accepts Extra! Extra!—Disillusioned by the Peace—Becomes a Pacifist—Votes for Harding, His "Bit in the Great Betrayal"—Turns Playwright

As a matter of fact, he did find the time to get a surprising amount of outside writing done during his years on *Life*, before and after he became its editor and notwithstanding the pressures of his various jobs as a movie critic. He had to. There were the two Marys, his wife and daughter, to be considered as well as his own assumptions of a more than plentiful plenty. Lytton Strachey quotes one of Newman's disciples as saying, when the Cardinal had sat down to four fish courses at lunch during Lent, "I am sorry to say that there is a lobster salad side to the Cardinal." Most decidedly Sherwood had his lobster salad side.

Although he was making what for those days was good money, the $10,000 which *Life* paid him was not good enough for Mary Brandon or really for him. He liked his comforts and the fleshpots too. But though he was thriftless, Mary Brandon was his superior at least in extravagance. Her awareness of her wants was as strong as his financial sense was weak. Pouts and tears, tantrums and scenes were the weapons she used to get her way, and at each of these she was an expert. He had an aversion to emotional explosions and unpleasantness and, except when he had had a few drinks, retreated from them, silently submissive. He was confused and mystified by anyone whose values and instincts were drastically different from his own. He gave way to Mary Brandon by giving in to her. Since her demands were many and his refusals few, the wolf could at first have served the Sherwoods as a butler because he was so often at their door.

Fortunately, Sherwood could make money even if, with Mary's aid, he could not keep it. Like his father and his grandmother, M.E.W.S., and many of the Emmets, he had a talent for summoning dollars when emergencies arose rather than for saving and investing them in between times. But the dollars he summoned during these years were never enough.

In his days on *Life* he was a young man, up to his high neck in living high, who went about his diversions as earnestly as if he were being paid for the time they took. These were so numerous that they would have shattered most schedules and to some have seemed a labor in themselves. Yet, in spite of his lingering over morning newspapers, his insatiable night hunger for books, his long lunches, the hours he had to spend in movie theatres, his afternoons at ball games or the track, his croquet bouts, his constant theatregoing, his dinner parties, his grim sessions at cards, his ardent participation in parlor games, his outpourings of "The Red, Red Robin" on late evenings, his appearance in such Dutch Treat Club shows as Ring Lardner's *Dinner Bridge,* and his increasing bouts with sinusitis, he did, from the abundance of his energies and the greater drive of his economic needs, somehow manage to grind out an incredible amount of stuff that brought in supplementary cash. Since his finances in the twenties were always open at the seams, he had no other choice than to keep on calking them. He had no illusions about this kind of writing. It was hack work as he was well aware. But the checks it brought in were literature, however minor.

The movies also came to his aid. It was an eased day for him when in 1924 he was asked to rewrite for $2,500 the subtitles for *The Hunchback of Notre Dame,* a request which persuaded Rosina that Hollywood producers must be mad since it seemed to her that "Victor Hugo had so much to say on the subject that he rather covered the ground." Encouraged by this commission, he collaborated with Bertram Bloch on three scenarios, one of which, *Oh, What a Nurse!* a complicated slapstick affair, actually reached the screen in 1926 with Syd Chaplin, late of *Charley's Aunt,* impersonating the nurse.

Since it was brightened by such subtitles as "He's got calves only a cow could love," it was widely and understandably panned, though Sherwood confessed in *Life* that he found it "pretty funny . . . in spite of its genesis." He even attempted a musical comedy, *Horse-Shoes*, for Jackson, Clayton, and Durante, but it died a-borning.

Then there were the short stories. Although his mother had been begging him for quite a while to try his hand at fiction, his invariable reply had been that he did not know enough to write it and was no good at it. She was doubly pleased, therefore, in 1924 when she could inform Jane de Glehn in London that *Munsey's* had paid him $400 for one story and had accepted another. Sherwood was more pleased with the money than with his work and thought the $400 story "very poor." He was poorer. In spite of all his money-making efforts, Rosina could only report at the time of his sales to *Munsey's* that "Bobby never has a spare cent and goes about in a shabby old suit he had in college. When Mary came to see me the other day, she said, 'I wish they would send the check for that story because we had to borrow $70 from the baby this week.'"

By the end of the next year Sherwood had reason to feel gratified with the progress he was making. It was then that he wrote *Extra! Extra!* which he came to look back on as his "one respectable story." Short, lean, and acid, it had to do with a clerk who, after having endured his complaining wife for seven years, at last walks out on her and their little son and ships as a sailor. This occurs on an evening, which proves one too many, when she badgers him once more into going down the five flights of stairs to buy an extra that is being hawked. He does not see her again for twelve Enoch Arden years during which she has remarried. At their brief encounter he recalls, when prodded, that the earth-shaking headline which changed their lives and set him free was merely that the Red Sox had won.

Only a man who knew about a nagging wife could have written the story with such smoldering feeling. It could, in fact, have been a tenement version of what Sherwood faced with Mary Brandon, especially in such a paragraph: "If only there had been a slight variation in his wife's techniques . . . but there never was. At first, he had

tried to be frightfully sporting about it, assuming the blame at the
first hint of trouble and doing whatever was demanded of him with
all possible grace; but that pose, and it had not been long before he
admitted that it *was* a pose, was worn away by a process of erosion,
a process that had kept up for seven years. . . . Seven years of
listening to those endless scoldings and complaints at home. Whatever of gallantry had existed in Mr. Whidden's soul had crumbled
before the persistent and ever increasing waves of temper. He knew
that now, if he gave in, he did so because of cowardice and not
because of any worthily chivalrous motives."

With misgivings Sherwood sent *Extra! Extra!* off to Robert
Bridges, the courtly editor of *Scribner's*, making clear that he would
not "for an instant resent its rejection because, in this form of composition, I have not even reached the point where I think my stuff is
any good." He did not have to live long with the anxiety of a writer
hoping for a phone call or on the lookout for the postman. Four days
later Bridges wrote him, saying, "I think you have surely pulled it off
with *Extra! Extra!* It is a good character and an excellent situation,
and we are glad to have it for the magazine." He offered a fairly
remote publication date and $150. The real pay was Bridges's
words.

When the story appeared in the July issue, 1926, Sherwood received a heartening number of congratulatory letters and was pleased
to find in F.P.A.'s *Diary of Our Own Samuel Pepys* one Saturday
morning an item which noted, "Read a tayle in *Scribner's* called
Extra! Extra! by Rob Sherwood, and I deemed it as finely bitter a
tayle as ever I read, and one having a fine economical brevity, too."
He had the further pleasure of having the story included in Edward J.
O'Brien's *The Best American Short Stories of 1926* and finding himself teamed there with such authors as Zona Gale, Ernest Hemingway, Ring Lardner, Manuel Komroff, and Wilbur Daniel Steele.
With flattering frequency *Extra! Extra!* found its way into several
other anthologies, American and European, no copies of which,
Sherwood confessed, he had kept.

Although he thanked Bridges by assuring him, "Your generous
encouragement will probably spur me on to frantic efforts in fiction,"

his doubts hung on. The month after the publication of *Extra! Extra!* he was admitting to one of its admirers, "I have written very few short stories because fiction is a medium in which I am ill at ease because of an utter unfamiliarity with the technique, whatever that is. The story, *Extra! Extra!* is the first one I have ever written that did not entail years and years of agonized work. When I say years and years I am not exaggerating. I have just finished a story called *Armistice Day*, which I started to write in 1921. I should like nothing better than to write a great many short stories, but the ideas just won't come."

The postscript to his letter to Bridges when he submitted *Extra! Extra!* was revealing. "I might add," it said, "that the enclosed story is not intended to be funny." It was neither so intended nor was it funny, but Sherwood felt obliged to make its seriousness clear, knowing that, because of his association with *Life*, he was thought of, except as a movie critic, as a professional funny man.

This is what he had been in most of his light verse, his fillers, his sketches, his published political gibes, and in many of his laughing movie reviews. This is what he was condemned into being by the very nature of the magazine. His readers knew the locust only by the shell, and Sherwood did not as yet know himself. They knew the lunge of his opinions, the unrestrained collegiate heat of his enthusiasms, the sanity of his approach to the arty, and his accuracy as a deflator. If they knew him only in print, he must have seemed to them a bright member of the younger generation who took an unconscionable time ceasing to be "younger," a party person whose only grave determination was to be gay, and whose smile in type was caught in fixative.

Occasionally, what was going on within him broke through as when, at the very time he was finishing *Extra! Extra!* he described the Great War as "that grim travesty." He did so in more detail in a review of *The Big Parade* when, after saluting Laurence Stallings as its scenarist, he praised King Vidor as its director. Writing hot from his own recollections as a combatant who had had to do some killing, Sherwood said of Vidor, "He has made war scenes that actually resemble war. . . . He has shown an American soldier, suddenly wild with the desire to kill, trying to jab his bayonet into the neck of a dying German sniper. He has shown the look on the sniper's face and the horrible revulsion that overcomes the American boy. I doubt that there is a single irregular soldier, volunteer or conscript, who did not experience that same awful feeling during his career in France—who did not recognize the impulse to withdraw the bayonet and offer the dying boy a cigarette."

For the most part Sherwood appeared in *Life* without permitting his full or inner self to follow him there. What was shaping him, the stresses to which he was subjected, the shifts in his feelings and convictions were not expressed, even as what he was shaping into was no more suspected by his readers than by him. His talents, though forming, were unformed; his depths untapped. The war and his disillusionment with the peace had changed him greatly, along with many another, but he was writing, especially for *Life*, from that portion of himself which remained unchanged.

He had marched off an innocent from an innocent America, aglow with idealism, mesmerized by recruiting slogans, and as convinced as Gibson and millions of others were that getting rid of the Kaiser would solve the world's problems. At the war's end he was still briefly confident that its sacrifices, terrible as they were, would be justified by the victory they had won. Wilson, whose long neutrality had disgusted him in college, had stirred him into confidence by his War Message. He had been drawn for a while to the President because his noble ideals, nobly phrased, raised echoes in Sherwood's heart. For a time he thought, out of the hope of a tired spirit in need, that Wilson had really fought a war which would end war and make the world safe for democracy.

Sherwood was "instinctively enthusiastic" about the idea of a League of Nations. He had not forgotten the kinship he felt with the paralyzed South African Jew and the scalded Australian who had been next to him in that hospital overseas. He wanted to believe that there would be some world medium for the expression of the good will which he shared with them and servicemen of many kinds and nationalities. He became internationally minded at a time when on the tongues of isolationists the word "internationalist" was synonymous with "warmonger." He did not care. He had been taught by war to hate it. To his way of thinking, the surest way to make a start at peace was through some sort of union of the English-speaking peoples who were already united by the advantages of a common language, common traditions of freedom, common ethics, and a common desire for peace.

His early internationalism was swift in fading. It died with his belief in Wilson. It vanished after the peacemaking in Paris and the battle that was waged for the League. It perished when Wilson, with his genius for chilling a warm principle, became for Sherwood another toppled hope and his fall brought down all the great, high hopes he had raised. He realized Wilson was "unquestionably a prophet," "essentially right," and "far ahead of his time." But Sherwood came to see him as a man, tactless and arbitrary, who "as the tragic result of his university background" could not cope with nor tolerate short-sighted stupidity, and therefore made the fatal mistake of playing directly into the hands of his enemies in the Senate, thus contributing to the defeat of his noble purposes.

On his return Sherwood felt at first the superiority which comes easily to veterans. But not for long. Although his fondness for The Black Watch and the satisfaction he took in having served with it never left him, his pride in having been a combatant was soon replaced by a sense of outrage at having been duped. The soldier who had thought of himself as a crusader came to feel that he had been a sucker. The internationalist turned isolationist; the pleader for our being in the war came back from it a pacifist; the champion of preparedness, a passionate advocate of disarmament.

By 1919 he was convinced by the writings of George Harvey and other Wilson-haters of the futility of the League. "I became," he wrote ruefully in his preface to *There Shall Be No Night*, "a rabid opponent of the League—which means that whenever I engaged in a discussion of major political issues in some speak-easy I would say, 'The League won't work because it's impractical. I agree absolutely with Senator Henry Cabot Lodge that Article XVI stinks!' I had a very hazy idea of what Article XVI actually provided for, but I was young and free again and it was much more fun to be a critic than an adherent."

Sherwood, in other words, returned from the war a Republican in good standing with his Republican family. The youth who in Boston had marched for Hughes in 1916, and would have voted for him had he been old enough, cast his first vote as an American citizen for Warren G. Harding in 1920. "Thus," he admitted in the confessional which was that same preface, when twenty years later he was looking back on all that had happened to the world, America, and himself, "I did my bit in the great betrayal. I voted for the proposition that all the American soldiers who had given their lives in the Great War had died in vain. And what I and all other Americans got from Harding's victory was a decade of hypocrisy, corruption, crime, glorification of greed and depravity, to be followed logically by a decade of ascendant Hitlerism."

In the mid-twenties Sherwood was an author in search of his own changing self. He was eager to find a medium, comfortable and congenial, in which he could write as the man he had become. He had many journalistic outlets which he—and the bank—knew he needed and in which he had made a name. He, however, wanted something more. Restless and driven, he was convinced, in spite of the mild success with *Extra! Extra!*, that short stories were not his affair. His curdled estimate of *The Dawn Man*, after he had dashed it off three years before, had persuaded him that the drama also was not for him. Nonetheless, in 1926 he came back to it, forgetting the resolution he had made to abandon playwriting. It was hard for a member of the Algonquin group *not* to be writing a play.

16

AT THE GATES OF ROME

His Reasons for Writing The Road to Rome—*An Evening with Sidney Howard—Mommsen Reread and an Old Hero Rediscovered in Hannibal—Why Did Hannibal Not Take Rome?—The Dramatization of a Guess—His Writing of the Comedy—Paul Hollister's Mugs—The Reviews Good and Bad—Modern Slang and Ancient History—"Shaw in Short Pants"—The Black Watch Attends—Mary Brandon and Some Drama Backstage*

Sherwood was in retrospect to give various explanations for his change of heart. In his preface to *There Shall Be No Night* he pretended that in *The Road to Rome* he had written his first play. "My main reason for doing so was that I was about to be thirty years old, and I had read somewhere—I think it was in F.P.A.'s column—that all young newspapermen promise themselves that they will write that play or that novel before they're thirty and then the next thing they know they're forty and still promising. I didn't have time for a novel. When I wrote *The Road to Rome* I didn't know what sort of playwright I might be, provided I might be a playwright at all. So I tried it in every style of dramaturgy—high comedy, low comedy, melodrama, romance (both sacred and profane), hard-boiled realism, beautiful writing—and, of course, I inserted a 'message.' That message was that I was opposed to war."

To his valued friend Edna Ferber he gave another explanation since he considered her involved in the play's getting written. A week after its New York opening late in January, 1927, he wrote her from *Life*, "A year ago last summer I was engaged in conversation with you at the Swopes' summer White House, with crap games to the left of us, chemin-de-fer games to the right of us, Irving Berlin in front of us and the usual jolly round of volleying and thundering from our host. You said to me, 'The best thing that could happen to you would be to have you snatched out of the Algonquin and exiled to Kansas City for two years. At the end of that time, you'd come back with some fine work.' That casual observation so impressed me that I left the Hotel Algonquin, where I had had lunch practically every day for six years. I didn't go to Kansas City, but I did go to work and wrote two plays—*The Road to Rome* and a dramatization of Ring Lardner's *The Love Nest*. Furthermore, I feel a great deal better because I wrote them. The object of this letter is not, presumptively, to suggest that your glowing prophecy has been fulfilled—but to thank you for giving me a shove in what unquestionably was the right direction."

To William K. Zinsser, movie critic of the *Herald Tribune*, he confided still another explanation in 1955. This was when Zinsser wrote an hilarious review damning *Jupiter's Daughter*, a movie, wet with a swimming pool and much more, which M-G-M had somehow extracted from *The Road to Rome* for Esther Williams. "Years ago, when I was a critic, I expressed something less than wild enthusiasm for a Russian film about *The Cruiser Potemkin*. That caused me to be attacked savagely by a young upstart on the *Herald Tribune* named Richard Watts. He described me as 'the dean of motion picture criticism,' and added that, like most deans, I was suffering from hardening of the critical arteries. I was then 28 years old. Dick's cruel words hurt me so that I felt a finished motion picture critic and, in desperation, went to work on the script which eventually gave you the opportunity to write that marvelous review."

Sherwood's answer to a woman reporter a few weeks after *The Road to Rome* opened was perhaps closest to the point. Her question was why had he written it; his reply, "a house—and two mortgages." He was $14,000 in debt, enough to start anyone's pen pushing.

Coincidence nudged him into work one evening when, while looking over the books in the library of his friend Sidney Howard, he happened to come across a set of Mommsen's *History of Rome*. Taking down one of the volumes, he turned to the chapters on Hannibal and, as he flicked the pages, the magic of that name caused a fire long cold within him to blaze again.

Since his schoolboy days Hannibal had been Sherwood's "pet

hero." Why, he did not quite know. Certainly because of the Carthaginian's valor and greatness. Perhaps, as he told an interviewer, because Hannibal had about him, in the manner of Mary Queen of Scots and Robert E. Lee, the romantic sadness which the young find irresistible in the leader of a lost cause. More compelling was a question to which history gives no answer. It had nagged at Sherwood's curiosity for years after he had been coerced at Milton into studying "the confusing history of the First, Second, and Third Punic Wars." Suddenly it plagued him again. Why had Hannibal, after his long trek from Spain, his crossing of the Alps, and his fifteen years of defeating Roman might in Italy and striking terror to Rome's heart, failed to move in for the kill when, following his victory at Cannae, the city lay within his grasp?

At Milton Sherwood had contemplated writing an epic on Hannibal, the length of which he had to admit was not determined by the greatness of his subject. A rival had submitted to the *Orange and Blue* an Arthurian epic four pages long. Sherwood's must be two pages longer, "quantity being our undebatable standard." Somehow Sherwood left his epic unwritten, and over the years the image of his hero naturally dimmed. That night at Sidney Howard's, however, with Mommsen open in his hands, his old curiosity and excitement seized him, and he asked Howard if he could borrow the book.

"What are you digging into Rome for?"

Sherwood was evasive in answering this tall, handsome Californian who was nearly five years his senior. He was very fond of Howard. Their spirits met. Lean and alert, with a boxer's bounce and an aviator's dash, Howard looked at life with unblinking gray eyes. Physical fear was a stranger to him. Everything about him spoke for strength and created confidence. His face, all amusement when he laughed, as he loved to do and did well, was formidable when his thin lips thinned and his pointed jaw shoved forward. No one had to glance at his hands to sense that they would clench into fists to fight for anything or anyone he believed in.

He and Sherwood had many bonds. Prosperous families interested in the arts. Harvard, where Howard had studied playwriting with Baker and Sherwood had taken Baker's courses in the history of the theatre. The war, in which Howard had served first as an ambulance driver on the Salonika front and then as a captain in an American bombing squadron in France. Illnesses, since Howard had spent a year in Switzerland because of a lung ailment. Disenchantment with the war, having seen it and the peace plain. *Life,* which Howard had left in a huff as a book reviewer within a year of Sherwood's becoming its movie critic. Love of the theatre. Journalism. Short-story writing. And Edward Sheldon's friendship.

Close as he was to Howard, Sherwood had a reason for being evasive with him that evening. Howard was a success in a profession in which Sherwood was not even a beginner. He was married then to the patrician and uncommonly gifted actress, Clare Eames, the niece of Emma Eames. He had had two plays in verse, *Swords* and *Bewitched* (the latter with Edward Sheldon), produced on Broadway, and several adaptations. In 1924 he had won the Pulitzer Prize with *They Knew What They Wanted,* which he had followed the next season with *Lucky Sam McCarver.* Moreover, the very year that he asked Sherwood, "What are you digging into Rome for?" he had sold *Ned McCobb's Daughter* and *The Silver Cord,* both of which, when produced within a month of each other by the Theatre Guild that fall, were to be highly respected hits. Understandably, Sherwood could not bring himself to tell Howard that he was thinking of writing a play and felt he might have found its subject in the hero of his youth. Instead, he muttered, "Short story." As he put it, "I wasn't going to get myself laughed at by admitting that I was soon to be numbered among the would-be playwrights of Broadway."

He took the Mommsen volume home and devoured it. Then he pored over a map tracing the course of Hannibal's great march. The more he thought about the Carthaginian the more absorbed he became in the question Hannibal had raised for him at school. Hungrily he sought an answer in other books, his reading ranging beyond Mommsen to Livy and Juvenal and Frazer, William O'Connor Morris, and Wells. Still the question, still no answer.

Sherwood refused to accept (he had Napoleon's authority for this) the claim of the Romans that Hannibal had been frightened and bluffed away by them or awed by portents from the gods. For fifteen years Hannibal had been doing the bluffing and the frightening, and he was, as Sherwood saw him, "unquestionably far too intelligent" to "have been diverted from his purpose by divine intervention." It seemed unthinkable to Sherwood to believe that a pompous politician like Fabius Maximus, or even a determined young fighter like Scipio, "could have wheedled him from the main object of his life's efforts." Why, then, did Hannibal refuse to listen to the pleas of his officers and march away from Rome when he was at the gates?

Sherwood's answer was a guess, and *The Road to Rome,* as he described it, his dramatization of that guess. It seemed possible to him that "Hannibal, after the battle of Cannae, was suddenly afflicted with an acute attack of introspection—that he paused to ask himself the devastating question, 'What of it?' and was unable to find an answer. In resolving this idea into a three-act play, I realized that I couldn't express it all in the form of a soliloquy by Hannibal; there would have to be a character to put these disturbing thoughts into Hannibal's mind. As there was no record that such a character existed at the time, I took it upon myself to invent one in Amytis, the purely fictitious wife of Fabius Maximus. *The Road to Rome,* therefore, has its principal being in the person of a character who did not exist."

To take on Hannibal successfully in Italy had been a task beyond the Romans' reach. That fact did not make it any easier for Sherwood to confront Hannibal as a dramatist. One figure in Mommsen came to his aid. It was Fabius the Roman Senator and newly elected Dictator, Fabius the Delayer, and Sherwood felt he caught his character almost at once. "What a boring existence his wife Amytis must have had!" he thought, she young, beautiful, born in Athens of a Greek mother, and strong in her dislike of the Roman virtues of her husband, who was always too tired for love but never for platitudes. Perhaps it was she who, fascinated by the fame of Hannibal, went forth and stopped him at the gates of Rome?

His comedy began to take shape in Sherwood's mind on his way to the movies which he had to review, during them, at *Life,* and when he could get away from the magazine. The first act would be in Fabius' home in a threatened Rome. The second and third acts would be in Hannibal's tent where Amytis would tempt Hannibal to spend the night with her. By persuading him to take her rather than Rome, she would have him prove to himself that he was not a machine but a man, a man who, in forswearing the conquest of a city so easily his, had found his true greatness and his soul.

To a very few friends Sherwood confided that he was planning to write a play. Among these was the Titian-haired Lewis ("Tish") Martin, his intimate at Milton, who had become an actor. One day Martin could not resist asking, "When are you going to start writing that play you've been talking about?"

"I am going to the Harvard Club next Tuesday afternoon," was Sherwood's reply. "Have dinner with Mary and me at our house that night and I'll read you the first act."

Martin arrived as requested, and after dinner Sherwood read the first act. At its conclusion Mary Brandon said, "It stinks." Undiscouraged because he was used to Mary, Sherwood invited Martin for dinner the next Tuesday. "I'm going to the Harvard Club that afternoon to write the second act." This time Mary Brandon thought better of the first act when she heard it read again with the second, though two hours was a long time for her to surrender the center of the stage.

The following weekend Sherwood went up to Stockbridge to stay with his mother and, while a cocktail party was going on, sat down at a desk in the corner of the room and wrote the third act. According to Martin, who appeared in the comedy as a Carthaginian corporal and, in Sherwood's phrase, "was present at the firing of the first gun in the Second Punic War," this was the way *The Road to Rome* got written.

A good story, made the better by seeming to limit the writing time to three afternoons, Martin's version was in essence accurate. Sherwood *did*, when possible, take his afternoons off from *Life* to dig in at the Harvard Club. Martin *did* hear each act as it was finished. And, in the midst of other tasks, Sherwood *did* dash off the play in three weeks and in a form so final that only a few alterations were made during rehearsals.

His power of concentration was dismaying, and so was the speed with which he wrote. What made his pauses as a conversationalist frequent and formidable was the very thing that made him write with ease. He liked to know what he was going to say before he spoke and, by the time he formed his thoughts, the talk had raced on to other topics and he was discussing a station two stops back when still another station had come into view. When he sat down to write, he usually knew with floodlight clarity what he was going to write and his hand moved swiftly as it took the fluent dictation of his mind.

He sent the manuscript off to be typed and, when it came back, left a copy of it, with an apprehension he was never to forget, at the Sutton Place home of Elisabeth Marbury. Miss Marbury, rotunda-round but with a dynamo's drive, was one of the best of agents and Sherwood shared the common respect for her judgment. His agony of waiting for her opinion was short. She read the play that night—read it three times in fact—and called the next day to tell him of her enthusiasm.

Selling the play brought its early discouragements. Sherwood, an ardent admirer of the Lunts, had them in mind when he wrote his Hannibal and Amytis. Having them in mind was to become a habit with him, as fortunate from their point of view as his. Although they shared Miss Marbury's enthusiasm for the script, knowing how suited it was to their gifts, the Theatre Guild, under whose management they then were, turned it down. Gilbert Miller rejected it, too, with the comment, "I don't like even *first-rate* Shaw," and the Shuberts took an option which they dropped. Then, when things looked darkest, they brightened. Two young producers, William A. Brady, Jr., and Dwight Deere Wiman, bought the play, and gave it a fine, resourceful production with Jane Cowl as Amytis, lilting, lovely, and not a little coy, her hands fluttering around her mouth like doves around a cote; with Philip Merivale magnificent in the tired strength of his Hannibal, and Barry Jones uproarious as the general's younger brother who, against his will, was serving as keeper of the elephants.

After three weeks of rehearsal *The Road to Rome* company headed for its Washington tryout, all hope and nerves, and Sherwood went with it in the same condition. As his train pulled out of the Caracallan grandeurs of the Pennsylvania Station he was no more concerned with what was going on in the White House than Calvin Coolidge was with what would go on at the Belasco. He chuckled, however, as he stuffed into his overcoat pocket the farewell present which Paul Hollister, his friend from Harvard and New Rochelle,

handed him unwrapped. It was a standard shaving mug on which
Hollister had had reproduced his corny drawing of a signpost with
four indices all pointing to different roads and reading "Rome."

Act by act, the first performance in the city of American Fabiuses
was plainly a success, and after the curtain calls many surged backstage with congratulations. When they cleared out, someone thought
of a drink. Only a bottle of rum was available and no paper cups or
even grimy tumblers could be found. Sherwood had an inspiration.
Remembering the shaving mug, he hauled it out from his overcoat
pocket. For one and all it served as a flowing bowl which did run
over.

What was meant as a gag suddenly became for Sherwood a mas-
cot, a bringer of luck, a portent, and the beginning of a first-night
ritual. From then on, in the long years ahead, Hollister's ingenuity
and friendship (both large) were tested by his having to think up a
new mug for each Sherwood opening. Sherwood became so fond of
these mugs that he took most of them to England with him after he
bought a house in Surrey. One night there he and Mary Brandon
descended to the dangerous game of saying honestly what each of
them would save first in case of fire. Her jewelry was Mary Brandon's choice; her difficulty was deciding which of the best pieces
she had persuaded him to give her she would rescue. When Mary
Brandon, thinking he would name her, asked him what he would
save, his immediate reply was, "My mugs." What is more, as he later
told Hollister, by this time he meant it.

After a decade of playwriting Sherwood was to remember his
Washington notices as being the best he had ever received and recall
them with that blur of pleasure which time brings to praise. If his
memories of his New York notices two weeks later were more vivid,
it was because a few of them were so bad that in retrospect they all
seemed "bitterly disappointing." The severity of the bad ones mysti-
fied him, as the audience at the Playhouse that last night in January,
1927, had been uncommonly responsive. The applause was vigorous,
the laughter continuous, Miss Cowl and Merivale took numerous
curtain calls, and there were heartening cries of "Author!" "Author!"
although Sherwood did not appear.

Actually, the next day's notices were "mixed." Most were favorable, even those tepidly so. The *World's* was a rave. In it Woollcott saluted *The Road to Rome* as "wise and lofty and searching and good," and said that, as a drama inspired by the war, it belonged "side by side" with *What Price Glory?* However, as is the way with authors, including critics turned authors, it was the bad reviews, with their savagery and condescension, which stuck in Sherwood's mind.

As the decades slipped by and he outgrew *The Road to Rome*, Sherwood's own enthusiasm for it cooled. In his *There Shall Be No Night* preface he dismissed it by saying that anyone who remembered it in 1940 remembered it principally for one line near the end of the last act. The line was Hannibal's and spoken by him when Fabius, having come with a delegation to the Carthaginian's tent to sue for peace, found Amytis there, not knowing she had already achieved his purpose by spending the previous night in Hannibal's arms. "Fabius," says Hannibal when he is about to turn his troops away from Rome, "I wish happiness and prosperity to you, your wife, and your sons." "Thank you," replies Fabius, "but I have no sons." Hannibal's answer is, "You may have."

The Road to Rome invited recollection for more reasons than that capping line, so typical of its other innuendoes. Critics have a relish for identifying the fingerprints of a followed example. With them (as well I know) this is at once a compulsion, a flexing of knowledge, and a quick way of suggesting the style and manner of the work at hand, it being so much easier to say what something is like than to say what it is. *The Road to Rome* provided the reviewers with a precedent-hunters' field day by its irreverent handling of history and its use of modern attitudes and colloquialisms in dealing with antiquity. Sherwood, according to Behrman, came to regret the means he had used in his comedy. Once in the forties when he spoke of the play slightingly, someone asked him why he was so hard on his first hit. "Because," said he, abandoning his earlier defense of his methods, "it employs the cheapest sort of device—making historical characters use modern slang."

The critics were quick to point out that in taking his liberties with the past he was in good and numerous company. Landor's *Imaginary Conversations* and his letters to Pericles and Aspasia, Anatole France's *The Revolt of the Angels*, Andreyev's *The Sabine Women*,

Maurice Baring's *Diminutive Dramas,* Philip Moeller's *Helena's Husband,* John Erskine's *The Private Life of Helen of Troy,* and, above all, Shaw were used to take reckonings even in the most favorable of the reviews.

Although he admired Shaw greatly, Sherwood became worn down by the point, made again and again, that he had borrowed Shaw's method without having his mind to sustain it. "Shaw in short pants," said in a variety of ways, were hard words to swallow. In his preface to the play he not only defended himself against the charges of imitating Shaw or anyone else, but insisted that he was following—as indeed he was—the disrespectful attitude both past and present which was very much in the spirit of the defrocking twenties.

Deliberately, he had his Carthaginian Expeditionary Force talk the soldier talk of *What Price Glory?* which Sherwood himself had known in The Black Watch. He did not hesitate to have one of Hannibal's privates say, "I don't do no turn with no elephants, see?" This was his way, his *Life* and still Hasty Pudding way, of establishing in his audiences a sense of the nearness of the remote. In his opinion his use of modern colloquialisms in classic dress no more indicated that he had imitated Shaw than introducing a seduction scene would mean that he had imitated Elinor Glyn.

For Sherwood *The Road to Rome* was not only a welcome ally in his battle against the two mortgages but a successful entrance to a new career. Audiences flocked to it, relishing its performances, delighted by the flippancy with which it dealt with history, smirking at its audacities, and roaring at its togaed versions of contemporary speech. During its long run, however, no audience was ever closer to its humor than the one for which Sherwood arranged a special matinee and at which he spoke briefly from a moved heart. The audience was made up of a large detachment from The Black Watch which had come down from Canada to march in full regalia in the Memorial Day parade. These Highlanders were at home with Sherwood's kilted Carthaginians. They were messmates in their attitudes and slang, and howled with particular glee at Hannibal's tough Sergeant of the Guard, modeled as he was on a warrant officer in the 42nd who happened to be in the theatre that day.

Many playgoers preferred to overlook the comedy's deeper reachings, or at best put up with them. Their search was for laughter and romance, with both of which it provided them bounteously. At its core there was more to *The Road to Rome* than that. This became manifest after the first act when, regardless of the questions he left unanswered, Sherwood changed his manner. Possessed by the largeness of his concerns, he began to write with the smooth-flowing, simple clarity which was later to distinguish his best dialogue and endow it with a cadence, style, and eloquence very much his own.

The Road to Rome was, as Charles Brackett described it in *The New Yorker*, "a hymn of hate against militarism—disguised, ever so gaily, as a love song." It was Sherwood's first sustained public antiwar statement, written from the deepening disillusionment which the peace had brought him. Although his subject seemed to be an enthralled leader, a lightheaded charmer, and brazen coquetry or sacrificial adultery, his title could have been *What Price Glory?* as Woollcott noted. Through Amytis he was seeking to point out, in terms however smiling, the futility of battle and that "every sacrifice made in the name of war is wasted." His Hannibal was a genius unable to explain to himself why he fought or to find a reason for the countless deaths his conquests had caused.

The Road to Rome was Sherwood's first contrast between the idealism and love of beauty of the Greeks and the success worship of the Romans. His case against Rome was weakened because his Rome was weak and his Hannibal strong, his defense of Greece enfeebled because his Amytis was foolish. Even so, he was grasping for a theme which was to be a favorite with him. To most theatregoers his comedy was a spoof on Rome; to Sherwood it was an oblique attack on America. He, like many another, saw a "deadly and disturbing" parallel between the materialism of ancient Rome and Coolidge's America. His fear was that the Roman faults rather than the Roman virtues were in the ascendant in this country, his hope that audiences would recognize the similarities between our gogetters and his antique Romans, and come to question their efforts and their values.

It was typical of him that, having taken his legitimate liberties with facts in his play, he should feel obliged "to do the right thing by history" in his preface. The tugs within him were always many, and just then the historian was beginning to emerge with the dramatist. For thirty-one of the thirty-eight pages of his able and informative preface it was the historian who took over, and Sherwood was as grave as only he could be in his approach to gaiety.

With almost undeviating earnestness he devoted himself to explaining the rivalry of Carthage and Rome, untangling the complexities of the Punic Wars, and following the "magnificently eventful life" which Hannibal lived "in vain" from its beginnings to its tragic end in Bithynia when, still hounded by the Romans twenty years after he had left Italy and about to be betrayed, he opened the seal ring he always carried and took from it the poison with which he killed himself.

One bit of drama occurred on the opening night of *The Road to Rome* which was unseen by the audience. Like the comedy's success, it gave great pleasure to Sherwood's friends at the Algonquin. It, too, was a hit that he scored, but it had to do not with Rome but with Mary Brandon. According to the version of the story most widely told, she arrived at the Playhouse, a cluster of orchids, and took her seat in the second or third row while he paced up and down at the back of the theatre. She was all assurance, Sherwood all nerves. She did not mind being conspicuous, his wish (though the odds were against him) was to be invisible. Unable to endure the agony, he stole out soon after the curtain went up to find peace and courage in a nearby speakeasy, where he sipped out his ordeal.

He returned to the theatre at the end of the performance, elated to hear the applause and wise not to heed the calls for "Author! Author!" He lumbered down the aisle to Mary Brandon to take her back to congratulate the cast. His success had not gone to her head. Her mood, to put it mildly, was ruffled. The play had been his, but she saw to it that the next scene was hers.

For such a little person she began, at the sight of him, to make a very big noise. "Where have you been?" she started screaming. "In a bar? You're drunk!" Somehow Sherwood got her and himself backstage and into Jane Cowl's dressing room. There, when he gave the beautiful Miss Cowl a grateful kiss, Mary Brandon's screams grew in volume. Mortified and angered, Sherwood reached down for Mary's orchids, snatched them from her dress, and handed them to Miss

Cowl. As he bowed his apologies to her, he made a wide gesture with his windmill arms and Mary Brandon, who happened to be in the way of one of them, toppled to the floor.

Some say that at a party later that evening Sherwood achieved the same result with the same provocation but without the same innocence. Mary by then had changed her role. Sensing the play's success, she now wanted to be part of it and from virago turned loyal wife. One witness recalls that she sidled up to Sherwood in front of everyone to proclaim, "Bob, I always knew it would succeed." This playacting of hers was more than he in his condition could stand. "Don't be such a god-damned liar!" he snarled and, stepping completely out of character, struck her.

All agree that, when the stories of his other hits got around, Sherwood was for the next month the hero of the Algonquin and was deluged with congratulations in person or by telegram from most of the Tablers. Among them Mary Brandon was no heroine. As Sherwood remembered the evening a decade later, it was "a disgraceful performance, especially by me." Even so, there were those ready to cheer him.

17

MARY, QUITE CONTRARY

The Incredible Mary Brandon—Her Self-Absorption and Unfortunate Talent for Scenes—"What Did You Bring Me, Bobby Dear?"—Their Good Times—Geoffrey Kerr Describes Christmas with the Sherwoods—Overdrafts on His Fortitude—Her Spending Forces Him to Earn—Sherwood on What It Takes to Make a Playwright

Considering Mary Brandon, the wonder was not that Sherwood divorced her but that he remained married to her for twelve years. They were strange, bitter-sweet years, those years between 1922 and 1934. Sweetened for him by his productivity, his mounting success and the glamorous life it brought him here and abroad, and by his daughter Mary, his family and friends, they were made bitter by Mary Brandon. To their end these years continued to hold for him their palliative pleasures which were many and varied. But it soon became clear, even to Sherwood, that almost all of these pleasures existed in spite of Mary Brandon rather than because of her.

The storm warnings were not long in going up. Within a few months of their marriage Sherwood appeared one morning at Mary's father's office to say, as Mr. Brandon told the story, "I've always had bad luck in picking roommates and now I'm afraid I was a poor picker in my wife." This was when Mary Brandon and he were living in a tiny apartment at 71 West 12th Street, which Rosina described as being "very pretty and filled with new furniture and wedding loot."

When they moved uptown to a charming little house, only twelve and a half feet wide, at 153 East 71st Street, they were followed there by tensions which mounted and ructions which multiplied. The reason for their increase was not that as a young wife

Mary Brandon found herself swamped in a sea of in-laws. To be sure, Rosina and Rosamond lived across the street, the Townsends were a block down, and Aunt Lydia and the young Arthur Sherwoods had apartments in the same building on 70th. This was Emmetry indeed, but it had no effect on Mary Brandon. She was beyond being swamped, and almost beyond being touched. In her withholding way she liked the Emmets, and her frequent pleasure was to have the whole populous clan for dinner. As for the Emmets, they, being family-minded and affectionate, did their loyal best to like Mary Brandon, and at the outset Rosina even persuaded herself that she did.

The trouble was Mary Brandon. Born to be a trouble to herself, and to almost everyone else, she more than fulfilled her fate. Her talent for failing others was part of her genius for failing herself. Small as a doll at the base of a Christmas tree when she stood beside Sherwood, she seemed as guileless as one, and was as pretty. Although she had no moral sense, she had a look of pert innocence. With her dimples, her dark bright eyes, her child's complexion, her pleasant voice, and the interest in others which she was able to simulate, she had the power in those years to charm almost anyone for a while, especially during a first meeting. Her facility in building people up was one of her more successful deceptions because building herself up was her obsession. At times she could be the greatest fun, but the delight she could give she could not sustain. She loved to entertain, in part because she hated being alone, yet her gift for giving good parties was counteracted by her ability to ruin them by the "acts" which she put on.

The spotlight was to Mary Brandon what the sun is to an invalid. She could affirm her existence only by winning attention for herself and she was unable to relate herself to other people. The separation was total from what she was and what she thought she was. She was sure that she was happy and convinced she was enticing. Her life was a lie told to herself, in the truth of which she believed; her "scenes" were proofs to her of her reality. Money was one of the few facts she faced. Sherwood's money, not hers. She assumed his and saved her own. She knew more than most about the number of pennies in a dollar, and seldom parted with one of hers.

If her detractors were plentiful and her defenders few, one reason was her habit, whenever possible, of turning everything she did into a production of which she was the star. None of her productions caused more annoyance among her already annoyed familiars at the Round Table than Mary Brandon's one venture in maternity. This was a year after her marriage when she gave birth with the aid of a Caesarean to a daughter, Mary, and provoked one of Dorothy Parker's best known lines.

Long after the daughter's advent Woollcott remembered her coming. "It seemed to some of us," he wrote, "that she was forever being born. For months the whole town had been kept uneasily aware of her approach. For months the little mother had filled the public eye with a kind of aggressive fragility." At first nights Mary Brandon would "pointedly rise" and "conspicuously leave the theatre whenever the play became too intense for one in her assiduously delicate condition." Things grew so portentous that Marc Connelly at one point took her aside "on behalf of the exhausted neighborhood" and "gravely advised her to drop the whole project." At last the news of little Mary's arrival reached the Algonquin and telegrams of relief and congratulation poured in from all directions. Mrs. Parker's perennially quoted wire said, "Good work, Mary. We all knew you had it in you," and was sent collect.

Another role which Mary Brandon relished was that of "Wife of a Distinguished Broadway Figure." It was part of the "image life" in which she indulged, and she had notions of her own as to what the role entailed. They were not self-denying. They meant that, in fairness to Sherwood, she must dress well, live well, entertain well, and glitter with good jewelry.

Sherwood's increasing success obliged her, as she saw it, to increase her self-indulgence. When he became recognized as a playwright, though she showed scant interest in hearing about his plays, she enjoyed her own enhanced importance as a playwright's wife. Typical of her attitude was her behavior one night when Roger Burlingame and a group of Sherwood's friends were sitting around waiting with Mary for Sherwood to bring them news of a manager's decision about *The Road to Rome*. When he did arrive and started his story, Mary Brandon interrupted almost at once to send him downstairs to get her a glass of water. The scene had been hers as literary hostess and he had stolen it, which was more than she could bear. He had spoiled her party, and parties were her realities. She had to have people around her and found in them what she was unable to find in herself. She needed them so deeply in her dodging of life that during the long twelve years of their marriage she was rarely willing to dine with Sherwood alone.

Her almost daily greeting to him when he came home was, "What did you bring me, Bobby dear?" Once in a shop window she saw two pear-shaped blue vases traced with silver. Coveting them with her usual passion for things, she begged him to give them to her. When he explained that he could not afford them, she cried and stormed so that the next day he bought them—and peace, too. Sherwood's friends realized her shortcomings sooner than he did and for his sake tried to put up with them. But Woollcott, whose tongue was sharp and patience short, once found himself driven beyond his slim control. "Mary," he said, "I've decided to write a play about you." "How wonderful," she cried. "Yes," he added, "and I've even decided on the title. It's to be called *The White Man's Burden* or *Bob Sherwood's Cross*."

Mary Brandon was a burden and became a cross. She was not exactly a help when he tried to work at home and she would knock on the door, saying, "You've been in there fifty-five minutes! Don't you love me any more?" Naturally he retreated to *Life* or the Harvard Club to get his writing done. In the early days he was entertained by her and found some pleasure in her cruelty. "Kinda enjoy a little spitfire," he would drawl, his mouth twisted in a smile. He was amused, too, at the outset by her lack of knowledge about matters unrelated to her own interests. To him it was drolly cute, a part of her attractive girlishness. He laughed when soon after their marriage she came to him and said, "I want to ask you a question. Now promise me you won't think me stupid. I just want to ask you how and what is Lenin and Trotsky." This was flapperdom come true, as was the time when, according to F.P.A., she confessed to Sherwood that she thought the Riviera was a street in Paris, and he said, "You don't really think so, do you?" and she replied, "No, I know it is a big store."

Neither he nor anyone else found anything except horror in her performance one night at a party when she was tight and got mad at Sherwood and stood up on a chair beside him so that she could hit him in the face. Nonetheless, Sherwood loved her at the start, and to the end she loved him as much as she was capable of loving anyone else. More than being pretty, she could be companionable and had her talents as a sorceress, even if the magic at which she excelled was really bitchcraft. But, difficult as she was and disastrous as was her personality, Sherwood put up with her with the same fortitude with which Lincoln put up with Mary Todd.

During their first years they seemed so happy that Woollcott, a bachelor, sneered at Sherwood as one who "unfortunately became extremely married." This was because he had dropped out of the Thanatopsis Club, preferring to spend those evenings with Mary Brandon, which was another form of gambling and one at which he lost. The bad times she gave him soon routed the initial illusions of bliss eternal and came with increasing frequency. Yet even after she had chilled his love and lost it, and when, though they continued to live and move as a couple, he found himself more and more alone in her company, Sherwood did have his good times with Mary Brandon.

They came fitfully, these good times, were sudden and brief, and the intervals between them grew until they did not come at all. They came because of Sherwood's eagerness to believe that they were always there and because of Mary Brandon's unpredictable lapses into charm. They came because, though he lived with the ugly facts of their marriage, Sherwood sought to dodge these, being, as he put it, "always hopeful of escaping the inevitable." They came when he and she traveled abroad or to Hollywood with their daughter Mary, and Mary Brandon could play the role of "Visiting Playwright's Wife." They came at home at parties where she could act "Hostess," though in both parts she often blew up in her lines. Above all, they came at the family gatherings with which the Sherwoods celebrated Christmas, because at them Mary Brandon, tiny as Tim, tried her frail best to be on her good behavior by playing her Park Avenue version of Mrs. Cratchit.

Old Thomas Addis Emmet, who loved "the bustle of company" in his house, would have felt at home at these family gatherings. So

would those other early Emmets who more than a century before had
crowded into his living room to talk, eat, and drink, to sing and play
the fiddle or the clavichord, and to amuse themselves with cards and
other games. The spirit remained the same, and neither Prohibition
nor Mary Brandon could parch it. They were huge parties, made the
larger by the inclusion of a few friends who seemed like family. They
buzzed with happiness, were enlivened by songs and stunts, and
crowded with people, young and old, who in the presence of the
lighted tree became one age, eager to have fun and ready to provide it.

Rosina, lean and patrician, was, of course, a pivotal feature, and,
though by then in her early seventies, was among the youngest
present. Laughing, eager, and vital, she held court at the same time
that she was the best of audiences, with her ear trumpet twisting
snakelike toward every center of interest. Aunt Lydia, percolating
vivacity, was also there. And Sherwood's brother Arthur and his wife
and children. And his sister, the lovely Cynthia Townsend, with her
husband and children. And all Sherwoods and Emmets who were
able to make it. Essential to the evening's gaiety was Rosamond
because of her amazing gift for playing by ear on the piano or the
accordion any tune that might be called for. These included all the
songs from *Barnum Was Right* which Sherwood, invited to do so or
not, was sure to sing with ferocious intensity, beating the time with a
giant foot that pounded like a drum.

The size of these Christmas Eve parties was guaranteed by the
magnitude of the family, their meticulous planning by Sherwood who
took Christmas with the seriousness with which he took all festivities
and fun. As a sentimentalist, his love for it was special. He approached it not only as if he believed in Santa Claus but as if he
were Santa Claus, and, since the act of giving gave him deep pleasure, Mary Brandon also found the day pleasant. He was no last-
minute shopper. Christmas was on his mind for weeks before its
coming. He spent days looking for presents certain to be right and
hours trimming the tree and decorating the house. According to
Geoffrey Kerr, no Fifth Avenue shop window was ever dressed with
such a painstaking attention to detail as the Sherwood Christmas
tree, and none was ever lovelier.

Kerr's knowledge was firsthand because he and June Walker, to whom he was then married, were among the outsiders enfolded in the family at these parties. June Walker, the diminutive actress with heartbreak in her voice, who was well known for her work in John Howard Lawson's *Processional* and Molnar's *The Glass Slipper* and was to play in Sherwood's *The Love Nest* and *Waterloo Bridge*, was Mary Brandon's intimate. And Geoffrey Kerr, the young English author and actor who had succeeded in many Broadway comedies such as Philip Barry's *You and I*, A. E. Thomas's *Just Suppose*, and as a rich playboy in Sherwood's *This Is New York*, had become and was to remain one of Sherwood's closest friends. As couples, the Sherwoods and the Kerrs were so close in those days that, when possible, they dined back and forth with each other at least twice a week.

A high point of the Christmas Eve celebrations came when Sherwood and his young nephew Jim Townsend, then in his teens, gravely danced and sang as always "The Red, Red Robin." Another was when Kerr would take over, at Sherwood's urging, and do card tricks. The third was Sherwood's passing of the punch. This was an ordeal in suspense which Kerr never forgot. Soon after dinner Sherwood would descend to the basement and be gone for a long time. Eventually he would reappear, his lengthy arms spread wide, carrying a tray crammed with glasses of punch. Although the times were numberless that he had made the punch, he always was zealous in sampling it downstairs to be comfortably sure that it was up to standard.

His entry with a second brew at about three o'clock in the morning was nerve-racking. Would he, could he, possibly make it up the narrow stairs? Apparently he always did, and each year his doing so, without spilling either the punch or himself, was a miracle. The evenings were late and so were the breakfasts the next morning when everyone reassembled and presents were exchanged while the kids prattled and some of their elders nursed their hangovers. These Christmases, being truly merry, were interludes which meant much to Sherwood. The only trouble with them from his point of view was that they did not come often enough or last as long as he would have liked.

Between Christmases there was always Mary Brandon, more often

for worse than for better. Occasionally he asserted himself decisively
as he did when in London she balked at going down an escalator in
the Underground. "I won't, Bobby, I won't," she cried until he
grabbed her firmly and lifted her onto it with a "Yes, you will." Or
there was that crisis very late one night at a party in New York
when she refused to go home, and he picked her up, tucked her under
his arm, and went around the room saying, "Good night. I've had a
very nice time." Mary Brandon kicked and screamed, of course, but
he patted her gently on the head and said, "Shut up, Mary," while
continuing his good-byes.

Lifting Mary Brandon was as easy as lifting a doll, but carrying
her day in and day out year after year was another matter. Sherwood
tried to lighten the load by placating her, hoping for peace, acting as
if he had it, and doing his best to make the best of the abundant
happiness he had, regardless of Mary, with his friends, his career, his
trips, his mode of life, and in watching the growth of his daughter
Mary. His relationship with Mary Brandon meant for Sherwood
being with her but without her, having her painfully present at times
and painfully absent, though present most of the time. It meant
traveling with her with friends to whom he had to turn for true
companionship. As he became increasingly aware, it meant not
shared pleasure, but joint solitude threatened always by possible
turbulence.

The changes in Sherwood's feelings for Mary Brandon could not
be guessed at from his dedications to her of his five plays published
during their marriage. These dedications scarcely tapped his heart or
taxed his ingenuity. "To My Wife" each of them said as if printed
from a stencil, and each was accurate as a statement of fact, though
their precision ended there. Sherwood's feelings for Mary Brandon
had changed even before the first of his plays was published. He
was forced to admit this to himself and in time most of his friends
sensed the change almost with relief. All too soon he discovered that,
instead of loving her, he was enduring her. He continued to do this
with patience, humor, kindness, and hope until he at last found her
unendurable.

Looking back on his life with Mary Brandon in the spring of 1938
at a moment when he was feeling depressed, nervous, and exhausted,

he wrote in his diary, "Perhaps in the years from 1922-34 a large part of me was burnt out, and with what's left I'm capable of doing a small amount of work and nothing more." This was not to prove true. He had a great deal of work left in him, and some of it his best. But such were the bruises left by those years with Mary Brandon and his final decision to leave her that to the same entry he added, "It's encouraging to reflect that I felt far more despondent, more sterile in 1932-33."

Mary Brandon's overdrafts on his fortitude were emotionally impoverishing. Yet, impossible as she was, in certain respects she was good for Sherwood in her bad way. Although as a writer he made his understanding of character clear, as a man he was inclined to think in terms of humanity rather than humans. People loved him, admired him, and huddled around him, but he found it hard to get close to them. No man was ever more widely cherished by those who had to admit that, though they had known him long and intimately and prized his friendship, they never quite felt they knew him well. He had pity and love, loyalty and kindness, gaiety and strength to give, and he gave of these unstintingly. At the same time he could make others ill at ease, not because of any lack of manners or warmth on his part but because he often seemed ill at ease himself.

Due to his shyness and because of the slowness of his speech, the boldness of his pauses, his want of the small change of conversation, and his habit of abruptly withdrawing into himself, he often had his difficulties reaching other people and made it difficult for them to reach him. Eloquent as he was in the presence of an audience, he could develop the emotional equivalent of a stammer when confronted with an individual. Mary Brandon was an individual who saw to it that he did not ignore her. She was once likened to the tree that falls in the forest without making a noise unless someone is present to hear it. She was always making some kind of noise to call attention to herself, and Sherwood's fate for those twelve years was to be present and hear it.

Her demands were many and insistent, and silence was not a weapon she employed to get her way. She wanted money and what money bought and goaded him into making it. He was extravagant, she was more so. He tried to keep his checkbook but could not; she did not try to keep their expenses down. He liked the life she liked to live, and she saw to it that he worked so that they could live it. A governess for little Mary, an attractive home in New York with two servants, pretty clothes, jewelry, parties, incessant entertaining at restaurants, large tips to win smiles, trips abroad with an entourage, charming houses rented in London, in the English countryside, and at Montreuil-sur-Mer, cars and chauffeurs to meet them, the best of suites at the Beverly Hills Hotel, a home in Hollywood complete with swimming pool, and finally the purchase of Great Enton, Sherwood's lovely country place in Surrey—all these, after *The Road to Rome*, were part of his enjoyment and her demanding. Before then, when they were in debt, she did not hesitate to live as if they were not.

Fortunately, his gifts were the equal of his needs. His productivity was immense, his facility uncommon, and his resilience such that, in spite of battles with sinus and other ailments, it enabled him to survive both Mary Brandon and the peripheral work which mainly because of her had to be done. Without meaning to do so, she performed a service for him. By temperament Sherwood could easily have played with the arts in his father's fashion, had it not been for Mary Brandon. Her ability to spend made it imperative for him to earn. The necessity with which she confronted him was at least in part the stepmother of some of his invention. She dislodged the dilettante in him and drove him into becoming a professional.

He was not long in discovering the special endowments which in his opinion a playwright must have. "To be able to write a play, for performance in a theatre," he wrote, "a man must be sensitive, imaginative, naïve, gullible, passionate; he must be something of an imbecile, something of a poet, something of a liar, something of a damn fool. He must be a chaser of wild geese, as well as of wild ducks. He must be prepared to make a public spectacle of himself. He must be independent and brave, and sure of himself and of the importance of his work; because if he isn't, he will never survive the scorching blasts of derision that will probably greet his first efforts."

That was in 1928 in his preface to *The Queen's Husband*. Twenty-one years later in the *Saturday Review* he stood by those words, noting with amusement that during the Second World War in his OWI days they had been used against him on the enemy radio.

Someone in the Japanese propaganda ministry picked them up, twisted them patriotically, and referred to Sherwood as an American propagandist "who once admitted that he was something of an imbecile, something of a liar, something of a damn fool." This apparently went over so big in Japan that to Sherwood's delight Goebbels also used it in Germany.

18

PLAYWRIGHT IN THE TWENTIES

Sherwood's Ten Favorite Modern Plays—The Complex Twenties—High Points in Fiction and the Theatre—A Latecomer in a Crowded Field—Disillusioned but No Debunker—"The Muse That Wears a Green Eye-Shade"—A Lusty Romantic—Champion of Hokum and Defender of a Painted Moon

When with *The Road to Rome* Sherwood at thirty first faced the hazards of being a professional playwright, the twenties were within a little less than three years of coming to their end, not with a bang but with a crash. In the theatre, however, the decade began and ended with a bang, since it started with *Beyond the Horizon*, the first display uptown of the brooding, fearless genius of Eugene O'Neill, and concluded with *The Green Pastures*, that heavenly fish fry in which a Negro Lawd walked "de earth in de shape of a natchel man" and Marc Connelly (with Roark Bradford's aid) wrote a miracle play which in itself was something of a miracle.

Both plays were among the ten modern "favorites" which Sherwood listed for Ward Morehouse in the *Sun* in 1934. The others were *The Playboy of the Western World*, Eva Le Gallienne's version of *Alice in Wonderland*, *Yellow Jack* by Sidney Howard with Paul de Kruif, Somerset Maugham's *The Circle*, *What Price Glory?*, *The Wisdom Tooth* (also by Connelly), *Journey's End*, and *Show Boat*. Significantly, all of these except the first three were products of the twenties.

As is the way with decades, the twenties were many times at one and the same time. Certainly they were to Sherwood. Though he participated happily in the fun they offered and enjoyed their frivolities, he was appalled by their excesses. No wonder. The twenties in America were the years of flaming youth, flapperdom, and the Charleston; the roaring wet-dry years of Prohibition, of bathtub gin, the flask, the speakeasy, and bootleg "hooch," when the whole country seemed to have gone on a spree. They were the years of Al Capone and gangsterdom, when the Volstead Act was an invitation to lawlessness. They were the years of Harding's "normalcy" and the Coolidge boom; the years when the first Henry Ford was making automobile history by selling Model T's for $310. They were the years, too, according to Sherwood, of "the preposterous High Priests of Babbittry" and of "the arrogant ignorance [and] the Bourbonesque insensitivity of many of our leaders, political and industrial."

They were the long, humiliating years of the Sacco-Vanzetti agony and of "the Big Red Scare" when Communists, known as "Bolshies," were represented in cartoons as bearded and carrying bombs. They were the shameful years when the Ku Klux Klan rode again for a while; the crazy years of dance marathons, flagpole sitting, and such a sorry sideshow of bigotry tangling with enlightenment as the Scopes trial. They were the years when sensation lovers gorged themselves on such an old man-young girl sex orgy as "Daddy" Browning's pursuit of "Peaches," and on the Hall-Mills, Loeb-Leopold, and Snyder-Gray murder cases. They were the decade darkened by such a national scandal as the Teapot Dome and brightened by finding in Lindbergh a sorely needed national hero.

The twenties were all these things and many more just as crass and just as foolish. Although it took time for him to do so, Sherwood later saw that their character could not be caught in a catalogue of their faults and absurdities. He never denied, because no one could, that they were "one of the most sordid of periods," and confessed that one of his reasons for writing his first plays was to escape from that sordidness. But when, in the general "gloom" which he felt about the twenties, he condemned even their theatre as being "dismal," he came to see—and say—two decades later that he was "just plain silly."

By then he recognized that the twenties had their high points as well as their low, and that in the arts, particularly in literature and the drama, these high points were very high indeed. Sinclair Lewis,

Fitzgerald, Hemingway, Willa Cather, Ellen Glasgow, Sherwood
Anderson, Wilder, Wolfe, Stephen Vincent Benét, Frost, Pound, and
Eliot were among the Americans who in prose and poetry were the
shadow-casters. As for the theatre in this country, it was in what
proved to be its golden age. In the midst of its abundance Sherwood,
like everyone else, took its productivity for granted, assuming also
that it would continue. When it did not and a marked shrinkage
occurred in the decades ahead, Sherwood looked back on that theatre
with unabashed nostalgia, saluting it as being "a wonderfully exciting
place in which to work and to progress . . . as wide open as a virgin
continent, and as teeming with chances of adventure and fortune."

It was a theatre ignited by new impulses and as yet unmenaced by
the talkies and television, a theatre which on many memorable evenings became "the dwelling place of wonder" that Sherwood thought
the theatre should be. Its aims were high, its costs low, and happily
its offerings were not condemned to being flops because they had
failed to be hits. Its lower-priced economy enabled moderate successes to survive. This is one reason why it bubbled with activity,
averaging 225 productions a year in the ten-year interval and reaching 268 in the peak season of 1927-28.

Its diversity was a part of its health and a proof of its strength.
There was room in it for Ann Pennington's knees and John Barrymore's genius, room for the comedies of Kaufman and Connelly
and the tragedies of Eugene O'Neill, and room for such pioneers as
Winthrop Ames, Arthur Hopkins, the Provincetown Playhouse, and
the Theatre Guild as well as such routineers as the Brothers Shubert
and Al Woods. The Broadway that had venerated David Belasco and
suffered *Abie's Irish Rose* gladly for five years had not died by any
means but it had met its determined challengers. A different kind of
theatre, astir with fresh talents and aiming at new goals, was fighting
for its place in the spotlight, and the excitement of its arrival was in
the air.

In this theatre the American dramatist had achieved a prominence
which had not previously been his and what he had to say for himself
mattered as much as the actor to whom he had given something to
say. As Sherwood noted, "the ancient and frequently vulnerable
theory that a play that was 'arty' could never get by in the box office

was forever discarded." As proof of this he cited the success of *John Ferguson, Beyond the Horizon, Liliom, Anna Christie, Saint Joan, The Show-Off, Beggar on Horseback, What Price Glory?* and *They Knew What They Wanted.* He could have named dozens of others.

When Sherwood entered this teeming theatre, he came as a late-comer on a crowded field. By 1927 all of his friends and acquaintances were writing plays or had written them—Kaufman and Connelly, Sidney Howard, Philip Barry, Edna Ferber, Edward Sheldon, Stallings and Anderson, Elmer Rice, S. N. Behrman, George Kelly, John Howard Lawson, George Abbott, Paul Green, Ben Hecht, Charles MacArthur, and so many others that, according to Arthur Hopkins, you could ask the postman, "How's your second act?" and he would tell you.

Sherwood's turning playwright was part of his immersion in the twenties, and few people were more immersed in them than he. After his first plunge on *Vanity Fair* into what they were to be, he swam midstream in those currents which became part of their legend. As *Life's* motion-picture critic and editor, as a regular first-nighter, as Will Rogers's campaign manager, with his intimates at the Algonquin and the Thanatopsis Club, on lively weekends with the Swopes or the Harrimans, and as a party boy equally at home with the glitter groups of Broadway, Hollywood, or London, Sherwood was at the center of the twenties. This did not mean that he fitted into them with total comfort. Much as he enjoyed them, and his enjoyment was lighthearted and huge, a fundamental part of him refused to fit into them at all.

At their beginning he was profoundly shocked by the revelation that six members of the Chicago White Sox, including the great Shoeless Joe Jackson, had sold out to gamblers and thrown a World Series. To him it seemed that "the last illusion had perished for us Americans when Jackson, emerging from the Court House, could only hang his head in reply to the little Chicago boy who pleaded, 'Say it ain't so, Joe.'" That episode became for Sherwood the epitome of the twenties and that boy's cry his own when he surveyed the world in which he found himself.

Like many another, he felt betrayed by the peace which the victory had brought. He saw clearly, and passionately resented, the corruption and materialism, the vulgarity and violence of the years that followed, and shared the widespread disillusionment. But he did not have it in him to join the ranks of the "debunkers." He was not built that way. He had faith and needed illusions. The twenties, as he recalled them, were a dreadful decade for anyone idealistically or romantically or even hopefully inclined. He was all three. Hence, though he marched gaily in the procession of those times, he was often out of step, happy to be in the company of his fellow playwrights yet disapproving of the direction in which they were heading.

He was thirty-one when in 1928, in the preface to *The Queen's Husband*, he raised his voice in protest, still smarting from some of the notices which that comedy and *The Road to Rome* had received. Rereading this preface two decades later, Sherwood could not make out the sort of person he was when he wrote it. One thing he did recognize and admit. Its author was young, much younger in his thinking than in his years. He was guilty of "evidences of such juvenilism" that Sherwood felt inclined to borrow from the critic who had dismissed his earlier plays as "knee-pants" dramas, and to describe his preface as being "knee-pants," too.

He had a point. All his life he was to be a romantic but never again such a Cyrano in short breeches as in this preface. In it he was most decidedly feeling his youth. To him the theatre was then the theatre of Rose Trelawney and Fanny Cavendish and the Crummles family, and (having no way of knowing how it or he was to change) he was sure it always would be. He deplored what he saw going on in it. The theatre seemed to him to be turning its back on itself. Romance, sentiment, and enchantment were being driven from it by the tough journalistic tradition which had come to dominate our literature. "We have developed a literature that is hemmed in on all sides by city desks," he sadly noted, "a literature that is not literature but 'copy,' and dedicated to a muse who wears a green eye-shade, wields a blue pencil, and asks in a cold, contemptuous tone, 'Have you verified this?'" There were exceptions, he admitted, and more of them in the theatre than in the novel, but wisely, as a deplorer, Sherwood did not dwell on them.

He blamed the critics who had told the American writer that

romance is hokum, that fantasy is hokum, and that sentiment is the lowest of all. Because of this instruction the American writer had come to know that he must be literal. He must be an iconoclast, a misanthrope, and a fearless exposer of the mediocrity and hypocrisy of life. He must be "hard-boiled" and " 'sophisticated' (in the Broadway rather than the dictionary sense of the word). He must be illusionless and, like all other successful Americans, he must be 'he.' "

To Sherwood these "musts" meant denying the theatre the diet upon which it has to feed. The theatre to him was "no place for consciously superior persons." It was a place for "those incurable sophomores who have not been blessed by God with the power to rise above their emotions," "the nursery of the arts," and "a romping-ground for man's more childish emotions." Ibsen, the most relentless of realists, said he, realized this. He was not afraid of hokum. He equipped little Eyolf with a crutch to gain a legitimate theatrical effect. He wanted the audience to be chilled by the description of that crutch floating on the water when the child was drowned. O'Neill sensed the same need for theatricality. The distant beat of the tom-toms in *The Emperor Jones* or the roar of the airplane in the final act of *Strange Interlude* was the recognition "by an astute and sympathetic dramatist of the eternal juvenility of the theatre."

Ibsen and Chekhov stand out, not because their tragedies are written from "the cool, calculating scorn of reporters" but because they spill from "the intense, aching sympathy of artists." As for Shaw, supposedly all head and no heart, those who said he eliminated the hokum of "love interest" from his plays overlooked "the obvious fact that Shaw won't permit his heroes to marry his heroines because he is so passionately in love with them himself." His plays are "glamorous romances, with tender and lovely heroines" who have various names, but in them there is only one "stalwart, dominant hero," and his name is Shaw.

Sherwood was tired of the ex-newspapermen who, as essayists, novelists, and dramatists, were forever giving the lowdown on religion, the lowdown on love and marriage, on patriotism or motherhood, the lowdown on anything and everything. His conviction was that hokum was "the life blood of the theatre, its animating force, the cause and reason for its existence"; his contention that "a playwright should be just a great big, overgrown boy, reaching for the moon." Why? Because "the moon is not unattainable. Playwrights have reached it in the past; they have even brought it down to earth, and pasted it on a back-drop. The moon is never more beautiful than when it is seen shining down on an insecure balcony, in a painted Verona." Youth could scarcely be younger, romanticism carried further, or anyone more stage-struck.

When he dashed off the preface to *The Queen's Husband* just in time for publication, Sherwood was something of a great big, overgrown boy himself, proud to be reaching for a make-believe moon in the beauty of which he firmly believed. Although in the years ahead he smiled at the exuberance of this early preface, certain of his abiding articles of faith were in it. To him life was one thing, the theatre another, and neither reporting nor debunking was the theatre. He wanted the theatre to be theatre. He did not want it to reject its special possibilities as a medium. He wanted it to rejoice in them, unashamed of sentiment, unafraid of glamour, unintimidated by romance, a release for the emotions, a dispenser of wonder. He was growing up when he was young enough to swear allegiance to a painted moon, and growing up in many ways, but he was never to outgrow completely the boy within him. That boy, who relished greasepaint and illusion and had to believe in spite of doubting, was to remain part of the man into which he grew. Fortunately there was room enough in Sherwood for both. His theatrical muse never wore a green eye-shade.

19

"IDEA MINT" AT WORK

Playwright's Progress—Dark Thoughts and Light Comedies—His Remarkable Prophecy about the Future of Television—Good Lardner, Poor Sherwood—Marie of Romania and The Queen's Husband—*Wartime London Remembered in* Waterloo Bridge—*His Admiration for Al Smith—Sherwood Becomes a Democrat—Resentment of Intolerance in 1928 Campaign—Prohibition, Gangsters, Politicos, and* This Is New York

He had always been stage-struck, and the success of his first play did not make him less so. With *The Road to Rome* he had tasted at the start of 1927 the heady delights of a new profession. After that, and for almost the next five years until *Reunion in Vienna*, he faced without quite solving it the problem always faced by those who, because of having once succeeded, must succeed again to the same or to a greater extent.

Not that he was idle. Far from it. As the twenties reached their final years and slipped into the thirties, he was writing with an energy which appeared to be inexhaustible. Outwardly he seemed as self-confident as a man-about-many-towns. Inwardly, as he later confessed to his diary, he was "insanely critical and insanely uncertain" of himself. He cited his preface to *The Queen's Husband* as an example of this uncertainty and could have given many others. Why not? These were his years of stretching intellectually and spiritually, and seeking to discover the reach and true aim of his grasp. His quest was twofold—for his craft and for himself, and he found the former before he located the latter. The conflict was stubborn within him between the playwright who, after thinking dark thoughts, wrote light comedies and the man who, having finished these comedies, was apt to precede them with prefaces ever deepening in their melancholy.

At this time Sherwood knew the sweetness of success, the bitterness of failure, and the heartbreak of near-success. He was learning, too, that the "hair's breadth" which separates the three in theatre is "a terrifying thing." Nonetheless, these were exciting if frustrating years for him, and agreeable, too, in spite of Mary Brandon. He was thought of as a success whether he had a current one or not. His reputation was growing at home and abroad. Royalties from Europe, the road, and stock companies were pouring in, and sometimes from Broadway. Hollywood was buying film rights, regardless of the wrongs done to what was bought. Life was cushioned, and the worldly pleasures which Sherwood loved were coming more and more within his unworrying command.

What he called his "Idea Mint" was working overtime and he rejoiced in the period of "intellectual promiscuity" which this made possible. He was trying his hand at every kind of writing—magazine articles, poems, his monthly book-review page for *Scribner's Magazine*, a novel, and as a scenarist in Hollywood. He even found time to turn soothsayer in "After the Talkies—Television," an article which in 1929 led off the July issue of *Scribner's*. He had written it on order early that spring for *McCall's* but, when some revisions were asked for which he was unwilling to make, he sent it to his old friend, Robert Bridges, who had encouraged him three years before by accepting his short story, *Extra! Extra!* "It is, in so far as I know," he assured Bridges, "the first attempt to indicate (publicly) what Television will be. . . . Most of it will be news to the reader."

And news most of it was, because at that time the popular response to rumors about something called television was disbelief and smiles. The mere idea of sending through the air into everyone's home pictures which talked seemed a crazy man's pipe dream or so much science fiction. Sherwood knew and noted that in dozens of laboratories in the United States and Europe electrical engineers were working frantically at making this possible, and that all the big radio and electrical companies, backed by farsighted businessmen, were drawing up staggering plans for it. But the engineers were working behind closed doors and the planners refused to be quoted. Because of their crudity the few actual broadcasts that had been made from Pittsburgh, Washington, New York, and Whippany, New Jersey, appeared to justify the scoffers. The widespread feeling about television was very simple—and familiar. Since it was not, it *therefore* never could be.

This was not Sherwood's attitude. His was a welcoming mind. He realized at once that a birth was taking place and that the baby aborning was a giant. When it was still in its crib, he treated it as if it had grown up. He accepted it as readily as he had accepted the "flickers" when it was fashionable to scorn them and he as a reviewer took them seriously. Or as he had sensed at their outset the potentiality of films in color. Or recognized from their first tentative releases of sound that the "talkies" would revolutionize the movies. With the planners he was convinced that television, more than "approaching," was "inevitable and imminent," and saluted it as "one of the most fantastic of all the scientific miracles." He prophesied that within five years, more or less, it would be an accomplished fact, so taken for granted that the doubters would forget that they had ever doubted and that a huge public, at first amazed by it as a novelty, would be assuming it as a commonplace.

Satisfied that "the major problems of Television have been solved," Sherwood reached for his crystal ball to see in it a world as yet unknown which in the years ahead (though he did not foresee this) would be another of the many worlds in which he was to be involved. He knew a huge revolution in communications was at hand and proceeded to point out in detail the transforming effect it would have on the home, on advertising, political speeches, news coverage, the radio, the talkies, and the theatre.

"It will be possible," wrote he when all this seemed impossible, "to watch the actual enactment of news events without having to wait for them to appear [shades of another era] in the rotogravure sections or in news reels days or weeks later." Actors will face new challenges and have new chances. Scripts, being meant for the eye as well as the ear, will be different from what they were on radio. Humor, too. Politicians, facing a camera, will have to alter their styles.

Radio, for the most part, will concentrate on news and music, and leave storytelling to the recently arrived medium. More and more thousands, when able to get entertainment for nothing at home, will not face the inconvenience of going out to pay for it. As a result, the theatre, already an "impractical institution," will suffer from an increasing lack of audiences. So will the movies, which will not operate on their former scale, and a great many movie palaces will close and be torn down, along with many legitimate theatres.

Moreover, commercials (he called them "paid propaganda") will become so numerous that they may "cause the public to revolt against the national advertisers and institute a disastrous boycott of nationally advertised goods." This was a revolt which unfortunately has never occurred, but on the subject of lessening its causes Sherwood offered some reassurance. "I can state, on the best authority, that all Television sets will be equipped, as all radio sets are now equipped, with control switches. Thus, when anyone decides he has been fed to the teeth with visible and audible salesmanship . . . he has only to turn the little switch and shut the darned thing off."

Attempting to prophesy the future of a future medium was fun which he enjoyed, but what mattered was Sherwood's finding himself in the old medium which he was seeking to make his own. Often during these years of self-discovery he was seen deep in thought, pinching at his close-cropped black mustache. This was always a good sign. It meant that he was writing a play, not writing it down at first when he was unpredictably seized by a new idea, but composing it so completely in his head that he could quote long scenes from it before committing it to paper. Some of these plays reached production. Some were bought but not produced. Others, after being hoped for and fussed over, were consigned to that oubliette known to him as his "bureau drawer."

The Road to Rome had been running for nearly eleven months when Sherwood's second play, *The Love Nest*, opened just before Christmas in 1927 to notices as indifferent as the general public proved to be, and closed after twenty-three performances. It was a dramatization, made the year before, of Ring Lardner's astringent story about a famous movie magnate's wife, an ex-star, who in her wretchedness has become a secret drinker when forced by her husband to play the role of a perfect homebody presiding over a supposedly ideal home.

Sherwood sought to solve the dilemma of expanding a short story into a long evening by first showing the magnate in all his pomposity directing a banal film, and by writing a melodramatic last act in which the wife ran off with the butler. In spite of such padding, the play in three acts remained a one-act play, and Lardner proved right when he wrote F. Scott Fitzgerald, "This ain't my play, though of course I shall share the royalties. (There won't be many.) I saw a dress rehearsal last night. Bob has done some very clever writing and the second act is quite strong with June Walker great as a drunk. But I'm afraid most of it will be over people's heads. This, of course, is under your hat." Looking back on *The Love Nest* decades later, Sherwood's only comment was, "The Lardner part of it was good."

His next three plays to reach the stage were *The Queen's Husband* and, two years later, *Waterloo Bridge* and *This Is New York*. All showed marks of his strengthening skill and all suffered from his unconquered uncertainties. In the first his delight in theatrical fabrication was the most apparent, in the second his heart was sunk deepest, and in the third he edged nearest to his times.

Of the three *The Queen's Husband* came closest (though not very close) to duplicating the success of *The Road to Rome*. *The Love Nest* had barely closed when toward the end of that same January in 1928 his new play opened in New York. More than a failure and less than a hit, it ran there for only 125 performances. It did, however, succeed on the road, and in England and Canada, where Barry Jones and Maurice Colbourne delighted audiences in it for some eighteen months. In time, too, it became a favorite with the Little Theatre groups that were then as plentiful as goldenrod. And within three years, which was at least good for the till, it was made into a less than mediocre film that Hollywood, in Hollywood's happy fashion, chose to call *The Royal Bed*.

Had an unloving critic described *The Road to Rome* as "George Bernard Shaw in short pants"? To *The New Yorker*'s Charles

Brackett *The Queen's Husband* was "George Barr McCutcheon in a beard." And Graustarkian it was, Graustark with Ruritania thrown in, with a revolution breaking out, a crown in peril, a wicked minister about to take over, and a domineering Queen put in her place by a mild, ineffectual, lovable little King who proves to be a royal worm that turns. He is a reluctant monarch, this Eric VIII, quite capable of cheering the revolutionists. He prefers watching penguins at the zoo to reviewing parades and playing checkers with a flunkey to ruling his people. He does assert himself at last, thereby holding his throne and saving his daughter from the loveless state marriage planned for her by the Queen, and making it possible for her to elope with the man she loves, a commoner who is the son of a plumber, albeit a wholesale plumber.

Sherwood's setting was "a mythical and anonymous kingdom, situated on an island in the North Sea, somewhere between Denmark and Scotland." He was quick to point out that it was not the usual Graustark-Ruritania or musical-comedy type of kingdom, even though it did possess "the usual quota of anarchistic plotters." Instead, it was "a sort of pocket edition of Great Britain." With this exception. Its never having become a dominant world power had prevented its people from developing "the British point of view." Accordingly, the average citizen of this mythical country could be described "as an Englishman with an inferiority complex, if one can imagine such a thing."

It was not of the English as a people that American audiences thought when they sat before the play, although Roland Young gave as the King a performance which was as dryly English as a back issue of *Punch*. Instead, it was an English woman, a granddaughter of Queen Victoria, who came inescapably to mind. A little more than a year before, Queen Marie of Romania with her daughter, the Princess Ileana, and her younger son, Prince Nicholas, had come to the United States and Canada on an unofficial forty-four-day visit. The trip, which was more in the nature of a circus than a Royal Progress, was the most regal of the vulgarities of the twenties. It had amused Sherwood as it had diverted millions. With his strong awareness of what was dramatic in the news, he had tucked it into his romantic melodrama as a contributor to its laughter and its plot. The world knew what Queen Marie was like. She had seen to that. What entertained Sherwood was guessing at the kind of man that might be married to her. Disregarding the real King Ferdinand, Sherwood made up a King of his own, stressing his shift in emphasis by calling his play *The Queen's Husband* rather than *The King's Wife*, though the Queen and her journey to America were very much an offstage part of it.

Marie insisted to suspicious bankers in New York that she had not come with a golden cup in her hand. Her excuse for her trip was an invitation from her old and quixotic friend, Sam Hill, to dedicate an unfinished museum which he was building at the little town of Maryhill in his native state of Washington. Her purpose, she explained, was to persuade Americans to love her so that they would love her country; her aim to put Romania on the map.

No one could deny that this handsome, strong-willed, and enervatingly energetic woman had put herself all over the map as, dripping with pearls and diamonds, she whistle-stopped her way around the country from one red carpet to another on the luxurious trains which the railroads put at her disposal. Her countless clothes were costumes; her costumes, as she wore them, royal robes. She was feted everywhere. No presidential candidate could have been more indefatigable. Thousands flocked to see her, and hundreds, delighting as democrats in royalty, paid good money to curtsy to her or kiss her hand. "There are not half a dozen actresses in America who could fill the role as well," wrote Heywood Broun, who was among the many who spoofed her royally.

Marie's visit was at least dramatic in its results. One of these was *Rosalie*, a musical in which Marilyn Miller as the Princess Ileana twirled merrily in front of her mother and a chorus of Ziegfeld beauties dressed up like plebes at West Point. Another was *The Queen's Husband*. Audiences laughed heartily when, at the end of Sherwood's first act, his Queen Martha said on leaving for America, "I shall come back with the money that we need—even if I have to go straight to the President of the United States himself." After she swept out, there was a moment of silence. Then the King brought down the curtain, and the house, by muttering, "God help the President of the United States." The audience knew Sherwood's Queen by then, but the King did not seem to realize that the President of the United States was Calvin Coolidge.

Another woman, not a queen in the news this time but a London streetwalker remembered over the years, was the inspiration of his next play, *Waterloo Bridge*, which opened in New York at the start of 1930. Sherwood was outfitted in the hospital blues of the British wounded when he had found himself jammed against her in Trafalgar Square in 1918. The two of them were in the midst of a riotous mob which was celebrating the Armistice by stoking a bonfire at the base of the Nelson Monument. She was very short, quite pretty, and wearing a blue tailored suit. He spotted her at once for what she was.

He was surprised to notice that pinned across her shirtwaist was a silk American flag. To his "Why?" her reply, in a voice that suggested nothing but Broadway, was, "Because it belongs to me, you big Limey." When he asked her how, with that flag and that voice, she happened to be in London of all places, she told him that she had come over years before in the chorus of *The Pink Lady* and had stuck through no choice of her own. She also told him she had a nice little flat in Leicester Square, and added, "Why not come up some time soon?" In the turmoil Sherwood unfortunately forgot her address, so he did not see her again. But he never forgot her or the London he had known during the war, and from the two of them wrote *Waterloo Bridge*.

His preface, in which he re-created the England he had seen during the dark time when victory had seemed impossible and the delirious days when at last it had somehow been achieved, was the serious and able work of a man haunted by memories of a war which would not leave him. It was stronger than the play into which it led. To some, *The Queen's Husband*, with its mixture of royal romance, court intrigue, cannonading melodrama, and farce-comedy, interrupted by occasional serious political comments, had seemed too many plays at one and the same time for its own good. To most, *Waterloo Bridge* appeared to be not enough of a play to sustain an evening. It told of a young American who, while serving in the Royal Canadian Regiment, had been wounded in France and hospitalized in

England, in Sherwood's fashion. He comes to London on a sick leave, meets on Waterloo Bridge the streetwalker who is the chorus girl from *The Pink Lady* in the preface, hears her voice which is home to him, and falls in love with her and she with him.

He is a small-town Y.M.C.A. type, so innocent over and beyond the call of virtue that he does not suspect the way in which she is serving the Armed Forces; she a prostitute with a heart which is a mine of gold. When his leave is abruptly canceled, he asks her to marry him, having asked for nothing more, and she, out of love for him, begs him to forget her and tells him what she is. His love is such that he does not mind, and, before heading back for the hospital and France, he settles her overdue rent, sees that part of his pay will be assigned to her, and makes out his insurance in her name. Her future is as unclear as his, though it seems certain that, if she survives the air raids, she will return to her past. *Waterloo Bridge* was as simple as that; a duologue which, as acted and magically acted by June Walker and Glenn Hunter, was at moments touching in its tenderness. But it was a frail love story, unheated by desire and too innocent for belief, which was filled in with secondary characters whose chief business seemed to be to keep the curtain up.

Sherwood had realized before its Boston tryout that it "would require an enormous amount of 'strengthening' as it was palpably frail and insufficient." How to do this he did not know, though he thought he might have some new ideas when he saw it on the stage. If these came he did not use them, contenting himself instead with a few cuts and revisions. He had the best of reasons. H. T. Parker in the Boston *Transcript* had surprised him by giving the play a notice festooned with superlatives. Praise from H.T.P. was praise indeed, because this remarkable little man of fine perceptions, with his dark eyes burning quizzically in a head bent forward with a sleuthing thrust and emphatic in its nods, was a giant among critics. Sherwood felt (as he wrote me after the Broadway opening, long before we had met, correcting a column of mine in the *Post*) that he would have been "a sap to tamper with such a masterpiece." His realization, following his bad press in New York, was that "anyone who goes in for play writing, which is necessarily so profoundly affected by critics, has a hard time knowing just who to believe."

He had written the play late in 1929 "while Prime Minister Ramsay MacDonald was visiting President Herbert Hoover, offering 'Faith, Hope and Parity,' and Wall Street was getting ready to crash." It had for him a personal importance which he did not claim for it as a drama. "What's the war, anyway?" his Canadian soldier had cried. "That war's over for me. What I've got to fight is the whole dirty world. That's the enemy that's against you and me."

His quickened interest in American politics was for him a first step. The Harding and Coolidge administrations, more than adding to his disillusion, had pried Sherwood from his inherited Republicanism. The campaign he conducted for Will Rogers as president was only his joking way as *Life*'s editor of registering a protest. His serious candidate in 1928 was Al Smith. It was Al of the florid complexion, the gravel voice, the shaky grammar, the strong honesty, and ready wit; Al of "The Sidewalks of New York," the "Happy Warrior" whose helmet was a brown derby, who turned Sherwood into a Democrat. It was "humble, reverent Al," as he called him, and all that he stood for. It was also those against Al, men as different as Senator Borah, Charles Evans Hughes, Henry Ford, Bishop Cannon, and "Big Bill" Thompson, and organizations as unappealing to Sherwood as the Anti Saloon League, the Methodist Board of Temperance, Prohibition and Public Morals, the Woman's Christian Temperance Union, and the Ku Klux Klan.

Sherwood was disturbed to find William Allen White, that "sane and civilized Kansan" of the Emporia *Gazette*, among the most vociferous who, in championing Hoover, endowed Smith with a "satanic significance." Sherwood admitted that White did not attempt to disguise his admiration for Smith's integrity, executive ability, and good nature. He did not join in "the fantastic chorus of Heflins and Simmonses who promised Protestantism that a vote for Smith was a vote for the Pope." Neither did he help to circulate the rumor that "a tunnel was being dug from the Vatican in Rome to the White House in Washington for the purpose of smuggling in His Holiness together with a large stock of contraband chianti." But, according to Sherwood, White darkly warned that Smith, as the protagonist of the New York idea even more than as a Catholic, was "a menace of inestimable potency to the church-going, saloon-hating, monogamous spirit of America."

Since most Americans seemed to share this feeling, Hoover was swept into office ("and reaped the whirlwind"). Manhattan, in the person of Al Smith, was repudiated even by New York State, and the nation, thereby, was supposedly made safe for the old-time religion. Sherwood was revolted by the religious intolerance which disfigured the campaign. He was irritated, and amused, too, by the clarity with which the election expressed the country's distrust and dislike of New York, his New York, the city which most Americans angrily insisted was not America but which to him was, faults and all, for better or for evil, precisely that. The hinterland's antipathy for Manhattan and the suspicion with which it viewed it supplied him with a subject for his next play, *This Is New York*. This was produced two years after Smith's defeat and one year after the stock market crash, when it had become clear to Sherwood and millions of others that "God's country was anything but safe," and that the old-time religion was "suffering more than ever from a malignant form of senile dementia."

"I've finished one act of a new play, tentatively called *New York Is Not America*, which looks as though it might be good," Sherwood wrote his mother from London in the summer of 1930. "It's an out-and-out comedy, almost a farce, and extremely modern. It contains no preachments against war." It was his answer to the old saying, quoted by him in his program and on the title page of the printed text, "New York is all right for a visit—but I wouldn't live there if you gave me the place."

This Is New York turned out to be a melodramatic comedy in which the very independent daughter of a windy, New York-hating Senator from South Dakota and his D.A.R. wife becomes involved in the suicide of a bootlegger's moll while paying an unexpected call on her fiancé's blackmailing mistress. Some critics greeted it as Sherwood's best comedy to date, though Atkinson and others found it genial entertainment which was not especially fervent about anything. There was no question but that Sherwood's Senator from South Dakota was fervent in stating his hope that New York would be kicked out of the Union before it had a chance to secede, and would be towed across the Atlantic to the Europe where he thought it belonged. Sherwood was no less fervent in championing New York City as the microcosm of the country and "the American spirit in concentrate form (add grain alcohol and serve)." The trouble was that the Senator launched his attacks on Manhattan in the play itself whereas Sherwood rose to its defense in his preface. The result was a fight in which the two contestants seemed to be sparring in separate rings, and a play which, in spite of its good scenes, lasted only 59 performances. Sherwood did not look back on *This Is New York* with pride. Actually, he considered it a warning. Years later he thought of it as "full of tough guys, gags, profanity—synthetic."

His luck changed with his next play. It was *Reunion in Vienna.*

20

DISILLUSIONED CRUSADER

The Road to Rome in Vienna—Sacher Hotel Suggests a Play—Unhappy at Home—The Crusades Win His Interest—Writes a Play and a Novel about Them—Failure of The Virtuous Knight—His Love of England—Summer in Surrey—Sherwood Seen Through the Eyes of a Boy—Reunion in Vienna Suddenly Takes Shape

An idea for a new play is for a dramatist among the pleasanter dividends of a trip. The idea for *Reunion in Vienna* was such an unexpected dividend. In the summer of 1929 Sherwood was in Europe for the first time since the war. England was his initial stop, and from there he went with Mary Brandon to Vienna to see *The Road to Rome,* produced under the title of *Hannibal Ante Portas.* The comedy's being produced in Austria was a measure of how far his reputation had spread.

He did not enjoy the Viennese performance, keyed as it was from start to finish to very low farce. But plainly the audience loved it. Success was in the air. He could not, he did not, object to that. The audience had been informed of his presence, and at the end of the second act he was asked to appear on the stage alone where he took eight bows to the accompaniment of cheers. The news he had was as encouraging as the reception of his play. It was one of the most popular in the Volkstheater's repertory. The great Max Reinhardt had wanted to stage it and would have done so had his schedule permitted. Other productions were planned for Munich and Berlin.

All this was agreeable, but what stayed in Sherwood's mind was not the triumph of that night but his impressions of the city in which it occurred. It was Vienna he remembered, haunted by reminders of

its departed grandeur; Vienna, its gilt tarnished and its imperial
eagles plucked, in which a dead past was stronger than a living
present. To a romantic such as Sherwood the contrast between the
two was stabbing in its poignancy. The Opera House, for example,
where Socialist burgomasters sat beneath the golden crown of the
royal box. The great gateway of the palace of the Hapsburgs topped
by a glaring Mobiloil advertisement. Then, there were the leading
intellectuals—"a pathetic, down-at-the-heel lot"—that he met at a
reception given for him at the Rathaus after *Hannibal Ante Portas.*
"Poor Vienna," he wrote his mother, "is a depressing place these
days—hopelessly broke and gone to seed, and yet still trying to
persuade itself that it is the gay, opulent capital of all Europe."

He was particularly impressed when taken to the Hotel Sacher,
that plush monument to former gaiety, intimate dinners, and royal romances in the rooms upstairs. With its high ceilings, its corridors
flanked with statues and paintings, and its sense of rich Victorian
stuffiness, this venerable hostelry nonetheless suggested to him "a
wicked intimation of Viennese caprice." For him it still sparkled with
"happy imaginings of frivolities which no longer are—and perhaps
never were—but which eternally should be." In it he sensed the
setting for a play and in Frau Sacher, who still presided over it, a
character crying to be written. When he came to write that play, he
described her as "a formidable old party absurdly dressed in ancient
clothes." Her voice was "gruff, her expression unchangeably hostile,
her manner toward all arrogant and despotic." He was told by a
Viennese, as he later wrote Ward Morehouse, that old Frau Sacher
still gave parties secretly for her aristocratic patrons who were down
and out. She insulted and browbeat them just as she had done in the
old days when they, entrenched in their position, were sufficiently
assured to be amused by such treatment. Now they were sensitive,
left defenseless by their fall, and enjoyed neither her manner nor her
parties at which they assembled, feeding on memories and pretense,
as frail followers of a dead religion.

Frau Sacher, barking and smoking her cigars? These aristocrats in
faded finery, musty leftovers of once glittering society? Perhaps a
returned Archduke, hot-blooded and imperious, as a means of con-
fronting the past and present? His former mistress and a party for all

these ghosts in an upstairs room? To Sherwood it was at once obvious that somewhere in this mélange of contrasts was an idea for a
comedy. But where? The search for the plot and the theme was a
problem that was to tease his mind for the next two years until to his
delight he stumbled upon a solution, the result of which was a
comedy waltzlike in its lilt.

His thoughts during the years that preceded the writing of *Reunion*
were anything but gay. They were, in fact, as black as the comedy
was bright in which he sought to escape from them. Such contradictions were at the center of his being. Relishing fun, he was tormented
by misgivings and apt to retreat at any moment, even at a party, into
a stockade of solitude.

The tensions of his life with Mary Brandon contributed to his
unhappiness. Part of his talent for make-believe was spent in pretending that these tensions did not exist. In addition, there was his
despondency about the world. He could not get the war's broken
promises and betrayed ideals out of his mind. The war made him a
pacifist; the peace, a pessimist. His deepening conviction was that a
dark present was leading to a darker future.

Always a hungry reader of history, he turned to the past for warnings and parallels. In *The Road to Rome* he had gone back to
Rome's Babbittry at the time of Hannibal and dealt smilingly with a
conqueror who learned to question the conqueror's role. His comedy
had scarcely opened when he concerned himself with the past again,
this time the Third Crusade. With it in both play and novel form he
lived and labored, in the midst of his other interests and activities for
four years. In both cases he approached that Crusade with the disenchantment of a soldier who, in the First War, had himself approached the shores of France as a crusader.

In the Crusades, he wrote when reviewing three books on them for
Scribner's, "one may observe, and in heroic relief, all the major
strengths and weaknesses that have ever promoted mortal man's pride
and his degradation. They formed the greatest of all wars, which
continued steadily for a hundred and fifty years. No other period of
history contained as much of gallantry, treachery, selfless devotion,
corruption, sublime faith or unspeakable horror."

With these aspects of the Crusades Sherwood grappled in both his

play *Marching as to War*, which was never produced, and his only
novel, which was published in this country under the title *The Virtuous Knight*, and in England as *Unending Crusade*. The hero of each
was a Crusader too virtuous for belief or interest, who remained
trapped in a tapestry. In both the play and the novel knighthood
was wintrily out of flower. Both had shattering things to say about
Richard the Lion-Hearted and his Crusade; about the venality of his
deputies; about prelates, using inquisitorial methods, who fattened
themselves on the lands of those they had sent abroad; the barbarism
of the times; the costly squabbles of little men in big places; the
blood price and agony of warfare; and the sorry fate of idealists who
in the name of King and Church were tricked into heading for the
Holy Land. The novel in particular was merciless in rusting Richard's shining armor and showing him in all his selfishness, arrogance,
sloth, and cruelty.

Both ripped the plumes off the casques of Scott's warriors in *The
Talisman* and each, in spite of its attempts at rugged realism in a
World War I vein, contained scenes of slashing swordplay, great
leaps, miraculous escapes, winging arrows, and cornered men win-
ning against odds, that would have delighted the senior Douglas
Fairbanks. Each, in its own way, reached an identical conclusion:
Marching as to War that the Crusade turned believers into heretics;
The Virtuous Knight that Crusaders "must never again be seduced
by a fraudulent faith." Both ended by ruefully admitting that in the
future there would be other Crusades. This was a point close to
Sherwood's heart. He had been on one of them.

As was necessary, Sherwood's hopes for *Marching as to War* were
high when he started it. "It is in the same vein as *The Road to
Rome*," he wrote Maxwell Perkins in the summer of 1927, adding,
"I think it is a great deal better . . . and so apparently does everyone
else." His faith in it persisted for the next four years during which
Leslie Howard expressed interest in it, Winthrop Ames said he would
like to produce it, two other managements bought it, and its production was announced each fall, only to come to nothing. Finally,
having revised it again and again, he wrote his mother in 1930, "I've
reached the stage of refusing to fuss with it any longer. I know it isn't
quite right, but I've done so much embroidery work on it that I can
do no more for the time being." He never did.

The more he came to know about the Third Crusade the more he wanted to know. His appetites were strong, and history was one of them. Fiction another. In spite of his playwriting, he was eager to get at *The Virtuous Knight*. He sought to face the challenge of a novel. By writing an historical novel he satisfied two desires at one time. *Marching as to War* was a theatrical fabrication quickly thrown together. *The Virtuous Knight*, as it followed Richard's Crusade from England through France and the Mediterranean to the walls of Acre, was the product of protracted research.

Unfortunately, in spite of its graphic battle scenes, its colorful evocation of places, its contrasts between the Christian and Moslem worlds, the vividness of some of its characters, and its deeply felt passages, the narrative floundered, weighted down by its cargo of history. Begun as an adventure, it ended as a chore. Its writing tired Sherwood, and he tired of it. As he wrote to Woollcott when at last he began to see the end of a tunnel which seemed endless, "I'm still toiling laboriously on my first 100,000 words novel, and thanking God with every word that it will never have an opening night."

Most of his friends, having forgotten or ignored his preface to *The Road to Rome*, had no reason to suspect the intensity with which he could burrow into history. Nor would they recognize it until he made his gift clear in 1938 in *Abe Lincoln in Illinois*, and clearer still a decade later in *Roosevelt and Hopkins*. Even Mary Brandon appears to have been unaware, while he was slaving at the novel, of what so occupied Sherwood's thoughts. When at last it was finished and about to be published in 1931, he asked Perkins to send him two copies to Hollywood. One of these was for Mary Brandon to read on the train east because she "has yet to know just what it is that's been causing so much trouble for the last two and a half years."

He had not been able to start working on *The Virtuous Knight* until he felt financially free to do so. This was why he wrote Perkins early in 1929 and with some embarrassment asked for an advance, saying that unless he got it he would have to postpone the novel "until I have piled up a sufficient surplus from my hack work or I have another successful play going." Such was Perkins's confidence in him, and in the book, that a week after they talked it over he sent Sherwood a check for $2,000, with promises of more to come. When *The Virtuous Knight* did appear, it was somewhat better received in

England than in America but a failure in both places. The advance from Scribner's, however, served an unforeseen purpose. More than enabling Sherwood to undertake the novel, it helped to make possible the visit to Vienna which started *Reunion* percolating in his mind.

It did even more. It altered the pattern of his life by making England part of it. It was from England that he had headed to Vienna in 1929 and to England that he returned. He had liked Vienna, Munich, and Paris on that trip but, as he wrote his mother, "I must say that I like London the best of all." A reason noted in his diary was "One feels so God-damned rich in London & one had God-damned better be." That was some years later when money was flooding his way. Even before then, with him it was a case of easy go no matter how hard come. He had no fondness for garrets. There was no Chatterton blood in him. He was always amenable to comfort. Money, as money, never mattered to him except to have enough of it to spend or give away. Since his gift for conjuring it was real, he assumed its coming in and for the most part was unbothered by its going out.

He loved England, the England he had first known as a boy in its full majesty of Empire, and then in the desperate testing of the war years. He was glad to return to it. He loved the English people, too. Their stodginess could amuse him, their ways perplex him, their arrogance enrage him. But he admired them and got along with them at every level. Affection brought him back no less than work. England was for him the more delightful because it was a stage setting for Shakespeare, Scott, Jane Austen, or Dickens which just happened to be real. Like many another American, he kept feeling he had read what he was seeing there. The traditionalist in him found the comfort of continuity and the nonconformist a manorial Bohemia in which, in the years ahead, he was able to live as he liked.

Much as he relished England, he occasionally rebelled against its manicured perfection which made him long for the United States. "It's too God-damned neat, too set," he could grumble, "I crave the stimulus of irregularity. My thoughts and my plays are American in impulse but English in form (well made, compact) which is a good thing—but God help me if form triumphs over impulse." In spite of such moments of revolt, he could not resist the English countryside or the people who had given it order. "The sensuous thrill of the sight of England after coming from anywhere else is, for me, extraordinary. The may trees are in bloom, & the chestnuts, & they're playing cricket on the fair green lawns. But it's much more than the beauty of the landscape. Other scenes are beautiful, too. The Adirondacks—the high places of Arizona—the Monts des Maures [near St. Tropez] . . . But here—the fact that it's England. You feel that people who can keep their own home land so orderly, so neat, are competent to do the same for the world."

Surrey was the part of England which became a part of Sherwood. He first knew the delights of living there that summer after the Scribner advance when, at Witley, he rented Polshot Farm, an old, low-ceilinged, many-roomed place, and started to work on *The Virtuous Knight*. Though he spent the next three summers in London or France or Hollywood, Surrey remained rooted in his mind. And to it he returned to live after he purchased Great Enton in 1932, and for the next twenty years divided his time between it and America except during the war.

The London summer in 1930 started out with high hopes but was not a success. He and Mary Brandon and little Mary shared with the Paul Hollisters and their young son and daughter an attractive, luxurious, well-staffed house in Hanover Terrace, facing Regent's Park. As his study Sherwood took a large room at the back overlooking a garden, and conditions seemed at first ideal for work. But the children, all three of them, came down almost at once with measles. Two noisy doves in the garden proved "far more disturbing than the gentle cooings of the traffic at 5th Ave. and 48th Street" where he was accustomed to work. The distractions of London were many and beckoning, and the atmosphere inside the house at times was so strained that even the Hollister boy realized that Sherwood was having his troubles with Mary Brandon. Though he managed to write an act of *This Is New York*, revised *Marching as to War*, and mailed his monthly column of book reviews to *Scribner's*, Sherwood confessed to his mother at the end of July that he had not "done a lick on the novel, due to an insufficiency of opportunity for extended concentration."

To Sherwood the summer, as it was drawing to a close, seemed

"rather disorderly." One sharer in it, seeing it through the unworried
eyes of youth, had a different view. This was Paul Hollister, Jr., who
was eleven years old and wonder-struck. From the moment the
Sherwoods and the Hollisters (the elder Paul joined them later)
boarded the *Lafayette* for England at the end of May, Sherwood
became the boy's friend and hero. Though no relation, he was to him
Uncle Bob. The boy marveled at this tall man, the tallest he had ever
seen, and, in his newfound loyalty, was proud because he did not see
a taller all summer. He tried to take steps as far-spread as his, and
dipped his fingers in hot water, hoping afterward to stretch them out
to Uncle Bob's length. He stooped without need when he went
through doors and, having heard Sherwood complain, curled up in
his bed so that he could pretend to himself that it was also too
short.

He watched and listened, and felt as close to the giant he admired
as a child can be to a grownup, and Sherwood found pleasure in his
companionship. Young Paul loved to hear the tall man roll out the
names of English history—Drake, Richard Coeur-de-Lion, and the
rest—speaking them always with a ponderous deliberation which
seemed to add to their importance even to Sherwood. The boy was
one of the few permitted to sit in his study when he worked fitfully at
The Virtuous Knight. And Sherwood, when free, loved to take him
by tube and taxi, or walk him dogtrotting after, to the Guildhall, the
Tower, or any of the old sights which Uncle Bob made new as he
talked about them.

The youth rejoiced in Sherwood's long and elaborate comic stories
and his ever-spilling puns, such as the one he got off one chilly day
when Mrs. Hollister, who was going to the races, asked if she could
borrow his scarf, and his reply was "Yours for the Ascot." He never
forgot the kindly intense older man carrying an enormous Graflex
camera around with him and stooping over to scowl into it, "like a
horse with its nose in a feedbag." Or suffering from excruciating
headaches when they had all moved on to Paris. Or carrying maps
with him everywhere and shouting whenever they went on an excur-
sion, "Who's got the maps?" until the question became a group
joke.

The map of Sherwood's career was changed during the year ahead.

Back in New York, unbothered by the doves in Hanover Terrace and shut away at will from people, including Mary Brandon, he dug into the office he used at Scribner's and sweated out the final chapters of *The Virtuous Knight*. He felt uncertain about the novel even when he had turned it in and submitted many revisions with the galley proofs, including one long insert at the end because he felt "the story was coasting down hill . . . and needed an emphatic dramatic jolt." The added last pages did not solve the problem. But Sherwood had no reason to brood long over his disappointment. By the time the book appeared he had solved another problem. After all his fretting about those people he had met at Frau Sacher's hotel, he suddenly hit upon the character needed to bring them together and supply *Reunion in Vienna* with its plot.

21

AN EXILED ARCHDUKE COMES HOME

The Problem in Reunion *Solved—Comedy Accepted—"The Chief" in the Age of Railroads—Working for Howard Hughes and Douglas Fairbanks, Sr.—Joys of Working with the Lunts—Troubles with the Theatre Guild—Eruptions in Baltimore—Praise from Deems Taylor— A Despairing Preface—The Tug of War in Sherwood's Nature—Doubts about the Play's Ending—Helen Westley's Off Night*

With Sherwood his characters came first, his plots later. He was convinced that a dramatist should be able to write a searching biography of each character, even though only scraps of it were conveyed in the play itself. "In the case of any play of mine that was any good," he wrote his niece, Lydia Sherwood, when she asked his advice about writing a comedy, "I knew the principal characters intimately—had lived with them and slept with them—long before I had any remote notion of the plot."

As an example he offered *Reunion in Vienna.* He saw Rudolf, the exiled Archduke, and Elena, his former mistress, with absolute clarity before he knew how he was going to use them. He also knew several of the lesser figures. He had, of course, met Frau Sacher, that unlikely reality, who was to become his Frau Lucher. The others, too, were all as real to him as if they had been alive. He could even hear "a lot of snatches of dialogue."

One character, however, eluded him, the man he needed as Elena's husband. His first thought was to make him a famous surgeon, but since as such he refused to come into focus the play got nowhere over the lengthening months. Then one day it dawned on Sherwood that, if psychoanalysis was (in his Rudolf's phrase) Vienna's "sole remain-

ing industry," there was no question. Elena's husband must be a
psychoanalyst. He could then apply his professional theories to ex-
tinguishing the fires of an old romance and have a reason for urging
Elena to go to Frau Lucher's secret party for the fallen aristocrats.
Her going would be in the nature of a cure. Seeing Rudolf there after
he had been a taxi driver in Nice for ten years would destroy her
haunting memories of him as an Archduke. At least it would according to the theory of Elena's psychoanalyst husband. The differences
between what he thought would happen and what did happen was
the gay concern of *Reunion in Vienna.*

Once the doctor became clear to him, Sherwood raced through the
writing of the comedy in two weeks and sent copies off to the Theatre
Guild and to the Lunts who, under its management, were touring in
Elizabeth the Queen. Years later he said, "I suppose every playwright at the end of the second act or so thinks, 'Now this won't be
so bad if I can get the Lunts to appear in it.'" He again had them in
mind as when he wrote *The Road to Rome.* In his enthusiasm he told
them to toss *Reunion* into the wastebasket if they did not like it. Miss
Fontanne, as was their practice with scripts, read it first, then Lunt,
and both of them liked it. The Guild liked it, too. Indeed, the Lunts
liked it so much that they chose it rather than *Mourning Becomes
Electra* when the two plays were submitted to them by the Guild that
May. Fine as they knew O'Neill's tragedy to be, they were eager to
frolic again in a comedy and sensed at once that this one was as
suited to them as they were to it.

The good news about *Reunion* was followed for Sherwood by a
period of waiting for rehearsals to begin in far-off September and
for the publication that same month of *The Virtuous Knight.* To ease
the anxieties of this period when time would have dawdled, he decided to go to Hollywood and take there any stopgap job his friend
and agent, Harold Freedman, might find for him. "If I do sell my
soul to the cinema," he told his mother, "it will be for a tidy sum."

Money was, as usual, a need that spring and summer. Distraction
another. A third was the ever-deepening necessity of trying to find a
more stable peace with Mary Brandon. She could make things pleasant but she did not make them easy. Because of her prettiness, her
gusts of gaiety, and her mechanically summoned charm, many close

to the Sherwoods had no suspicion of the vexations she caused Sherwood by her sudden scenes and steadfast self-absorption. Though he saw her through increasingly impersonal eyes, he remained pleased when she was admired and grateful when she was kind or gay. He even pretended to be amused when she was difficult or cruel. An illusionist by profession, he still preferred to live with the illusion that his hopes were facts and that he and Mary Brandon must be having a good time together because they so often had good times with others.

Since there were lots of "others" to have good times with in Hollywood, old friends such as Geoffrey Kerr, Sidney Howard, and Douglas Fairbanks, Sr., to be seen again, and glamorous new friends to meet, the Sherwoods were in high spirits when, with little Mary and her Mademoiselle, they set out toward the middle of May. On the way they stopped over in Indianapolis to see John Marble Judah, Mary Brandon's grandfather, and Sherwood was delighted to observe how fond the old man was of both Marys, and particularly of Mary Brandon, and noted, almost with surprise, how "marvelously kind" she was with him.

After a stopover in Chicago the Sherwoods and June Walker, who was going out to join Geoffrey Kerr, started west on "The Chief." The Chief had much more to recommend it than the fact that, as Sherwood pointed out, it went through Kansas at night. In that golden age of railways it was a train among trains. It was the Santa Fé's pride, and the joy of those who boarded it as if it were a liner which just happened to travel overland. It sped westward, a model of luxury blissfully isolated from the world, averaging fifty-five miles an hour to Sherwood's proud amazement and covering over a thousand miles a day.

It was a glamour train headed for a city in which glamour had ceased to be a word and become an industry. As the rails hummed, Mary Brandon played backgammon with June and "giggled incessantly," and "was actually beginning to be excited by the prospect of California." Little Mary, who had been obstreperous, was subdued by the seven-year-old's curiosity with which she surveyed everything. Sherwood read and wrote and looked forward with eagerness to going to the dining car, not only because the food was delicious but because the steward had been a waiter at Frau Sacher's.

Reminders of his plays traveled with him; his reputation had preceded him. When he had gone to Hollywood in 1922, he was twenty-six, a newcomer to the new profession of movie criticism, and a glib star-questing reporter with a name to make. He now returned nine years later with his name made. Widely recognized for the work he had done as *Life's* motion-picture critic and editor, he was still contributing his monthly page of book reviews to *Scribner's*. More important by far, he was a playwright who had had five plays produced on Broadway and written a sixth in which the Lunts were scheduled to appear in the fall. *The Queen's Husband* had been made into a film. *Waterloo Bridge* had gone before the cameras just before his arrival. Paramount was planning a production of *This Is New York*, and there was talk of doing *The Road to Rome*.

The Hollywood he came back to was as different as the Sherwood who returned to it. The industry, like the country, was deep in a depression, though one would not have guessed it from the way he lived. The talkies, as Sherwood had predicted, had taken over. Some of the older stars, lucky enough to have voices as well as looks, had managed to survive. But a new generation of actors, directors, and technicians was emerging, equipped to meet the demands of an altered medium. There was room, too, for new authors who, theatre-trained as Sherwood was, were able to write the dialogue which had replaced subtitles.

For their first weeks the Sherwoods stayed at the Beverly Hills Hotel and then moved into a furnished house. It had the inevitable swimming pool, a garden, a charming Negro couple who came with it, and "some of the worst interior decoration ever conceived." But it was less expensive and spared little Mary the risks of becoming a "hotel child," as her father feared she might. Getting around was made easy for them by the Buick they rented and their chauffeur who, sent out ahead of them, had learned the locations of all the stars' homes.

Fortunately, Sherwood found himself at once with a good job. "I am already at work," he wrote his mother three days after his arrival. "I am employed by Howard Hughes, producer of *Hell's Angels* and *The Front Page*, among others, and the story for which I am writing snappy dialogue is called *Age for Love*, though why, I wouldn't just know. It's pretty good fun, however, and the job lasts for only two weeks and nets $7500. Hughes is quite an interesting character—a young man, whose father made millions in oil, and who is fascinated by the movies. I have an enormous office and two stenographers, one of whom isn't so bad looking and is named Miss Brandon. So Mary had better watch out. Sidney Howard works in the same building, but for Samuel Goldwyn, who is also a United Artists producer."

Sherwood's next assignment, after finishing his task for Hughes on schedule, was *Around the World in 80 Minutes with Douglas Fairbanks.* The film was a record of Fairbanks's recent trip, and Sherwood, who had a financial interest in it, helped with the editing and wrote the commentary. The world supplied the settings, Doug the bounce, and Sherwood the puns and gags. He found his job "unusual and fascinating," and had his fun larding the text with "nifties" about Indians dying to get into a funeral procession or elephants bathing with nothing on but their trunks. Nonetheless, it won its laughs and its public both as an entertainment and as a travelogue.

Another commission came Sherwood's way, again from Howard Hughes. Sherwood was eager to fill in his time while waiting for more reels of the Fairbanks film to arrive from the Orient. With Charles Lederer he was asked to collaborate on a madcap screen play, *Cock of the Air*, in which Chester Morris as a lieutenant defied all Air Force regulations by flying from Italy to Paris with his girl because she had a longing for a champagne cocktail at the Ritz bar.

Trivial as these scripts were, they were well received and Sherwood enjoyed doing them. A job was to him a job and entertainment was entertainment. He respected both, and his facility in meeting the demands of the film work which came his way was to prove one of the most lucrative aspects of his career. In Hollywood, as usual, he worked feverishly when he worked and played no less feverishly when he played. When not studio-bound, he was always on the go. He saw a lot of the Geoffrey Kerrs and not as much as he wished of Sidney Howard and his second wife, Polly Damrosch, because they went to Santa Barbara. He and Mary Brandon attended two concerts at the Hollywood Bowl as the guests of his old friend Walter Damrosch. Until seriously stricken with water on the knee, he played his determined tennis with Kerr. He lunched, too, with Bobby Jones when Jones was making one of his golfing films.

Sherwood enjoyed watching a rehearsal of *Waterloo Bridge*, though he had "a hard time choking back the tears" when he saw Roy Cronin in his Canadian uniform. He and the two Marys played happily with their new coal-black Scottie, a four-month-old pup with "parenthetical legs," called "Blackie" though his name was Black Watch. He was pleased to note that Mary Brandon was "actually beginning to have a good time" and had "even deigned to buy some California clothes which look great." Night after night he and she dined with the King Vidors, the Adolphe Menjous, the Roland Youngs, the recently returned Doug and Mary, his former guide to the studios, Adela Rogers St. John, the Richard Barthelmesses, John Gilbert, Dolores Del Rio, or Virginia Cherrill, "the lovely girl who was with Charlie Chaplin in *City Lights*."

Much as he liked these people, he did not like California. To Max Perkins he wrote, "California is certainly kind to the body, though not to the mind or the moral structure." To his mother he complained, "The weather is cool and clear, the flowers are gorgeous, and only man and his works are vile, and how! It's just as awful-looking as I remembered it to be, except that the filling stations, roadeterias, etc., have been breeding and one never escapes from sight of them." Or, later in his stay, "We'll be glad to get out of this place. The people are very nice and the work is interesting, but there's a horrible pall of boredom hanging over everything. The stench of stagnation assails the nostrils. It may be ideal for the natives, but it's no place for a white man." Writing to Kyle Crichton at *Scribner's*, he said, "The industry, by the way, doesn't seem to me to be half so insane as it was in the old De Mille days. The people here are for the most part very good company, and the literacy rate is going up all the time. But the place itself—and by that I mean California—is deadly dull."

This did not mean that the parties were dull. In the same letter to Crichton he reported, "Last night we went to Roland Young's to dinner. Mr. and Mrs. Alfred Lunt, Mr. and Mrs. Geoffrey Kerr and John Gilbert were there. At midnight the party broke up, and Gilbert took the Kerrs and ourselves to his house where we went for a swim in the illuminated pool. The next thing we knew it was beginning to look like dawn, so we all dashed down to Gilbert's other house, on Malibu Beach, some twenty miles away and leapt into the surging Pacific, had breakfast, and got back to the hotel at 12 noon."

That kind of night-to-noon party was the popular notion of life in Hollywood. It was the legendary twenties persisting into the depression and the new-born thirties. It was young middle-age holding onto youth and a reaching for the kind of release that, grim-faced as he was, was to be an abiding need of Sherwood's.

The arrival of the Lunts toward the middle of June made him the more impatient to have the period of waiting over. Their enthusiasm for *Reunion in Vienna* rekindled his. They talked it, breathed it, embodied it. Being perfectionists, they had already started to learn their lines and run through their scenes. Hearing and seeing them increased Sherwood's eagerness to be back in New York, with the three of them working together as they had dreamed of doing.

Much as he had liked Alfred Lunt and Lynn Fontanne when they first met eleven years before, he had shared the feeling about them which, according to him, was then general among theatrical people. Acclaimed as they were, they were regarded as "gifted grotesques, sure to shine in the sideshow but doomed never to achieve prominence in the Main Tent." Both were labeled "eccentrics" and for that reason would be "denied access to the heights reserved exclusively for romantic leads." Lunt had had his "Big Chance" as the comic ex-rookie in *Clarence*; Miss Fontanne hers as the feather-brained and dowdy Mrs. Malaprop in *Dulcy*. Even so, "all Broadway felt sorry for them," being certain that "in each case this would be the only Big Chance."

The right people could scarcely have been more wrong; the wise-acres less wise. Since then, Alfred Lunt and Lynn Fontanne had come so long a way that they had become the Lunts. Not "Mr. and Mrs. Lunt." Never that, though on a May morning in 1922, five months before Sherwood's marriage to Mary Brandon, they had, without telling anyone, taken a subway down to New York's Municipal Building to get married. There they had persuaded two strangers not only to serve as witnesses but to lend them the money they had forgotten which was needed for the license. Although it was the law which made them man and wife, it was something beyond and above it which in the years following their marriage made them the Lunts. "What the Lunts have joined together Dartmouth will not set asunder," read the citation for the joint honorary degree they received in Hanover in 1954. Joined together on and off stage they truly were, two people who as a couple were singular, each so good that there was no better half. In the public mind and in their own they were a union, one and indivisible, set free rather than fettered by this fact. So uninhibited was the abandon with which they played their love scenes that a respectable old lady, observing them at a performance of *Caprice*, was heard to whisper to her neighbor, "It's nice, my dear, to know they really are married, isn't it?"

No players in our theatre had acted in plays of greater variety or merit than they during the years since *Clarence* and *Dulcy*, and the first false forebodings about their careers. None had been given greater opportunities to demonstrate and develop their skills, thanks largely to the Theatre Guild. Separately, Lunt had proved his ever-growing abilities in dramas as different as *Outward Bound*, *Juarez and Maximilian*, *Ned McCobb's Daughter*, *Marco Millions*, and *Volpone*; Miss Fontanne her emotional power in *Strange Interlude*. It was jointly, however, that they had walked into the public's heart in scripts as demanding and dissimilar as *Arms and the Man*, *Goat Song*, *The Doctor's Dilemma*, *Pygmalion*, and *Elizabeth the Queen*.

Adept as they were at converting everything they touched into theatre, including life, they had shone with a special brightness in such comedies of manners as *The Guardsman*, *The Second Man*, *Caprice*, and *Meteor*. In these romps they had proved how triumphantly far they had come since the start of the twenties, Miss Fontanne in transforming plainness into the ultimate in stylish beauty, Lunt in replacing ingenuousness with the most authoritative sophistication. Of pottery she had made Lowestoft while he had converted pewter into silver. Both loved dressing up and putting on a show, the showier the better. Their work was their play, their play their work, and the curtain never lowered on the theatre which was their lives. To them good acting, as Sherwood soon observed, was the good life and that was the life they lived. From his first talks with them on the West Coast about *Reunion* he realized that they had complete understanding of his script and their characters in it, even as, during rehearsal, he came to realize that they always knew what they were doing—and why. For Sherwood working with the Lunts on a play was not only a high privilege. It was "the best possible training in the art and craft of the theatre." It was also a "lot of fun."

Fun it might have been all the way through when the three of them remet in New York in September to start rehearsals, had Sherwood not run full tilt, as Lawrence Langner put it in *The Magic Curtain*, into the Theatre Guild's Board system and disliked it heartily. The Guild had been making theatrical history for twelve years when *Reunion in Vienna* went into rehearsal. It was different from most other theatres in that it was run by a committee, not an autocrat, and its plays were the choice of a majority instead of an individual.

The strength of this committee system was that the six members of the Board of Managers, because of their own differences in temperament and interest, tended to represent the varied tastes of audiences. The weaknesses of the method were human. They were the result of clashes in opinion so unsparingly stated in the presence of authors that some offended playwrights felt, as Sherwood did, that they were appearing in a police line-up rather than at a conference. Even by the admission of the Guild's Executive Director, Theresa Helburn, the initial exposure of a dramatist to the Guild system came as "a difficult ordeal." The members of the Board, said she, were so concerned with correcting faults that they forgot to mention virtues and their disagreements were often so intense that the battles became violent. Their taste was better than their manners, their convictions than their consideration. They fought family quarrels, failing to remember that the playwrights they included in them were not members of the family.

When Sherwood first faced this committee system, the Guild's Board of Managers consisted of: Langner, a well-known patent lawyer, a dramatist, and a man of foresight with a sharp eye for a script and a genius for nurturing a growing organization; Miss Helburn, a small, spirited, button-nosed woman with a sphinxlike head, an inscrutable smile, and a mind as bright as her twinkling eyes; Helen Westley, an actress, tough fibered and informed, who had become widely acclaimed because of the factory-whistle shrillness with which she played overrouged and underwashed old vixens; Philip

Moeller, a playwright-director of much temperament and perception, who was a Marchbanks thirty years later; Maurice Wertheim, a suave, stage-struck banker, whose graciousness matched his business acumen; and Lee Simonson, an admirable designer and writer on aesthetics, full of knowledge but capable of being tactless, whose face was like a voodoo charm done in ivory.

The procedure of the Board was simple, however complicated the results. A play was bought if four out of the six members voted for it; if only three favored it, its purchase was delayed. In the case of *Reunion in Vienna,* the meager minutes of the Board reveal that Langner, Moeller, and Miss Helburn were strongly for the comedy; Miss Westley was "lukewarm"; Simonson against it, feeling it "very superficial"; and Wertheim did not vote because he had not received a copy. Even so, it was "decided to buy the play immediately as a vehicle for Mr. Lunt and Miss Fontanne."

The division in the vote was a portent of trouble, especially since the dissenter was Lee Simonson. Simonson, amiable at heart and blessed with many gifts, was on occasion very difficult to put up with. "Charming" was not the adjective one reached for to describe him, though when put down a peg or three he could be likable. His unfortunate habit was to defend his point of view by attacking instead of persuading those who opposed it. His bullhorn voice did not make his attacks the easier to take or his bluntness the more palatable.

From the start he made clear to Sherwood his dislike of his play in terms so noisy and vehement that they surprised Sherwood and even embarrassed the Board members, accustomed as they were to the ferocities of frank opinions. Sherwood was not quick to anger. His height made him seem above battle. He appeared as imperturbable as a monolith. One would not have guessed that his wide-spaced, slow-coming words were handy weapons for the quick parries of verbal dueling. Once provoked, however, he was an impressive combatant. His eyes blazed. His face froze into a frown that loomed over his attacker. The very deliberation of his speech supplied it with thunder. Simonson provoked him.

The Guild's practice was to assign two members of its Board as a production committee for each of its offerings. This did not mean that the other members were not free and expected to give their opinions at a run-through rehearsal or on the road. *Reunion in Vienna* was entrusted to Langner and Miss Helburn. Worthington Miner was called in to direct, Aline Bernstein to do the settings, and a cast chosen in which Miss Westley, as the termagant Frau Lucher, was to give one of her most memorable performances. Everything seemed set, and the pleasure Sherwood had long awaited of having the Lunts in one of his plays was at hand.

Sherwood's scripts, because of his sureness as a craftsman, required few revisions. "With the exception of Eugene O'Neill," Langner noted, "I know of no playwright who produces a manuscript which, on first reading, is so ready for production."

More revisions than usual (with him) were needed in *Reunion in Vienna*. Even before rehearsals started, the Lunts and Miner made some suggestions which Sherwood found "tremendously helpful." On the road it became clear that still more changes were necessary. Most of these Sherwood, by then a veteran of the vexations of rehearsals and try-outs, made cheerfully with his customary speed and dexterity. Working with the Lunts proved the joy he had anticipated. He never failed, as he put it, to be surprised by their humility and the enthusiasm with which, unmindful of their past successes, they plunged into his play as if it were going to mark their advent on Broadway.

If he remembered the experience of readying *Reunion* for New York as "just one long quarrel," most certainly it was not because of the Lunts. Instead, it was because of the debating society approach of the Guild's committee system, and, more particularly, because of Lee Simonson's conduct as a debater. Simonson was a sullen opponent. He fancied himself as an authority on psychoanalysis and at the very start got into what Langner described as "an acrimonious argument" with Sherwood as to whether his analyst in the play was orthodox or not. Langner tried valiantly at first to oil the troubled waters, and for a while succeeded. But there were other flare-ups, bitter, angry, and wounding, the worst of which occurred in Baltimore where the comedy had fared so badly that there was some discussion about abandoning it on the road.

The Baltimore eruption took place in the Hotel Belvedere after an evening performance and could have served as a model of how *not* to conduct a peace conference or a meeting of any kind. At it Simonson was in a state of aroused belligerency. He tore into Sherwood and his comedy, and delivered lengthy harangues on psychoanalysis and Sherwood's inadequate understanding of it. Miner left the room after taking as much as he could stand. Sherwood remained a little longer. Then he strode out, haggard and filled with fury, swearing, "I'll never give a play of mine to the Guild again." Although in the future he did relent and let the Guild produce one of his plays and co-produce another, the fight that night in Baltimore was "terrible," according to Miner. Even seven cooling years later, Sherwood recalled his Guild experience with *Reunion in Vienna* as an ordeal. "Because of the never-ending wrangling and jangling," he told the *Sun*'s Ward Morehouse, "I came out of it so shot that rather than go through with it again, I would prefer to work for Zanuck or Goldwyn or Selznick or the Cohn brothers or anybody."

Clashes in temperament are as commonplace in the theatre as waves in the ocean. Had such difficulties as Sherwood ran into with the Guild been limited to him, they would have been no more than mishaps in personal chemistry. But in the years ahead there were other playwrights—S. N. Behrman, Sidney Howard, and Maxwell Anderson, for example—who resented having to run the gauntlet of the Guild's committee system. By Langner's admission this irritation added up from author to author until it contributed considerably to forcing a group of malcontents to band together and form a self-producing organization, the Playwrights' Company.

That was seven years later. The troubles *Reunion* encountered before its opening did not end with Sherwood's with the Guild. No play that he had written had such a fluctuating life in its tryout period. He soon discovered one of the inexplicable laws of the stage in these theatrically divided United States, and that is that each city, however inland, can be an island unto itself. As the weeks on the road were extended, the same play, or practically the same play, and the same performance seemed different in different cities. It looked bad in Pittsburgh where it opened, good in Buffalo, bad again in Cleveland, was a near-flop in Baltimore and a huge success in Washington.

Then it swept into the Martin Beck Theatre in New York on

November 16, 1931, as one of the big hits of that year and of the Lunts' and Sherwood's careers. It was quite a season, enriched as it was by Ernest Truex in *Whistling in the Dark* and Philip Merivale in *Cynara*; by Katharine Cornell in *The Barretts of Wimpole Street* and Leslie Howard in Philip Barry's *The Animal Kingdom*; by Paul Muni in Elmer Rice's *Counsellor-at-Law* and Helen Hayes in Molnar's *The Good Fairy*; by the grandeur of Alice Brady and Alla Nazimova in *Mourning Becomes Electra*; and by such musicals as George White's *Scandals*, Earl Carroll's *Vanities*, *The Cat and the Fiddle*, *The Laugh Parade* with Ed Wynn, and, most especially, by Victor Moore's performance of Throttlebottom, the timid Vice President, in *Of Thee I Sing*, a political lampoon which Brooks Atkinson saluted as being "funnier than the government and not half so dangerous."

In those days, when a dollar had a longer reach, legitimate productions which grossed over $10,000 a week could be well in the clear and those which grossed between $20,000 and $30,000 were sizable hits. *Reunion in Vienna* moved at once into the latter category. The advance interest in it was immense. Two hundred orders for the opening could not be filled. Standees flocked immediately to the theatre for matinee as well as evening performances. The first-night reviews ranged from favorable to excellent. They were of that summoning kind known as "good box office." "An exuberantly humorous comedy," "dapper and diverting," "nostalgic and yet gaily satirical," "a cause for much rejoicing," "the Lunts in topnotch form"—such garlands were tossed at it. Yet, in spite of their warmth, the notices were oddly withholding, considering the enthusiasm with which the comedy came to be remembered long after the reviews had been forgotten even by the critics. Sherwood was no stranger to notices of this grudging sort. He had been exposed to them since *The Road to Rome*. I know because until *Reunion* I was one of the grudgers, bothered by something undergraduate in his humor and cloudy in his serious interludes.

One notice stung Sherwood in particular. It was written by Arthur Ruhl who, at the opening, was pinch-hitting for the *Herald Tribune*'s Percy Hammond. Ruhl called the comedy "tortuous and foggy . . . thin and dry and rattling," and said it was hard to imagine what the play would have been without the Lunts. The question was beside the point since the Lunts were in it, and gloriously in it.

One of Sherwood's favorite memories of the Lunts dates from the morning after the New York opening of *Reunion in Vienna*. He woke up late and started to read the notices, picking, with his usual uncanny accuracy, the worst notice to read first. "I was half way through the second," he recalled, "when Alfred telephoned and asked, in a very discouraged voice, 'How is the press? Don't tell me what they said specifically, because Lynn and I never read them and we don't want to know what they say about it. But what's the general opinion?'

"'Well,' I said, 'I haven't read much yet. The *Herald Tribune* is pretty bad, and the *Times* seems a little better as far as I've . . .'

"Alfred interrupted, shouting that I should pay no attention to the *Herald Tribune*, because it was only a substitute critic and anybody could tell from reading his review that he hadn't understood one word of the play. 'But,' he asked, 'did you see Gabriel in the *American?*'"

The conversation went on for a long time. Before it was over Lunt had told Sherwood just what Kelcey Allen had written in *Women's Wear*.

When the ordeal of the testing night was past, Sherwood for a short euphoric time enjoyed the elation of success. Not fully, and not for long. He had a huge hit on his hands. "Such gay and exciting entertainment . . . that you must go, budget or no budget," *The New Yorker* said. Everyone seemed to be doing just that. In spite of the spread of the Depression and increasing unemployment, the weekly receipts soared. The enraptured response of audiences was heartening. There were immediate nibbles for foreign rights, and the sale of *Reunion in Vienna* within two months to Metro-Goldwyn-Mayer for $85,000 was sweet additional proof of the comedy's popularity.

Notwithstanding all this, the letdown for Sherwood came almost at once. He was more exhausted than he realized by his battling with the Guild. There was a sudden emptiness in the fullness of his present. The reviews that filled his pockets wounded his pride. He was delighted by their praise of the Lunts' acting but disappointed by their reservations about his playwriting. He was hurt, too. How hurt he made clear in his reply to a letter which, some weeks after the opening, he received from Deems Taylor.

Since Taylor recognized qualities in his comedy which neither the public nor the press had noticed, he read the letter with "filling eyes." Answering it, Sherwood said, "I knew before I wrote the play—before I had any notion that it might be superficially amusing—that it would contain a number of things that its audiences would overlook; and I still know this, now that the play has become a highly popular frivol, 'thin as cellophane,' as one of the more favorable notices described it. In short, I had and have a high opinion of the body of *Reunion in Vienna*—an opinion which was not fortified, despite the pleasant noise of the box-office smash, until I read your letter."

Sherwood had been melancholy when he started *Reunion in Vienna*. It was the old melancholy, Mary Brandon, and the doubts about himself and the world, which had deepened in him over the years and in the midst of gaiety or success could suddenly engulf him. His despair had been confirmed by reading Joseph Wood Krutch's eloquent abandonment of hope, *The Modern Temper*, which was so black in its mood that by some it was referred to as *The Modern Distemper*. Of all unlikely pacemakers for a comedy Krutch's lament for the living would seem the most improbable. But in it Sherwood found a "fine expression" of a point of view which had become his own. He remembered it as a book that "affected me deeply & led to *Reunion in Vienna* & *The Petrified Forest*." It was typical of him that out of his despair—and Krutch's—he should evolve *Reunion in Vienna*, a comedy which he described as "another demonstration of the escape mechanism in operation."

He was even more despondent when he wrote the preface. In addition to being thoroughly worn out and somewhat disappointed, he was a dramatist between plays. He was drifting. He had no work in progress and was not to go to Hollywood again until the next fall. He was plagued by doubts about his abilities and feelings of displacement and uncertainty which he could not shake off.

The unexpected vent for his dejection was his preface to *Reunion in Vienna*. It was as if "The Emperor Waltz" had been introduced by Chopin's "Funeral March." In this preface he spoke as a member of a generation that had "the ill-luck to occupy the limbo-like interlude between one age and another." The First World War was still with him, its wreckage around him. "Democracy—liberty, equality, fraternity, and the pursuit of happiness! All the distillations of man's maturing intelligence" had "gone sour."

The worst of it was, as Sherwood saw it, that man had been so full of hope. The age of reason had led to unreason and man, the individual, had been coerced into being a struggler in an anthill by such systems as Mussolini's and Stalin's. Having lost his religion, man had become the victim of his politics and of science, too. He was "a sick animal" and the chief symptom of his malady was "an embittered distrust of all the physicians who would attempt to heal him."

"The impulse to be an artist and a damned fool" was being neutralized by the disciples of Lenin and Freud. The prospect was one of "unrelieved dreariness." Perhaps man knew that he was "doomed anyway" and "riding to oblivion in a vehicle of antiquated design." But there was "hope, after all. Man may not have time to complete the processes of his own undoing before the unknown forces have combined to burst the bubble of his universe."

With these green-apple words Sherwood rang up the curtain on the printed version of *Reunion in Vienna*. Fortunately for the audiences, his actors played the play instead of the preface. But Sherwood had to get stated for himself the apprehensions from which his comedy, "with the help of God and a few Lunts," supplied an escape. Later he was to dismiss his melancholy, along with his "disorderly thoughts, impelled this way and that by a futile indignation," as "God damned adolescent introspection" and "a product of infantilism."

Nonetheless, he was to quote at length from his *Reunion* preface in his introduction to *There Shall Be No Night* (1940). "In it," he said, "I came closer than ever before to a statement of what I was trying to think and write. . . . It has a considerable bearing on all that I have written since then." Despairing as he would often be in the future, he never again indulged in the luxury of such wholesale gloom as in his *Reunion* preface. In fact, he was soon to be in rebellion against his own despair, a revolt which was to continue through the years immediately ahead.

Due to the tug of war in his nature, Sherwood went into *Reunion* with what seemed to him "an important if not strikingly original idea—science hoist with its own petard—and came out with a gay, romantic comedy." The comedy, once the Archduke and his former mistress were reunited, was all bounce and energy and exuberance. The only purity it bothered about was to be pure theatre. It was contrivance triumphant, the merriest of waltzes executed *con brio*, boisterous in spirit and unblushing in sophistication.

"He is not one of the wits, of whom we have several," said Brooks Atkinson of Sherwood in his follow-up Sunday piece after the opening, "but he is one of the humorists, of whom we have very few." It was from a spilling sense of animal vitality that Sherwood built, and the Lunts played, his two principal characters in *Reunion*. They were too swept away by emotion to take time out for epigrams. They slapped or kissed, wilted or waltzed, eluded or loved in a series of tumultuous scenes that came as answers to some very simple questions. Would Elena go to Frau Lucher's as her psychoanalyst husband urged her to? Would the Archduke return for the party? Would their former love flame again? Had Rudolf conquered her as he seemed to when he swept her into the Imperial suite? Would he conquer her the next time when, she having fled to her home, he followed her there? When it was all over, and Rudolf had returned to Nice to be a taxi driver again, would Elena recover from this interlude and return contentedly to her husband?

So many people felt this last question was left unanswered that Sherwood wrote one correspondent, "I have almost been compelled to prepare a form letter, explaining things that I had hoped would be obvious in the play itself. Even before the play opened—during the rehearsals and the discouraging try out period—this was a subject of endless discussion. The directors of the Theatre Guild wanted me to be much more explicit, but I could find no way to do this short of parading some chorus girls across the stage with placards. However, a certain amount of obscurity seems to be a valuable property in the theatre in these odd times; and, to the surprise of all concerned, the lamented element of doubt in *Reunion in Vienna* has contributed a great deal to its success. . . .

"There are those who feel sure that the wife, Elena, will again hear the old call and will dash off to Nice in answer to it. I've had one letter saying 'I'm positive that the doctor's prescription turned out to be not a cure but a pleasant, habit-forming drug.' A psychiatrist told me that I should have added an epilogue showing how completely the cure had worked—that the ghost of the past is forever dispelled and that all is serene in the Krug household.

"All of which is extremely flattering but also embarrassing, as I'm forced to confess that I don't know what happens after the final curtain. I do know that she has yielded herself freely and without fear or compunction to the Archduke, and that she is all the better for the experience—but the ultimate results of this provide a problem which it would take several more plays to settle, and I'm not going to attempt to write them."

One incident occurred early in the run of *Reunion* which amused Sherwood and many others, including Woollcott, who reported it to Paul Hyde Bonner. It happened during the scene at Frau Lucher's when "the returning Hapsburg has his first encounter with the old beldame (played, of course, by Helen Westley) who runs the restaurant where the reunion is effected. He can be heard speculating idly as to whether she still wears her old red flannel drawers, and at an opportune moment lifts the skirt to see. The glimpse of Helen's behind incarnadined in flannel is a nightly joy to the Guild subscribers. The other evening, unfortunately, even Helen knew by the gasp of the minor actors on the stage that she had forgotten to put them on . . . Alfred came out of his catalepsy at last unable *not* to speak the line which was then due. It was, 'Well, thank God there is one thing in Vienna that hasn't changed.'"

22

OF MEN AND BOOKS

"Literary Sign-Posts" as a Monthly Column—Old and New Contributors to Scribner's Magazine—A Self-Revealing Reviewer—The Harvest of Those Writing Years—Praise for The Green Pastures—Meeting with Madeline Hurlock Connelly—Her Career—The Connellys and Sherwoods Become Inseparables—Luncheon at the Shaws'—A Happy Summer—Hints of the Future—Buys Great Enton

Eight months after the opening of *Reunion* Sherwood made his last appearance in *Scribner's* as its book reviewer. From September, 1929, to June, 1932, missing only two numbers, he had contributed, busy as he was with his own writing, the lead reviews in a department called "Literary Sign-Posts." One says good-bye to regular reviewing with mixed feelings, sorry to relinquish the transitory authority which goes with it yet entranced to be released from the bondage a column entails. Meeting a monthly deadline had for Sherwood been at times a chore. Often his copy arrived at the last minute accompanied by harried notes full of apologies. But Sherwood liked the job even as he—and Mary Brandon—liked the hundred dollars it paid each month.

Naturally he took pleasure in the surprising freedom which *Scribner's* granted him. He was not tethered to an office. His notices did not have to coincide with the publication dates of the books he was reviewing. He had no editorial responsibilities except to get his copy in. He wrote from wherever he happened to be—England, France, Hollywood, or New York—and about such books as he chose, whether they had been sent to him by the magazine or had attracted his attention in England when they were published there.

The reading he had to do was no hardship. Always a compulsive reader, not given to reading but addicted to it, he would in any case have read many more books a month than the three or four he reviewed. By his own confession he was a plodder rather than a skimmer, and usually stuck to what he was stuck with. "It is my quaint notion," he said in *Scribner's*, "that before reviewing a book I must read every word of it. About those volumes in which, after several pages I cannot detect matter of interest, I maintain silence." As a rule he did. On the few occasions when he did not, he was quick to admit that he was unable to finish the books he was discussing.

He enjoyed having an outlet in a magazine of *Scribner's* prestige. With *Harper's*, *The Century*, and *The Atlantic* it had long occupied a cushioned place in the affections and esteem of its readers. It had fed them richly, in its great days before the turn of the century and down to the First War, on Meredith, Stevenson, Barrie, Quiller-Couch, Kipling, William Dean Howells, Galsworthy, Edith Wharton, Theodore Roosevelt, Austin Dobson, Kenneth Grahame, and Richard Harding Davis. These authors, British and American, had spoken admirably for the world that had been, the assured world in which Sherwood had grown up.

In the decade after the peacemaking *Scribner's* faced a changing magazine field even as *Life* had done when Sherwood was its editor. The times were ultimately to prove too much for both, though each made valiant efforts to keep up with them. Holding onto the old, *Scribner's* reached out bravely for the young who spoke for a new generation and an altered world. These it found in such writers as James Gould Cozzens, Sherwood Anderson, Oliver La Farge, W. R. Burnett, Thomas Beer, John O'Hara, Kay Boyle, F. Scott Fitzgerald, William Faulkner, and Ernest Hemingway whose *A Farewell to Arms* was being serialized when Sherwood started "Literary Sign-Posts." It was as a *new* critic and a *modern* writer that *Scribner's* introduced Sherwood, though it was careful to comfort older readers by saying it would continue William Lyon Phelps's chatty pages of book talk called "As I Like It," in which Galsworthy and Barrie were gods and Robert Browning was always news.

As a movie critic Sherwood had been an innovator, a pioneer almost alone in an unexplored country. As a book reviewer he was only one in an army that had been foraging on print for centuries. He faced new challenges because writing about Aldous Huxley, Rebecca West, Kafka, or Edmund Wilson was bound to be very different from writing about Jackie Coogan, Gloria Swanson, Harold Lloyd, or Cecil B. De Mille.

Reviews seldom outlive the moment they were meant to serve. Sherwood's were no exception. As purveyors of information and honest reaction, they did their duty in a forthright, unpretentious way. They were the products of a highly literate man who loved books and happened to be capable of seizing upon the essence of what he read and conveying it vividly. Reviewing was a needed release for his journalistic impulses, another anchorage in his times, and a form of happy hackdom which found him being paid, however little, for what he enjoyed doing.

Inescapably, while writing about what others had written, Sherwood said much about himself. The boyishness of his movie criticism had almost vanished, though the old gaiety often asserted itself in the same personal terms and the same conversational tones. He made his copy easy for the reader because he made it seem as if its writing had been easy for him. His enthusiasms continued to be exuberant and his rejection of the arty and highbrow resolute. Honesty remained his only policy and sanity his chief attribute. His personal loyalties were strong but friendship neither softened his attacks nor made him afraid to praise. As a Democrat who loved Al Smith, an enemy of Prohibition, or a vehement pacifist, he never hesitated to make his private convictions public.

Sherwood's first contribution to "Literary Sign-Posts" was a review of two German war memoirs which so burned themselves into his memory that eleven years later, when war had come again and he had just heard of the Fall of Paris, he recalled them in his Prize Day address at Milton. One of these was Ludwig Renn's *War*, a chronicle of a private's experiences which ached with truth in expressing the point of view of "all inarticulate, reluctant soldiers." The other was *Storm of Steel* by Ernst Junger, a bloodthirsty Prussian officer and future Hitlerite, who glorified the sacrifices of war with an eloquence that was "brilliant and horrible." Along with these Sherwood discussed *All Quiet on the Western Front* with the sympathy of one who shared Remarque's antiwar feelings. In his every comment his own hot hatred of war made itself felt, right down to his hope that these three books would be available to young men "when the 'Give Till It Hurts' posters are again displayed."

The real compensation for Sherwood of his job at *Scribner's* was that it stretched his mind in many directions, forcing him to read not as a casual reader but with the alerted attention of a person who knows he has a review to write. The books he chose ranged from Marshal Foch's *Memoirs* to Dorothy Parker's *Laments for the Living*, from *Hard Lines* by a newcomer named Ogden Nash to Kafka's *The Castle*, and included Marie Stopes's *Married Love* and Calvin Coolidge's *Autobiography*, Thornton Wilder's *The Woman of Andros* and Colette's *The Gentle Libertine*, Will James's *Lone Cowboy* and Mencken's *Treatise on the Gods*, Edith Wharton's *Hudson River Bracketed* and Michael Gold's *Jews Without Money*, Margaret Sanger's *My Fight for Birth Control* and Evelyn Waugh's *Vile Bodies*, Mabel Walker Willebrandt's *The Inside of Prohibition* and Edna Ferber's *Cimarron*. All these he reviewed during his three years on *Scribner's*, and nearly a hundred more, not to overlook the fourteenth edition of the *Encyclopaedia Britannica*, which under its new editors he described as the *Encyclopaedia Americana*, lamenting the passing of the old volumes engagingly entitled "Bis to Cal," "Har to Hur," and "Pay to Pol."

As a romantic rooted in the past, Sherwood was no admirer of "the intestinal school which Hemingway founded." He respected Hemingway and recognized his qualities though he was not sympathetic to his chest-combing toughness. It was Hemingway's talentless imitators that annoyed him, the host of young writers who aped him without being artists, the undergraduates who, having gulped down *Men Without Women*, were fooled by its simplicities into believing that they could write like that if only they employed a "staccato, riveting-machine style" and turned out stories which consisted "principally of periods." They made Sherwood long for an American novelist who wrote in the "elegantly passemented manner" of Henry James and believe that there was "ample room for a revival of the Victorian novel, with all its gregarious adjectives and its impressive sentence-structure. . . . A way must be found to restore the belief (discredited by the spectacular example of Ernest Hemingway) that writing is no cinch. Something must be done to convince the young part-time authors that the novel and the night letter are two separate and distinct literary forms."

One of the least likely of Sherwood's enthusiasms, considering his respect for tradition, was William Faulkner, whose *Sanctuary* was published in 1931. He confessed that he had never heard of Faulkner until a short time before in England when he read an article about him by Arnold Bennett, that eager greeter of new talents, acclaiming Faulkner as "the new American genius." Sherwood, reporting this in person to Faulkner a year later when they occupied adjacent offices in Hollywood, was startled to have Faulkner acknowledge such praise by saying, "Bennett's about the only man I have ever heard of who deliberately set out to be a second-rate writer and succeeded." In his review of *Sanctuary* Sherwood had already admitted that Bennett was right, or almost right, when he said Faulkner "writes like an angel." He added, "I don't say that William Faulkner writes like an angel, for I don't know much about the literary standards prevalent in the celestial hierarchy. It would seem to me that he writes rather like a fiend out of hell. But this doesn't much matter. All that does matter is that he writes, and with a power that disrupts the most well-ordered entrails. I don't think that I've ever read a more terrible book than *Sanctuary*—terrible in its marked reality, its relentless conviction, its unspeakable beauty—and I'm not sure that I care to read another like it. But whether I like it or not, I shall be compelled to pay the strictest attention to everything that Mr. Faulkner ever has to say."

In "Literary Sign-Posts" during 1930 two men were touched upon, Adolf Hitler and Marc Connelly, who had never been linked before and never will be linked again, and would not now be if in their different ways they had not altered Sherwood's life. The one was born to bloody the world; the other to give it pleasure. The first was already an enemy, however underestimated; the second, an old friend extravagantly esteemed, soon to marry the woman who became Sherwood's second wife.

Sherwood's first mention of Hitler occurred in his review of Lion Feuchtwanger's *Success*, a novel about the Munich putsch, which sent the Jewish author into wisely timed exile since it later put him on the Nazi death list. In their fictional guises, Sherwood reported, many of the characters were instantly recognizable "even to one who knows little about Bavarian politics." But when he gave the real name of "the preposterous leader of the True Germans' Ku Klux Klan," it appeared, believe it or not, as *Rudolf* Hitler.

Sherwood had relished Marc Connelly from the Algonquin days and his early comedies written with Kaufman. He had taken excited pleasure in *The Wisdom Tooth* (1926) which Connelly wrote alone. In its gentle way that fantasy was the embodiment of Sherwood's own romanticism and his protest against the "lowdown" and the "hard-boiled." *The Green Pastures*, four years later, reaffirmed his faith in the American stage and in Connelly's "pre-eminence" among native playwrights. To Sherwood there was no one to match Connelly "in breadth and depth of imagination, in appreciation of those qualities that are of the essence of the theatre, in understanding what the theatre is and always has been and ever will be."

Early in the morning of October 4, 1930, nine months after the triumphant launching of *The Green Pastures*, Marc Connelly slipped down to the Municipal Building to be married, and some months later Sherwood, who had been out of town, met his old friend's wife for the first time. The meeting occurred at one of those celebrity-strewn Sunday brunches over which Woollcott loved to preside at his East Side apartment that Dorothy Parker had christened "Wit's End." Among those present was the Grand Duchess Marie who, as a "real live" Romanov and the author of *Education of a Princess*, was creating quite a stir in democratic New York that season. It was for her that Sherwood mistook Madeline Hurlock Connelly when, across the room, he saw a woman of marked chic and commanding vitality at the center of a group.

She was tiny, almost as small as Mary Brandon, had deep brown eyes and dramatically black hair, and, though prettier by far, did bear a certain resemblance to the Grand Duchess. There was something about her—was it her seeming self-possession, the erect way in which she held her head, or the sense she created of being unfazable? —that in time caused her intimates to typecast her in their charades as "Her Grace" and refer to her affectionately as "The Duchess." No stage queen could have been more regal, no real one so earthy. Her tidiness was glistening, her figure worthy of the Mack Sennett beauties of whom she had once been one, and she as feminine in her looks as she was tough in her thinking. Soft and hard-boiled at one and the same time, she had a pleasant voice, diction that could bite in its precision, and a sharp, laughing mind. Plainly, and with the winnng eagerness of a girl, she wanted life to be a party. No less plainly, she tolerated no nonsense, was quick to puncture pomposity, and stared at the world with unblinking eyes. A friend's wife can end a friendship but, to the relief of both Sherwood and Connelly, Madeline and Sherwood became friends at once, never guessing that their friendship would lead to love and marriage and, five years later, give S. N. Behrman cause to quip to Madeline (to Sherwood's delight), "If you had lived in the beginning of the seventeenth century, you would have married both Beaumont and Fletcher."

When, as Mrs. Connelly, Madeline Hurlock first met Sherwood, she had amply demonstrated her powers of survival. She had been born in 1899, the eldest of four daughters and two sons, in a family to which she was strongly attached. This was in Federalsburg, a small backwater town on the Eastern Shore of Maryland, which in feeling was much more Deep South than Border State. It was a place which meant much to her sentimentally and which she was often to revisit alone. From it she was sent to a school in Philadelphia called Neff College, after which, being already stage-struck, she came to New York and landed, and briefly held, a job as "Miss Java," a show girl on the old Century Roof. This led nowhere except back to Federalsburg which, fond of her family as she was, she had outgrown. She stood it as long as she could and early in 1921 set out for Hollywood, persuaded of its wonders and her chances there by a girl she had grown up with.

For the first two and a half years she found fitful employment as an extra. Then someone told her to report to the Mack Sennett lot for a test. Soon she started to appear, impish and imperious, in slapstick Sennett two-reelers, each of which was ground out in ten days to two weeks. Chiefly she played, with a lacquered gift for burlesque, the vampire who caught the more than usually wayward eyes of Ben Turpin. This was rough-and-tumble work, but it provided a living and an outlet and was fun. It presented its hazards such as the several films in which she was forced to be playful with a lion that stretched across her or jumped into her lap. The lion, Gladstone-old and sleepy, had to be prodded by her to make him snarl. His ferocity was not the test of endurance. His breath was. To her adventures in Hollywood was added a brief and most unhappy marriage to John S. McGovern, a professional soldier with whom she had nothing in common and from whom she was divorced in 1924. Four years later, fed up with her movie career, she headed for New York where she was introduced by Howard Dietz to Marc Connelly, who found her "a very beautiful and storm-tossed girl," tender and gay, and proceeded to fall in love with her.

When she married him, Connelly was at the peak of his career as a dramatist; when she met Sherwood, he was well advanced—and steadily advancing—in his. Although Sherwood knew her only from the movies as a Sennett girl or a Ben Turpin vamp, she was not unfamiliar with him. She had seen *The Road to Rome*, read some of his movie reviews, was acquainted with New York as a Hollywood subscriber to the *World*, and through F.P.A.'s "The Conning Tower" had followed the doings and the sayings of the Algonquin set.

The Sherwoods and the Connellys began to see a great deal of each other. From being friends, they became so inseparable that, by the end of April, 1932, they put their friendship to the acid test of taking a trip together, heading for France, next England, then back to France. They were an odd foursome, each couple seemingly happy as a couple but needing the other's company to maintain that happiness. Both men were romantics, each had a sense of humor, Sherwood masking his in his somber looks and slow-crawling speech, Connelly spilling his volubly with unfatiguable wit. Theirs was a happy fellowship, the result of years of good evenings and good laughs, and made stronger by the admiration each felt for the other's work. Both were riding high on the waves of their recent successes. They had the time and money to spend, and the inclination, too. Their wives, stylish and lighthearted, were also in a holiday mood, so eager to enjoy what the trip brought that they got along together as if they also were friends.

Mary Brandon found by traveling in a group the audience she needed. The Connellys put up with her for Sherwood's sake. Sherwood, as usual, pretended to himself that everything between him and Mary Brandon must be all right because that was the way he wanted it to be. Connelly was a waggish pontificator and a much-talking dear who wrote fantasy and lived it. By his own admission he had "never been on realistic terms with life." Madeline always had been. By temperament Connelly was a performer, and an able one, whose compulsion to be forever "on" was so strong that Madeline, with her sharp eye for the ridiculous, found that she was beginning to laugh at him rather than with him. Yet, as a group, they had a good time. All four were young, at least youngish, and blessed with a stamina which enabled them to work as hard at having fun as if the twenties had never ended and the depression never begun.

The high point of their stay in England was their meeting with Shaw at the end of May. Sherwood had thought when it was first arranged that it would be a brief interview. He was surprised and the more pleased, therefore, when the Shaws asked the four of them for lunch at their flat in Whitehall. Also invited was Sir Barry Jackson, the producer of Shaw's plays at the Malvern Festival, who was soon to put on *The Road to Rome* at his repertory theatre in Birmingham.

Approaching the Shaws' apartment for the first time was in those days a cause for great excitement and not a little nervousness. Pilgrims coming to Ferney to see Voltaire a hundred and sixty years before must have known the same exhilaration tempered with the same self-doubts. What could one say that was worth the saying? How much duller would dullness seem in the presence of such brilliance? Shaw, after all, was Shaw, a Superman of his own creation, self-described as "a professional man of genius," with decades of performance to justify the description. As a playwright, polemicist, critic, speaker, iconoclast, jester, Ibsenite, Wagnerite, Fabian, reformer, and tom-tom beater in his own cause, he was a world figure who had appointed himself headmaster to the universe. No wit was sharper than his, no intellect more dazzling, no employer of the language more eloquent, no statesman more quoted, and no movie star more photographed or willing to be. Ringing his doorbell was an intimidating act. His claim was that he happened to things rather than they to him, and that he was therefore unable to write his autobiography because he was himself an event.

Sherwood was one of the hundreds of thousands to whom Shaw was just that, and had been since his boyhood. Though he was discomforted when *The Road to Rome* was described as "Shaw in short pants," he was flattered to have Shaw mentioned in connection with any comedy of his. He had gone the night before his luncheon at the Shaws' to see a revival of *Heartbreak House* and found it "very good." Six months earlier in a review for *Scribner's* of the Shaw-Terry letters, he had mocked those "who, parrotwise, protest that the author of *Candida, The Doctor's Dilemma,* and *Saint Joan* is a monster of exaggerated intellect and no heart." To him Shaw's greatness was as Olympian as his capacity to annoy. "There are moments," said he, "when you want to kiss the hem of his tweed mantle, and other moments when you want to wring his neck. You are torn between the desire to beg him to go on talking, forever, and the impulse to request him to shut up."

At luncheon that day Sherwood experienced to the full the unexpected kindness and courtesy of the Shaws. "It was a great experience," he wrote his mother, "as the old gentleman ran completely true to form. He even talked Marc Connelly under the table, which is no inconsiderable feat." He found Mrs. Shaw "very nice, cordial, and homey," and was pleased to see that she and Mary Brandon, who was on her best behavior, "hit it off splendidly." The tension of arriving at the Shaws' was eased at once by Charlotte Shaw, who started things off agreeably by saying that she and her husband had enjoyed *The Queen's Husband* "more than any play they'd seen in years, because of the good taste it left in one's mouth."

Shaw, as usual, waited until the others had arrived before making an entrance, tall, lean as a soda straw, his blue eyes twinkling, and his prophet's beard held high. He "talked a blue streak—being incredibly witty on all manner of subjects, particularly Russia," and of his trip there the year before with Lady Astor. On it Sherwood concluded that most of the important observations were not made by Shaw (he was too closely guarded by Soviet officials) but by Julian Huxley, the biologist, who went along and sneaked off from the main party.

"I believe," wrote Sherwood, "that Shaw is an unconscionable poseur—that he says a great deal, emphatically and of course effectively—that he doesn't really mean. He affects to approve wholeheartedly of the Russian system. Telling how they dispose of all recalcitrant nonconformists by simply blowing their heads off from behind, he said he thought that an excellent idea—but it goes without saying that under such a system Shaw himself would be the first to suffer decapitation." It seemed to Sherwood that Shaw, always "a superb josher," but once, for all his kidding, passionately sincere in his attacks on Victorian complacency, was "just going through the motions of being a radical, a hurler of monkey-wrenches." He was "determined to be shocking and revolutionary at all times," and at the moment his espousal of extreme Communism gave him his best opportunity. Actually he seemed "pretty appalled by the prospect" and admitted, in an off moment, that his professed enthusiasm for Communism was "strictly under control."

The question came up of the Soviets' rigid regulation of literature, and Sherwood asked Shaw whether his own works were acted and read in Russia. The Elderly Gentleman said he believed they were to a considerable extent.

"Do they permit the young to read *An Intelligent Woman's Guide to Socialism and Communism?*"

Shaw laughed. "Oh, I don't think they'd ever allow that—it's much too reasonable."

When the conversation drifted to physical exercise, Shaw proudly announced that he never took any.

"But you do swim a great deal, don't you?" asked Madeline.

"I'm popularly supposed to," replied Shaw. "At the age of 76, I have become formally 'a great man.' Thus, whenever I gingerly, trepidantly step off a small rock into one foot of water, some press photographer records the event, and then the picture is published with the statement that I am shown poised for a twenty foot dive." Shaw, as always unfettered by consistency, then conceded that when in London he went each morning before breakfast to a swimming pool and that every day for the past forty years or so he had done setting-up exercises which he learned from an acrobat.

There was one long moment, to Sherwood it must have seemed an hour, when he wished Shaw had gone on talking, forever. He did not refer to it in his letters to his mother, but later on it was a source of amusement to him and to his friends. In S. N. Behrman's telling of the story, Shaw was holding forth with wonderful fluency on the main currents of nineteenth-century liberalism and Sherwood listening enraptured as he ate. Suddenly, to his horror, Sherwood realized that the torrent of fascinating talk had ceased. Silence had settled on the room and everyone, including Shaw, was looking at him.

"Don't you agree, Mr. Sherwood?" Shaw asked, wanting an American opinion. The question hurled at him so unexpectedly was a challenge which offered Sherwood the chance to make an answer worthy of his host. American letters were on trial. American wit, too. Sherwood panicked. Not a thought came to his mind, not a word to his tongue. After swallowing the food he had been enjoying, he managed at last to summon such a brilliant assent as "I certainly do," and murmured that in tones so low that no one heard it.

Shaw, hopeful and insistent, did not let him off. "What did you say, Mr. Sherwood?" he inquired. With the table's attention still focused on him and Shaw surveying him intently, he sought again to conjure an answer, pleased to have a second try. Once more he recognized the challenge and the opportunity at hand. Once more inspiration failed him. Speech, too. All he could finally muster as the silence lengthened was a slowly muttered, "I said, 'I certainly do!'" Shaw came mercifully to the rescue by erupting with ease and wit into talk that was more Shavian. Everything was not lost, however, because at the lunch's end Shaw invited the Sherwoods and the Connellys to go with him to the Malvern Festival to see *Too True to Be Good*, which was to have its first British production there in August.

The summer for the Sherwoods and Connellys was as carefree a suspension in time as a vacation should be. It had a pleasant lilt. Plays, friends, and sights to be seen in London, plus projects discussed that raised professional hopes. Expensive restaurants in Paris, and giddy, hot-spot nights there, Fitzgerald in their mood. A wine- and food-tasting motor trip through Burgundy, accompanied by Gus Edwards, Sherwood's classmate at Milton and one of the closest and dearest of his friends, who was then a dealer in rare books in Paris.

A stop on the way back at Vézelay, a place which for Sherwood glowed with personal meaning since it was haunted by the ghosts of the Crusaders he had written of in *The Virtuous Knight*.

Above all, there was *La Maison Grise*, the large and charming house, part medieval but mainly Louis XV, at Montreuil-sur-Mer, which the Sherwoods rented from Gilbert Miller. With its cobbled courtyard, terrace, and walled gardens, it was as French as Polshot Farm was English. To it the Connellys came for happy weekends, and Sherwood's sister Rosamond, and such friends as Gus Edwards, Cass Canfield, the publisher, and the Louis Bromfields. From it Sherwood set off on his rambles about the ramparts of Montreuil, with history and his own thoughts as his companions when Connelly and Edwards were not with him. Nearby were the battlefields of Agincourt and Crécy. And Étaples too, where during the First War his Canadian Black Watch regiment had paused on the way to the front and he had learned the perils of playing baseball in a kilt.

He walked the walls of Montreuil, happier recollecting the past than thinking about the present. Outwardly he seemed cheerful in his morose way, but inwardly, as he later confessed in his diary, he thought disordered thoughts and brooded ominously on "the soft uselessness" of his life. He was assailed with the old doubts about himself, his work, his future, and the melancholy plight of man. He was still cursed with the feeling of emptiness which had been his since the success of *Reunion* and still tormented by the black thoughts he had expressed in its preface. The world of reality was beginning to invade the cottoned world in which he was enjoying himself. Already he had started a new play, *Acropolis*, about one of the fundamental and abiding cleavages in that world. By August he had finished a first draft.

Two incidents stand out from Sherwood's European interlude which proved to be more significant than its passing pleasures. One occurred early on the first visit to Paris when the two couples went dancing at the Bagdad, a small night club. Sherwood and Madeline created such a sensation dancing a tango, he so tall and awkward, she so small and graceful, and both so energetic and assured, that the floor was cleared and coins were tossed at them. This may have been the first time that Sherwood looked at Madeline with more than friendly eyes. However valiantly he fought against looking at her that way again, he *had* looked. The second evening which cast its shadow on the future was the night in Paris when Sherwood read the Connellys the first act of *Acropolis* and aroused Connelly's interest in the play. On his return to America Sherwood sent him a completed script and Connelly's enthusiasm was such that he said he would like to direct it. This he did when in London *Acropolis* was at last produced a year later and his doing so altered in ways unforeseeable the lives of the Sherwoods and the Connellys.

The summer outlasted itself in another of its happenings. Before sailing home Sherwood and Mary Brandon went to England again, and in Surrey saw—and bought—at Witley, near Polshot Farm, a lovely old-new house called Great Enton and its beckoning twenty-five acres. With Sherwood it was a case of love at first sight and the beginning of a lasting romance. He had found what was to be his second home.

23

ROOSEVELT TAKES OFFICE

Sherwood Writes Acropolis—*Charade of a Happy Marriage—The Grand Duchess Marie and John Barrymore in Hollywood—Sherwood Persists with* Acropolis—*Farewell to Hoover, Doubts about Roosevelt—F.D.R.'s First Inaugural—Paul Hyde Bonner to Produce* Acropolis—*Connelly Wants to Direct It—Gathering Storms—London Opening—Symbol of an Age-Old Split—"A Fine Failure"—Hitler, Lincoln, and Periclean Athens*

When he returned to New York in 1932, *Acropolis* was very much on Sherwood's mind. It was on his mind when early in September he set out with Mary Brandon and little Mary for Hollywood and six weeks of script writing for Metro-Goldwyn-Mayer. On his mind, and in his heart, it was to remain for the rest of his life, particularly during the next seven years when, haunted by it, he was to revise it again and again.

Never published, never written in a version which quite satisfied him, and a failure when given its single professional production, this drama about Periclean Athens, imperiled from within and without by the militarism of Sparta, was the central play of Sherwood's career. It marked a dividing line both in his work and his attitude toward it and the world from which it sprang.

In *Acropolis* he found the man he had become and started to speak for the man he would grow into. In it for the first time, as Behrman shrewdly noted, he achieved the integration between what he was and what he wrote. He thought it by all odds the best play he had so far written and the most positive affirmation of his own faith. It was a reaction, a rebellion, said he, against the despairing spirit of the *Reunion in Vienna* preface, a rebellion which he thereafter continued. Out of it, he acknowledged, came *The Petrified Forest, Idiot's Delight,* and *Abe Lincoln in Illinois,* and from it he took lines for them and his paraphrase of the noble words spoken by Pericles over the Athenian war dead which he included in Dr. Valkonen's letter of farewell in *There Shall Be No Night.*

In Hollywood that year he was a man waiting to hear a jury's verdict. In spite of his resolve after *Reunion* not to face again the ordeal of its committee system, he had submitted *Acropolis* to the Theatre Guild, believing and hoping it would be accepted. Before he reached Los Angeles he had had two favorable reports. These only made him the more impatient to hear from the other three directors.

On the Coast he and Mary Brandon went through their usual charade of pretending to be happily married. If they had their tensions, they also had their fun, and, to have it, avoided being alone with each other. They played a lot of tennis and enjoyed being entertained by such figures from the marquees as Mary Pickford, Douglas Fairbanks, Jr., Joan Crawford, Ronald Colman, John Gilbert, Charles Farrell, Richard Barthelmess, and even Theda Bara. This time Sherwood did not utter his usual complaints against the horrors of life in Hollywood. The people there seemed to him to be "pleasanter and better company . . . than in any other community on earth." They were "completely wise to themselves and to the frailties of their art," and were the more ingratiating because they were "all puzzled as to why the inevitable collapse of the whole works has been delayed this long."

He was not happy in his assignments. Asked to do at first a film treatment of the Grand Duchess Marie's *Education of a Princess,* and then, when nothing came of it, to help with the scenario of *Rasputin* in which John, Ethel, and Lionel Barrymore were to appear, he found himself, as he put it, up to his neck in Romanovs. "I frequently long," he wrote, "for the good old days when I was an unshackled critic of the cinema, instead of its hireling, as I'd like to disgorge a number of embarrassing views."

He did enjoy the Grand Duchess Marie for whom he had mistaken Madeline Connelly. At times it gave him a start to realize, as he discussed one melodramatic situation after another with this vital, strong-chinned woman, that what he and she were "hashing about," in the usual "story conference" manner, was the life of the person with whom he was working. He was touched to have Marie admit that she had wept buckets at *Reunion*, particularly when the exiled Hapsburg said, "We deserved to be thrown out, not because we were tyrants but because we were all at heart rotten sentimentalists," and even more touched when she added, "That was so true." He was pleased, too, when struggling on *Rasputin*, to have John Barrymore tell him that there had never been a part in which he gave such a good performance as he planned to give in the scheduled film of *Reunion*. "Why, that character is autobiographical!" exclaimed Barrymore. "A crazy, conceited, arrogant, offensive egotist—flaunting himself about, hogging the center of every stage, devising magnificent exits for himself—why, that's *me!*"

Back in New York toward the end of October, Sherwood lived with his disappointment over the divided reaction that had reached him of the Guild's directors to *Acropolis*. Although they liked the play, they did not like it enough to produce it unless revised materially. "I agree that it needs to be made more theatrical," he wrote his mother, "but how to make it so without ruining it is a problem I can't yet solve. However, I intend to keep at it." And keep at it he did.

While waiting to hear the fate of *Acropolis*, he had found time to finish *The Oxford Accent*, a modern comedy about life in an English university town, but it turned out so badly botched that he gave it a hasty burial in his bureau drawer. *Acropolis* was different. Although over the years he was to consign it from time to time to the same bureau drawer, Pericles, Cleon, Phidias, Socrates, Alcibiades, Aristophanes, and Aspasia were characters who refused to stay there. They would not let him alone. Neither would the opposing ideals of Athens, freethinking, democratic, beauty-loving, and of Sparta, with its austere dedication to strength, totalitarianism, and the military. As 1932 slipped into the past, the ancient division between the two grew again into a present reality. Events saw to that. On January 30, 1933, Adolf Hitler became Chancellor of Germany, and on March 4 Franklin Delano Roosevelt President of the United States.

On that 4th of March, Sherwood, at George Kaufman's, was one of the millions waiting eagerly for Roosevelt's address. He was not expecting much. Al Smith was still his idol, the Al Smith because of whom he had ceased to be a Republican and become a Democrat. Although he voted for Roosevelt, he had his doubts about him. "All Coolidge had to do in 1924," he was to say, "was to keep his mean trap shut, to be re-elected. All Harding had to do in 1920 was repeat 'avoid foreign entanglements.' All Hoover had to do in 1928 was to endorse Coolidge. All Roosevelt had to do in 1932 was to point to Hoover."

On the day before the inauguration Sherwood wrote Gus Edwards in Paris, "Things here at the moment are so bad they're funny, with 'bank holidays' prevailing in a majority of states. The crisis is imminent. . . . Tomorrow the world at large will be literally suspended on Roosevelt's inaugural speech, but it's my guess that he won't say much. The other day Al Smith made a brief speech before a Senate committee in which he said *everything*. Al, however, is too honest and forthright to be an efficient politician. Roosevelt is cagey and will play his cards deliberately and, we trust, with the utmost finesse."

Sherwood expressed the same misgivings, tinctured with the same hope, in "Inaugural Parade," a thumping jingle of his which appeared on the front page of the *Saturday Review of Literature* on March 4. He had first submitted it to *The New Yorker*'s Harold Ross who, after the attempted assassination of F.D.R. in Miami in February, returned it to him, saying he could not take a chance on Roosevelt's being alive on Inauguration Day. With strong beats on Vachel Lindsay's tom-tom, it began:

> *Plodding feet*
> *Tramp—tramp*
> *The Grand Old Party's*
> *Breaking camp.*
> *Blare of Bugles*
> *Din—din—*
> *The New Deal is*
> *Moving in.*

In name rhymes as ingenious as those in a Frank Sullivan Christmas salutation, it catalogued the list of those who would be present, including

Huey Long with galloping tongue;
Owen D. and Tammany Young;
Admiral Grayson, Major Domo;
Walter Lippmann, sapient homo;
Bishop Cannon, the Methodist Pope;
Bernard Baruch and Herbert Swope.

Finally it came to Hoover and Roosevelt.

But—hold!
Sit *down!*
Yes—meaning you!
Sit down in front!
Here come the bearers of the terrible brunt
One incoming—the other out-going.
Which is the luckier?
There's no way of knowing.
But though it's a hollow platitude
To speak of a nation's gratitude,
The mob today should be nothing loath
To offer plenty of same to both.

To you, Lord Hoover—we would mention things
    more relevant
To peace of mind than all their votes or vetoes;
There's climate that is bracing and benevolent
Twixt Palo Alto's hills and Sausalito's,
Where one may calmly dwell, relieved of onus,
Watching in eastern skies the new Aurora—
Deaf to the shrill demands for Beer or Bonus—
Deaf—best of all!—to belchings out of Borah. . . .
So bless the vengeful voters who evicted you,
Discard the hairy shirt that has afflicted you,
And find the solace that detachment brings
To those who once were presidents and kings.
And you, Mr. Roosevelt—our nation-wide selection—
We know that smiles of confidence enwreath
Your cheering face. Each rotogravure section
Reveals that you have Cousin Teddy's teeth;
But are we sure that you have fixed your eyes on
A goal beyond the politician's ken?
Have you the will to reach the far horizon
Where rest the hopes of men?

We know not now, but as you gird your loins,
We'll think about the motto on our coins—
And leave the full solution of your mystery
To that relentless epic poet, History.

The sky was dull and threatening and the wind chill when Roosevelt began his address. By the time he was through, the dark clouds hanging over not only Washington but what he described as "a stricken nation in a stricken world" appeared to have lifted. Long and straight of spine, his shoulders and chest so powerful that his braced legs were forgotten, his handsome face free of the vacuities of campaign smiles and resolute in its dedication, he stood behind the presidential seal the embodiment of the confidence in itself that America had misplaced. He stood there a patrician inviting the country to share in his privileges. He had reached only his fifth sentence when it became plain that the weather was changing. "So, first of all," said he, his diction precise, his voice warmly resonant, "let me assert my belief that the only thing we have to fear is fear itself— nameless, unreasoning, unjustified terror which paralyzes needed efforts to convert retreat into advance."

The "fear" phrase, as he spoke it in his Groton-Harvard accent, leapt from his manuscript into every listener's memory. And into history. One did not need television. To hear the new President was to see him and to recognize at once that in him democracy had found its defender in an hour of seeming defeat. In something under two thousand words he had made it abundantly clear that he would "act —and act quickly."

Sherwood, who expected little from the speech, found in it a new world, or rather an old world made new and fresh again. Looking back on it fifteen years later when Roosevelt had been dead three years, he wrote in Roosevelt and Hopkins, "No cosmic dramatist could possibly devise a better entrance for a new President—or a new Dictator, or a new Messiah—than that accorded to Franklin Delano Roosevelt. . . . As the occasion of his entrance was tremendous, so was the manner of his rising to it." Hoover, said he, "was in the parlance of vaudeville, 'a good act to follow.' Roosevelt rode in on a wheel chair instead of a white horse, but the roll of drums and the thunderclaps which attended him were positively Wagnerian as emotional stimuli and also as ugly warnings of what might happen to American democracy if the new President should turn out to possess any of the qualities of a Hitler or even of a Huey Long. . . . The American people were literally starved for leadership." On that March day Roosevelt had already started to supply it. That leadership proved ever-widening in its influence on men and events. Seven years later it reached out to include a surprised but eager Sherwood among those working closely with Roosevelt.

For Sherwood 1932-33 was the long year of waiting for *Acropolis* to find a producer. To fill his time, he turned to versifying, writing in addition to "Inaugural Parade" two other "poems" ("serious poems" he called them) in the same vein. One was "Hymn to the Citadel of Static," a rueful salute to Rockefeller Center and its "vertical austerity," which appeared in *The New Yorker* in December, 1932. The other, published in *Vanity Fair* the next July, was "Independence Day Oration" in which, as if ventriloquizing for Roosevelt, he mockingly reminded Americans, particulary the D.A.R., that their forebears were "Reds," "rebels," and "lawless." But *Acropolis* was his real concern.

The Guild remained firm, though friendly, in its decision not to produce it until he had revised it. Restive under this postponement, Sherwood showed the play to Jed Harris, who wanted to put it on. This made him the more eager to get the script right. He was hard at work revising it when in May, with Mary Brandon and little Mary, he sailed for England to take possession of Great Enton. There he did some remodeling and furnished the house completely. There, too, during that summer *Acropolis*'s sole professional production had its beginnings.

A neighbor was Paul Hyde Bonner, who was living three miles away at Polshot Farm which the Sherwoods had rented four years before. Bonner, the son-in-law of a fabulously rich silk manufacturer, was a retired businessman who, long before he worked for the State Department and wrote such novels about international life as *SPQR* and *Hotel Talleyrand*, was so ambassadorial in his looks that one would have sworn he was born wearing striped pants. He and his wife Lilly possessed to a degree denied most people, rich or poor, a talent for living. With them wealth was not dulling nor comfort corroding. They had been Sherwood's intimates since the old Algonquin days. Indeed, they were friends of all the Algonquin Group and Woollcott's particular pets. Fortunately for *Acropolis*, the Bonners were stage-struck. Better still, in a worldly sense they were in a position to be angels.

One day, when Sherwood was playing his earnest tennis at Polshot Farm, Bonner inquired what he was working on. When he said a new play and described *Acropolis*, Bonner asked if he could read it. The authors are few who can resist such a request. Sherwood was not one of them. The next day he took the manuscript over. When the Bonners read it, they were so enthusiastic that Bonner said that if Jed Harris did not produce it he would.

In August the Connellys had their first view of the green lawns and blazing flowers of Great Enton. Before arriving in England, they, with Edna Ferber, Peggy and Ralph Pulitzer, and Alison and Russel Crouse, had taken a North Cape cruise on the *Kungsholm*. During it no midnight sun was needed, except for Connelly, to make it clear that all was not well with their marriage. Madeline stayed in her cabin for days; Connelly, avoiding reality, believed that she did so only because she was not well. Since the Sherwoods' marriage was in a no less shaky condition, the Connellys' long visit at Great Enton invited complications. These were not slow in coming. Though he struggled against it, by the end of the month Sherwood was again looking at Madeline with more than friendly eyes. By then the two of them had had what they knew as their "Declaration of Love Day." The real storms lay ahead.

Acropolis hastened their coming. When the Connellys and the Sherwoods were back in New York in September, they learned that Jed Harris was unable to go ahead with his planned production. Sherwood remembered Bonner's offer and cabled him, and Bonner, true to his word, said that he would gladly produce it with Connelly directing. After much discussion and many cables, it was decided to do *Acropolis* at once in London before offering it in New York. The decision was reached on the basis of lower costs, greater ease in casting, and the chance of getting the script in final condition for Broadway.

This West End production meant that toward the middle of October the Connellys and Sherwood were once again in London, with Mary Brandon conspicuously missing from the erstwhile foursome. Never interested in Sherwood's plays except for the money they made and the position their success gave her, she did not bother to go over for *Acropolis*. She had interests of her own which were neither literary nor theatrical. One of them, according to Rosina, Sherwood's mother, was a rich, rather fashionable, dissipated man who cared no more for her than she for him. Her fortunate indiscretion, from Sherwood's point of view, was that, when drunk, she boasted to some of her friends of her infidelity and even informed Sherwood of it in England, oddly believing that her being attractive to other men would make her the more attractive to him. Her strategy, worse than being perverse, was unwise. The ironic result of Mary Brandon's not being in London was that Madeline and Sherwood were thrown together particularly during the long hours of rehearsals when they sat in the balcony of the Lyric Theatre.

Acropolis was a play which required close listening but there were chatterers in the stalls when it opened on November 23. There were late-comers, too, who were noisy in debating whether or not they should push on to their seats. And promenaders who throughout the evening strolled about talking at the top of their voices. The first-nighters gave the more audible performance, prompting one occupant of the pit to say as he left the theatre, "What them stalls want is a machine gun." There was also a silly fellow who shouted "Rubbish" at the curtain's fall. He, however, was soon silenced by the roaring applause of those who respected what had been attempted even if they had their reservations about what had been accomplished.

"Rubbish" *Acropolis* plainly was not. The discerning recognized its merits in spite of its faults. James Agate of the *Sunday Times*, though alert to the play's flaws, found it interesting and "highly intelligent." To *The Observer*'s Ivor Brown it was "a noble experiment in the playhouse world," fine and bold in its theme, if inadequate in developing it. To Jane de Glehn, who with an aunt's affection saw it twice, it was a "beautiful, witty, strange play" which, as she reported to Rosina, put Sherwood "in a very high class *indeed*."

The joking attitude of *The Road to Rome* was gone, the easy device abandoned of having ancient characters employ modern slang. The romantic, though still present, was defending something higher and more luminous than a cardboard moon. The confectioner of comedies, his wit persisting, had more on his mind than laughter or contrivance. In *Acropolis* Sherwood was writing "straight." If his characters, in spite of their Grecian costumes, spoke as moderns, it was because their conflicting hopes and fears and beliefs have always been contemporary. He was as serious as his subject, unafraid of eloquence and able to rise to it in sentences clear, simple, and flowing.

Playwrights may or may not make history but they have the right to remake it. Sherwood exercised that right. In a stage direction he returned for a moment to his old collegian mood, describing Cleon as "the most violent of the citizens," and the one who, through his facility in preaching the doctrine of "mass terror," was to become "the most influential with the people." These, he pointed out, were quotations from Thucydides which he had inserted "to impart to this play, if only momentarily, a semblance of historical accuracy."

Was the Parthenon, which was still being built in *Acropolis*, its columns rising higher and higher in each act, really finished some years before the war between Sparta and Athens broke out? Was it straight invention to have Phidias (spelled Pheidias) condemned to die by drinking the cup of hemlock? To Sherwood these and his other many departures from history were rightly justifiable. His search was for those overtones of truth which refuse to become the prisoners of fact.

In the Acropolis he found a symbol of an age-old schism in the values and concerns of men. To Cleon, a Spartan in spirit, and to the members of his War Party, the work being done there represented a treasonable squandering of public funds which should have gone into armaments. Cleon's familiar cry, uncomfortable in its realism and always granted a new persuasiveness in times of emergency, was, "Can we eat beauty? Can we win battles with beauty? Look at the Spartans for instruction." This looking became the easier when the Spartan army, determined to destroy it, surrounded an Athens which

was crowded with refugees from an invaded and burned-over countryside and swept with pestilence.

Phidias, Socrates, Anaxagoras, and Pericles (influenced by Aspasia) took a different view in Sherwood's play. They persisted in
seeing the Acropolis through the eyes of Athenians. To them the
work on it must be finished even in the midst of war because it was
the embodiment of what Athens had offered to the world. It was not
art for art's sake but for the spirit's, the fruit which justified the
orchard. It provided a needed sustenance of its own, not by supplying the means of survival but the reasons which made it endurable.
Its noble beauty was proof that small, evil, and confused as man may
be, he has within him "divine powers of creation" which enable him
in his lasting works to rise above himself and to "defeat death."

The London critics, confronted with *Acropolis* as it was filtered to
them through the static of that first-night audience, were respectful
but lukewarm. They had praise for the demagogic passion of Raymond Massey's Cleon, for the artist's megalomania of Ian Hunter's
Phidias, and for several of the lesser performances, especially Eliot
Makeham's aged Anaxagoras. But their misgivings were strong about
Gladys Cooper as Aspasia, the hetaera who was first the love of
Phidias and then, to the outrage of Athens, the wife of Pericles. As a
famous courtesan, mistress of a famous house, she seemed to them a
goddess in beauty and an icicle in her sexuality who had chosen the
wrong profession. They found Marc Connelly's production academic
and lacking in vigor and Aubrey Hammond's massive settings stolid.
As for Norman O'Neill's incidental music, coming as it did from
records played over a loudspeaker, it made Agate think of cheap
salmon which tastes too much of the tin.

Naturally, the critics' major concern was the play. They made it
clear that they recognized *Acropolis* was not just another one. They
discerned and approved of the ambition of Sherwood's reach and
wrote glowingly of single scenes and the quality of the dialogue.
Some regretted the absence of Pericles, a pivotal figure who, though
much discussed, did not appear. Others wanted a Socrates who, as "a
dispenser of interruptions," was closer in scale to the wise Silenus
Plato drew. Still others wished that this character or that had been
amplified. All complained about the want of action and felt the play's

large theme needed clearer definition. The fatal flattery of criticism is that it raises its sights when faced with authors who have raised theirs. This seeming injustice is a compliment understandably unappreciated by those to whom it is paid. It means that to try for the indifferent is to gain tolerance and to aim at the best to invite dismissal. Sherwood became the victim of his communicated intentions.

Speaking for himself, the critic of the *Sunday Graphic* spoke in effect for his confreres when he said, "Sherwood's may not be a great play but there is enough profundity, wit and beauty in it to make the fortune of a half dozen plays conceived on less ambitious lines. For this must be judged by the highest standards. If one aims at the stars it is not enough to hit even the tallest lamppost. Complete triumph or a fine failure—there is seldom a happy mean."

Acropolis was "a fine failure," a *succès d'estime* which filled the stalls with swift-footed playgoers but left the pit and gallery empty. It had the shortest run of any play that Sherwood wrote and was the longest occupant of his interest. After only twelve performances, having cost Bonner some ungrudged $20,000, it closed, soon to be followed at the Lyric by the work of a rival playwright, Robert E. Sherwood, whose *Reunion in Vienna* in a return engagement with the Lunts was impatiently awaited by the manager. Four days after the opening of *Acropolis* Madeline and Marc Connelly sailed home with Sherwood, there to face troubles that were more than make-believe.

In the light of what was at hand, it seems odd, rather it *now* seems odd, that the English reviewers stopped where they did in pointing out the parallels between the past and the present in Sherwood's play. In the aesthetes of ancient Athens they saw precursors of those Victorians known as "The Souls." When discussing Cleon's objections to having work continued on the Acropolis in wartime, they recalled a project for a National Theatre in London which had been dropped after August, 1914. Edging into the contemporary, they likened the intellectual advisers of Pericles to the Brain Trusters who during Roosevelt's "First Hundred Days" had converged on Washington. But there they stopped with strange abruptness and a blindness stranger still, considering what we with hindsight can plainly see.

The year, after all, was 1933, and the opening of *Acropolis* late in

November. Sherwood remembered having read before then *Mein Kampf* (*My Battle*) which was the blueprint of what was to be the world's battle. It had recently been published in England and America in a diluted version; in Germany the uncut edition had sold over a million copies. In February, a month after von Hindenburg, that fossil of his Prussian self, had summoned Hitler to become Chancellor, Hitler had used the Nazi-set Reichstag fire as an excuse for putting a torch to German liberty and terrorizing all Germans, Communist or not. A month later he had made himself not only the head of the German government but its supreme legislator and had begun his boycott of the Jews. By July he had outlawed all parties except the Nazis. The *Sieg heils* of his followers filled the air and the goose-stepping of his Brown Shirts was thunderous in the land. But no one seemed to hear and no one seemed to see.

When the English critics wrote of Cleon, Sparta, and the War Party and left Hitler, or even Stalin and Mussolini, unmentioned, they only suffered from a lack of vision which affected most people, including those who should have known better. Among these was so perceptive an American correspondent as Dorothy Thompson who wrote, after her first interview with Hitler, "When I walked in Adolf Hitler's room I was convinced that I was meeting the future dictator of Germany. In something less than fifty seconds I was quite sure that I was not. It took just about that time to measure the startling insignificance of this man who has set the world agog."

To Sherwood, who had been reticent in stressing the threats to the present which had darkened the past, *Acropolis* was a statement of faith rather than a propagandist warning. For him it remained that during the years ahead when he rewrote it again and again, introducing Pericles and then omitting him, merging Anaxagoras with Socrates, seeking to humanize Aspasia, tinkering with scene after scene to strengthen it, and rereading Plato, Plutarch, Thucydides, Santayana, Sappho, and even *Mlle de Maupin* as pitch-givers for what he was writing.

He was sustained by having Gilbert Miller, Jo Mielziner and Kenneth MacKenna, the Theatre Guild again, Tallulah Bankhead, and Ina Claire show fitful interest in producing it, and delighted to have Maxwell Anderson like it, Edward Sheldon describe it as "a very fine play," and Eugene O'Neill write Bonner that it was "a damned sound piece of work and I can well understand your enthuiasm for it." He was grateful, too, to the Amateur Comedy Club of New York for giving it three performances in December, 1935, in a good production directed by Theodore Steinway in which he and Mildred Dunnock appeared.

Two years after that, when again working on it, Sherwood wrote in his diary, "*Acropolis* seems to be the persistent challenge to my desires & the exposure of my inadequacies." That same year he visited Greece for the first time and at last saw the Acropolis which had been haunting him. Its special meaning for him he explained to his mother in a letter, written when he was working on *Abe Lincoln in Illinois*, which was so personal that he begged her to keep its contents confidential.

"When you stand in the Parthenon and look through the columns (which have a strange, reddish tinge) at the surrounding mountains —Pentelicus & Hymettus—and at the sea and the Islands—you feel that you're seeing farther than you've ever seen before. When I think of all that I've read about the Acropolis—attempted descriptions of it by the greatest writers—I realize how completely inadequate are all the written accounts of it. But—standing up there and looking toward all points of the compass—the main feeling I had was one of a queer sort of patriotism; for I felt that in my country, more than in any other that has existed since the Age of Pericles, has been realized the ideal which the Parthenon symbolizes—and that is democracy, which the Age of Pericles invented. I felt that I knew at last what it is that has made me so absorbed in the play, *Acropolis*, what it is that has made me go back to that play again and again and slave on it although it had once been branded as a failure. It is the feeling that this is what I was born of, for and by—which is what leads me directly from a play about the Acropolis into one about Abraham Lincoln. But *please*, mother—consider this as strictly between you and me; and therefore keep this letter to yourself."

24

THE DIFFICULTIES FACED

*A Home No Longer Home—Tumultuous Divorce—"The Kidnaping"
—Rosina's Opinion of Mary Brandon—In Love with a Friend's Wife—
The Courtship—Sherwood's Breakdown—Fighting Against the Inevit-
able—Madeline Agrees to Sail*

Sherwood returned to a home that was no longer home. This time
he faced the reality he had long avoided. Mary's letter in London,
boasting of her lovers, brought an end to his somnambulism. Confused in his feeling about Madeline because of his friendship for
Marc Connelly, he was definite about three things. He wanted a
divorce, he wanted custody of his daughter, and for the sake of both
Marys he wanted to avoid scandal.

He had not taken Mary Brandon into account. Her response was
defiance, slander, hysterics, and scenes. Surprised by Sherwood's
anger, bewildered by his determination, she, the guilty party, acted at
first as if she were the injured one. Sherwood as a gentleman wanted
her to get the divorce. She as Mary Brandon refused to do so.
Though she felt no affection for little Mary, and little Mary none for
her, she put on a great show of mother love as a weapon with which
to wound and threaten Sherwood. She continued her melodrama until
she learned that his lawyer, Thomas K. Finletter of Coudert Brothers, had in his possession the needed incriminating evidence. She
then telephoned Sherwood to ask, "Can't this be settled out of
court?" His reply was certainly if only she would sign papers giving
him sole custody of their daughter. Bowing to the inevitable, Mary
Brandon signed but, while doing so, put on one of the biggest scenes
she had staged in all her years of embarrassing spotlight grabbing.

She burst into tears, groaned, spoke pantingly of her love for little Mary and Sherwood, and threw the pen across the room. Her performance might have been more convincing if at that moment a maid had not entered to announce the arrival of a beau. Instantly Mary Brandon forgot her tears, bounced up like a rubber ball, got herself fixed up, and in the highest spirits went downstairs. That night she went gaily to a big ball.

What she might do even after the signing remained unpredictable. To protect Sherwood legally, Finletter had advised him to leave his house and take little Mary with him. Accordingly, he and she, with her French governess, engaged in an operation known to the family as "the kidnaping." The three of them left home as if going for a walk and went into hiding at an obscure uptown hotel, and Sherwood hired a detective to watch over his daughter. Since they brought no suitcases, they depended for additional clothes on the few friends who were in the know. Geoffrey Kerr, a sharer of the secret, dropped by to find them having a cheerful dinner together, little Mary having struck up a warm friendship with the detective.

For little Mary, who was then a plump, precocious, imaginative girl of ten, "the kidnaping" was both an adventure and an escape. She was delighted to be with her father and away from her mother, for whom she could never recall feeling anything except dislike. This dislike was founded on many inerasable memories of tantrums and rages, during one of which Mary Brandon had evidently told little Mary that she had not wanted her. "Oh, mother does not care anything for me," she said during her stay at the hotel. "She did not want me but I just came."

Her feelings for her father were very different. "I can believe what he says and he is so good and I know he will never leave me and it's certain I'll never leave him. I asked him to take me away and he did." Mary Brandon's comment, made with great satisfaction a few weeks after giving up her only child, was, "Well, anyway they can't take my jewels away from me." As Sherwood's mother wryly observed, this was "a complete reversal of the well-known sentiments of the mother of the Gracchi." It was also a spiritual unfrocking of Mary Brandon.

What she had become was as clear to Rosina as the sitter for a portrait. "I used to be very fond of Mary," she wrote her son, "and understood why you were. She was appealing & attractive to me, and was very good company. She was responsible for ordering your common interests on a practical basis. Old Maria used to complain that 'Mr. Sam was mussy from childhood' and the same might be said of you. Mary made you careful of money. Also I used to think that she was a good & appreciative critic of your work & that she did not solely value it from a commercial standpoint. But as the years went on I came to realize that everything she did was for herself. She not only never wanted to give out anything—either in money or time or sympathy, but she despised in others the 'pulses stirred to generosity!' . . . And so she has made herself what she is, and I feel very sorry for her, God knows."

In another letter from the same period Rosina explained to Sherwood what her attitude and the family's had been to Mary Brandon. "For years I have known pretty well what Mary was & what she was not, but I have tried to be her friend, and, by dint of flattering and never the least criticism, to keep in her good graces. I have said to myself, 'Bobby loves her & I suppose she loves him in her way.' We have all pursued this policy for your sake and for little Mary's sake. Even on that dreadful Xmas day I was affectionate with her, & spoke of her to you as if there was nothing wrong, but I made up my mind that the atmosphere was dangerous and disastrous for the peace of mind of that blessed little child. She is sure to say things and do things before her that will leave scars."

Sherwood was to remember 1934, in a future moment of depression, as the year which shattered "the good old nervous endurance" and the "imperviousness" with which he had formerly been "blessed." Looking back on it was no pleasure for him, enduring it an ordeal. It was one of those "meanwhile" years when more crises occur simultaneously than are bearable. Its decisions were draining, its tensions incessant. There was the question of whether Mary Brandon would go into court against him before he could go to Reno to divorce her. There was her consent to be gained before she signed the papers. There were her tempers, whims, fantasies, and lies which required the most cautious handling. No one could anticipate what she would do or when she would abandon truth.

The lawyers faced the difficulty of agreeing on a settlement which would satisfy her, Sherwood the problem of meeting its demands. "I suppose," said his mother, "you will have to give Mary a lot of money." He did. To her went the house in New York, the car, half the securities bought from his savings, and half the future royalties, amateur as well as professional, from all the plays he had so far written, including *Acropolis*. Fortunately, Great Enton was in his name and so were the full rights to his future works. Sherwood did not care. He wanted his daughter. He wanted the "lovely, beribboned decree" which, when handed to him in Reno, would set him free. And he wanted Madeline.

The idea of being in love with a friend's wife and breaking up his home disturbed him. Sherwood was a moral man, sinewy of conscience. When some time later he read about a famous man, well known to him, who had taken a friend's wife for his wife, he found it "pretty horrible," adding, "Of course, I'm a poor one to view with righteous indignation—but this makes me rather sick." In his case the circumstances were scarcely the same. Madeline, though slow to make up her mind about leaving Connelly, had made it clear that she was not in love with him, and Sherwood, though fighting against wounding Connelly, was very much in love with Madeline. He saw her constantly from January until November whenever he was in New York, but, since they were able to meet only for lunch, tea, cocktails, and an occasional dinner or movie, these meetings, however pleasant, proved teasing and frustrating and got them both down.

The year was made the more upsetting by the news which reached Sherwood when he was forced to be out of town. In February and March, while in Hollywood working at M-G-M with Irving Thalberg on *Marie Antoinette*, he learned that Mary Brandon was again lying about him. She was telling her new friends in New York that he had been a brute to her and knocked her down and blacked her eyes. Then, while he was in Reno for the obligatory six weeks and writing *The Petrified Forest*, he was distressed to discover that Mary Brandon was also expressing herself in make-believe. She was assuring everyone that Sherwood was still in love with her, that he would remarry her on his return, and that they would go to England together the coming summer as if nothing had happened.

Mercifully she did not turn up at Great Enton that summer, but Rosina and Rosamond did, and Madeline came for two short visits. After the first, when she went to the Continent with nothing settled, the year took its toll on Sherwood, who in July had a breakdown. He described it afterwards to Paul Bonner when explaining his inability to do a satisfactory revision of *Acropolis*. "I just simply haven't been able to work on it, and before I can do so I must achieve some degree of calm detachment. Ever since Reno my mind has been a bloody mess. Indeed, in mid-summer, I went to pieces so completely that I had to go to bed for three weeks and submit to the tyranny of doctors and nurses. I had lost twenty-five pounds from my all too skinny frame and was really exhausted. Recovery from that has been slow and it will be quite a while before I'll feel like working again. . . . But you must understand the extent to which uncertainty has oppressed me ever since that dreadful disruption of my home last winter."

Madeline in Paris was persuaded by phone to come back to Great Enton where, with Rosamond, she stayed for several days before she, little Mary, and her governess sailed for New York with Sherwood, who was deep in the worries of readying *The Petrified Forest* for Broadway. The two of them met for a few times in October under the same inhibiting conditions and finally agreed not to see each other again. But meet they did, drawn together irresistibly, although with a surface chilliness hiding the warmth of their real feelings. By then *The Petrified Forest* had opened in Hartford and Boston, and was heading for New York where on January 7 of the next year it was to score a huge success. On December 30 Sherwood had his crucial meeting with Madeline. He could stand it no longer. He told her he was weary of waiting for her to divorce Connelly and that, after the opening, he was planning to leave with little Mary, her governess, and Geoffrey Kerr for a long stay in England. He hoped she would sail with them and get her divorce. She said she would.

In May, 1935, when she and Sherwood were at last about to be married, Sherwood wrote to Woollcott, hinting at the difficulties they had undergone and not foreseeing those which lay ahead. "As you may possibly have heard, from any one of eleven thousand authoritative sources, the turbulent and often unbearably harrowing romance between Madeline and self is about to be solemnized at the altar. (The altar will probably be located in Budapest, as that seems to be the only place in Europe where we can obtain a license to wed without going through all manner of diplomatic negotiations. They don't think much of Reno divorces over here.)

"When I saw you at dinner at the Lunts' one evening last Fall, and Madeline was referred to, all hope seemed to have been lost. I had made a determined effort to be ever so noble, and had refrained for two months from pressing my suit or even communicating in any way. But that phase didn't last much longer, and I was soon back in the saddle of Lochinvar. There is no way of disguising the fact that this business has hurt Marc sorely, or that from certain points of view I must inevitably appear a prime shit. But the only answer to everything is that I love her very much indeed and want to make her happy. And I believe that the emotion and the motive have your approval. Time heals all wounds—as I think I said in one of the sub-titles of *The Hunchback of Notre Dame*—and it's possible that eventually Marc will forgive. But Time will have to do some mighty drastic therapy."

In *The Petrified Forest* the garrulous grandfather insists, "There ain't a woman alive or ever did live that's *worth* five thousand dollars." To this Alan Squier answers, "Let me tell you one thing—you're a forgetful old fool. Any woman is worth everything that any man has to give—anguish, ecstasy, faith, jealousy, love, hatred, life or death." Sherwood did not have Mary Brandon in mind when he wrote that speech. He could have been thinking of Madeline Connelly.

25

FREEDOM AT LAST

Reno as a Restorative—A Road Map Gives The Petrified Forest *Its Name and Direction—"At Last—I'm Started!"—The Intellectual, "A Vanishing Race"—Humphrey Bogart Becomes Typecast as a Gangster —Leslie Howard Fine but Unreliable—Divorce, Riga; Marriage, Budapest—Happy Ending and a Productive Year—Ideas for* Idiot's Delight

Sherwood's unhappy 1934 had for him, in terms of the theatre, two happy endings—Madeline's decision and *The Petrified Forest*— and Reno made them both possible. He had realized he had to have a new play for the fall, and this knowledge was one of the pressures under which he had lived. But the dislocation of his life had robbed him of his writing energies. His one attempt, *Milk and Honey*, a comedy laid in France, turned out to be such a proof of fatigue that he buried it at once in that bureau drawer.

Reno came as a temporary restorative. It was like no place he had seen, and the impact of its differences brought back his zest for work. In a jubilant letter to Geoffrey Kerr, he described its climate as "bracing," its scenery as "marvelous," and it as one of the "oddest" and "most fascinating spots" he had ever visited. He liked it because it was "a genuinely and unashamedly wide open town." He liked it because its gaiety restored his own and because it was "natural" and "uninhibited." He reported with pleased amazement that a population of only 22,000 could support what seemed to him enough bars, night clubs, and gambling houses for five million people. He was interested, too, that, though parents and children went as families to these places, there appeared to be nothing that was vicious and very little that was sordid about their doing so.

Four out of five of the hungry women waiting to be divorced seemed to him a sorry lot, and a few so sorry that their husbands must have been "heaving with relief" at the thought of being parted from them. The decree-waiting men struck him as being even sorrier, the kind of men who "tell their troubles to the bar-tenders." Even they, however, were better than the gigolos, dressed up like cowboys, who stalked the incipient divorcees.

He took to the natives, the social leaders and big businessmen who looked just like their counterparts elsewhere but behaved differently. They were "hearty and cordial." He liked the health of their laughter, the imprint of the sun on their faces, the clink of their silver dollars, and the way in which they referred to paper currency as "Los Angeles money." He loved the bars and the gambling and the sense of adventure he experienced each day when playing tennis with a bartender from San Salvador, who was trying to organize a treasure hunt on Cocos Island. In Reno he found the spirit of the vaunted Old West. The echoes of the Gold Rush and the footprints of the Forty-Niners were all around him. These stimulated and excited him.

On the day he arrived, after a flight that was agony to him because of his fear of planes and his dread of flying over the Rockies, Sherwood dug in at the Riverside Hotel, which could claim among its many advantages that it was next door to the Court House. The following day Lester Summerfield, his lawyer, a companionable and understanding man, took him for a drive to nearby Carson City. Summerfield was an old-time resident of the region, sprung from authentic pioneer blood, and Sherwood liked him immediately. He was a yarn spinner, full of tales of the area, and on the way he told vivid stories of the Comstock Lode and Virginia City, and of Mark Twain when he lived there.

Sherwood listened eagerly, his imagination as fired by what he was hearing as by what he was seeing. Suddenly, from the nowhere that ideas come from, an idea for a play came to him. Vague as it was, it was urgent enough for him to say on the way back to Reno, "I'd like to rent an office and a typewriter somewhere in town and try to spend my time doing some work." By the next morning Summerfield had found him a furnished office, for which he was to pay $25 a month if, after the first two weeks, he found he could write there and nothing if he could not. Fortunately he could, and within a week was confiding to Kerr that he had a play half done.

His recollections of how he dashed off *The Petrified Forest* he later wrote to Ward Morehouse. The day he took the office Sherwood started writing dialogue without much idea of where he was going. "My only reference library was a road map, and for some reason (I forget just what it was) I decided to put the scene in the Arizona desert instead of Nevada. I arbitrarily figured out on the road map just what was the exact location. In the First Act, I came to the point where the girl says to the man, 'Where do you go from here?' and the man replies, 'That all depends on where this road leads.' I thereupon looked at the road map to see where it did lead, and found some little criss-crosses on the map and the words, 'The Petrified Forest.' From that point on, I knew just what the whole play was about and within four weeks I finished it and shipped it on to Arthur Hopkins. That left me two weeks in Reno with nothing to do but play roulette and keno and the slot machines and I think I just about broke even."

Though these last two weeks dragged, his memories of Reno were agreeable—eating steak at the Grand or the Elite, catching 18-pound trout in Pyramid Lake with Summerfield (whose name he used for an unseen lawyer in the last act), playing tennis with his bartender friend, dining at the Town House, dancing at the Tavern, where one night he was thrown out for falling down, all six feet seven inches of him, and in general savoring the town's bizarre gaieties. Some wondered when he worked because they saw him so frequently looming large at play. But work he did and feverishly, and his chief memory was the excitement he felt while writing *The Petrified Forest*, his mind fired by the scale and strangeness of a part of America that was new to him, and his own problems for the moment dwarfed and seen in a different perspective.

"At last—I'm started!" he thought when he completed the play, and because of this he always had "a great fondness" for it, even when he had come to think of it as "negative and inconclusive." "It pointed me in a new direction and that proved to be the way I really wanted to go." He was pleased with the play because it contained its own preface, and proud of it because it was his first real attempt to speak out directly and have his say about his own country in his own time.

Among the reasons for the success of *The Petrified Forest* when it opened six months later in New York was that in the best Pauline manner it was all things to all men. Each theatregoer discovered in it the kind of play for which he was looking. To those whose search was for a melodrama it supplied one, plentiful in its suspense, about a famous killer Duke Mantee, who with his gang shoots it out in the lunchroom of a lonely filling station in the Arizona desert on the way to the Petrified Forest. To those with a taste for the sentimental it provided a tender romance about a futile intellectual, Alan Squier, who gives his life for a pretty young waitress so that she can go to France and become a painter.

Written from the grim mood of the depression and yet filled with the romantic disillusionment of the twenties, it managed to say stark things gaily. Indeed, melancholy has seldom taken a sprightlier form or seriousness been more lightly expressed. Truth, treacle, and tension it mixed freely and with success. In one breath it approved of the bitter vision of T. S. Eliot, in the next it quoted with rapture from the love poems of François Villon, but at no time did it refer to the strivings for rebirth and renewal of the New Deal, though rebirth and renewal were its concern. If it did not quite make rational sense, it did what was of greater importance theatrically. It caught audiences in the web of its illusion. One of its delights was that it not only made the impossible probable but made it seem real.

There was more to *The Petrified Forest*, however, than gunplay, romance, comedy, and mesmerizing theatre. At least, there was more for those who chose to look for it, and these were many. The play was an allegory, tantalizing if sometimes elusive in its symbolism, in which Sherwood had his grave comments to make. His petrified forest was no mere natural curiosity in far-off Arizona. It was the whole of American civilization which he believed had become petrified. All of his characters, except for the young waitress, were people turned to stone by having outlived their usefulness. The one thing that Alan Squier, the panhandling intellectual, and Duke Mantee, the rugged individualist and killer, have in common is that both of them are condemned.

The old, old man, who is the waitress's grandfather, is the most ancient of the obsolescent, an Indian fighter who, since he can only look back to the days of Billy the Kid and a vanished West, deserves to die because he is no longer living. His American Legionnaire son has long since ceased to be the man he was in the emergency that created him. The glorious years of the eternal halfback who works at the filling station were those he spent in college. The stuffy banker who turns up at the Black Mesa Bar-B-Q is the victim of his own success, and his wife, who wanted to be an actress, has been robbed of her life by living with him. Only the waitress, who may yet become a painter, has anything to give the future. She is its sole hope. Therefore the defeated writer persuades the killer to shoot him, without letting her know of his request, so that she, by getting his insurance, can escape from her present and bring to life in herself the dream that has died in him.

For Sherwood the essence of his play was contained in the scene in which Squier says to the girl, "You see—the trouble with me is, I belong to a vanishing race. I'm one of the intellectuals. . . . Brains without purpose. Noise without sound. Shadow without substance." Then, after mentioning *The Hollow Men* and the intellectuals who thought they had conquered Nature and dammed her up and sold her in cellophane, he explained the cause of the chaos in the world. "It's nature hitting back. Not with the old weapons—floods, plagues, holocausts. We can neutralize them. She's fighting back with strange instruments called neuroses. She's deliberately afflicting mankind with the jitters. Nature is proving that she can't be beaten—not by the likes of us. She's taking the world away from the intellectuals and giving it back to the apes."

As honest about his own work as he was about the work of others, Sherwood knew he had not quite said what he had in mind. Two years later, when he came across the same ideas in H. G. Wells's *The Croquet Player*, he wrote in his diary of his own "garbled expression" of them in *The Petrified Forest*. His later conviction, as he told Edith J. R. Isaacs, when thanking her for a piece she had done on him, was that the first act was "much better than the second, and there was no conclusive way of ending the play." Even soon after the first night, with the cheers of the audience still in his ears, with the praise of the press fresh in his mind, and long lines forming at the box office, he felt a sense of "almost" rather than of "all right" about the play.

"The trouble with me," he said to the *Herald Tribune's* Lucius Beebe, "is that I start with a big message and end up with nothing but good entertainment." Admitting that some of the critics were right in their reading of the meaning of his allegory, he asked, dragging out his words, "Do the great run of theatregoers peel off their banknotes to see an Indian fight, a gunman, a millionaire, and an American Legionnaire symbolizing the passing of a world order? In a pig's eye! They come to see two parts of a highly improbable and sentimentalized romance stirred, like a martini, with one part gunplay. They don't want a message and, anyway, perhaps I didn't give it to them as I should have." In the character of the waitress he had tried to express the renewal of courage and vitality and fresh ideas. "But I lost control of the idea, to a certain extent, just as I lost control of the theme of *Reunion in Vienna*, and made Lynn Fontanne's husband a man instead of a scientist."

Regardless of his feeling that he had failed his subject in *The Petrified Forest*, Sherwood had not failed his audiences. "If it is not unethical to say so in the first sentence," wrote Atkinson in the *Times* after the opening, "Robert Sherwood's new show is a peach." It was as "a peach of a show"—a lusty, gay, literate, and tender melodrama "written by a man . . . mentally restless in a changing world"—that the public hugged it to its heart. It was as all these things that it was directed by Arthur Hopkins, that amazing, moon-faced little cherub, who, looking like a small-town banker and thinking like an artist, had in such productions as *The Jest*, the Barrymore *Hamlet*, *What Price Glory?*, and many another given the American theatre some of its biggest hours. He brought to it the largeness of the West and the magic of the theatre, and an excellent company headed by Humphrey Bogart and Leslie Howard.

According to Geoffrey Kerr, who had it from Sherwood, the inspiration to cast Bogart as Duke Mantee was Hopkins's, not Sherwood's. Bogart had played Latin lovers with some success but at the moment was down on his luck. He felt suicidal and looked it and was the object of his friends' concern. One of these was Sherwood. In the hope of getting him some kind of job, he suggested him to Hopkins for the thankless part of the ex-football player. He had the build. He bulged with strength. He was all male.

Hopkins sank into one of his silences during which time seemed to stand still. He thought of more than Bogart's masculinity. He thought of his driven power, his anguished dark eyes, the puffs of pain beneath them, and the dangerous despair which lined his face. As if coming out of a coma, Hopkins said a half hour later that he believed Bogart was not right for the ex-football player but thought he would be ideal as Duke Mantee. He was. In fact, he was so ideal that Sherwood later blamed himself for having written in the killer the kind of tough guy part from which Bogart was not allowed to escape. Leslie Howard's share in making Bogart the Humphrey Bogart known to millions was even greater. Wanting a big name for the gangster role, Warner Brothers was eager to give it to Edward G. Robinson. Howard had promised Bogart during the New York run that he would not appear in the movie if Bogart were not the Duke Mantee. He kept his word and Bogart got the part.

For Leslie Howard's Alan Squier, Sherwood felt enduring gratitude and an admiration which chagrin could not diminish. Blond, handsome, with a sad wry smile and a gift for quietly spoken comedy, Howard was a player supreme as a water-colorist but without the strength for oils. Of a negative he made a positive; of diffidence, an act of caring. No one could write of him, or talk of him, without falling back on the word "charm," which he had in such easy abundance that he could turn nighttime theatregoers into matinee audiences. Immaculate, quizzical, and stylish, he had in Savile Row terms something of Chaplin's pathos. Women doted on him the more because, in addition to being attractive, he seemed to need and invite their protection. His performances in such plays as *Outward Bound*, *The Green Hat*, *Berkeley Square*, or *The Animal Kingdom* were almost installments in a delightful serial. Into this serial Alan Squier fitted perfectly. Sherwood knew this and Howard realized it as soon as he read the copy of the play which Sherwood gave him on the *Majestic* when they were sailing for England to work on *The Scarlet Pimpernel*.

In the screen version of this novel of the French Revolution by Baroness Orczy, Sherwood (aided by Arthur Wimperis) wrote one of the most successful of his motion-picture scripts, and in it Howard gave one of his best performances. As Sir Percy Blakeney, the Eng-

lish gentleman who cheats the guillotine of the lives of French aristocrats, he remained Howard, which proved a fine thing, but he was
Howard with a difference. He brought a new devil-may-care energy
to the part and a new sense of character in distinguishing between a
man who at home is a foolish fop and abroad a coolly fearless secret
agent. This British film, in which Merle Oberon, Raymond Massey,
and Nigel Bruce also appeared, was affectionately referred to as
"good hooey" by those who collaborated on it, and captivating
melodrama it proved to be in both England and America. It took
time in the making because Alexander Korda, its producer, was the
kind of man who would call off work if the day were beckoning and
sunny, and Howard the kind of person who was as interested in his
polo ponies as he was in his acting.

Looking back on his experiences with him, especially in *The Petrified Forest,* Sherwood wrote twenty years later to Geoffrey A. Johnson, "Leslie Howard was a brilliant, sensitive, natural actor. He was
also one of the most thoroughly unreliable artists that I have ever
known. You could not count on him to show up for a rehearsal or
even for a performance after the play had opened. Nor could you
count on him, once the play had been established, to deliver the lines
as written and not ad lib improvisations in order to relieve himself of
doing the same thing night after night. I knew Leslie for a long
time—from his first arrival in New York to appear in *Just Suppose* in
1920. I saw him emerge as an exciting new acting talent, together
with such other new talents as Alfred Lunt, Lynn Fontanne, Helen
Hayes, Katharine Cornell, Tallulah Bankhead. I don't think I ever
saw him give a bad performance."

On January 30, 1935, three weeks after the opening of *The Petrified Forest* and one month after Madeline reached the decision to
leave Connelly, she and Sherwood, along with Mary, Mademoiselle,
and Geoffrey Kerr, boarded the *Manhattan* to embark on what was
one of the oddest of odysseys in quest of divorce and marriage. New
York was a mass of snow and slush, the harbor choked with ice, and
the wintry air chilling. The travelers did not mind. They were
warmed with a sense of adventure. Little Mary was released from
school. Kerr, who had been down on his luck, was heading home.

Madeline and Sherwood were deeply in love and impatient to marry. Sherwood had already won his freedom; Madeline was in search of hers.

Early in January Kerr had learned of Sherwood's plans when dining with him in his apartment at the Carlyle. At the end of the meal Sherwood got up abruptly and without apology or explanation went into another room. He returned in a few minutes carrying one of those lined yellow pads he always used, tore off the top sheet, and handed Kerr the note written on it. It said that Sherwood was sailing to England on the *Manhattan* with Mary and Mademoiselle and that also on the boat would be "a Certain Party." She was not named and did not need to be. This announcement was followed by the suggestion that Kerr accompany them and the statement that Sherwood would lend him money for the fare. Kerr accepted the offer, touched by this new proof of friendship. To him the writing down of what, between most close friends, would have been spoken seemed "curiously characteristic" of Sherwood and his way of evading what might have been an embarrassing discussion.

In London Madeline went to the Dorchester and Sherwood stayed in Isobel Jeans's house on Avenue Road. Ahead of them lay four months of waiting. They were months filled with fun, but made exasperating by delays and even comic in the problems these raised. Sherwood's Reno decree proved in Europe an invitation to legal difficulties which quickly appeared. Madeline's divorce obtained in Riga (Reno's Baltic counterpart) presented no obstacles except arduous travel and an irritating postponement. Within two weeks after reaching England, Madeline and Sherwood set out on a turnaround trip to Latvia, leaving London on February 15 and arriving in Riga on the 17th. The next day Madeline petitioned for her divorce, and on the 20th they were back in London. It was, however, not until May 13 that the Riga decree came through. Two weeks later they were on their way to Budapest, it seeming to be the only place that would accept these law-crossed lovers, and there on June 15 they were at last duly married. "We have had the god damnedest time finding a place in Europe where we can have it done respectably," Sherwood wrote Bonner in a moment of despair. "The prospects are that we shall have to travel about a thousand miles to achieve a legal ceremony. However, such difficulties are trivia in the history of this particular romance."

The Sherwoods were entrapped in red tape until the very end. "We had almost abandoned hope in Budapest," he told his mother, "when finally a prominent Hungarian author and editor—by name, Lajos Zilahy [later author of *The Dukays*]—went to the Prime Minister and said that if they denied us the license it would be accepted as an insult to the U.S.A. It was then granted, on June 14th, and the following morning, at 12:30, we were married by some official who wore a red, white and green sash." The witnesses were Mr. and Mrs. Zilahy, the Sherwoods' lawyer and his wife, a Mr. and Mrs. Ellis from the U.S. consulate, and a Mrs. Woodward Jelke whom Sherwood had met in Reno. "There was also an official interpreter and two camera-men, who snapped pictures all through the proceedings. The ceremony was simple and dignified, which was a relief after all the opéra bouffe nonsense we had been through."

Little wonder that when they were at last handed the certificate Madeline's comment was, "How do you know this isn't a permit to fish in the Danube?" Some of their friends enjoyed teasing them about the Riga decree and the ceremony in Budapest, saying that their marriage would not hold up in America. Among these was Averell Harriman, who offered to legitimatize their union by giving them a large wedding at Arden. After the procedure at the registry, the Sherwoods went back to the hotel, toasted their good fortune in champagne, and took the Zurich express for Paris. When Sherwood discovered that the train had an hour's wait in Vienna, where Madeline had never been, he rushed her to the bar of the Hotel Sacher, where they downed a bottle of Grinzinger in honor of a certain play. Then they pushed on to Paris for three days, staying at the Crillon in the apartment overlooking the Place de la Concorde in which Lansing, Colonel House, and Wilson (his one-time hero) had drafted the covenant of the League of Nations.

Back in London, they were met by little Mary, who looked pale and seemed nervous. "I think she felt that we'd be entirely different, now that we're married," he wrote his mother. But she began to brighten and suddenly burst out with, "My father has gone back to being what he used to be—I thought I'd lost him." Sherwood had the feeling she could see that he had been "relieved of the burden of uncertainty that has oppressed us all in the last bad years."

Personally and professionally, he had every reason to be happy that June. After a long series of harassments and frustrations, he was married to Madeline. *The Scarlet Pimpernel* had triumphed on both sides of the Atlantic. *The Petrified Forest*, a hit in New York, had been sold to the movies for a comforting $110,000. For Korda and René Clair he had finished the script of *The Ghost Goes West*, which he was certain would prove honey at the box office. And since April 24 his adaptation of *Tovarich* by the French dramatist Jacques Deval had been the reigning success of the London season.

Tovarich was the most gilded, delightful, and deliberate hokum, about an impoverished Russian Grand Duchess and her princely husband who rejoice in working as servants for a Parisian banker, come near to being dismissed when recognized, and finally give to a Soviet commissar the fortune which the Czar entrusted to them to be used for the good of Mother Russia. Sherwood had been asked by Gilbert Miller to make an English version of the comedy and, according to Kerr, tossed one off in three or four days while staying at Avenue Road. Theatregoers were delighted with his adaptation. Only Deval objected to it. From the time of the Edinburgh tryout he maintained "his standard of complete ungraciousness." But after he saw the London reviews and the first box-office reports, Deval was mollified and—success being the final persuader—agreed, as Sherwood put it, that "the fine qualities of his play had been strong enough to survive even my process of mutilation."

Tovarich was pure theatre of an older kind, born of an earlier day when royalty was dearer, when the murder of the Imperial family at Ekaterinburg was a horror fresher in everyone's mind, when Paris was overrun with White Russians, and any taxi driver could turn out to be a prince or any *vendeuse* a grand duchess. It was contrivance for the sake of contrivance, not what could happen but what audiences with all their hearts wanted to have happen. It was a Sherwood comedy that Sherwood did not write; a script so Lunt-like in its mood that it seemed as if the Lunts must be playing in it even when it was being admirably acted in London by Eugenie Leontovich and Sir Cedric Hardwicke, and in New York by Marta Abba and John

Halliday. There was something about it, in or out of Sherwood's adaptation, that won tears and laughter everywhere.

In his travels across Europe Sherwood noticed that there were only two ways in which the countries through which he passed resembled one another—the munitions plants were doing capacity business and so was *Tovarich*. In Paris it ran for some 800 performances. It was played in nearly every city in Europe outside of Russia. In Berlin it had been so successful that Hitler, according to John Gunther in *Inside Europe*, was supposed to have seen it four times, having first, of course, had his secretaries telegraph Paris to make certain that M. Deval's ancestry as far back as his grandparents was kosher Aryan.

The Lunts were among those delighted with Sherwood's marriage and his hits, including *Tovarich* which they had reluctantly turned down to do a revival of *The Taming of the Shrew*. In his letter of congratulation Lunt sent Sherwood one of the most welcome of wedding presents—an idea for a new play. He was looking for something with which to follow Shakespeare's "old flapdoodle farce." "Seems to me, Mr. Sherwood," he wrote, "you'll really have to do something about *that!* You could put us in Budapest this time—say a Chicago punk on his way to Bucharest to put in those slot machines or a former 'barker' now managing a troupe of midgets—who meets the elegant Hungarian fakiress between a couple of hot violins & a zimbalum. Easy! Bobby, you could do it on your ear."

Sherwood was "greatly tickled" with this suggestion and asked Woollcott to tell the Lunts, who were staying with him at Lake Bomoseen in Vermont, that he would "write a play along the lines they require with a lot of good two-scenes for the right team." As a matter of coincidence, Sherwood had been thinking for some time along somewhat similar lines, groping for the play which was to become *Idiot's Delight*.

He wrote Ward Morehouse in 1948 that, when in Reno, he already had the idea for *Idiot's Delight* but it took a long time to work it out. "In November, 1933, I was coming back from England and on the ship (the *Majestic*) I ran into my old friend, Harry Carr, of the Los Angeles *Times*. He had been on a trip around the world and he said that the supreme hotspot was Harbin, Manchuria. He described the hotel there and the dramatic mixture of nationalities, including always, some beautiful, phony White Russian girl who was formerly a Grand Duchess (the supply of Grand Duchesses must have been unlimited). All the people there were continually looking up into the skies for the bombers that would herald the start of the Second World War, which would begin, presumably, between the Soviet Union and Japan. So I decided to write a play about that hotel in Harbin, but I could not work it out until the summer of 1935 when I was at the Club Arizona in Budapest and saw battered-looking American chorus girls doing an act. I asked the proprietor of the joint where he had found them and he said, 'Oh, they have been touring the Balkans for years.' Those girls provided the line on which the whole play could be strung. I moved the hotel from Harbin to the Italian Alps."

The ingredients were all there for him to put to his own uses. The Chicago punk became Harry Van, the American hoofer that Lunt played. The chorus girls Sherwood had seen in Budapest replaced the midgets as members of Van's troupe. The phony White Russian (Lynn Fontanne) emerged as the mistress of a German munitions manufacturer, and a woman with whom Van had spent a night at the Hotel Bryan in Omaha years before when they were both in vaudeville. The "hotspot" of international trouble in Manchuria was transferred to Fascist Italy. And the bombers for which the people at a resort in the Italian Alps searched the skies were Mussolini's planes from a nearby airfield on their way to attack Paris, and French aircraft striking back.

26

THE SHAPE OF THINGS TO COME

Darkening Headlines—Mussolini into Ethiopia, Hitler into the Rhine-land—Lippmann on Dictators—Sherwood's Persistent Hopes for Peace —Idiot's Delight and the Coming of War—Harry Van and Sherwood— Edward Sheldon as a Friend—On the Road and in New York—The Triumph of the Lunts—Wins Pulitzer Prize—The Mayor of Omaha and the Lord Chamberlain—Idiot's Delight in London and as a Film—The War Comes Nearer

The Second World War was four years off when Sherwood drama-tized its outbreak in *Idiot's Delight*. When it was six years away and most people were talking about peace and disarmament, and the League of Nations continued to offer some hope, Laurence Stallings wrote the stabbing captions for a collection of battle horror photo-graphs called *The First World War*. To many, especially in this country, the mere hint of another war then seemed ghoulish and unthinkable.

There were those who knew better, and among these the one who knew best was Winston Churchill. As early as 1932 he had risen in the House to mock the policies of the MacDonald government and give the first of his many formal warnings of the approaching war. His later conviction was that, until the middle of 1934—the "cardi-nal year" he called it—"the control of events was still largely in the hands of His Majesty's government without the risk of war." Britain, in concert with France and through the League of Nations, could, he felt, by decisive action have brought an end to the Hitler regime. After that it was too late. The hopes, which proved a house of cards, had begun to collapse.

Sherwood was well aware of the menace of events when he wrote *Idiot's Delight* late in 1935. But for him, as he looked back on that

year in his diary at the beginning of the next, it was "a large year."
He was at the peak of his productivity and earnings and at last
happily married. He and Madeline had had a fine summer at Great
Enton, where they had built a new wing. On their return to New
York in the fall they had taken and completely furnished an apartment at 120 East End Avenue, and he had done some doctoring for
Max Gordon on the stage version of *Pride and Prejudice*. "I must
have spent more last year," he told his diary, "than ever before—
how much I have no idea. Some $30,000 on Great Enton & new
apartment. But whatever the total sum was, it was well spent. Never
before have I got so much living out of twelve months."

Furthermore, he had written *Idiot's Delight*. He began the play on
November 25, writing so swiftly that by December 19 it had been
typed, submitted to the Lunts, and accepted by them. When he
started it, Mussolini had already invaded Ethiopia. By the time it
opened in March of the next year, Hitler had occupied the Rhine-
land. Japan, Italy, and Germany were aggressor nations nakedly on
the move. In the House of Commons Britain's Foreign Secretary,
Anthony Eden, had said the situation was "dreadfully similar to
1914."

With Madeline and the Bonners, Sherwood was boarding the noon
train for Washington and the tryout there of *Idiot's Delight* when he
saw the news that Hitler had ordered the German Army into the
Rhineland, thus "shattering the Versailles Treaty (what remains of
it) & Locarno pact. This is the most serious news yet," he wrote in
his diary, "and it seems if *I.D.* waited another week to open it would
be utterly out of date."

If he began *Idiot's Delight* unable to foresee what the headlines
would do to it, he waited for its Broadway opening with increased
uncertainty. "What will happen before this play reaches print or a
New York audience," he admitted in his postscript to the published
version, "I do not know. But let me confess here the conviction that
those who shrug and say, 'War is inevitable,' are false prophets."

In the months between finishing *Idiot's Delight* and seeing it into
production he hung on his radio and devoured his newspapers. He
was familiar with the facts which lent persuasion to the prophets of

doom. He knew the darkening picture drawn by foreign correspondents. In January, at a dinner at the Thomas Finletters', he listened with great interest to Walter Lippmann as he talked about foreign affairs, pointing out that dictatorships reach a point of strength beyond which economic law makes it impossible for them to go. Lippmann's contention, according to Sherwood, was that then they either use their strength or decline. "Japan reached that point some time ago. Italy reached it this year. Germany is soon to reach it. So it is pretty much now or never for Mussolini, Hitler and the Jap war leaders." But Sherwood, out of the strength of his naïve faith in the goodness of man, did not, would not admit to himself that a Second War had to be.

Few intricate men have been simpler in their essential beliefs than he, few worldlings so unworldly. The Commencement orator at Milton remained, bafflingly and sometimes disconcertingly, at the core of the grown-up, brooding man. This was a source of his strange strength even when his decencies befuddled him. "I believe in two things," he wrote in his diary during the rehearsal period of *Idiot's Delight*, "true Democracy & true Christianity. I hope to God neither of them dies before I do. Certainly nothing can kill them but brutal stupidity. . . . All I want to do with my life is to go on and on attacking such betrayers of the human race [Hitler, Beaverbrook, the Comité des Forges, and Hearst were for him then the villains] and expounding the simple doctrines in the Sermon on the Mount."

In his postscript he publicly repeated his conviction that the world was largely populated by decent people who, mindful of "the persistent validity" of that Sermon, did not want war, had not forgotten the twelve million men who died between 1914 and 1918, and could, without fighting, defeat the megalomaniacs of the Fascist countries by a proper show of "calmness, courage, and ridicule." It was a pretty faith, expressing a fine hope but based on everything except recognition of the imperiling realities.

In *Idiot's Delight* Sherwood lowered his final curtain on the crash of bombs, acknowledging that the whole world had gone to war, and having his hoofer and the phony White Russian welcome death ironically by singing "Onward, Christian Soldiers." Though he admitted a Second War could come by imagining that it had, his play was not meant as a prophecy. Instead, it was a condemnation of war itself and what it does, once it breaks out, to the minds and values of men who cease to think as individuals and start to feel as nationalists.

His characters are people who hope to be allowed to take a train that will get them out of warring Italy and into neutral Switzerland. They are, including the six chorus girls, a wisely mixed lot. A young English artist who, because of the war, forgets his painting and his honeymoon and is impatient to get home and join up. A munitions manufacturer who escapes to safety and his profits after arranging it so that his Russian mistress is left behind. A distinguished German bacteriologist who, though he may be on the verge of finding a cure for cancer, prepares to return to his Fatherland so that he can serve it by dealing out death. And a French pacifist, an avowed radical and internationalist, who cries, "Vive la France!" when he is about to be shot by some personally charming Fascist troops who have surrendered their wills to the Duce. At the end only Harry Van, the small-time American showman, and Irene, the disillusioned White Russian adventuress, elect to remain, ready to die because they can find no justification for survival in a world gone mad.

Strongly antiwar, *Idiot's Delight* was also violently anti-Fascist. It was the last play Sherwood wrote as the pacifist the First War had made him; the last, too, of his serious plays in which his leading characters choose to die without rising to defend their beliefs. Serious as it was, it was a "show" first of all, entertainment shrewdly fashioned with comedy and calamity juxtaposed. To Sherwood, as he said in his *There Shall Be No Night* preface, "it was completely American in that it represented a compound of blank pessimism and desperate optimism, of chaos and jazz."

In one speech of Harry Van's, Sherwood spoke more directly for himself than he had spoken in any of his other plays. "I've remained an optimist," says Van to the German scientist, "because I'm essentially a student of human nature. You dissect corpses and rats and similar unpleasant things. Well—it has been my job to dissect suckers! I've probed into the souls of some of the God-damnedest specimens. And what have I found? Now—don't sneer at me, Doctor —but above everything else I've found Faith! Faith in peace on earth and good will to men—and faith that 'Muma,' the three-legged girl, really has got three legs. All my life, I've been selling phony goods to people of meagre intelligence and great faith. You'd think that would make me contemptuous of the human race, wouldn't you? But—on the contrary—it has given *me* Faith. It has made me sure that no matter how much the meek may be bulldozed or gypped—they *will* eventually inherit the earth."

There was one person to whom Sherwood was particularly anxious to read *Idiot's Delight*. This was Edward Sheldon, the author of *Salvation Nell, The Nigger, The Boss, Romance,* and other plays, a man who by then, though unable to see, saw everything, and without being able to walk moved deep into the lives of countless friends. Arthritis in its most merciless form had stricken this handsome devotee of the theatre, books, music, and life when he was in his thirties and at the height of his career. He, however, had made a new and even richer career out of the strength his invalidism brought him.

Geraldine Farrar, Ruth Draper, Walter Damrosch, Woollcott, Katharine Cornell, Sidney Howard, Helen Hayes, Charles Mac-Arthur, Cornelia Otis Skinner, Jascha Heifetz, Helen Howe, Anne Lindbergh, and a hundred others of all kinds and interests dropped in at his penthouse in East 84th Street for counsel, comfort, and stimulation. They came to him to read what they had written, to play or sing for him, and just for the joy of talking with him. He lay immobile on a high canopied bed, immaculately dressed, with only his head and shoulders showing, his eyes bandaged, and a red-and-brown Paisley shawl spread across his body. His voice was warm with welcome. He rarely, very rarely, mentioned his condition. Instead, he referred to the books he had "read," meaning books that had been read to him, talked of the world outside as if he were still a part of it, which indeed he was, and addressed his unseen visitors as though he saw them. Most people approached him the first time dreading their meeting, but after five minutes, due to the resonance of his mind and spirit, the barrier of timidity which can separate the healthy from the ill disappeared, and they were aware only of how alive he was and of how much he added to their living.

Sheldon had been blinded and paralyzed for some years when, at the time of *The Road to Rome,* Jane Cowl took Sherwood by to meet him. The two men hit it off at once, and Sherwood soon began having dinner by that bedside, sharing ideas with Sheldon, reading him his plays, hoping for his praise, and listening with interest to his criticism. Friendship with Sheldon was a creative act, and it was as a friend who had this genius that he followed the younger dramatist's development. He admired Sherwood's wit, recognized the depths of his capacity for indignation, and sensed that there was a deeper dimension to him than his early comedies revealed.

With the blinded Sheldon, a friend, though always out of sight, was never out of mind. Constant telegrams and long letters, as lively as the best of talk, showed how close Sherwood was to him. They also make clear how remarkable were Sheldon's insights. He, of all people, could write after Sherwood's divorce, "There are worse things than pain and I feel sure you have the ability not only to endure it, but to turn it to some magnificent personal use." Himself an awesome demonstration of fortitude, he did his best to encourage the younger man when he surrendered to despair. "I get frequent cables from Ned Sheldon," Sherwood wrote Woollcott in the summer of 1935, "all of them so eloquently friendly and cheerful that they make me feel well toward the human race. It is an achievement for a species to have produced him." Sheldon knew Sherwood well enough to realize that beyond his doubts lay belief. This is why he spotted at once that Harry Van was in essence Sherwood and told him so—an optimist in spite of everything.

Sherwood noted this comment in his diary, underscoring its validity by writing just ahead of it, "No generation that ever lived has seen as much history being made as has mine. Born in the last years of Victoria, with limitless security in prospect—and then, all of human life completely disrupted by emancipation of women, great war, automobiles, airplanes, radio, Communism, Fascism, prohibition, Freud, movies, economic collapse. And the result so far? Emphatic improvement."

Work on the production of *Idiot's Delight* began in earnest in January, 1936. The weeks ahead were crowded for Sherwood because he found that he had to do much more rewriting than was usual with him. It was not a matter of keeping up with the headlines so much as guaranteeing that the meaning of his play would be heard above its laughter. The Lunts, as he well knew, were perfectionists always eager to better what they were doing. For Sherwood this was one of the joys and challenges of working with them. He welcomed, or nearly always welcomed, the comments or suggestions of the Lunts, recognizing that these were not so much criticisms as creative acts of collaboration.

The Theatre Guild's directors were concerned with the same pursuit of the best. *Reunion* had been Sherwood's painful introduction to their committee system; *Idiot's Delight* reintroduced him to their tactlessness. Lee Simonson remained a person Sherwood admired but "could not love." He was to do "a magnificent job" on the set, "really wonderful—just right in size, arrangement and spirit," and suggesting "a vague kind of horror" called for in the stage directions. But Sherwood's liking for him was not increased when, at their first discussion of the scenery, Simonson told him that he had been wrong in choosing the declaration of war as the background for his play. "It may kill the comedy," said he, and Sherwood listened, chagrined though consoled by remembering that Simonson and others at the Guild had said psychoanalysis would kill *Reunion*. "How they underrate me! But I ask for it. I'm so scared of being overrated."

At one of the earliest run-through rehearsals Lawrence Langner also raised some objections to *Idiot's Delight*. Admitting that it was "delightful," he found that it drifted perilously between the somber and the comic and was "too light for its significant content." It needed more weight. Other directors agreed with him, and Sherwood, seeing their point, was grateful to Lynn Fontanne when, with her instinct for the theatre, she suggested a scene between herself and Weber, the munitions manufacturer, which would supply that weight.

"I've been thinking about the character of Weber, the Comité des Forges magnate in *I.D.*," wrote Sherwood before Miss Fontanne made her suggestion, "wondering whether I should make him more sympathetic, more human. The answer is No. I believe that such people are the arch-villains of mortal creation, and since I believe that, why am I scared to say so? It's just that recent theatrical tradi-

tion decrees that villains must be charming. What has clinched my
determination is reading in *Time* a quotation from Sir Herbert
Laurence of Vickers: 'The sanctity of human life has been exaggerated.' Such men are sons of bitches & should be so represented."

He left Weber a villain, loveless, cold, and cruel, because Sherwood was among the many at that time who believed munitions
manufacturers were the "merchants of death," responsible for the
First War and in their own interests working for a Second. But,
taking Miss Fontanne's advice, he decided to draw Weber more fully.
On February 4 he was writing in his diary, "I also did the work that I
have been wanting to do—realizing the character of Weber in *I.D.*
Completed the scene with Irene in Act II, beginning with the line
'I'm beginning to wonder about that.' This I think rounds the play
out. Oh God I hope so!"

To Irene he had given a speech depicting the horrors of war in
terms of what would happen to the young English couple if war
came. "I saw him in his nice, smart, British uniform, shooting a little
pistol at a huge tank. And the tank rolls over him. And his fine
strong body, that was so full of the capacity for ecstasy, is a mass of
mashed flesh and bones—a smear of purple blood—like a stepped-
on snail. But before the moment of death, he consoles himself by
thinking, 'Thank God *she* is safe! She is bearing the child I gave her,
and he will live to see a better world.' But I know where she is. She is
lying in a cellar that has been wrecked by an air raid, and her firm
young breasts are all mixed up with the bowels of a dismembered
policeman, and the embryo from her womb is splattered against the
face of a dead bishop. That is the kind of thought with which I
amuse myself, Achille. And it makes me so proud to think that I am
so close to you—who make all this possible."

For Weber, Sherwood now wrote a reply, not absolving him of his
guilt, but showing that it was not his alone. "Ask yourself: why
shouldn't they die? And who are the greater criminals—those who
sell the instruments of death, or those who buy them, and use them?
You know there is no logical reply to that. But all those little people
—like your new friends—all of them consider me an arch-villain
because I furnish them with what they want, which is the illusion of
power. That is what they vote for in their frightened governments

—what they cheer for on their national holidays—what they glorify in their anthems, and their monuments, and their waving flags! Yes —they shout bravely about something they call 'national honor.' And what does it amount to? Mistrust of the motives of every one else! Dog in the manger defense of what they've got, and greed for the other fellow's possessions! Honor among thieves! I assure you, Irene —for such little people the deadliest weapons are the most merciful."

As Sherwood put it, "Every day I do some more crocheting on I.D." He continued to do it throughout the rehearsals and tryouts and even after the New York opening. It was a tricky business, this constant redrafting of single lines or scenes, but Sherwood faced it as undaunted by writing them as the Lunts were by learning them, seeking only to get the play as right as all of them could make it. He recognized that the problem, as the Guild directors had pointed out, was fusing the night club atmosphere of Harry Van the hoofer and his six blondes with the tragedy of a second world war. It was a matter of finding the proper balance between Harry's indestructible faith and Irene's disillusioned image of God as a "Poor, lonely old soul. Sitting up in heaven, with nothing to do, but play solitaire. Poor, dear God. Playing Idiot's Delight. The game that never means anything, and never ends."

It is common practice to say, by way of simplification, that an author *wrote* so-and-so just as if his life stopped while he was writing it. Sherwood, more than most, wrote in the midst of living. Although his concentration was utter when he was writing or thinking about what he was to write, he was not one to shut out the world entirely, nor did he do so when under the strain of readying *Idiot's Delight*. The radio and the newspapers were very much his concern, and would have been even if his play, by its very subject, had not brought them closer to him.

As usual, after working hard each day, Sherwood renewed himself by playing hard. Both he and Madeline loved parties. Both relished good talk, good food, chic women, pretty rooms, laughter, games, and days that had evenings. Together they enjoyed dining with such old friends as the Bonners, the Walter Damrosches, the René Clairs, the Finletters, the Littells, and the Gilbert Millers, or going to late parties (2:30 A.M. was an early evening for Sherwood) with the Swopes, the Pulitzers, the Guinzburgs, the Backers, the Kaufmans, the Oelrichs, and the Harrimans.

Then there were the movies new and old to be seen, such as *Modern Times, The Informer, The Scoundrel, The Guardsman,* and his own *The Petrified Forest* and *The Ghost Goes West.* And the theatre to be caught up with—*Three Men on a Horse,* Gladys Cooper and Philip Merivale in *Call It a Day,* Helen Hayes in *Victoria Regina,* and Raymond Massey, Ruth Gordon, and Pauline Lord in *Ethan Frome.*

In the midst of rewriting Sherwood continued to read as avidly as he did when reviewing for *Scribner's.* Often he was a book-a-day man, reading almost anything that was at hand. Although unable to finish Sinclair Lewis's *It Can't Happen Here,* he found much pleasure in Anne Lindbergh's *North to the Orient,* Stanley Walker's *Mrs. Astor's Horse,* Colette's *Duo,* and Santayana's *The Last Puritan.*

Three books in particular meant a great deal to him because of *Idiot's Delight.* One was H. M. Tomlinson's *Mars His Idiot,* an eloquent pacifist plea which Sherwood found "wonderful, beautiful, stirring," and relied on when revising his play. The second, Thomas Mann's *The Magic Mountain,* he thought so fine that he had his German scientist quote from it in the second act, even though Sherwood himself, bogged down by "all those billions of tubercles," could get through no more than half of its nine hundred pages. The third was John Gunther's *Inside Europe,* "a magnificent book," especially welcome to Sherwood because it was written by a reporter who was not a cynic. "This book tells me a hell of a lot that I want to know. And it certainly verifies *I.D.*"

Naturally it was *Idiot's Delight* which absorbed Sherwood during these weeks of rehearsal and rewriting. In 1936 he started to keep a diary, factual and unliterary but always honest. In it, while recording his thoughts and doings and the growing threats of the news, he gives a running account of the play's fortunes and fate.

Jan. 5. Alfred and Lynn and several others of their company had a rehearsal of *I.D.* today, going all through it and being highly pleased —especially with the way Lynn's part works out.

Jan. 8. Alfred, Lynn and Russel Crouse [then the Theatre Guild's

press agent] today inspected 200 chorus girls looking for the 6 for
I.D. They plan now to open Washington, March 2d. The ideal spot, I
should guess.

Jan. 11. Saw Lynn's ravishing blonde wig for *I.D.*

Jan. 13. Mad. went to Valentina's in the afternoon and saw Lynn's
clothes and that glorious wig. I went to the Alvin Theatre and helped
Alfred in the momentous selection of 12 out of some 250 chorus
girls. Russel Crouse & Vinton Freedley there and it was pretty funny.
Some of the others thought we ought to be influenced principally by
the dancing talent of the candidates, but I voted steadily for physical
allure. They can learn all the dancing that's necessary.

Jan. 14. Finished another revised script of *I.D.* I am going Friday to
hear it read through for the first time. They have been rehearsing it
for about ten days.

Jan. 17. Went in afternoon to Guild Theatre to hear, for the first
time, reading of *Idiot's Delight* by the cast. They sounded fine. Only
worries are some of the accents. Slightly fearful that Lynn's may be
too thick. Must talk to her about this—she should never fish for
words.

Jan. 22. Went to see Miss Stringfellow at Chapin School. She is
O.K. Reports on the daughter still lamentable. No concentration, no
spirit of cooperation. I delivered a stern lecture to Mary, without
much conviction, because of my own shameful scholastic past. I have
a fearful time keeping a straight face when admonishing her about
her duty to her arithmetic teacher and me.

Jan. 28. [Boston] Went to rehearsal in afternoon at Colonial Theatre, scene of so many glamorous evenings when Harvard undergraduates approached the *Ziegfeld Follies* with the same reverence displayed by Crusaders at Jerusalem. And, in 1915, it was just about as
hard to get into. Rehearsal went fine and show seems O.K. Cast
excellent. They have over half the play all staged & memorized.

Jan. 29. [Boston] Mad. & I to rehearsal at 1:30. They did Act I &
two scenes of Act II, and then read through Act III. Mad. says she
never saw a rehearsal in such fine shape. I telephoned to Irving
Berlin, in the Beverly-Wiltshire, Beverly Hills, Calif., asking him if
he would write the song needed for Act II. He thinks he might. I
hope so. Irving is one of my heroes.

Feb. 3. Did some work on *I.D.* today and sent it airmail to the

Lunts in Chicago. Everything new I do for the play seems good to me, and I feel very confident that this is the best chance I've ever had to discharge ideas that have long been boiling in my mind & heart. In fact, this play is like a 100% orgasm.

Feb. 22. Saw Irving Berlin today. We decided to do his old song "Puttin' on the Ritz."

Feb. 26. To rehearsal, where I found that things are going fine.

Mar. 7. Arrive in Washington for opening at the National Theatre. Lunts & entire company in high spirits and advance sale in Washington enormous.

Mar. 9. I.D. opened fine—audience excited & enthusiastic but severely surprised. The Lunts terrifically happy, and so am I. But— again I've failed to say as much as I want to say. Again I see a burst of indignation accepted as a gag-fest. At least, too much as a gag-fest.

Mar. 10. Some of the notices bad—betraying bewilderment & confusion which was evident in last night's audience. Went to the theatre and the atmosphere about Alfred is very blue. This improved materially, however, when the second performance turned out to go far better than the first. Restaged end of Act I & wrote some new stuff, mostly for Lynn, which should help. When the audience leaves the theatre they are greeted by newsboys shouting threats of war in Europe. The headlines are terrific lies—like "French Attack Nazi Planes"—as is the way of Bulldog editions. But it seemed as though these newsboys were characters in the play, heralding a 4th Act.

Mar. 11. All is now lovely. The matinee was riotously successful— the few new lines in the play help considerably—and there doesn't seem to be any doubt now that we're in. After the matinee I gave Lynn a new line in her Act III scene with the Captain. He says: "I realize, madame, that politeness means nothing now. But—under these tragic circumstances, what else can I do?" To which she replies: "I'll tell you what else you can do. You can refuse to fight! You can refuse to use those weapons that they have sold you!" If that doesn't sum it up—the hell with them. Lynn used the lines in the evening performance. The audiences are now taking the play more seriously & the main points are getting over.

Mar. 16. [Pittsburgh tryout] Flew from Newark, 4:30 P.M., in

Douglass plane—a magnificent ship . . . We ran into fearful fog & I was scared. I was the only passenger for Pittsburgh & they thought they would be unable to land there, but they tried it, against my better judgment, & made it. I went to the Wm. Penn Hotel, dined with R. Crouse, & then saw *I.D.* It went well, though the Pittsburgh audience was unresponsive. Had supper later with the Lunts & I told them the ending of the play was still not as effective as we had hoped. They agreed & resolved to work on it.

Mar. 17. Pittsburgh notices very favorable but dull. One of them, Harold Cohen, said it ended in confusion. I resolved to talk to him about this & went to his office but failed to see him. Went to rehearsal at 3, and for over two hours we worked tiresomely (and with frequent displays of irritability) on the finish. All manner of suggestions made & some tried. Good results accomplished. Dined with Crouse & Cohen & latter said some things of value. Wonderful performance tonight, appreciative audience, the revised ending went fine. I felt that for the first time the show had really clicked. Thrilled & pleased. . . . Floods have been rising hereabouts at an alarming rate. The natives are speculating whether the 1907 record of 35 feet will be equalled. They doubt it. But there was a fearful snow storm today which will swell the rivers.

Mar. 18. The flood reached 48 feet today. It fills the streets to within a few blocks of the hotel & the theatre. No trains are running. Luckily, I booked a place on the 4 o'clock plane this afternoon. Went to the theatre to say good-bye & found them all wondering how soon the lights would go out. Two of the orchestra are in the Roosevelt Hotel, waiting for a boat to take them out of 2d story windows. I returned to the hotel to get my suitcase & found that the elevators have stopped running. I have a grievous hangover today & won't walk up 9 floors. So I told Larry Farrell to get the suitcase when & if he could. It took a long time to get transportation to the airport. While we were on the way there all lights in Pittsburgh went out, and another blizzard started. Airport chaotic—frightened people trying to get away from the disaster. No light, no water. When my plane took off, in darkness & blinding snow (5:00 P.M.), only light was provided by a man waving a kerosene lantern. It was like The Age of Frustration in Wells's *The Shape of Things to Come*. Exciting and scaring.

We climbed to 8000 feet, ice forming on wings in the dense snow clouds. We landed in Camden, N.J., & were told there would be no further flying. So rushed by car to North Philadelphia and caught train for New York. Just had time to shout to Western Union boy to telegraph Mad. Arrived home 9:15 to find that evening papers & radio news flashes are full of blood-curdling stories about the frightful flood in Pittsburgh. I am mighty glad to be here.

Mar. 19. R. Crouse, who left Pittsburgh Tuesday night, got home this morning (Thurs.). I was lucky. Telegram from Larry says they played matinee & evening performance, thanks to emergency generator in Nixon Theatre. No word about my suitcase, but the hell with it.

Mar. 20. Saw in paper that the *I.D.* company had given up & left Pittsburgh tonight. Thank God for that! Report is that typhoid has broken out there, & I telegraphed Lunts begging them to come home.

Mar. 22. The *I.D.* company reached New York late last night. I met them at the theatre this afternoon & heard awful tales of horror in Pittsburgh. It seems that after I left, the flood rushed into the cellar of the Nixon. They could hear it under their feet while they played the matinee. During the number in Act II, the lights went out, but they went right on, using Alfred's cigarette lighter & electric torches, until the generator got going. The worst of it all was that water was shut off and so they couldn't bathe or flush toilets. Some of them feel sick, but they're awfully happy. The scenery arrived today, escorted by George Greenberg, who evidently acted with great intelligence & courage, as did Larry & all of them.

Mar. 24. [New York opening at the Shubert] Felt very nervous at first today—that old stomach trouble. Went out & bought flowers for all, sent telegrams, had a haircut, joined Mad. at Valentina's. She was trying on a fine new print dress, white on black, and also experimented with a round, broad-brimmed straw hat—alluring. After fitting, Mad., George Schlee & I had brandy flips at the Savoy-Plaza, & then home and into bed for a nap. But sleep was elusive. We dined at home, peacefully. The nervousness is virtually all gone, but Mad. says her stomach is tied in a rather loose bow-knot. I gave Mary the lecture, & then Mlle. came in and quite a scene ensued. On top of this, we went to the theatre, arriving about 9:30 in the middle of Act II. Instantly we knew it was going beautifully. Standing at the back, we watched it through to the end, then rushed backstage and thrilled to the sounds of the greatest demonstration any play of mine has ever received. Nineteen curtain calls, vociferous cheers—what I have been hoping for ever since I saw *What Price Glory?* twelve years ago, and decided it would be wonderful to be a playwright.

Mar. 25. Read notices. First I read was Atkinson's, in the *Times*, & it was lukewarm. The others seemed not much better. Disappointed. Anderson's in the *Eve. Journal* was marvelous, & so was Lockridge's in *The Sun*. General opinion is that all notices were superlatively good for box-office—but except for the last two mentioned they're far from satisfying me. God damn it—why do they deliberately close their ears to everything of importance that is said in a comedy? You'd think it was a crime to state unpleasant truths in an entertaining way.

Though disappointed in the reviews, Sherwood was overjoyed by the success of *Idiot's Delight*. The play came as the climax to one of the Theatre Guild's best years, a year during which it had presented *The Taming of the Shrew* with the Lunts, *Porgy and Bess*, *Call It a Day*, and *End of Summer*. It came, too, as a high point in an exceptional season. In addition to the Gershwin classic and the Behrman comedy, it included such other plays by American authors as *Winterset*, *Dead End*, *Boy Meets Girl*, *Ethan Frome*, *First Lady*, and *Bury the Dead*. From among these it was Maxwell Anderson's verse tragedy *Winterset* which in March won the New York Drama Critics Award for the best play (with three of the seventeen members holding out fiercely for *Idiot's Delight*). But it was *Idiot's Delight* which in May carried off the Pulitzer Prize.

Sherwood was in England at Great Enton when on May 5 a cable from Columbia University brought him the news. He was pleased to be the winner, though only mildly pleased at first because he did not as yet know what the winning meant. He knew the Pulitzer Board had that year altered the terms of the award, reducing it as an honor by deciding to exclude from consideration plays by previous winners. This would have made acceptance humiliating because many of the best playwrights would have been debarred.

Before he left New York, Sherwood had told Russel Crouse, who on reading *Idiot's Delight* prophesied it would be the winner, that, if these terms persisted and the prize chanced to come his way, he would refuse it. A transatlantic talk with Crouse reassured him. The Board had decided at the last moment to ignore the new provision. *Idiot's Delight*, as Sherwood noted in his diary, had won honorably "in real open competition." In the statement he gave Crouse, he again made his position clear. "Had not these restrictions been removed, I would have been forced to refuse the prize and believe any self-respecting dramatist would have done the same." As things turned out, he could say with truth, "I am terribly happy . . . and consider it a high honor, particularly this year."

He had had successes before. Now he had recognition and a success. It was no hardship. He had not guessed how exciting it would be. Theatre people must by long addiction be among the major sources of Western Union's income. Telegrams and cables are to them what back-fence talk used to be to neighbors. He was flooded with congratulations on the day of the announcement—cables from the Guinzburgs, Masseys, Freedmans, and Edna Ferber. Especially welcome was the one from Ralph Pulitzer saying "decision was unanimous." Others poured in from Rosamond, the Bonners, Ned Sheldon, Philip Barry, Donald Klopfer, Philip Merivale, and Gladys Cooper. This was just the beginning. There were calls also from the AP, INS, the *New York Times*, and the *Daily Mail*. In the next weeks the mail was sweet as well as heavy. Letters from his mother, his brother Philip, Noel Coward, and Harold Finn (unseen since they had been in the same squad at Plattsburg in 1916), and, of course, from the Lunts.

Lunt said in his letter, "I didn't even cable after the awarding of the Pulitzer Prize as I didn't feel you generally cared whether you got it or not & personally I didn't give a Goddam. It was all so obvious and the only thing that gave me a glimmer of pleasure over it was that people just settled back & said, 'Well for once that committee did the right thing.' The award didn't affect business (which is its 'stimulating' purpose, isn't it?) as it couldn't affect business. The public just knew it was good—all by its stupid little self." So did

Eugene O'Neill from whom, shortly before the Pulitzer announcement, Sherwood had a note saying, "I like *Idiot's Delight* immensely! It's grand stuff! Congratulations on a fine job!"

The published play was "lovingly dedicated" to Lynn Fontanne and Alfred Lunt, and they in their playing of it returned this love. She, in her blonde Garbo wig as Irene, was a fascinating enigma, beautiful in the clinging costumes Valentina designed for her, her head held high, her face a mask, her shoulders thrown back, her arms and body flowing, and her Russian accent as borsch-thick as Valentina's own. He, as Harry Van the other and franker illusionist, was wonderfully shiny in his brashness, very human and touching, too, and had for himself the fun he gave others by proving that a "serious" actor, cast as a shoddy hoofer, could sing and strut with the glibness of a veteran song-and-dance man.

"Had Professor Copeland appeared in a Hasty Pudding show dressed as a girl," reported Benchley in *The New Yorker*, the Guild subscribers could not have howled with greater glee. This overhearty laughter irritated Benchley because it seemed to him to mean that the Guilders had overlooked the play's basic seriousness and underestimated Lunt's long-proven versatility. Fortunately, however, for Sherwood as well as for the Lunts, this "audience enthusiasm" continued wherever the play traveled up and down the United States.

There were dissenters, not many but a few. Meaning to harm *Idiot's Delight*, they aided it by denouncing it with such beckoning words as "scandalous," "salacious," "profane," and "immoral." Most publicized and publicizing among these was Mayor Dan Butler of Omaha, Nebraska, who had a taste for censorship. He was a one-man reform party, given to banning shows he had not seen. He had done this with the foreign film *Ecstasy* and had tried to do it with *Tobacco Road*.

In May, 1937, when the Lunts were scheduled to appear in Omaha, His Honor was ready to step in again. He demanded that the text of *Idiot's Delight* be cleaned up, insisting that no one would dare to take a seventeen-year-old child to see "such garbage." His most serious objection apparently was to Irene's and Harry Van's admission that, though unmarried, they had once spent a night together in Omaha at a hotel Sherwood called the Governor Bryan. According to the *Herald Tribune,* there was no such hotel. But the Mayor thought the use of such a name besmirched the reputation of a beloved Nebraska statesman, former Governor Charles Bryan, brother of the late William Jennings Bryan. This was more than he could put up with. This was immorality indeed.

Woollcott gleefully described the crisis to his friend Dr. Gustav Eckstein. "Yesterday at two-thirty New York time frantic calls from Omaha where the Lunts had encountered a Mayor who forbade their show unless they made some sixteen deletions from the text, which has since been referred to by some New York scrivener as *Idiot's Delete.* Lynn had written a statement she wished to make to the public before the rise of the curtain but I denounced them both as poltroons not fit to be trusted with a play by Sherwood or anybody else if they didn't have the gumption not to play at all. This advice entranced them so they told the Mayor to go to hell and he collapsed at once. The play was therefore given last night as written."

Even before Woollcott got into the act, *Idiot's Delight* had found a powerful defender in G. Bromley Oxnam, Bishop of the Methodist Episcopal Church in Nebraska. He publicly regretted that the Mayor had made their city, Omaha, "ridiculous" and stated he was going to take his fourteen-year-old daughter to the play. He reminded His Honor that "Persons or organizations that turn to censorship are turning . . . toward the dictatorships of Europe," and suggested that as a theme song for his next campaign the Mayor adopt, "Every Little Damma Must Be Taken from Our Drama." As goes without saying, the theatre was packed that night in Omaha.

His Honor was not the only one to raise objections to *Idiot's Delight* in its different incarnations. His were merely the most foolish. Both the Lord Chamberlain, when the play was to be produced in England, and the powers-that-were at M-G-M, on its being made into a film, asked for alterations which in neither instance were limited to cleaning up the language. The Lord Chamberlain's eye was on Europe, Hollywood's on a world market. *Idiot's Delight* was against war. This was all right. It was also violently anti-Fascist. This was not. The Lord Chamberlain sought to avoid "any complaint from the Continent." In courtly terms he asked that specific references to Fascism be deleted, that the locale and the uniforms be unspecified, and that an imaginary language, concocted by Sherwood, be substituted for the Italian used by the officers and servants. Hollywood made its own alterations. The Italians still spoke Italian ("courageously," said the *New York Times*), but the Alpine hotel was vaguely located, all references to dictators were removed, the officers' uniforms were unidentifiable, the nationality of the raiding planes was unnamed, and a happy ending suggested.

Sherwood worried about the changes he had to make for the English text, the preparation of which he called "a damned nuisance." In his diary he wrote, "Read through *Idiot's Delight* for purposes of submission to the Lord Chamberlain. Cut all lines that seemed dangerous to me—but there are too many. Play didn't seem to have enough good language in it, but, I should say, excellent construction and the chief virtue the distinctness and economy of the character drawing." He worried, too, about the toning down in the movie version. In each case he worried needlessly. Both the English production and the American film succeeded as if they had not been toned down at all. One reason was that it was impossible to tone down the actualities of a darkening world which, month by month, were bringing reality nearer to *Idiot's Delight*.

Sherwood and Madeline were returning from California via the Panama Canal when they learned how recent events had again caught up with the play. They had been in Hollywood where he had labored on the movie of *Idiot's Delight* for which M-G-M was paying a palatable $135,000. His time there had been a pleasant make-believe interlude during which, as usual, he combined work and fun. After long hours at the studio, he dined with such friends as Polly and Sidney Howard, the Irving Berlins, the Goldwyns, Clarence Brown, and George Oppenheimer. One very pleasant evening stood out for him because it outlasted its pleasures. It was the night he spent playing "the Game" at Dorothy Parker's and Alan Campbell's with Dashiell Hammett, King Vidor, Sam Hoffenstein, James Hilton, and F. Scott Fitzgerald. He was delighted to see Fitzgerald again, a "ghost" unencountered since he was writing *The Beautiful and Damned*. Saddened, too. "A marvelous writer, a first rate mind & a tortured spirit. If he could only get back into his stride."

This good evening at the Campbells' was plainly too good. The next morning when Sherwood set out for Santa Monica to read the script to Norma Shearer and Clark Gable (his new Irene and Harry Van), he had "a gruesome hangover." His eyes were "bleary," his head was "splitting," the reading an "ordeal." He was glad when it was over, and glad to feel at its end that the script gained by the omission of some of the antiwar arguments which he feared had been repetitious in the play.

Sherwood and Madeline were cruising slowly home on the *Virginia* when *Idiot's Delight* tried out in Glasgow, and were in New York when it opened in London. His diary tells the story of what happened to the impact of the play at that time because of what was happening to the world. It also tells the story of what was happening to him and for the same reason. He had no access to inside information. He had access only to his own hopes, fears, and conscience as an intelligent man who devoured each day's news and whose convictions were being shaken and changed by it.

Feb. 20, 1938. Hottest day so far, off coast of Costa Rica. Thick jungle, in contrast to bare brown hills of Mexico. Captain told us today that Anthony Eden has resigned, which certainly marks the end of idealistic pacifism in Europe. In my uninformed opinion, Eden was the best man in the British government, certainly the most honest.

Feb. 23. Sensational news these days. Evidently Hitler delivered another momentous speech last Sunday, but we missed any report of that. Same day Eden resigned. Monday Eden made a fiery speech in Commons, denouncing Italy. Chamberlain then spread soft soap. Lord Halifax (pro-Nazi churchwarden) new Foreign Minister. Col. Blimp is now in the saddle for sure. . . . Incidentally, the international political background for the opening of *I.D.* in Glasgow was apparently as terribly appropriate as it was at the Washington opening in March, 1936.

Mar. 12. Hitler has completely seized Austria—has even moved in himself. The British government is deeply pained. There is no government in France, Blum having failed to form a cabinet. It's pretty close to chaos at the moment. But all will probably be straightened out, with Austria extinct & Hitler more powerful than ever and the rest of the world (including Mussolini but excepting Japan) more jittery. Looked at map of Europe. Poor Czechoslovakia. Nothing to stop Hitler to the Black Sea.

Mar. 14. Austria has disappeared into the Nazi state. Jews & workers are being flogged into submission. Oh God, how I hope to live to see the day when those unspeakable barbaric bastards get their punishment.

Mar. 15. Read speeches by Chamberlain (in House of Commons) & Hitler (in Vienna). Chamberlain is in a tough spot, but his speech sounded as if the old British iron were still in it. Now there is no more equivocating, for the time being. With Hitler in power, there is no further doubt (as if there ever was in any sane mind) that anything can happen at any moment. But—for the time being—*watch out for Mussolini.* His prestige has had a severe slap. He's not the fellow to take it sitting down. He may well vent his egomaniacal rage on anyone, most of all on Spain. Reports from there very alarming.

Mar. 18. Read all newspapers today. It's absolutely bewildering. Germany, Italy, Japan are really riding over civilization, and apparently no one is prepared to make any real attempt to stop them. The entire world war is being wiped out with hardly a sign of resistance from the supposed victors. France & England seem disorganized, disunited. Russia has liquidated most of its leaders & is generally discounted as a force. Yesterday Sec. Hull gave a speech which was admirable but didn't mean much of anything. What price pacifism now? More bombings in Barcelona—incredible brutality. I've been optimistic for a long time, but now I actually believe that we're being driven straight toward a war far more terrible than anyone could imagine—and I suppose the sooner it comes, the better. What a dreadful thing to be writing.

Sherwood saw *Idiot's Delight* in London six weeks after its opening on March 22, 1938, with Raymond Massey and Tamara Geva in the parts he had hoped the Lunts would play there. He was as pleased with the play's performance as with its reception. "No decent seats available, so we sat in an upper box. Ray Massey has given it a fine production and a fine performance. Really thrilled to see its effect on the audience." He was human enough to be delighted to have his play succeed even without the Lunts, and touched by Miss Fontanne's saying, when she heard of its English success, "It proves just what she & Alfred have always said: it's the play that counts & it makes no difference who acts it." He knew better. So did she. But he was grateful for her generosity which he called "typical."

A year passed before he saw the screen version in New York with Clark Gable and Norma Shearer, and much too much had happened for his happiness and the world's. He found Norma Shearer's Irene "beautiful" with her mystifying speech, her blonde wig, her slinky clothes, and long cigarette holder, and Clark Gable "very funny" as the hoofer. However, he was more approving than enthusiastic. Something was missing. Perhaps it was the ultimate pathos which the Lunts ensured along with the comedy. "Quite a good picture," he reported, "early parts excellent—but so much cut from play it seems confusing." The critics did not share his reservations. "At long last, an adult picture," said the *Times*, "one of the year's major events— as timely as tomorrow's front page."

By the beginning of February, 1939, *Idiot's Delight* had become just that. Chamberlain had met with Hitler at Berchtesgaden and Godesberg and signed the Munich Agreement. The bloody Civil War in Spain was drawing to an end, bringing another dictator into power. The German-Russian Pact was six months away; the declaration of war by England and France, seven. Events were overtaking *Idiot's Delight* as a script. They had begun to do so at a disturbing rate even in December, 1938, when Lunt was in Chicago rehearsing a new company to take on the road.

"You will be amazed," he wrote, "how even more up-to-date it is now than it was three years ago, and we are really thrilled at getting back into it again. When we rehearse next week, if you don't mind, I will make little notes where you can add a line here and there, although I would rather you would do it. References to Ethiopia for instance, which we changed to Spain, and later to Czechoslovakia. Now where do you want it? You certainly have a wide choice."

27

PRESENT LAUGHTER

*The Solacing Delights of Great Enton—Hospitality as an Architect—
Sherwood's Love of Flowers—A World Apart—Graham Robertson, a
Victorian Neighbor—The Old Savoy Croquet Club—A Madcap Court
—Edward VIII's Abdication—Prize Days, Games, and Drama Festivals
—Problems in Logistics and Patience—Sherwood's Double Tic Doulou-
reux—Talented Loafer and Productive Writer—At Work on Abe
Lincoln in Illinois*

Those years during which the circle of tragic choices was widening
were paradoxically among Sherwood's happiest. Not that he was
indifferent to the news—far from it. His absorption in it grew, his
depression because of it increased. He brooded over it, hopeful one
day, despairing the next. He was torn and confused, fighting a fierce
struggle within himself. His awareness of the menace which the dictators presented to the free world forced him to re-examine his deepest
convictions and drove him little by little to abandon his pacifism. In
spite of his anxieties, however, he had a solace to look forward to
each year, and that was Great Enton and the long months he and
Madeline spent there from 1935 until the outbreak of the war.

Great Enton was more than a country place for him. It was a state
of mind, a condition of life, a spiritual need. At it he found the
escape for which he hungered and an illusion of peace which sustained him. He felt about it as he had felt about no other place
except Skene Wood on Lake Champlain which he had known as a
boy. Though he enjoyed New York, it wore him down. It was a city
in which he confessed he was "most of the time unhappy and uncomfortable in spirit." Amusing as Hollywood could be, it left him intel-

lectually starved. Great Enton was different. It soothed and satisfied
him and renewed his energies. After five months there he felt "like a
refilled fountain pen."

That Great Enton was *his* added to Sherwood's delight in it. It
meant that he had earned his own Skene Wood to which, as a man,
he brought a boy's gift for enjoyment. The Sherwoods loved the
city and liked the country; the Emmets loved the country and liked
the city. Sherwood was at home in both but had a special fondness
for his kind of country living, which was very special indeed. The
English countryside was in his eyes "the most satisfying sight on
earth" and no part of it more cherished than his twenty-five acres at
Great Enton.

On the subject of Great Enton he was rhapsodic. He embraced
its every aspect with his great long arms, and gave it his heart.
Again and again in his diary and letters he referred to it over
the years as a "lovely" and "beloved" place. He never tired of
its spread of greens, its lawns and woodlands, and the changing
procession of its flowers and flowering shrubs. Was the house pretty?
Lord Beaverbrook, after he had visited it, thought not, adding that
for comfort it was much too near the railway over which, though
hidden, trains passed every half hour. The Sherwoods did not hear
the trains, neither did their guests. What they heard was puns and
quips, and incessant roars of laughter. Or country quiet broken by
the sounds of croquet and tennis balls in use or of darts striking
against a board.

As for the house, it belonged to no period, yet it was as much a
part of the landscape as the great oaks which surrounded it. Hospitality was its architect, comfort its decorator. Its predominant effect
was that it was welcoming. Brick and stone, and sharply gabled, it
was begun in the early seventeenth century, added to in the nine-
teenth, and given a new wing by the Sherwoods. Its walls were
festooned with wisteria, its wide windows eager to embrace the sun,
its majestic chimneys proofs of the warmth within. With its bricked
terrace, its friendly hall, its four large rooms downstairs, its seven
bedrooms, and its five bathrooms (not to forget the sturdy old W.C.
by the stair landing known affectionately as "Victoria," or another at
the end of the hall above called "Ethelred the Unready"), it was a
house meant to be filled with people. And filled with them it was

when the Sherwoods owned it, people drawn to it by their remembrance of the fun they had had there and their eagerness for the fun they knew they would have again.

Except on the rainiest days, the outdoors bloomed everywhere indoors in the flowers which were Fantin-Latours painted by Madeline's skill in arranging them. With Sherwood, as with her, flowers were a passion. He never ceased to marvel at their beauty and could never get enough of them. He was amused when he heard that a sour-tongued maid, commenting on his habit of tagging along after Madeline in the garden carrying a large flower basket, called him "Old Fetch and Carry." "*Don't miss that, biographers,*" he wrote in his diary. It has not been missed.

Did he often return to the house with his hands and forearms ripped and torn? He did not mind. Cutting roses was "good fun," and he was delighted that there were close to a thousand bushes on the place. He noted the flowers "in use" as scrupulously as he commented on the books he read, the plays and movies he saw, the day's news, Madeline's new dresses, the money he lost or won on the races and rummy, his progress on his scripts, or meals which he particularly enjoyed. To him flowers were a kind of nourishment. An entry for a June day, which could have been written on any of his June days at Great Enton, runs, "All sorts of lupines, of which the bush lupines (white & pale yellow) are the loveliest; peonies; delphiniums (just beginning); huge red poppies; irises; a few snapdragons; sweet williams & carnations just beginning; rhododendrons; Queen Anne's lace. Front hall looks wonderful with new stands for flower pots. Some wonderfully fragrant Balsam."

At each season's end when he sailed for home he gathered "bales" of gladioli and roses with which to fill his cabin, doing his best to make Great Enton last by taking a part of it with him. One flower he hated—the autumn crocus. From his boyhood it had been a herald of unhappiness, announcing that the holidays were almost over and that he would soon have to head back to school. As a man, he felt again this schoolboy melancholy at the sight of the first autumn crocus. It meant the luggage would presently emerge to be packed for the return voyage to New York, and that for another half year Great Enton would be a memory and a hope.

His reasons for loving the place were many and contradictory. He, the Irish Emmet and ardent American Democrat, enjoyed playing the role of English squire. He was entertained once to walk around his "property" after tea with the British general who was a neighbor, discussing their "frontiers" and being "frightfully pukka." "Pukka" was the last thing Sherwood was except when he was play-acting and keeping back a smile, though he was not unaware of the satisfactions of being a "sahib."

Servants at the time cost little and therefore could be numerous at Great Enton. It gratified Sherwood to have a staff which, until the coming of the war, included a butler, a cook, a kitchen maid, a parlor maid-waitress, two upstairs maids, a gardener, a gardener's boy, and a chauffeur. The setup was amusingly Trollopean no matter how Algonquinish were the antics of those served. Sherwood admired the "semi-stately" homes of England, in spite of finding one he visited "teeming with ancestors and inconveniences." But he and Madeline took pains to supply Great Enton with conveniences, to have it teeming with theatrical friends, and to see to it that its mood was as unstately as they could make it. He lavished money on it, buying silver, china, and furniture to give it a traditional atmosphere, and then spent jubilant weekends (and more money) turning tradition topsy-turvy.

Great Enton under the Sherwoods was not enclosed by high walls, though from the point of view of the neighbors it might just as well have been. Being suspected of stuffiness, they were not encouraged. They had called punctiliously at first and left cards, but Mary Brandon had not returned the calls. When Madeline took over two years later and found the cards dusty in a bowl, it was too late. She solved the problem by throwing them out. Great Enton undisturbed, Great Enton apart, Great Enton as a refuge for work or chosen friends, a little Monaco for games and merriment, that was the way the Sherwoods wanted it and that was the way it was.

An exception among their English neighbors was Graham Robertson. He was welcome even if at times he did appear for tea when the Sherwoods and their guests, in a frivolous mood, were unprepared for the prim courtliness of this tall survivor of the days of the *Yellow Book*. Robertson was a witty flaneur who in his talk could bring to life such of his former intimates as Rossetti, Burne-Jones, Wilde,

Swinburne, and Ellen Terry (with whom he had once been in love). A painter, a devotee of Blake, the author of children's books and beguiling letters, he had mastered the art of converting small things into large, and could afford to do so.

With his *capa* flowing from his shoulders he was no citified dandy, in the manner of his friend Max Beerbohm who was six years his junior. Rather, he was "picturesque" in a country sense, seeming always to have been a feature of the landscape. Tougher than his fragile looks betrayed, he thought nothing of walking the three miles to Great Enton from his home Sandhills. There, in the midst of paintings, books, silver, mahogany, and brass, he lived a refugee from the present and a recluse, coddled by his servants, coddling himself, and proud that his house was uncontaminated by electricity, modern bathtubs, or a telephone.

To Woollcott, who also was an oddity, Robertson seemed "the most enchanting man that ever lived." Sherwood found him less than that, though he liked him and was drawn the closer to him because he was flower-struck in Sherwood's fashion. Better still, since seeing the Lunts in *Reunion*, Robertson had become stage-struck again, as stage-struck as he had been twenty years earlier, almost as stage-struck as Sherwood himself. He had come to know Sherwood in Surrey before he saw *Acropolis*, to follow the fortunes of his plays with keen interest, and to await eagerly his annual return to Great Enton, as he recorded in his *Letters*.

To his friends as the summers passed Robertson wrote, "It will be nice to see the whole six foot eight of him again"; or "I came in a few days ago to find Robert Sherwood coiled up carefully in the dining-room (he always looks like Gulliver in Lilliput in any room of ordinary dimensions) and quite pleased so far with the progress of his play [*Acropolis*]"; or "Bob Sherwood comes over sometimes. I really think he has grown; he can hardly creep into my front door." His friendship with Sherwood grew when he was whisked off to the London opening of *Reunion* by Hamish Hamilton, the English publisher, whose first publication had been the old gentleman's autobiography *Time Was*. He surrendered at once to the "glamourie" of the Lunts, being reduced by them to "such a state of helpless idiocy" as he had not known since years before as a young man he had seen

Ada Rehan. Though a little shocked by some of it, he found *Reunion* to be "fine 'theatre,'" reporting that Sherwood's "sense of the stage is wonderful."

He was interested in Sherwood's "queer, rather child-like nature," but he recognized his qualities. "He is shy, and seldom lets the casual acquaintance really know him, but though he says little of any moment one can sense the deep underlying seriousness of his nature and a certain bigness in the man, which impresses one almost unconsciously. . . . I remember Alfred saying suddenly to me (at an early stage of our acquaintance), 'You are fond of Bob.' I said, awkwardly, 'Oh, I wouldn't venture to say that. I know him so little.' Alfred observed simply, 'If you are fond of him you *do* know him.' And there is much truth in that."

Robertson was fond of him, in addition to admiring him. Even so, his sense of relief could be real when after one of his weekend calls at Great Enton he returned to Sandhills. Its hush and peace seemed "intensified" when he got back. Too much was going on at Great Enton for the old man's taste. The tennis was furious, the croquet determined, and the air apt to be sliced by model airplanes propelled by mouse-power motors consisting of tautly wound rubber bands. There were too many people and they too active, and their talk was shuttlecock fast. He referred to them as "the usual crowd that always collects around Bob," adding, "which I don't believe he really enjoys."

In this Robertson was wrong. He was speaking for himself. Of all the people, mostly American, Sherwood enjoyed having at Great Enton during these prewar years, none were closer to him than the little group of regulars, English, Canadian, or French, and most of them connected with the stage or screen, who banded together to form the Old Savoy Croquet Club. The O.S.C.C., as it was known, took its name from the sobriquet "Old Savoy" which Ladbroke's, the bookmakers, suggested that Sherwood use when placing his racing bets by telephone, as he did almost daily and usually with draining results.

If the O.S.C.C. got its name by chance, the club itself was by choice the begetter of nonsense. Its reason for being was fun, fun of the singular kind created of, by, and for the people included in it.

Surely the members of no fraternities have dedicated themselves with more frenzy to the pursuit of happiness than did this few, this happy few. None have been graver in their devotion to the zany. Or competed with grimmer earnestness at croquet, tennis, darts, rummy, hearts, flying model planes, jingle-writing, word games, pun-making, or the staging of burlesque sketches. To them laughter was a serious business, and each year they scampered after it with greater seriousness and in rituals which grew in elaborateness.

All the members of the O.S.C.C. were exuberant hams, and none more so than Sherwood even when he did not mean to be one. They were blood brothers in finding the same things entertaining and shared the same passion for dressing up. All were equally disinterested in whether Queen Victoria, or Graham Robertson for that matter, would have been amused by what delighted them. And unsparing treatment of each other was their way of showing how sturdy was their friendship. Fortunately their stamina was the equal of their energies, and their ability to amuse each other as strong as their hunger for amusement. They refreshed themselves by doing what would have exhausted others. For the clock they had scant regard. The passing hours mattered little, the drained moments much. Unable to get enough of the theatre during a week's hard work, they worked with equal intensity every weekend at playing, particularly when staging one of their Drama Festivals. On these scurrying occasions they, as adult professionals, threw themselves with the glee of children into playing "let's pretend," turning the court circular into *Uncle Billy's Whizzbang*, and cavorted like undergraduates at an initiation.

At the outset in 1935 the O.S.C.C. was a mere fivesome—the Sherwoods, Sherwood's old friend Geoffrey Kerr, and such other intimates among English actors as Richard Bird and his agreeable wife Joyce Barbour. Even then it took itself with enough mock seriousness to have officers. Sherwood, the somber wag, was The Founder; Bird, the blithesome, The President. The latter had played Marchbanks in New York to Katharine Cornell's first Candida and given an unforgettable performance there as Stanhope in *Journey's End*. Joyce Barbour had appeared on Broadway in *Havoc* and *Present Arms*.

By the next year a leaf had been tucked into the round table of this madly un-Arthurian court, and the circle had been widened to include Raymond Massey, the Cleon of *Acropolis,* and his wife Adrianne Allen, radiant though cozy as a kettle, who was known to New Yorkers for *Cynara, The Shining Hour,* and her Elizabeth Bennet in *Pride and Prejudice.* Other newcomers were Lady Anne Hunloke and her stage-struck MP husband Henry, and two junior members, Geoffrey Massey, a precocious fourteen, and little Mary Sherwood, a button-bright and button-round twelve. Later admissions were René Clair, the director with whom Sherwood had worked on *The Ghost Goes West,* Bronja his wife, and Kerr's new wife, the lovely Margot Kling. Occasional weekend guests, such as Bennett Cerf, Keith Winter, S. N. Behrman, the Ralph Pulitzers, and the Harold Guinzburgs, were active participants in the contests other than the Drama Festivals which at Great Enton were the order of the day and night. But the O.S.C.C., with its Drama Festivals, was a thing apart, an enclave within an enclave, a citadel within a citadel.

The first club meeting of the O.S.C.C. took place on a cold blustery day the year of the Sherwoods' marriage when they had arrived in London with Kerr. Ground was to be broken for the new wing at Great Enton, and a proper celebration seemed called for there. Compared to the rites which lay ahead, this ceremonial was a very simple affair, consisting of a surprise party for Sherwood at which Madeline and Joyce Barbour appeared dressed up as dowdy Lady Mayoresses and Bird and Kerr as seedy French town councilors, all of them carrying the largest cardboard brass instruments they could procure.

Later on in the spring, after the Sherwoods moved in, they were duly installed as the Duke and Duchess of Enton and known within the circle, with a squeeze of sarcasm, as Their Graces. To Madeline the role of Duchess was by then an old one; for Sherwood, being His Grace a new and entertaining indulgence in make-believe.

Like most Americans, he was a strong monarchist so far as England was concerned. In 1936 he was saddened to hear that King George V was gravely ill and, remembering his encounter with him in France, referred to him as "my old friend of wartime days." The accession of Edward VIII stirred him as much as the abdication moved and angered him. "The woman I love" broadcast was the stuff plays are made of, and Sherwood was one of the millions shaken by it. "I think," he wrote Paul Bonner, "it was the most moving and impressive—the most *historic* sound I have ever heard."

The emotions it aroused in him were "profound and complex." On one point, however, he was definite. Baldwin was "the most over-rated man on earth," a villain who with the Archbishop of Canter-bury had railroaded Edward from his throne. As for Edward, he was bafflingly appealing. Pictures of him made Sherwood "tearful." "It's inexplicable to me," he confessed, "how the abdication of Edward VIII has affected me. Reading about the present King, & Stanley Baldwin, I feel as bitter against England as an Irish Republican during the Black & Tan era. And this after 20 years (& more) of violent partisanship. I'm a complete romantic, I guess."

He was. He felt so strongly that he avoided being in England during the coronation of George VI by going with Madeline on a trip to Greece where he experienced the Acropolis. But he could not long resist the call of England and Great Enton. Two weeks later he was back in Surrey being crowned himself with a far larger crown than the King wore. The spoof ceremony, which took an infinite amount of planning, was held at Rosings, the Masseys' home nearby, where the O.S.C.C. assembled for the weekend. He described the event in his diary entry for Sunday, May 30, 1937.

"Again sunny & hot. At lunch, Adrianne gave us all handsome club pins. Then we opened the croquet season—Adrianne, Mad., & I against Bird, Kerr & Joyce. Couldn't finish the game as there was an elaborate program in store for us. In fact, the most elaborate of all, & far beyond description. Mad. & I dressed for a court ball, with numerous orders & decorations. We met the others in Ade's bed-room, they similarly attired. Then they went downstairs, we were summoned, & found ourselves in the midst of a coronation ceremony just about as grand in scale as that held recently at Westminster. I was crowned, anointed, sworn to oaths, kissed, etc., & so was Mad. Afterward, we went in to dinner—the whole house decorated mar-velously & even Newton & his assistant butler wearing medals. After dinner, the most terrific surprise of all. We emerged into the hall which was filled with the Coolham Town band (20 pieces, including four little boys, apprentices) in uniform, playing 'The Red, Red

Robin'—inaccurately but with fine inspiration. From then on, you
can imagine the hilarity. Mad. & I did some elaborate waltzes. It was
wonderful. In the morning Kerr gave prizes to all, a fine flower
collecting basket for me & for Mad. a flower cutter which will help
enormously in the main work of the summer."

During those prewar summers at Great Enton there were sometimes other guests, but weekend after weekend, with the regularity of
a clock striking, the O.S.C.C. turned up, needing no invitations,
waiting for none, and treating the place as if it were home. The two
major events for its members each year were usually the opening
"Prize Day and Fun Fiesta" at the end of May, and as September
approached a "Season's End" at which the Drama Festival and various contests were held.

With the O.S.C.C. anything that happened to be done was apt
thereafter to become a tradition. Its members were ritualists whose
delight was making fun of ritual. They put on airs to spoof them and
pretended reverence to be irreverent. They were proud of their exclu-
siveness and in various ways, both costly and unshrinking, pro-
claimed themselves a unit. They had their club colors, the croquet
colors of blue, red, black, and yellow, and a coat of arms. They flew
their own large flag at Great Enton and at the Masseys' more
grandiose home. When they chose they could write to one another on
their own embossed notepaper. Each had his own croquet mallet
with his name painted on the brass binding. Each possessed a large
key to the Oak Room at Great Enton and all received lavish silver
prizes on Prize Day. They also had their own song, sung lustily to the
tune of "There'll Be a Hot Time in the Old Town Tonight," which
they followed with an unchurchly chant recited with ecclesiastical
gravity. They had their printed handbills, for which Sherwood wrote
the copy, and in *The Rover* a club gazette which appeared once, and
then only after a printer was found willing to risk Britain's libel laws
by setting the type. They even had one member who appeared in
many of their sketches without knowing it because he was a store
dummy named Sir Cedric Hardwicke.

In addition the O.S.C.C. had in Geoffrey Kerr an official photographer who has kindly come to my aid by functioning as its court

historian. Kerr's mind took pictures too. He was Sherwood's closest friend, and has proved the depth of that friendship by the long, detailed letters in which he has described for me the Sherwoods, the O.S.C.C., and Great Enton. "Present mirth hath present laughter." That was the kind of laughter which rang out at Great Enton, and Kerr was *present*, contributing to the mirth and sharing in the passing laughter.

Take the weekend breakfasts. According to Kerr, these were apt to be late because going to bed was sometimes a dawn affair. They were purely male functions and the only times when seriousness was permissible in the smallest degree. The men's "mood was not, strange as it may seem, induced by the awe-inspiring appearance presented by Sherwood, the living embodiment of the Morning After, in a Black Watch tartan dressing gown. It was the one chance we had of a serious conversation—and by 'serious' I don't mean 'heavy'; I just mean that jokes were not compulsory."

It was at breakfast that Kerr sought Sherwood's views on any number of subjects. He sought them because Sherwood had "a mind of extraordinary clarity—the gray matter wouldn't slosh about, as Wodehouse would put it, in an untidy mess." Contributing to Sherwood's authority was the slowness of his speech. This Dead March pace, which enabled him to express himself with remarkable effectiveness, always surprised Kerr when he had not seen Sherwood for some time. Mainly, however, Sherwood's words carried weight "because of his power of concentration and because he always seemed to know *exactly* what he thought about everything."

After breakfast, weather permitting, there were the daily bouts of croquet. At Great Enton this gentle sport brought forth the most unbridled expressions of the deeper passions. "A stranger who chanced on the scene might well have tipped off the police that a murder might be expected any minute." The croquet lawn was actually quite a steep slope, which made the game different from the usual one. "At the third wicket, in particular, it was almost impossible, when the grass was dry, to take position. . . . Sherwood had to be closely watched when playing this one, to see he didn't rough up the grass, which was strictly taboo. . . . His face as he raised his mallet for the 'golf shot' was a study in brutal determination."

The evenings were given over with equal determination to rummy and darts. Kerr thought Sherwood the best darts player. Certainly he was the funniest. "He would lean his great height so far over towards the target that it seemed incredible he could stay upright—and, of course, occasionally he didn't. The only time he ever played really badly for several nights was once when he was on the wagon."

Each season a Treasure Hunt was organized by Bird, which took several hours to get through because of the diabolical difficulty of the clues. And one summer a Handicraft Competition was held in which Sherwood's entry was "The Martyrdom of St. Madelina," a colossal oil painting almost six feet square. "By refusing to give up and making endless trips to Godalming for more paint he managed to get into the picture about every single activity in which the members of the Club indulged. But Madeline's entry was the best. It was a special sort of wooden cabinet in which Bird, who was rather a messy eater, might take his meals. It was furnished with a curtain in front in which was a crescent shaped hole through which he might peer out."

The Wit Contest was another regular feature and another running battle. Each contestant, on getting off a pun, would say, "I enter that," and be graded "VG," "G," or "S" ("Very Good," "Good," or "Stinking") by the others on the score cards which were provided. The tradition was that Sherwood's entries, no matter how good they were, were always marked "S," much to his delight. The habitual winner was young Geoffrey Massey, but among the best was Geoffrey Kerr who, in Sherwood's opinion, at all times ranked "very high among the best wits."

At meals the game generally played was "getting words into sentences." Categories were assigned, such as vegetables, rivers, cities, or statesmen. The more elaborate the circumlocutions in getting the words in, the trickier the accents used, or the worse the puns, the better. At this exercise in fracturing the language no one was more inventive than Sherwood or proudly got off more atrocious puns.

The Poetry Competitions were held at teatime in the drawing room. At these the O.S.C.C. regulars, and the other guests if any, received silver prizes for their verses. The poems were often on the far side of bawdolatry and no less distant from poetry. They have not found their way into Bartlett. Nor were they meant to find their

way into print, though Bennett Cerf did issue an understandably private edition of the 1936 jingles (including his own). In
addition to writing an ode to Ernest Simpson, Esqr., each contestant
celebrated Sherwood's winning the Pulitzer Prize with *Idiot's Delight*. Typical of their spirit was Madeline's opening quatrain:

> A bunch of dumb guys
> Awarded a prize;
> Now, Sherwood, the sod,
> Believes himself God.

To Kerr this loving disrespect, though hard to explain to others,
was an important part of life at Great Enton and one of its friendliest
features. It was enjoyed by all and enjoyed most by Sherwood. Admiration lay behind it; affection made it possible. Of the countless
games worked at there, it was probably the most "in" game of them
all. Sherwood was the club's Founder, its patron, and "His Grace,"
but he was "also its goat. Led by Madeline, no member ever lost a
chance of insulting him." Knowing the devotion which underlay their
ribbing, he granted his "courtiers" the license of jesters, joining in
their jests with somber heartiness. He endured all this with the patience of a retriever being teased by terriers. The essence of the joke
lay in his sufferance and the knowledge of his playful attackers that
he was bigger than they were and could defend himself if he wanted
to.

This baiting game was one that Sherwood and Madeline had engaged in from the beginning of their courtship. Both relished the
sport and both understood its ground rules. Kerr noticed it, and
called it "curious," when he sailed with them on the *Manhattan* the
year of their marriage. If ever two people were in love, they were.
Yet even then he observed that they were "on almost precisely the
same terms on which they remained to the end—their deep love for
each other expressing itself most of the time in scathing insults."

Madeline, who liked to appear tough, could at heart be marsh-
mallow-soft. Sherwood, who according to her believed in both Santa
Claus and Cupid, was capable of toughness, too. Being passionately
in love, they had their stormy moments, but the basis of their love
was an understanding beyond storms, and their letters are awash

with "darlings," "X's," hearts, and "I love you's." This did not keep her from calling him "Sherwood" in front of people and dressing him down sharply. He did not mind. Her sarcasm amused him. He enjoyed her insights and the unsparing clarity with which she stated a point.

For fun in 1937 he made a list of the dinner companions who would interest him most. "Certainly Socrates & Aristophanes & Leonardo da Vinci & Abraham Lincoln & Shakespeare. Also Omar Khayyam & Voltaire. The only woman I can think of is Cleopatra & I'm not too sure of her." A few days later he returned to his diary full of contrition. "I think that Mad. should be included in my list. She could talk well to the best of them. I feel incompetent to make that fact sufficiently known. I wish I could write adequately a Hymn to My Wife. Whether I end up loving her or hating her with fierce intensity I'll know to my dying day that she is unquestionably the most profoundly interesting character I've ever known. From which you'd assume that she makes me feel inferior—which she does, in an unimportant way, and does not, in the essentials."

The kidding of Sherwood was just one of the endless games at Great Enton. It did not stop even during the weekends of the Drama Festivals. These were held each year shortly before the Sherwoods returned to America. According to Kerr, no production of *Hamlet* was ever staged with greater earnestness than they were, and Nathan's the costumers grew accustomed to accepting them as something that ranked at least with Glyndebourne. "One was greeted by the host and hostess with the usual affectionate cordiality, though perhaps a slightly faraway look in the eye. But then, instead of the usual chat in the Oak Room, there was a tendency on everyone's part to disappear. When you did run into someone else, he or she was always on his or her way to do something mysterious. Muttering lips showed that people were running through their lines or composing their prize poems."

After the reading of the poems came an excellent dinner. Cocktails and good wines played their releasing part, enough being consumed "to raise one's spirits but not enough to make one forget one's lines." Then the performance, held in the Oak Room or in the converted gardener's hut known as the Playhouse. This was the summer's climax, the attic theatre not of Greece but of childhood recaptured among professionals. At it a "Sea Breeze Fair" and the Hasty Pudding took over in Surrey, and a smaller audience than the smallest court theatre ever knew assembled with the Cratchits' zest at Christmastime.

Everybody contributed to the program. No one could have been stopped from doing so. With cool ease Kerr and Kling went through their magic act, which they had rehearsed furiously for at least three days. Bird, a last-minute man and improviser, threw himself with skill and frenzy into his protean act during which, seated at a card table, he put on wigs, beards, and mustaches to take on the appearance of twenty or thirty characters who were identified in couplets read by an assistant. Monologues were delivered, parodies acted out, and skits by Sherwood elaborately staged and costumed. In the last Madeline always stole the show which Sherwood had written for himself to steal. She appeared over the years in roles as different as the Dark Lady of the Sonnets, Queen Guinevere, Salome, and Dick Whittington's Cat, while Sherwood had his fun as Shakespeare, King Arthur, Herod, or a young Scoutmaster. Outstanding was his playing of a Naval Officer who carried on a long conversation with the store dummy that was Sir Cedric Hardwicke by saying, "Don't interrupt me, I haven't finished," "I know what you're going to say without your saying it," or "I don't wonder at your silence."

Summer after summer the festivities at Great Enton were presided over by Madeline with acidulous charm and by Sherwood with enveloping delight. Yet, fun as these weekends were, they did have their drawbacks, particularly when they had hardened into a routine and come to be assumed. They were weekends which took the week to get over. Privacy and quiet were not among their virtues. They cost money. The preparations for them were frantic, especially for the Drama Festivals. Though they were dispensers of pleasure, they were also problems in logistics. They required the endless planning of meals, a generously stocked cellar, an overflowing larder, and the arrangement of a profusion of flowers.

On Monday the house would empty, but in no time the next Friday would fill it again and the treadmill would be turning. The obligation to be *toujours gai* was draining, and in Sherwood's case

was one that, on occasion, he found hard to meet. In spite of his love
of laughter, he was a melancholy, brooding man who needed solitude. He always had a fine time when he and Madeline were alone.
He did not always have one with all the others, fond as he was of
them.

He was cruelly afflicted during these years with a serious sinus
condition which was not diagnosed as double *tic douloureux* until
September, 1939. For the rest of his life it was to plague him with
ever-increasing violence. Even then his bouts with it were terrible and
terrifying and sometimes of "screaming proportions." These attacks
meant nights of waking up at three and not getting back to sleep
until noon, or being wakened by a pain at 2:30 in the morning,
which grew worse at 4:30, was terrific at seven, and did not permit
him to go back to bed until midday. They meant dark hours of
floor pacing, depending on Bromo-Seltzer and sodium amytal, and
nights and days of becoming "panicky," of having his morale shaken,
and planning in his despair to go to Johns Hopkins "to get something
violent done."

No record of him would be complete which minimized his struggles against this illness, and no estimate of his character or behavior
fair which failed to take into account what he—and Madeline—lived
with and rose above. He mentioned it to few and for the most part
doggedly refused to let it interfere with either his pleasure or his
work. But when it did strike even during the summers, which were
usually the most merciful seasons, it left him exhausted, edgy, and
apprehensive.

More and more he came to question what he was doing with his
time and talents at Great Enton. Mutterings began to appear in his
diary. "The American theatre yells for new plays and here I am absorbed in the racing form and the momentous concerns of the Old
Savoy Croquet Club." This was in June, 1937. In August he was
writing, "It has been a very nice weekend and a highly welcome
change from the standard, even though it consisted mostly of croquet
& rummy & horses. . . . Thought rather grimly about the present
waste of my own gifts. After having been a model of industry for so
long I'm now the local loafer."

He reached a low point the next June after a day of "wonderful" flying with the model planes and a "memorable" game of croquet. "Rummy in the evening, and I was again nasty. What's the matter, anyway? Something seems to be terribly wrong with my nervous system. I get so tired and bored and impatient, and there's no reasonable, moral excuse for it." By the end of that July, shortly before the Sherwoods sailed for America, his patience was exhausted when the regulars appeared for the weekend with too many friends and relatives. "Beautiful weather—but general infuriation. . . . I got mad to the point of suppressed frenzy. We're actually looking forward to getting out of this."

Sherwood's disenchantment with the O.S.C.C. erupted most violently at the beginning of the 1939 season. "Rummy in the evening. I'm sick of that game & annoyed by it. It has become just a means of our distributing largesse to the courtiers. In fact, if I were to write the truth in this uneventful chronicle, I should add that I'm becoming somewhat sick of the O.S.C.C. It just seems to make trouble for and between my darling wife and me. Not that it's serious, but it's tiresome, momentarily, and permanently expensive. However, there are certainly glorious moments, as tonight when Bird made an after-dinner speech."

Such rebellions against the O.S.C.C. were momentary, mere flashes of heat lightning, and very occasional. They did no damage and never lessened Sherwood's loyalty to the club or his gratitude for the pleasure which it gave him. To him the thought of a year without the O.S.C.C. was "sickening." He had his other reasons for loving Great Enton. Among its advantages was that, besides being blissful green countryside, it was within daily reach by phone of his bookmaker. It was near Wimbledon, near Ascot, and near London and its theatres. It was also not too far from the studios of London Films which offered him congenial and profitable employment. Though an expert loafer, Sherwood was by no means the total loafer he feared he was becoming. He could work at Great Enton and, when quiet followed the turbulence of the weekends, work he did, in furious spurts, in his downstairs study with its windows opening on the Madonna lilies and the herbaceous perennials in the garden.

The amount he got done during these prewar summers was incredible. It included the preparation of a new text of *Idiot's Delight* for the Lord Chamberlain's approval; the writing of version after version of *Acropolis;* producing scenarios for such films as *The Scarlet Pimpernel, The Ghost Goes West, The Divorce of Lady X, Over the Moon,* and *Idiot's Delight;* tinkering with the script of *Rembrandt;* and struggling for months with the screen treatment of *Northwest Passage* (which he came to refer to as that "God-damned *Northwest Passage*").

In addition, he devoted hours to diligent and varied reading. Most unlikely of all, in the midst of the games, the frivolity, and the dressing-up, in 1937 he was wrestling with the fundamentals of his own convictions and poring over books about another tall and troubled man, this one from Springfield. He was passionately involved in the writing of *Abe Lincoln in Illinois.* He was to point out that, instead of being a play about Lincoln's achievement, it was about "the solidification of Lincoln himself." Without his suspecting it, the play revealed the solidification of Sherwood, too.

28

BOB SHERWOOD IN ILLINOIS

Why Abe Lincoln?—The Impact of Sandburg's The Prairie Years *on Sherwood—Lincoln, Flesh, Blood, and Fallibility—History without Hoke —The Writing of* Abe Lincoln in Illinois—*Founding of the Playwrights' Company—Maxwell Anderson, S. N. Behrman, Sidney Howard, Elmer Rice, and John F. Wharton—Sherwood Offers* Abe *to the Playwrights'— Early Reactions to the Play—The New York Opening and Reviews— World Events Cause Sherwood to Shed His Pacifism—A Letter from Eleanor Roosevelt—First Meetings with Harry Hopkins*

Why Abe Lincoln? Had Sherwood been a small man, he said he might, instead, have written a play about Napoleon. But Lincoln was a tall man outside and a giant within, and Sherwood a taller man who was growing inside year by year. This inner growth readied him for *Abe*—this plus the fact that, with the challenges to freedom multiplying throughout the world, Lincoln moved into the present with a new timeliness as "a man of peace who had had to face the issue of appeasement or war."

We say much about ourselves in our choice of heroes. They are the mirrors not only of what we would like to be but a reflection in part of what we are. From his youth Lincoln had occupied a special place among Sherwood's idols. As early as 1909, when he was twelve, he submitted an essay to a nationwide school children's contest commemorating the centennial of the President's birth. For some weeks he haunted the Fifth Avenue jeweler's window in which the prize medals were on display, confident that one of them would be his. He was genuinely surprised to learn when the awards were announced that he had not received even an honorable mention.

He saw Lincoln then and for many years thereafter through the usual fog of reverence, saw him as the myth not the man, as a statue that had somehow been alive. No other hero in our history reached so deep into Sherwood's heart as this figure of sadness, suffering, homely humor, and compassion. There was a kinship between them of temperament and beliefs, of bafflement and courage, and loneliness and eloquence. Like many another, Sherwood had been stirred by John Drinkwater's *Abraham Lincoln,* which he saw several times in 1920 and admired greatly as a "beautiful play." Two years later even the newsreel pictures of the opening of the Lincoln Memorial in Washington moved him, he confessed in *Life,* to a "state of maudlin lachrymosity."

He had read much on Lincoln, first learning the details of his early life from Ida M. Tarbell and of his period from Albert Bushnell Hart. His love for him grew as his knowledge increased. It was not, however, until he read Carl Sandburg's *The Prairie Years* that Sherwood "began to feel the curious quality of the complex man who, in his statement of the eternal aspirations of the human race, achieved a supreme triumph of simplicity." Sandburg introduced him to a new and human Lincoln and made him eager to know more about the forces, interior and external, which "shaped this strange, gentle genius."

For some fifteen years Sherwood had talked vaguely of writing a play about Lincoln's early life. *The Prairie Years* (1926), which he reread again and again during the next decade, eventually strengthened his determination to do so. "Can't open this wonderful book without feeling a rush of emotion to the imagination." Sandburg gave him an understanding he had not had before of the intricacies and contradictions of Lincoln's character and served as an invaluable guide to "the main sources of Lincoln lore."

This copious lore cracked for him the marble of Lincoln as a public statue, thereby permitting the man to emerge, flesh, blood, and fallibility, and all the greater for being human. Sherwood came to see, and state conqueringly in his episodic drama, the importance of Lincoln's frailties to his virtues. More and more he realized that, however heretical any admission of Lincoln's faults might seem to those who saw him only in Daniel Chester French or Gutzon

Borglum terms, these faults were a part of his size. As he put it, the doubts and fears that tormented Lincoln "could not have occurred to a lesser man" and his ultimate triumph over them was "in many ways the supreme achievement of his life."

In the winter of 1936 Sherwood began to write a play on Lincoln. At a Child's Restaurant on 48th Street he wrote the prayer for the recovery of a sick boy (really a prayer for America) which Lincoln speaks in the seventh scene. But he could get no further. His play had not formed in his mind nor his Lincoln come into focus. He needed more time in which to brood and plan and absorb. And greater and more intimate knowledge, too. Accordingly, led by Sandburg, he went to work in earnest.

Earnest in his case meant furious application. Never a decent student at school or college, Sherwood was always a painstaking researcher when, as a writer, he dealt with history. Before taking the license to which he was entitled as a dramatist, he had to know the facts from which he was departing. Hannibal, Richard Coeur de Lion and the Crusades, and Periclean Athens—all these he had read about with a scholar's zeal before handling them in his own unscholarly way. But never, until he wrote *Roosevelt and Hopkins,* did he immerse himself so deeply in history as when preparing to write *Abe Lincoln in Illinois.*

His supplementary notes, wisely printed not as an introduction but as a postscript to the play, are staggering in their thoroughness. Stephenson, Beveridge, Barton, Lord Charnwood, Evans, Baringer, the *Dictionary of American Biography,* Herndon and Weik (especially Herndon), and, above all, Lincoln himself as revealed in Nicolay and Hay's compilation of his *Complete Works* were among the sources upon which Sherwood drew with easy familiarity. He knew there were hundreds of other books which he could mention but did not, because, as he said in typical Sherwood fashion, "I haven't read them."

He had no desire in his notes to set himself up as a "learned biographer." But he was learned about Lincoln, drawn to his knowledge not only by the instinctive understanding he felt for him but by his theory of what a play about Lincoln should be. No one was more aware than Sherwood that "the playwright's chief stock in trade is feelings, not facts." A dramatist, he believed, was "at best, an interpreter, with a certain facility for translating all that he has heard in a manner sufficiently dramatic to attract a crowd." He felt, however, that in a play about the development of Lincoln's character a strict regard for the plain truth was both obligatory and desirable. "His life as he lived it was a work of art, forming a veritable allegory of the growth of the democratic spirit, with its humble origins, its inward struggles, its seemingly timid policy of 'live and let live' and 'mind your own business,' its slow awakening to the dreadful problems of reality, and its battles with and conquest of those problems."

His conviction was that, just as Lincoln's life needed no adornments to make it pertinent, his character needed "no romanticizing, no sentimentalizing, no dramatizing." To a reporter he said that, before he began, he made up his mind "not to have a line of hokum in the play. I love hoke in the theatre," he went on, "but this time I decided that, while they might say the play was dull, they couldn't say it was 'theatre.'"

To his Aunt Lydia he confided that he was "not concerned with Abraham Lincoln's position in history—because no one needs to elaborate on that. It was his remarkable character. It seems to me that all the contrasted qualities of the human race—the hopes and fears, the doubts and convictions, the mortal frailty and superhuman endurance, the prescience and the neuroses, the desire for escape from reality, and the fundamental, unshakable nobility—were concentrated and magnified in him as they were in Oedipus Rex and in Hamlet. Except that he was no creation of the poetic imagination. He was a living American, and in his living words are the answers— or the only conceivable answers—to all the questions that distract the world today."

Sherwood's shadowing of Lincoln when he was pondering his play did not stop with history or biography. Language, Lincoln's language public and private, the language of his period and of the authors who, having fed the hungers of his mind, helped to shape his style, became Sherwood's natural concern. To give authenticity to the dialogue in his scenes about the young Lincoln, he bought an English grammar of 1816. For period flavor he savored the *Pickwick Papers* and, to catch the swing and phraseology of common speech along the

Mississippi, he reread *Huckleberry Finn*. Again and again he searched the Bible, Shakespeare, Jefferson, and Whitman for an appropriately somber passage with which the student Lincoln could conclude the opening scene. Finding none, he used Keats' "On Death" as being right in spirit even if there was no record of Lincoln's having read it. The poem contained a phrase in "his rugged path" which stuck in Sherwood's mind. For a while he considered *The Rugged Path* for the title of his Lincoln play, which earlier he had thought of calling *The First American*, then *An American*.

In the midst of the activities at Great Enton Sherwood made another try at Lincoln in June, 1937. Again he found he was not ready and, after a few unsuccessful attempts, he put the project aside. But he was haunted by the play and continued to read for it and think about it. Not until the beginning of November did he actually settle down to writing. "Get to work on *Abe*, you lazy bastard," his diary exhorts, followed by "Got to work on Scene 2. Not too greatly pleased with progress."

Once started, Sherwood wrote rapidly, finishing the first draft in eighteen days. His diary reflects his exhilaration and relief.

Nov. 17. Wrote Scene 6 of *Abe*. Had quite a struggle with it, but think the finish is good. Not entirely happy about this scene or the whole play. Fear I have done too damned much reading & consequently regard it as an historical document instead of what it should be—a play by me. Also did a lot of work on Scene 9—the debate scene. This should be fine.

Nov. 18. This is unquestionably the best day's work I ever did. Up at 10, & during breakfast decided at last I must have Joshua Speed a character in play, filling need for someone to whom Abe can unburden his heart. Rewrote Scene 6, with Speed in throughout, & it's immeasurably improved. Then wrote Scene 7, 8 and 9. Scene 7 made me cry. Scene 9 difficult as it's a patchwork of lines from Lincoln & Douglas speeches, but if it doesn't read smoothly, that can be fixed. Quit at 11:45, never having stirred from the apartment where I'm alone, & annoyed by only one telephone call (a record). Read the *New Yorker*—a comical Profile by Wolcott Gibbs of Lucius Beebe who, I guess, represents the farthest conceivable cry from Abe Lin-

coln in Illinois. Later (2:07 A.M.). After calling my darling at
12:30, went back to work & wrote last scene, making Abe's last
speech a composite of his speeches at Springfield, Trenton & Philadelphia (1861). I cannot stop wondering at the perfection of his
style. "Not knowing when or whether ever I shall return." The placing of "ever." 2:45. I'm mighty tired. To bed.

Nov. 20. Finished first draft of *Abe Lincoln in Illinois.* Have really
worked harder and better these past four days than ever before in my
life. After two years of idleness, too. *Abe* needs a lot more work—
I'm certain of that—but I'm also certain that it's good. The tough
part is that I shan't know for a year whether it plays well enough to
fill a theatre. But thank God I've done it!

Abe Lincoln in Illinois was a turning point in Sherwood's career.
So were the happenings of an afternoon three days after he made that
entry in his diary. Sherwood presided then for the first time as president at a meeting of the council of the Dramatists' Guild. The day
was dull, as Elmer Rice remembered it in *Minority Report,* and so
was the meeting. The discussion of movie money in the theatre
dragged on for three hours. Little was accomplished, and to Sherwood the afternoon seemed "a terrible ordeal."

When it was at last over, he, Rice, and Maxwell Anderson found
themselves on the same elevator. They were tired men, and depressed. To raise their spirits, they went to a nearby bar where, over
their drinks, they shared their grievances against the American theatre in general and producers in particular. As Rice recalled,
Sherwood and Anderson spoke with special vehemence against the
Theatre Guild with which they both, while in the process of having
successes, had had painful experiences. The Guild had produced five
of Anderson's plays, including *Elizabeth the Queen, Both Your
Houses,* and *Mary of Scotland,* two of Sherwood's, and far back in
1923 Rice's Expressionistic drama *The Adding Machine.*

The Guild's committee system, which had irked Sherwood when
Reunion in Vienna and *Idiot's Delight* were being done, was attacked
by him and by Anderson. The two of them objected strenuously to
the fact that at the Guild they had been "harassed by disagreements
about casting, revisions, and the disposition of subsidiary rights."

They both expressed the wish that "their plays could be done as they wanted them done, without interference!"

In a spirit of fraternal revolt they revived a dream that for some years had come no nearer to reality than talk. This was a group of playwrights who, dispensing with the middlemen who were managers, would produce their own plays. Rice had long been a champion of such an idea, notwithstanding the failure of a previous association known as the Dramatists' Theatre which, after producing only one success among too many attempts, had died of dissension. Shortly after the hit of *Street Scene* (1929) he had suggested another project of the same kind to Anderson, Philip Barry, and George Kelly, without arousing their interest. This time the idea took root. Anderson and Sherwood committed themselves to it at once and asked Rice to join them, which he did with enthusiasm. Sidney Howard, whose *They Knew What They Wanted, Ned McCobb's Daughter,* and *The Silver Cord* had had hugely successful Theatre Guild productions, was also invited to be one of them, an invitation which he, as an ever-ready champion of new ideas, welcomed.

They had made a promising start. Then Thanksgiving intervened. This one was spent by the Sherwoods with the Averell Harrimans at Arden. During it Sherwood, while considering revisions for *Abe* and thinking about the newly conceived Playwrights' Company, spent his time bowling, playing badminton, parlor games and, in general, seeming to loaf. The Harrimans' guests included among others the Heywood Brouns, the William Paleys, the Donald Klopfers, Alice Duer Miller, Charles Lederer, Oscar Levant, Rosamond Pinchot, the George Backers, Peggy Pulitzer, the Harold Rosses, the George Kaufmans, and the Herbert Bayard Swopes. Someone said, "What a play this gathering would make," to which Kaufman replied, "Yes, the title would be *The Upper Depths.*"

Early the next week the four men, all quite excited by then, met at the Plaza's Oak Room to discuss definite plans. They decided to add another dramatist, feeling, according to Rice, "that five playwrights could presumably be expected to turn in three plays a year. If only one was even a moderate success, we would be on safe ground; a big hit every three years or so would provide a wide margin of safety." The candidate they tapped was S. N. Behrman who, in the

Guild's productions of *The Second Man, Meteor, Biography, Rain from Heaven,* and *Amphitryon 38,* had long since established himself as a comic dramatist. He took persuading, not wanting to involve himself actively in play production, but he accepted.

Such a separatist movement came near to giving the Guild a mortal blow. Lawrence Langner in *The Magic Curtain* tells how he called on Harold Freedman, the agent of Behrman, Sherwood, Howard, and Anderson, and suggested "somewhat bitterly that they take over the Guild's subscription as well," since he saw "little prospect" of its being able to survive without these playwrights.

The problems of management now descended on the five dramatists themselves. Anderson, a great, shy bear of a man, rich in humility and conscience, haunted by a high vision of tragedy, a better dramatist than poet, needing actors to lift his verse into poetry but bravely trying to bring back the music of language to a tone-deaf stage. . . . Behrman, a stylist wise and sensitive, the creator of worldlings made merry by their wit but miserable by the world outside their drawing rooms, a master of impeccable prose and dancing dialogue to whom polished talk was as important as plot. . . . Howard, with his mastery of theatrical device, his admiration for clarity even when pushed to obviousness, his belief that a dramatist is a "vicarious actor who happens to write well enough to be useful to real actors," and his brave response to any good idea that needed defense. . . . Rice, a rumpled, ardent man, sharply aware of the worsening conditions in the world, vehement and fearless in his response to social causes, a melodramatist whose gifts had been recognized since *On Trial* in 1914 when he was only twenty-one, and a virtuoso in realism as he had demonstrated in *Street Scene* and *Counsellor-at-Law.* These four—and Sherwood.

They named their organization the Playwrights' Company at the suggestion of Anderson, who had the medieval guilds in mind. Barry, a loner by temperament, believed it could not last. So did many skeptics along Broadway who foresaw conflicting egos and personal jealousies. But the five individualists who banded together were linked in ways more enduring than even they suspected. They were cemented by their shared discontent with the conditions under which they had had to work, by their respect for one another and their craft, and their dedication to the theatre. Their average age being forty-five, they were still young enough to welcome adventure. They had no distaste for profits, and each, because of his success, was in the happy position of being able to take a chance. In the terminology of the times, they felt they were launching a "New Deal" not only for themselves but for the stage.

Overnight their organization began to take shape. Money, of course, was a necessity. They thought that they could operate with a capital of $100,000, each investing $10,000 and with $50,000 more to be raised among their friends. Sherwood proved to be the most successful fund raiser, attracting on Long Island weekends such investors as Harriman, Dorothy Schiff, George Backer, Harold Guinzburg, Howard Cullman, Alicia Patterson, and Raymond Massey.

The agreement among the playwrights was that the Company would produce any script written by a member so long as the production budget was not in excess of $25,000, an amount then considered ample. According to Rice in *Minority Report*, "Plays calling for a greater expenditure required majority approval. Each playwright was to be in complete charge of his own production, calling upon his colleagues whenever he chose for script criticism, casting suggestings, comments at rehearsals and tryouts." All the plays to be submitted were to be new ones, unretrieved from trunks and dresser drawers. Each member, in Sherwood's words, "would get a straight ten percent royalty on his play and sixty percent of a picture sale. A dramatist would abandon hope for a play of his if his fellows all voted against it." In the years ahead all of them submitted scripts to the Playwrights' Company which were not produced by it. In such cases they were free to turn to other managements.

The next move, which they made swiftly, was to set up a working organization. The first person they called on was John F. Wharton, a quiet-spoken lawyer with strong opinions and sharp insights, who had been a theatre buff since he saw Maude Adams in *The Little Minister* as a boy. Pale of face, sandy of hair, and somewhat flat of voice, he had for years been as accustomed to reading scripts as to poring over briefs. In 1923, when Dwight Deere Wiman decided to be a producer, Wharton had had to learn about the stage in order to keep up with his client. Since then he had become increasingly in-

volved in the world of entertainment and, as general counsel for
David Selznick's company, was in Hollywood at the time when Sherwood got in touch with him. He was dubious about the project,
pointing out its obvious pitfalls. On returning to New York, however,
and talking with the playwrights, he became fired with their enthusiasm. By the end of December Sherwood was writing, "We decided
to take Wharton into the organization here and now so that we have
a lawyer, adviser, and mouthpiece—a very sensible move."

A business manager, a press agent, and an office were also imperative. The first they found in Victor Samrock, the second in William
Fields, and the third at 630 Fifth Avenue after having been for a few
months at 230 Park. Although Samrock was in his early twenties, he
was already wise in the mysteries of theatrical management, having
served his apprenticeship with Alfred de Liagre, Jr. Short, dark-
haired, and full of energy, Samrock had a healthy temper which he
kept under such control that he could deal smilingly with difficult
actors. Next to Sherwood he was to become the most popular member of the Playwrights' organization, and prove a welcome creator of
confidence and an easy winner of friends.

Bill Fields was different. His temper erupted awesomely at times,
belying his gentle appearance. No one could have looked less like the
stage stereotype of a press agent than this tall, reserved Texan about
whom there was nothing glad-handing or flamboyant. With his long,
thoughtful face he seemed closer to the bench than to ballyhoo. But
he was a master of his trade, who had handled shows of many kinds
since 1924, even serving the Ringling Brothers Circus as drumbeater
for its New York stand since the early thirties.

The cornerstone of the Playwrights' Company was, of course, the
playwrights themselves. To their self-interest as managers no less
than as dramatists, they wanted to put on the best possible productions with the best available actors. The future of their organization
depended chiefly, however, on the merit of their scripts and their
ability to turn these in with reliable frequency.

The first play offered to them was *Abe Lincoln in Illinois*. At the
initial discussion of their project Sherwood told Rice and Anderson
that, three days before, he had finished *Abe* and, as a show of

confidence, would "throw it into the hopper." With its twelve scenes, ten sets, and thirty-two characters, he was well aware that it would present difficulties in cost and casting. He was eager to have their opinion.

While writing *Abe* he had been torn between exaltation and despair. He had had days of being unable to start and days of being unable to stop. There had been nights when he experienced "such excitement" that it interfered with sleep. These were followed by periods of black melancholy. At times he felt "perfectly wonderful," convinced that "I've done at last what I most wanted to do with my work—express America." Then would come hours of torturing doubts when, laid low by attacks of *tic douloureux*, he found himself harassed by the episodic form he had chosen. "I'm geared to drive through an act, & so many starts, spurts & stops make it difficult for me to know whether I'm sustaining the interest."

One thing was plain. Even before his first meeting with Rice and Anderson, Sherwood had reached the climax of loneliness and uncertainty when a writer needs to discover whether all the effort and agony he has poured into his work have justified themselves. Early in December he retyped a lot of *Abe*, read it all through, and felt "terribly depressed. . . . It seems awfully, awfully dull. Fussed with it and stewed over it until suddenly I decided I should go nuts if it remained in the house another minute. So I packed it up and took it to Miss Simone to be typed. Lord—I hope this feeling of despair about it is only nervous reaction or something & that it's better than I fear it is now—a hell of a lot better." When the text came back, Madeline read it and, while she was doing so, Sherwood experienced the anxieties of an opening night. "Thank God she liked it & made some very good criticisms and suggestions which I shall act upon immediately."

Encouraged, he took a copy to his mother on her eighty-first birthday, read the play to Ned Sheldon, and sent copies to the other Playwrights, Edna Ferber, and Raymond Massey, who in England shared his with Geoffrey Kerr. The jailbound days of waiting for a verdict were mercifully short and all the responses fulfillments of Sherwood's highest hopes. The Playwrights were so enthusiastic that they decided to overlook the fact that the production costs would exceed the allotted $25,000. Anderson voiced their group reaction when he telephoned to say that *Abe* had given him "a lifting of the heart." Sheldon hailed it as "a noble portrait painted with a noble art." Miss Ferber thought it "an amazing characterization, touching, real," and "done with a masterly simplicity." Massey, whom Sherwood had had in mind for Lincoln since seeing him in *Ethan Frome*, cabled that he was "too moved for words" by *Abe*. Kerr was confident that he could see the play acted even as it then was and "have as good an evening in the theatre as I have ever had."

The praise of these first readers was plasma to Sherwood. He valued it the more because it included helpful suggestions. He had often said that of all kinds of criticism the one he hated most was "constructive." This time he was grateful for the advice given him. Miss Ferber wanted the dirtiness of the 1860 political campaign to be more sharply indicated. Kerr hoped for a few cuts, finding himself impatient for Abe's appearance during those scenes in which he made a delayed entrance. Anderson called attention to certain of Lincoln's speeches which might prove useful because of their applicability to the ever mounting tensions of the times.

Rice, who had never directed another author's play, was "astonished and flattered" when Sherwood asked him to direct *Abe*. He took on the assignment with excitement because the play seemed to him "one of the finest . . . ever written by an American." Naturally, in his director's role, he was more detailed in indicating possible improvements than the other Playwrights were. Among his many helpful suggestions, perhaps the most valuable was his pointing out that the Prairie Scene, in which Lincoln prays for the sick boy, should be more firmly integrated into the play as a whole. He advised that the boy's pioneer father be introduced earlier as an old friend of Lincoln's in New Salem, and that one of the town bullies, already known to the audience, should also be included. Sherwood was at first insistent that this was one scene he would not change. In time, however, he was persuaded and, as Rice put it in *Minority Report*, "by skillful interweaving . . . made the scene a logical step in the development of the plot and of Lincoln's character."

Some nine months were to creep by before the Playwrights inaugurated their first season. And a phenomenal season it turned out to be, with three hits and a near-miss. The first hit was *Abe Lincoln in Illinois*; the other two were *Knickerbocker Holiday*, the Anderson-Kurt Weill musical about Peter Stuyvesant, with Walter Huston, and Behrman's *No Time for Comedy* with Katharine Cornell and Laurence Olivier. The near-miss was Rice's *American Landscape*. The Playwrights, who had risked all, had not only amazed Broadway but exceeded their own expectations.

By May, 1938, Massey had signed the contract to play Lincoln. During July at Great Enton Sherwood reported, "Today Ray Massey read the whole part of Abe, I reading the other parts. We sat in the drawing room and there was beautiful sunshine on the delphiniums & roses outside the bay window. Ray will be fine, but Act I needs improvement in writing." Right down until its opening in Washington that October, Sherwood kept revising the script, finding that the Prairie Scene presented a problem to the very last.

One of the reasons for delaying the production of *Abe* was that Massey had to complete his London run of *Idiot's Delight*. Soon after this, on one of the most beautiful mornings he had ever seen, with New York at its best and his hopes high, Sherwood sailed down the bay on a revenue cutter at 6:45 A.M. to meet Massey on the *Queen Mary*. The rehearsals for *Abe* started the next day and to Sherwood the play sounded fine. Two weeks later came the challenge, which had been an ordeal when the Theatre Guild's directors met as a group to sit in judgment on one of his plays. This time it was no ordeal at all. "All the Playwrights' Co. assembled for the first time at the Cort Theatre—Anderson, Behrman, Howard, Rice, Wharton, Samrock, Fields & me—for run-through of *Abe*. It looked marvelous. Prairie Scene now fits in beautifully." After another two weeks of arduous rehearsing, which on one occasion lasted from 7 P.M. to 5 A.M., *Abe* opened in Washington to "superb" notices, "a triumph" for the play and for Massey, which was repeated the next week in Baltimore.

The gauntlet of the New York opening was still to be run. It was faced on October 15, a Saturday night, which meant an apprehensive Sunday spent waiting for Monday's reviews. Sherwood and Madeline watched the performance from the light balcony of the Plymouth Theatre with Rice and Anderson. Rice had last sat there seven years before when his *Counsellor-at-Law* opened, and Anderson in 1924 when he listened to the thunderous applause which greeted *What Price Glory?* All of them were nervous; all had much at stake. The first two acts seemed dull to Sherwood—"too many coughs." Rice, as the director, was relieved to see that the performance was dynamic and the mechanics smooth. But in *Minority Report* he confessed he was disturbed by his feeling that the audience, though attentive, lacked warmth and excitement. He saw that Sherwood was worried, too.

With the beginning of the first scene in the third act the atmosphere changed. There was, to be sure, a woman in the front row who created momentary consternation by talking as audibly as if she were one of the speakers in the Lincoln-Douglas Debate. She turned out to be Sherwood's mother, Rosina, proud and approving but so deaf that she was unaware that she could be heard. In spite of her, Rice remembered the scene "evoked a great round of applause" and "from then on the intensity of response increased." The evening's end, according to Sherwood, was "really thrilling—tremendous cheers—26 curtain calls."

The Sherwoods gave a large party at the Barberry Room after the opening. It was one of those theatrical parties which can be either a launching or a wake. Although the mood was jubilant, the congratulations flowed like the champagne, and the party lasted until five in the morning, Sherwood was dubious. From long experience he knew that the spoken enthusiasm of friends can be very different from the printed opinions of critics. Pleased as he was, he was impatient for Monday's papers and the reviews. The long, the unnerving watch lay ahead. He got through the blue Sunday as best he could. After dining with Madeline at home, the two of them went to Rice's apartment to wait for the early editions which were on the streets by midnight. The raves in the *Times* and *Tribune* put an end to the agony. By the next afternoon all the daily notices were in, and Sherwood summarized them in his diary by saying, "*Times, Tribune, World-Telegram*—fine. *Mirror, News, Sun, Journal*—fair. *Post* (John Mason Brown)—rotten."

I was rotten, and wrong, though not entirely so. I had some points to make which were not without their validity, though they now seem to me academic, ungrateful, and carping. One of these was that, if Sherwood had taken a curtain call, he would in all honesty have had to lead Abe on stage with him as his collaborator, because the best lines spoken during the evening were Lincoln's. I maintained that, failing Abe, Sherwood would at least have been compelled to enter carrying a copy of the Lincoln-Douglas Debates from which he had made his patchwork of quotations. I tried to establish, too, that in any play about Lincoln we read into simple sentences a significance which they would not have if it were not for our foreknowledge of John Wilkes Booth and the assassination. Another complaint of mine was that, instead of demonstrating Lincoln's greatness, Sherwood allowed it to overtake him during the intermissions.

I was decidedly in the minority with almost everyone against me, certainly everyone whose opinion I respected. I have come to know from his diary that what I challenged in *Abe* was what in part bothered Sherwood in his despairing moments while writing it. This was too much reading, too much homework, and too little playwriting by Sherwood himself.

In successive scenes Sherwood showed the young Lincoln as a student, a postmaster, the suitor of Ann Rutledge, a small-town lawyer, the reluctant husband of Mary Todd, a negligible Congressman, and a hater of war who long avoided the issue that might bring it about. Exciting and noble as the final episodes are, I still think there is a shadowy, pageant-like quality about these earlier scenes during which Lincoln emerges, in spite of himself, as the great, sad man who leaves Springfield to shape the nation's course in Washington. What I failed to sense on that opening night was the true dimension of Sherwood's play, his rightness in letting history speak for itself, and the skill with which he, aided by Raymond Massey's superbly moving performance, restated the American dream at a moment in the world when this restatement was dramatically needed.

During the writing of *Abe* Sherwood had had many dreams in which Lincoln appeared telling him he had done a good job. Although less authoritative, the critics and the public were of the same opinion. Few plays in our time have been greeted with such notices as *Abe* received.

"An inspired play—inspired by the sorrowful grandeur of the man it portrays. . . . A reviewer's only anxiety is that he may not herald it vigorously enough." (Brooks Atkinson, *Times.*) "One of the most stirring of American plays. . . . Not only the finest of modern stage biographies but a lovely, eloquent, endearing tribute to all that is best in the spirit of democracy. . . . Should become an American classic." (Richard Watts, Jr., *Herald Tribune.*) "It isn't easy to account for the feeling of rising excitement I had throughout the twelve scenes. . . . I suppose it was just the surprise and gratitude and somehow the sorrow of seeing a very great man exactly as he must have been." (Wolcott Gibbs, *New Yorker.*) "*Abe Lincoln* is the great American drama. . . . Marks an epoch in the theatre. It is also a political event of the first magnitude. . . . Thrilling and heartening . . . sounds a trumpet note. It is the very battle cry of freedom. . . . Should get the Pulitzer Prize and the award of the Critics Circle." (Heywood Broun, *World-Telegram.*)

Abe Lincoln in Illinois did not win the Critics Award—no play did that season—though it collected, after a session of furious discussion, five votes to the six for *The Little Foxes*, Lillian Hellman's brilliantly sulphurous melodrama about a decadent Southern family. *Abe* did, however, win him his second Pulitzer Prize. It did achieve a resounding run of 472 performances, and collect a cozy $225,000 when the film rights were sold to RKO and Max Gordon. Moreover the public found in Raymond Massey an Abe who still haunts the memory as the embodiment of the bumbling, humorous, tragic Lincoln, illumined by an inner light, who was summoned to greatness by events.

It did more than that. It marked, as I was too blind to realize at the time, a tremendous development in Sherwood himself and a reversal of the negative attitude which had been his during the years of disillusionment after the First World War. "It seems to me," he wrote when he was working on *Abe*, "there's one fundamental subject with which I am most concerned—*growth*. My own growth, and that of the characters I write about, and the ideas they express. No play seems worth writing if, at its end, its principal characters have failed to attain during its two hours greater stature. Of course, *Abe* is the supreme manifestation of that purpose so far."

The growth that Sherwood marveled at in Lincoln had in its own way occurred within him. Lincoln, opposed to slavery, was at first even more opposed to the idea of going to war to end it. He hated war with Sherwood's fervor, but in the end was forced to admit that the moment comes when men must fight for what they believe in. This moment was not to overtake Sherwood until after months of soul-searching during which he hoped and despaired, and finally recognized the inevitable was at hand.

As the New York first night of *Abe* approached, events clutched increasingly at Sherwood's conscience. That he, long articulate as a pacifist, chose to write about a man who was forced to wage a war which would cost thousands of lives, including his own, was in itself a change, a change in attitude as marked as the change in the form he used and the tone of his writing. Busy as he was rewriting his play, attending rehearsals and out-of-town tryouts, or following the fortunes of *Knickerbocker Holiday* on the road, he could not tether his interest to the make-believe of the theatre. The headlines preyed increasingly on his mind. More and more they pointed to the coming of that war the outbreak of which he had dramatized in *Idiot's Delight*.

Aug. 18, 1938. Thrilled by President's two speeches in Canada, in which he came as close as he legally could (if not closer) to telling the world, and Hitler and the Japs in particular, that if it comes to war they can consider us a partner of the British Empire. Roosevelt has made a lot more than his share of history, and damned good history, too.

Aug. 27. Things are happening at a ferocious rate in Europe. Evening papers carry sensational news of statement by British gov't. endorsing Czech gov't. and speech by Sir John Simon virtually announcing that the invasion of Czechoslovakia would bring England into war immediately with France against Germany.

Aug. 31. Present spectacle in Europe more mysterious and also more awesome than ever. Wholesale slaughter may begin at any moment.

Sept. 14. Our radio is practically inaudible, but tonight I heard it announce what is surely one of the most tremendous events of history. Neville Chamberlain has suddenly thrown a few things into a bag, stepped into a plane, and flown to Germany to see Hitler in a last minute desperate attempt to stop the war. God give him strength and wisdom, and Hitler at least one lucid interval.

Sept. 19. Dark, foggy Monday morning, & I ought to be working on the Prairie Scene, but I can't think of anything but the shocking news that French & British "statesmen," meeting yesterday in London, decided to yield completely to Hitler's loud threats and betray Czechoslovakia. Well—they were justified on one count: it was probably the only way of averting world war in 1938. But this is the absolute guarantee that the future history of the world—for a long time to come—will be a record of triumphs for nothing but brute force. . . .

Sept. 21. . . . I feel that I must start to battle for one thing: the end of our isolation. There is no hope for humanity unless we participate vigorously in the concerns of the world and assume our proper place of leadership with all the grave responsibilities that go with it.

Sept. 26. We're certainly trembling on the brink now. Now listening to radio—"the U.S. must stay out of this European horror—the U.S. cannot help but be involved eventually in this European mess . . ." If only I could look in some book to see what Abe would have to say. Jesus! It's dreadful.

Sept. 27. . . . Heard Neville Chamberlain broadcast from 10 Downing Street. A superb speech. . . . "I am a man of peace to the depths of my soul."

Sept. 28. This is one of the most exciting days in the history of the world. Another message last night from President Roosevelt, this one solely to Hitler & putting the finger precisely on him. More secret messages to Mussolini. Chamberlain was telling the whole, hopeless story to Parliament, Queen Mary present, when Sir John Simon handed him a note & Chamberlain announced to a spellbound world there would be a conference tomorrow in Munich between him, Hitler, Daladier & Mussolini. Who can say now that there has been no progress, that Woodrow Wilson lived & died in vain, that all died in vain who fought to make the world safe for democracy?

Sept. 30. Wipe out hopeful entries of two days ago. Democracy has bought peace by giving Hitler everything he wants.

Oct. 4. . . . Ashamed to read of the betrayal of Czechoslovakia.

The attitude he was later to make public with dramatic eloquence Sherwood had achieved painfully within himself.

Ten years later, when *Roosevelt and Hopkins* was published, Sherwood inscribed a copy to Jo Mielziner (who designed the settings for *Abe*), "If it hadn't been for *Abe Lincoln in Illinois*—to which you made such a marvelous contribution—I doubt that I ever would have become a friend of Franklin D. Roosevelt or Harry Hopkins, and would not have written this book."

Abe Lincoln in Illinois did alter Sherwood's life. He wrote it from basic beliefs that had changed, and it changed his career. From then on, more than being a playwright, he emerged in the public mind as a public man. As surely as it took years for Massey to escape from the part of Abe, Sherwood in the future was associated with the dimensions of his play about Lincoln. Having presented Abe as the embodiment of all that was challenged in democratic values, he himself came to be considered as a spokesman for those values. He did not carry Lincoln to the White House in his play, but his play was to bring Sherwood there, and in time make him a member of Roosevelt's inner circle.

Although they had never met, five days after the Washington opening Eleanor Roosevelt wrote him a longhand letter from the White House. "Dear Mr. Sherwood: I am just back from seeing your play and must tell you not only that I enjoyed it but that it moved me deeply. Mr. Massey acts beautifully, a difficult part, and the audience was more enthusiastic than I have ever heard them here. I hope the play has a long run. Strange, how fundamentally people seem to have fought on much the same issues throughout our history! My congratulations to you." Mrs. Roosevelt, whom Sherwood had long admired but never met, did not stop there. In her syndicated column "My Day" she wrote the first of her glowing tributes to *Abe*. Her generous enthusiasm was the beginning of a long and close friendship.

The person who did most to open the White House door to Sherwood was Harry Hopkins. Sherwood met this bright-eyed, intrepid, deeply loathed and deeply loved man early in September when *Abe* had just gone into rehearsal. Their first meeting took place on a Long Island weekend "under the hospitable roof of Herbert and Margaret Swope." He seemed taller than he was because of his ravished body. Plainly he was "a master of the naked insult," and no less plainly his fervor shone out in spite of his frailty. His laugh was "high and sharp and seemed to have an exclamation point in it."

In his diary Sherwood noted, "Long talk at breakfast with Harry Hopkins, the WPA Administrator, a profoundly shrewd and faintly ominous man." This was all he put down, but he remembered that on that occasion Hopkins talked to him "very agreeably, revealing a considerable knowledge of and enthusiasm for the theatre. He took obvious pride in the achievements of WPA in the Federal Theatre and Arts Projects," and Sherwood believed he had every right to be proud.

But, he added, "I did not quite like him. He used such phrases as, 'We've got to crack down on the bastards.' I could not disagree with his estimate of the targets in question but I did not like the idea of cracking down. I had the characteristically American suspicion of anyone who appeared to be getting 'too big for his breeches.' "

Nonetheless Sherwood was interested in Hopkins and Hopkins in him, though neither of them had the slightest notion that their acquaintance would lead to the closest friendship and bring Sherwood into intimate association with Roosevelt as one of his ghost-writers. This interest showed itself on the day when a nervous Sherwood was awaiting the opening of *Abe* in Washington. Hopkins considerately asked Sherwood to lunch with him. Then he took him to the White House where he showed him Lincoln's bedroom. "Furniture perfect. A great thrill," noted Sherwood.

He did not realize that in the years ahead he would on occasion sleep in that bed himself or the great thrills which were to be his at the White House. Hopkins, it might be added, was at the party at the Barberry Room after the New York first night of *Abe*. No one was more responsible than he for choosing Sherwood for the role he was to play at the heart of great events—and on a larger stage.

WORKS OF ROBERT E. SHERWOOD

Plays

The Road to Rome, 1927; 392 performances; produced by William A. Brady, Jr., and Dwight Deere Wiman; directed by Lester Lonergan; starring Jane Cowl and Philip Merivale; at the Playhouse.

The Love Nest, 1927; 23 performances; produced by Actor-Managers, Inc., in association with Sidney Ross; directed by Agnes Morgan; with June Walker; at the Comedy.

The Queen's Husband, 1928; 125 performances; produced by Brady and Wiman; directed by John Cromwell; with Roland Young and Gladys Hanson; at the Playhouse.

Waterloo Bridge, 1930; 64 performances; produced by Charles Dillingham; directed by Winchell Smith; with June Walker and Glenn Hunter; at the Fulton.

This Is New York, 1930; 59 performances; produced and directed by Arthur Hopkins; with Geoffrey Kerr and Lois Moran; at the Plymouth.

Reunion in Vienna, 1931; 264 performances; produced by the Theatre Guild; directed by Worthington Miner; starring Alfred Lunt and Lynn Fontanne; at the Martin Beck.

Acropolis (London), 1933; 12 performances; produced by Paul Hyde Bonner; directed by Marc Connelly; with Raymond Massey, Gladys Cooper, and Ian Hunter; at the Lyric.

The Petrified Forest, 1935; 197 performances; produced by Gilbert Miller and Leslie Howard in association with Arthur Hopkins; directed by Mr. Hopkins; with Leslie Howard, Peggy Conklin, and Humphrey Bogart; at the Broadhurst.

Idiot's Delight, 1936; 300 performances; produced by the Theatre Guild; directed by Bretaigne Windust; starring Alfred Lunt and Lynn Fontanne; at the Shubert.

Tovarich, 1936; 356 performances; adapted from the French play by Jacques Deval; produced and directed by Gilbert Miller; starring John Halliday and Marta Abba; at the Plymouth.

Abe Lincoln in Illinois, 1938; 472 performances; produced by the Playwrights' Company; directed by Elmer Rice; with Muriel Kirkland, starring Raymond Massey; at the Plymouth.

NOTE: All these plays were published by Charles Scribner's Sons except *The Love Nest* and *Acropolis,* which remain unpublished, and *Tovarich,* which was issued by Samuel French.

Films

Oh, What a Nurse! 1926; co-author with Bertram Bloch; produced by Warner Brothers; starring Syd Chaplin.

Age for Love, 1931; wrote dialogue; produced by Howard Hughes for United Artists; with Billie Dove and Edward Everett Horton.

Around the World in 80 Minutes with Douglas Fairbanks, 1931; wrote dialogue; produced by Mr. Fairbanks for United Artists; star, Douglas Fairbanks.

Waterloo Bridge, 1931; based on Sherwood's play; produced by Universal Pictures; with Kent Douglas and Mae Clarke.

The Royal Bed, 1931; based on *The Queen's Husband*; produced by RKO Radio; with Lowell Sherman and Mary Astor.

Two Kinds of Women, 1932; based on *This Is New York*; produced by Paramount; starring Miriam Hopkins and Phillips Holmes.

Cock of the Air, 1932; co-author with Charles Lederer; produced by

Howard Hughes for United Artists; starring Chester Morris and Billie Dove.

Rasputin and the Empress, 1932; extra work on script; produced by Metro-Goldwyn-Mayer; with the three Barrymores, Ethel, Lionel, and John.

Reunion in Vienna, 1933; based on Sherwood's comedy; produced by Metro-Goldwyn-Mayer; starring John Barrymore and Diana Wynyard.

Roman Scandals, 1933; co-author with George S. Kaufman; produced by Samuel Goldwyn for United Artists; starring Eddie Cantor.

The Scarlet Pimpernel, 1935; co-author with Arthur Wimperis of screenplay based on Baroness Orczy's novel; produced by Alexander Korda for London Films; starring Leslie Howard and Merle Oberon.

Rembrandt, 1936; extra work on script; produced by Alexander Korda; starring Charles Laughton, Elsa Lanchester, and Gertrude Lawrence.

The Petrified Forest, 1936; based on Sherwood's play; produced by Warner Brothers; starring Leslie Howard, Bette Davis, and Humphrey Bogart.

The Ghost Goes West, 1936; wrote screenplay; produced by René Clair for Alexander Korda and London Films; starring Robert Donat and Jean Parker.

Tovarich, 1937; screenplay by Casey Robinson based on Sherwood adaptation of Deval play; produced by Warner Brothers; starring Claudette Colbert and Charles Boyer.

Thunder in the City, 1937; wrote screenplay and dialogue with Aben Kandel; produced by Alex Esway for Atlantic Films; starring Edward G. Robinson.

Conquest, 1937; rewrote script and dialogue; produced by Metro-Goldwyn-Mayer; starring Greta Garbo and Charles Boyer.

The Adventures of Marco Polo, 1938; wrote screenplay; produced by Samuel Goldwyn for United Artists; starring Gary Cooper.

Marie Antoinette, 1938; worked on the script (1934); produced by Irving Thalberg; starring Norma Shearer.

The Divorce of Lady X, 1938; wrote screenplay with Lajos Biro upon whose play, *Counsel's Opinion*, the film was based; produced by

Alexander Korda for London Films; starring Merle Oberon and Laurence Olivier.

Idiot's Delight, 1939; wrote screenplay; produced by Hunt Stromberg for Metro-Goldwyn-Mayer; starring Clark Gable and Norma Shearer.

Abe Lincoln in Illinois, 1939; wrote screenplay; produced by RKO Radio; with Ruth Gordon, starring Raymond Massey.

Miscellaneous

The Best Moving Pictures of 1922-1923, edited by Robert E. Sherwood. Boston: Small, Maynard & Co., 1923.

The Virtuous Knight, a novel, published in 1931 by Charles Scribner's Sons.

WITH THANKS

Warm thanks, presented in this dreary but inevitable form, must appear cold. Nonetheless, mine are very warm indeed. And why not? In addition to the people already mentioned in the Introduction, they go to those who, by submitting to long interviews, writing illuminating letters, aiding in the gathering of newspaper clippings and photographs, turning over their files, giving helpful advice, and even listening to portions of this volume, have made its writing possible. Thanks unstinting, therefore, to:

Academy of Motion Picture Arts and Sciences, Elizabeth Franklin, Librarian; Dean Acheson; Adrianne Allen; Mrs. Winthrop Ames; Robert Anderson; Andrew A. Anspach; Brooks Atkinson; Dorothy Bartlett; S. N. Behrman; Mrs. August Belmont; Nathaniel Benchley; Mrs. Robert Benchley; Paul Bennett; Bertram Bloch; Lois Whitcomb Bohlig; Paul Hyde Bonner; Frederic Bradlee; Carl and Carol Brandt; Catherine Meredith Brown, my wife, who has put up with me gallantly during these long years of writing; Meredith Mason Brown and Preston Brown, my sons, who assisted me each for a summer in the research for this book; Roger Burlingame; Mrs. Richard Burton (widow of the critic); Edna Chappell; Mr. and Mrs. F. Maurice Child; René Clair; Columbia University, Butler

Library, Eugene Sheehy; Marc Connelly; Louis G. Cowan; Russel Crouse; Bosley Crowther.

Elmer Davis; Donald Day; Mary de Liagre; Mrs. Coert DuBois; Virginia Delano Dunphy; John Winthrop Edwards; John Farrar; Edna Ferber; William L. W. Field; William Fields; Gretchen Damrosch Finletter; Thomas K. Finletter; Lynn Fontanne; Mr. and Mrs. James Fosburgh; Mrs. W. G. Fraser; Harold Freedman; Donald Gallup; James G. Geller; Lillian Gish; Samuel and Frances Goldwyn; Jay E. Gordon; Ruth Gordon; Abel Green; Jerome D. Greene; Harold and Alice Guinzburg; Mrs. Helen Hackett; William Harlan Hale; Mrs. Emmet Hall; Hamish Hamilton; Mr. and Mrs. Averell Harriman; Jones Harris; Harvard University, William A. Jackson of Houghton Library, Sargent Kennedy, Registrar, William Van Lennep of Theatre Collection; Mr. and Mrs. Bernard Hawes; Serrell Hillman; Al Hirschfeld; Irving Hoffman; Paul Hollister; Paul Hollister, Jr.; Mrs. Frederick S. Hoppin; Mrs. Sidney Howard; Albert Weeks Hunt; Paul P. Hutchison.

C. D. Jackson; Barry Jones; Garson Kanin; George S. Kaufman; Geoffrey and Margot Kerr; Charles Kerlee; Thomas S. Lamont; Robert J. Landry; Norman McK. Lang; Armina Marshall Langner; Margaret Leech (Mrs. Ralph Pulitzer); Howard Lindsay; Mrs. Robert Littell; Alfred Lunt; Russell Lynes; Kenneth MacKenna; Mr. and Mrs. Archibald MacLeish; Tom Mahoney; Lewis H. Martin; Raymond Massey; David McCord; Drew Middleton; George Middleton; Jo Mielziner; Milton Academy, Mr. and Mrs. Arthur Bliss Perry, Dorothy F. Ayer, Margaret C. Osgood; Worthington Miner; Ward Morehouse; Agnes Morgan; Edward R. Murrow; Museum of the City of New York Theatre Collection, Sam Pearce; Robert Newcomb; New York Herald Tribune Library, Robert Grayson.

New York Public Library Theatre Collection, George Freedley, Paul Myers; New York Society Library, Sylvia Hilton, Helen Ruskell; Norcross, Inc., Esther B. Mooney; Maxwell Nurnberg; Mr. and Mrs. Donald M. Oenslager; George Oppenheimer; William S. Paley; John Patrick; Barbara Payne; Irvin C. Poley; Elmer Rice; Mrs. Eleanor Roosevelt; Victor Samrock; Elizabeth Schenk; Charles Scribner's Sons and Charles Scribner, Jr.; Samuel P. Sears; R. Baird Shuman;

George Sklar; Thomas Morrison Sloane; Mrs. Johnson Stoddard; Stonington Free Library; Lester D. Summerfield; Allene Talmey; Deems Taylor; Howard and Evelyn Teichmann; Time, Inc.; United Features Syndicate, Mr. Freeman; Irita Van Doren; June Walker; Clyde C. Walton; Richard Watts, Jr.; John F. Wharton; Yale Collection of American Literature, Theatre Guild Archive.

JOHN MASON BROWN

INDEX

395

ABOUT THE AUTHOR

JOHN MASON BROWN, author, lecturer, and dramatic critic, was born in Louisville, Kentucky, in 1900, and began his career in 1917 as a cub reporter with the Louisville *Courier Journal*. Following his graduation from Harvard, he was successively associate editor of *Theatre Arts Monthly* and drama critic, first of the New York *Post* for twelve years and then of the New York *World-Telegram*. During World War II he served in the United States Navy on the staff of Admiral Alan G. Kirk during the invasions of Sicily and Normandy, which he described in *To All Hands* and *Many a Watchful Night*.

In 1944 he began his column of play reviews and general comment, *Seeing Things*, which ran weekly until 1955 in the *Saturday Review*, of which he is still an editor-at-large. He is the author of seventeen books, including *Through These Men, Dramatis Personae, Daniel Boone: The Opening of the Wilderness*, the *Seeing Things* series, and *Morning Faces*; he has edited *The Portable Charles Lamb, The American Theatre as Seen by Its Critics*, and *The Ladies' Home Journal Treasury*, and has written the introductions to a number of books, including *The Portable Woollcott*.

He has also been a member of the Pulitzer Prize Drama Jury, a trustee of the Metropolitan Museum of Art, and Overseer of Harvard College, and has taught at many universities, including Yale and Harvard. He is also one of the judges of the Book-of-the-Month Club and is widely known as a lecturer and for his television appearances.

DATE DUE		